Instant PHP4

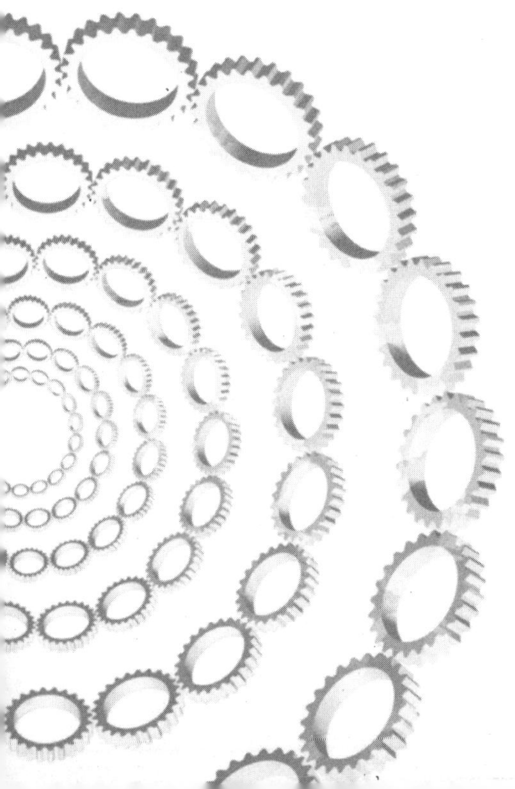

About the Authors

Robert Cox is the Director of Technical Support at Engage, Inc., a company that specializes in developing state-of-the-art online and offline advertising software. Robert is a graduate of Brigham Young University with a Bachelor of Science degree in Electronics Engineering Technology. He has designed many web sites, the bulk of them using PHP and ColdFusion. Robert has worked for more than ten years in the computer industry and gained most of his formal development experience while employed in the LAN Driver Developer Support Division of Novell, Inc. There he was able to learn the intricacies of C and C++ programming languages and gain valuable networking experience. Robert is the co-author of *PHP Developer's Dictionary*.

Robert's interests include all aspects of computer communications and development. He enjoys tinkering with networks, routers, and operating systems, and is comfortable with many different and diverse technologies. His love of computers dates back to 1980 when he continually snuck out of his high school American History class to work on programs in the local college computer lab. Robert grew up in Winslow, Arizona, and now lives and works in Raleigh, North Carolina, with his wife, Sheila, and three children, Kaitlin, Austin, and Dallin.

Michael J. Walker is a Senior Systems Engineer at Engage, Inc. He currently serves as a technical resource for the pre-sales engineering team. His previous work with Engage has included heading the consulting and custom development teams as well as being a developer of custom web applications using C/C++, HTML, JavaScript, and ODBC. He is a co-author of *PHP Developer's Dictionary*.

While at Engage, Michael has provided business and technical consultation to many of the top-tier web sites in the United States and throughout the world. He also has more than a decade of technology experience, which includes data processing operations, enterprise software implementation, and client/server development. He has developed software for many platforms ranging from micro-controllers to mainframes, using Assembly Language, C/C++, SQL, Visual Basic, PowerBuilder, and Java. Michael holds Bachelor of Science degrees in Theoretical Computer Science and Electrical Engineering from Northern Illinois University. He grew up in Batavia, Illinois, and now lives in Knightdale, North Carolina, with his wife, Kendra, and their two dogs, Merlin and MoneyPenny.

Neal Anders is an Internet Solutions Engineer for Engage, Inc. He holds a degree in Information Technology from Keiser College in Melbourne, Florida. Neal enjoys working with all aspects of the Web, with emphasis on graphical design and usability.

Neal's hobbies and passions include scuba diving, paintball, photography, hiking, medieval and Roman architecture, cryptography, and traveling to other countries.

Instant PHP 4

Michael Walker
Robert Cox
Neal Anders

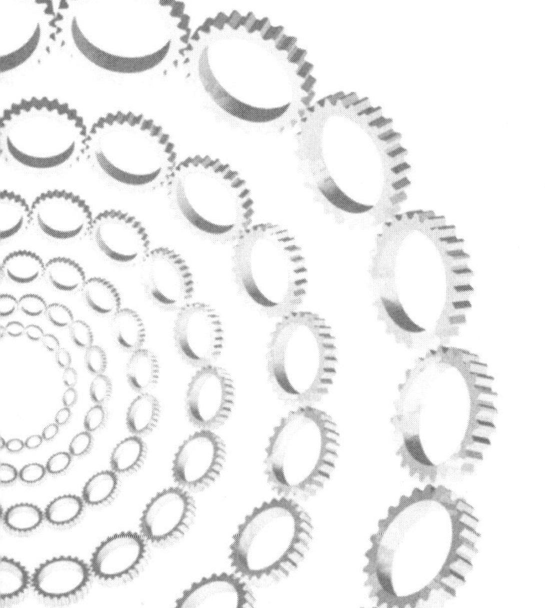

Osborne/McGraw-Hill

New York Chicago San Francisco
Lisbon London Madrid Mexico City Milan
New Delhi San Juan Seoul Singapore Sydney Toronto

Osborne/McGraw-Hill
2600 Tenth Street
Berkeley, California 94710
U.S.A.

To arrange bulk purchase discounts for sales promotions, premiums, or fund-raisers, please contact Osborne/**McGraw-Hill** at the above address. For information on translations or book distributors outside the U.S.A., please see the International Contact Information page immediately following the index of this book.

Instant PHP 4

1234567890 DOC DOC 01987654321

Book p/n 0-07-219009-4 and CD p/n 0-07-219010-8
parts of
ISBN 0-07-217074-3

Publisher	Brandon Nordin
Vice President & Associate Publisher	Scott Rogers
Acquisitions Editor	Jim Schachterle
Project Editor	Jody McKenzie
Acquisitions Coordinator	Tim Madrid
Technical Editor	Patrick McCarty
Copy Editor	Lunaea Weatherstone
Proofreader	Linda Medoff
Indexer	Jack Lewis
Computer Designers	Carie Abrew, Melinda Moore-Lytle
Illustrators	Michael Mueller, Lyssa Wald
Series Designer	Roberta Steele
Cover Designer	Greg Scott
Series Illustrator	Eliot Bergman

This book was composed with Corel VENTURA™ Publisher.

To my children, Kaitlin, Austin, and Dallin (Quinn) and
my best friend, who happens to be my wife, Sheila.
—Rob

To my grandfather Loyd Ruster, a man for whom I have
the utmost respect and admiration.
—Mike

For Nikki: Patience and perseverance—two very
important allies in our relationship.
—Neal

Contents at a Glance

Contents

Acknowledgments

Thanks to my co-authors, Mike and Neal, to Bob Kern and to the Osborne/McGraw-Hill team for this opportunity to write on a topic that I continually find fascinating. A special thanks to my wife and family—you put up with a lot during this writing, and I love you all so much. Also thanks to my parents: to my mom for her loving pats with the fly-swatter, and to my dad and his colorful ways of dealing with anger … remember that brick wall? Seriously, you gave me the solid foundation that I am continually able to build upon. Thanks so much.

I have many friends, co-workers, teachers, professors, and mentors who have, in their little way, molded my personality and talents. It is also to them that I am eternally grateful. You have given me the inspiration, enthusiasm, and vision of what I want to become. Thanks to you all, and God bless.

—Rob

I would like to thank my co-authors, Neal and Rob, for their hard work and dedication during such an eventful time. I also thank Bob Kern of TIPS Technical Publishing, along with Timothy Madrid, Jim Schachterle, Jody McKenzie, and Paulina Pobocha of Osborne/McGraw-Hill for their sensational efforts in bringing this book to life.

To Kendra, I thank you for your unconditional love, support, and understanding. I am grateful that you let me be the one.

"There is only one success—to be able to spend your life in your own way."

—Christopher Morley, playwright

—Mike

To my mother, for instilling in me the value of unconditional love, I shall make every attempt to do the same for my children someday. To my father, who enlightened me to the fact that the past, both good and bad, has got me to where I am today, and that I should acknowledge both. And for my grandmother, whose hard work and refusal to ever give up have inspired me so.

"Oh, you hate your job? Why didn't you say so? There's a support group for that. It's called EVERYBODY and they meet at the bar." —Drew Carey

—Neal

Introduction

Who Should Read this Book

Through experience, we have seen that many technical topics are best taught through example. This book uses that theory and takes it to the next level. We assume a couple of things in this book. The first is that you are familiar with web technologies and communications; the second is that you have some programming knowledge; and third, that you have a thriving desire to learn. With this foundation, we will take you through one of the most exciting programming languages to hit the Internet, PHP. You will be instructed, through example, how to build dynamic, web-based applications, using step-by-step instructions. If you follow the steps detailed in the chapters, you will have a working application when the chapter is complete. It is important to not limit yourself to the way the projects are portrayed in this book. Using the ideas and samples given, you can take these projects and add features and functionality. Some of our ideas for enhancements are included at the end of each chapter.

Each chapter contains a complete project or significant piece of a complete project. Each project is broken into files that contain the PHP code you will need to create your working example. We suggest that you briefly read the chapter and get the example(s) working in your environment. Once this is done, you can go back through the chapter, study the examples, and code more in depth. You will find it helpful to use the working example, the source code, and the text of this book to fully understand the items and techniques explained. Since this book has more than one author, you will probably notice slightly different programming styles, but each remains consistent with the same high standards of quality and is well explained.

We feel confident that you will find this book a valuable tool in your quest to learn PHP and the technologies, software, and techniques used to make dynamic, database-driven, or WAP-enabled web sites.

About this Book

Instant PHP 4 will guide you through some of the emerging trends of web applications working today—from database and administration tools, WML and WAP, online games and calendars, to address books and visitor polls. The book was written with the beginner to intermediate developer in mind, and has been laid out with specific steps to follow for each project.

Each chapter in this book concentrates on a particular aspect of building applications with PHP. As you read through each chapter, the projects get more complex. Beginners might find the first few chapters a good place to start. For the intermediate to advanced user, the projects in the middle and end of the book might be a more comfortable starting ground. Even if you are only somewhat familiar with PHP you should be able to read through each chapter, following the examples, and progress through the book nicely.

Some of the projects tie into each other or may be helpful in completing other projects in other chapters. For instance, if you are uncomfortable creating databases from the command line, you might try completing Chapter 5 first, and then using this application to create the databases for the other chapters. You can also take some of the existing projects in early chapters and apply concepts you pick up in later projects to them. For instance, in Chapter 15, we take the online address book created in Chapter 7 and WML enable it.

The appendixes of this book include an overview of source code control, Structured Query Language (SQL), and the process of setting up a MySQL database. These should be very helpful to those programmers who are new to the concepts of setting up a database and interacting with it, as well as tracking changes and revisions to your code.

What this Book Covers

This book contains 15 chapters and 3 appendixes. The majority of chapters contain standalone projects which illustrate how to use PHP to develop a variety of web-based applications. The projects are designed so that the subcomponents can easily be reused in other applications. Also, where practical, the code has been developed to be platform independent so you can implement it in whatever environment you happen to be working in.

Chapter 1, "Introduction," was written by Michael Walker. This chapter provides groundwork for the rest of the book, including prerequisites along with the software engineering plan followed throughout the chapters. In addition, a competitive overview is provided so you can be aware of how other technologies may work alongside PHP in a web development environment.

Chapter 2, "Developing in PHP," was written by Robert Cox. It covers three areas: version control, debugging techniques, and the Zend IDE. The version control discussion focuses on Concurrent Versions System (CVS) and its basic usage. The debugging techniques section covers useful debugging techniques along with common coding pitfalls. Finally, the Zend IDE and its unique debugging capabilities are covered.

Chapter 3, "A Simple PHP Calendar," was written by Neal Anders. This application presents a calendar as a web page for any month and year that the user selects. It utilizes the available PHP functions to handle date processing, such as determining which day of the week a month starts on.

Chapter 4, "PHP Connect 4," was written by Neal Anders. This project simulates the classic game of Connect 4 for two players. It highlights PHP's file access functions to save the game state between each player's turn.

Chapter 5, "Web-Based Database Administration," was written by Michael Walker. This application provides a web-based interface to a MySQL database. It allows a user to perform standard DBA-type activities along with executing raw SQL queries.

Chapter 6, "Interactive Visitor Poll," was written by Robert Cox. This application allows a visitor to a web site to cast their vote on a topic and see a running total of the other votes that have been cast. This chapter focuses on update and retrieval of data in a MySQL database.

Chapter 7, "PHP Online Address Book," was written by Neal Anders. This project takes contact data from a MySQL database and makes it available through the Internet.

Chapter 8, "PHP Online Store Administration," was written by Neal Anders. This is the first half of a project to create an online store. This chapter focuses on managing the products that the store is selling along with keeping track of a customer's order.

Chapter 9, "PHP Online Store Shopping Cart," was written by Neal Anders. This is the second half of the online store. This chapter covers account creation and management along with processing a visitor's shopping cart. It also handles the checkout process when a visitor is ready to make their purchase.

Chapter 10, "Administrative Tools," was written by Michael Walker. This project allows the user to remotely administer the machine on which PHP is running. It allows the user to perform various actions with files and directories that are on the host machine.

Chapter 11, "PHP Information Console," was written by Michael Walker. This project allows a remote user to find out more information about the PHP engine that is running on the host machine. The user is able to view information about PHP's configuration and examine the php.ini file directly.

Chapter 12, "NNTP Server Communications," was written by Robert Cox. This chapter shows how to create a Usenet news reader in PHP. It focuses on the socket communication functions available in PHP along with the interaction with a news server.

Chapter 13, "Message Board Application," was written by Michael Walker. This application lets site visitors create and view messages about various topics. The application is designed so that it can be readily adapted to any type of web site.

Chapter 14, "WML and WAP," was written by Robert Cox. This chapter provides a detailed background on the WML and WAP technologies. It also provides practical PHP experience in developing WAP applications using a WAP emulator.

Chapter 15, "WML-Enabled Address Book," was written by Robert Cox. This chapter extends on the work done in Chapters 7 and 14. It brings the online address book to the WAP world by utilizing WML and PHP.

Appendix A, "MySQL Database Installation," was written by Robert Cox. This appendix provides further details on how to set up a MySQL database in preparation for developing the projects that require database access.

Appendix B, "SQL Help," was written by Robert Cox. This appendix covers the basics of SQL for those readers who are new to database programming.

Appendix C, "CVS Help," was written by Michael Walker. This appendix provides an overview and quick reference information for using CVS as your version control system.

PART I

Background

OBJECTIVES

- Understand the approach of this book
- Learn the assumptions and prerequisites for the applications in this book
- Discover the process utilized in developing the projects featured
- Learn about PHP's major competitors and how it measures up
- Learn about setting up a process for controlling source code, specifically one using CVS and WinCVS
- Learn about the Zend integrated development environment
- Discover techniques for debugging applications
- Become familiar with the Zend debugger

CHAPTER

1

Introduction

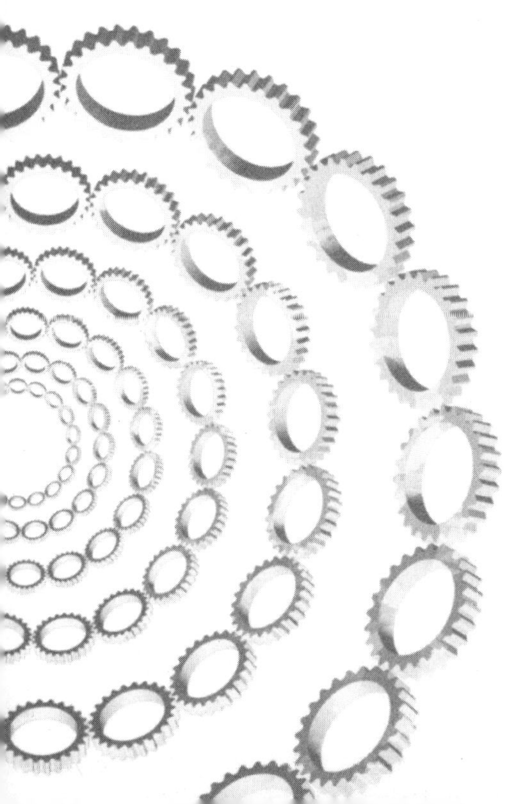

Welcome to *Instant PHP 4*! This book is designed to provide you with a well-rounded understanding of the PHP language by examining the development process of a broad range of web-based applications created with PHP. This book promotes learning the PHP language through examples and is not an introductory or reference manual; therefore, it is assumed that you have a basic understanding of PHP.

This book is designed for the intermediate to advanced PHP developer, and therefore does not cover all aspects of PHP. Rather, it teaches you about the language's features and capabilities through real-world examples. If you learn best by doing, then this is the book for you! Each chapter focuses on a specific project and includes all the development phases that are involved in completing the project. The chapters are organized in increasing complexity and generally build on preceding chapters; however, it is not required to read the book from beginning to end.

We hope that this book will provide you with an in-depth understanding of the PHP language and its applications so that you will be able to design effective solutions for any web-based project.

Groundwork

Before diving into the first project, we will provide the groundwork necessary for you to take full advantage of this book. This includes prerequisites, PHP environment requirements, and an explanation of the development process we follow.

PHP Environment

As the title of the book suggests, the projects included in the following chapters are designed for PHP 4 and higher. Because PHP runs on a variety of platforms, the projects are not developed for any specific operating system or hardware. Care is taken to point out any circumstances in which the platform chosen will affect project development. The reference platform we used to develop this book's projects consisted of Apache, Red Hat Linux, and MySQL on Intel hardware. We used the latest stable version of each product that was available at the time of writing.

Design Considerations

All the projects in this book follow the same overall development process. This process is commonly referred to as *software engineering*. There are many references available on this very important topic, and you are advised to become familiar with sound software engineering practices, as you and your code will greatly benefit from them. This section presents a brief synopsis of the process that we use throughout the book. The reason for following this process is to provide a systematic method for accomplishing the desired coding task. Following this process should ensure that each project is developed in a logical, efficient, and effective manner.

The process is divided into two phases, with the first phase being preparation, which includes requirements analysis and design. Requirements analysis is the most important step in the entire process because without a clear understanding of what you are trying to accomplish, you cannot develop a high-quality, robust, efficient solution, which should be the goal for each project you develop. The design step includes outlining the specific tasks necessary to meet the requirements. This generally includes establishing what information will be gathered from the user or users, as well as what information should be returned.

The second phase is development, which includes implementation and testing. During the implementation step, the actual code is written to meet the needs determined in the analysis step of preparation. Compartmentalizing functionality is a key method for ensuring successful implementation. This entails identifying each task that needs to be accomplished and then writing code to address each task separately. The benefits of this method are that it promotes code reuse and simplifies the debugging process. The last step in the process is testing. Testing includes verifying not only that the solution meets the requirements when it is operating as planned, but also that it handles all invalid data and error conditions gracefully. An application has no real value if it can easily operate in a manner that was not intended. An example of this is allowing a user to crash an application and bring down a web site simply by entering an invalid keystroke. Keep in mind that carrying out all the steps outlined in this process is necessary to achieve success and that overlooking any of them can derail an otherwise effective solution.

Competitive Comparison

The following sections outline the major competitors of PHP in the dynamic web page development landscape. This discussion will help you understand what the alternatives to PHP are, and when you may want to consider these tools as an alternative to developing in PHP. Although PHP is appropriate for many aspects of web page development, you may want or need to take advantage of these other technologies, rather than developing in PHP alone.

ASP

Active Server Pages (ASP) is a technology that was developed by Microsoft as an extension to its line of web server software that includes Internet Information Server (IIS) and Personal Web Server (PWS). ASP comes with the aforementioned software at no additional cost. Like PHP code, ASP code resides within standard HTML pages and is executed on the web server before a page is returned to the browser. ASP pages typically have .asp as their file extension. ASP simultaneously supports two entirely different scripting languages out of the box: JScript and VBScript. Note that you can even increase the number of scripting languages ASP supports.

JScript is the Microsoft implementation of the ECMA 262 language specification (ECMAScript Edition 3). In addition to being a server-side scripting language, JScript can be used for client-side scripting when Microsoft Internet Explorer is the browser rendering the page, whereas PHP is executed on only the server. An important consideration is that JScript is not a scaled-back version of Java, nor is it the same as JavaScript (although they have similarities). A major drawback of JScript is its inability to read from or write to files. JScript is available, or under development, for the following platforms: Win32, Win16, Sun Solaris, HP-UX, and Macintosh. In addition, Microsoft will license the source code of JScript to developers porting the language to platforms not already supported.

VBScript is a subset of Microsoft's Visual Basic language, and therefore shares much of the same features and functionality. VBScript can be used in web server and browser applications, as well as other applications that utilize ActiveX controls, automation servers, and Java applets. VBScript talks to these applications by using ActiveX scripting, which is an emerging technology being developed to allow scripting engines to be interchangeable. Developers can license VBScript source implementations for use in their products at no charge. VBScript is available, or under development, for the same platforms as JScript.

ASP is widely used for developing dynamically driven web sites in traditionally Microsoft environments. It is highly integrated with many other Microsoft technologies, such as ActiveX controls and Visual Basic. If you are developing for strictly a Microsoft audience and are very familiar with Visual Basic and ActiveX coding, you will need to examine whether PHP will be a more effective tool than ASP.

ColdFusion

ColdFusion is an Internet application server offered by Allaire Corporation. It is available on the Windows, Solaris, Red Hat Linux, and HP-UX platforms. ColdFusion's processing consists of both scripted pages and reusable components. It is available in three editions: Express, Professional, and Enterprise. The Express Edition is for individual use, the Professional Edition for small-scale deployments, and the Enterprise Edition for large-scale deployments. ColdFusion can be integrated with several other Internet technologies, including Simple Mail Transfer Protocol (SMTP), Post Office Protocol (POP), Hypertext Transfer Protocol (HTTP), Lightweight Directory Access Protocol (LDAP), File Transfer Protocol (FTP), Extensible Markup Language (XML), text search engines, and file servers. It is also extensible through Common Object Request Broker Architecture (CORBA), Component Object Model (COM), Java servlets, and JavaBeans. ColdFusion includes an IDE (integrated development environment), which features visual programming and database and debugging tools. ColdFusion includes many, if not all, of the features expected in a high-performance web application server, including multithreading, web server API support, database connection pooling, application-level dynamic load balancing, JIT (just-in-time) compiling, and caching, where applicable.

ColdFusion benefits from its strong integration with other Internet technologies, as well as the ability for developers to receive technical support. The major downside of ColdFusion is its cost, which can be upward of $5,000. Many of the advanced features are available in only the Enterprise Edition. In addition to being costly, ColdFusion typically requires a longer learning curve than PHP requires, and is not available on as many platforms as PHP.

JSP

JavaServer Pages (JSP) is a Java-based scripting language that is part of Sun Microsystems's Java Technology. It allows developers to create dynamic web pages by using XML tags and scriptlets. (*Scriptlets* are programs written in the Java programming language.) JSP is an extension of Java servlet technology. (*Servlets* are platform-independent server-side modules that are used to extend a web server's functionality by compiling the pages into servlets.) A key concept behind JSP is the separation of web presentation from web content.

Details on industry support for JSP can be found at the following location on the Internet: http://java.sun.com/products/jsp/industry.html. In addition, a reference implementation, Tomcat, is available through the Apache Software Foundation. More information can be found at http://jakarta.apache.org. JSP pages typically have a .jsp file extension and usually are compiled upon their first request from a web browser and then cached by the servlets engine in memory for further requests, offering faster subsequent page requests. Because JSP is an extension of Java, developers using JSP can take advantage of many of the features that Java offers, including integration with JavaBeans and the many APIs that exist for Java.

JSP usage seems to be on the rise and benefits from the usual hype that surrounds Java itself. For developers who are very familiar with Java, JSP is often a good choice; but it has some disadvantages, including, potentially, cost, depending on which vendor is chosen, as well as support on a smaller number of platforms than PHP supports. As PHP's support for Java grows, the differences between a JSP server's feature set and PHP's will continue to diminish.

Perl

The Perl language was originally developed by Larry Wall and has gained momentum through the contributions of thousands of developers. It has roots in C, sed, awk, Unix shells, and many other programming tools. Perl can be used for a variety of applications, not just web authoring. Besides web development, Perl is most often used for system administrator–level tools that require file and text manipulation. Perl is available free of charge and is supported by its user base. The major strength of Perl is its short learning curve. Perl can be used in a compiled state as well as an interpreted state, depending on the application it is being used in. Perl is very extensible and can be integrated with libraries written in other languages, such as C or Java.

Perl's major advantage over PHP is that it's been around longer, and thus has a wider development base. Like PHP, Perl is supported by the developer community, which typically allows for rapid progress and fast resolution of issues. Despite the many similarities between PHP and Perl, PHP often wins out as a web development tool because it was designed with the Internet in mind, whereas Perl is a general-purpose tool. Often, you can utilize both Perl and PHP in the same development environment, and there are many advantages to doing so.

Competitive Summary

Each of PHP's competitors offers many features and functional benefits comparable to those of PHP. Table 1-1 shows the approximate cost of the competing products and highlights some of the key advantages and disadvantages they have in comparison with PHP.

While the information presented in this chapter gives you a high-level view of PHP's competition, further exploration is necessary to determine which tool or tools are appropriate for each project you are working on. The positive responses to PHP that can be observed in many developer newsgroups and chat rooms suggest that PHP seems to be able to meet the needs of most web-based development projects these days. This is further evidenced by the growing adoption of it by many of the world's Internet sites, as seen in recent Netcraft surveys (http://www.netcraft.com/survey). Because of PHP's flexibility and openness, it should remain a serious contender in the web application development landscape for many years to come.

Product	Price	Key Advantages	Key Disadvantages
ASP	Free with Windows operating systems	Tight integration with other Microsoft products. Is flexible: supports two scripting languages.	Not open source. Not widely available on non-Windows platforms.
Perl	Free	Larger developer base because it has been in existence longer.	Not specifically designed for Internet development.
ColdFusion	Professional Edition—$1,300; Enterprise Edition—$5,000. Academic Edition available at a heavily discounted price	Robust IDE. Strong documentation and technical support.	Costly. Not open source.
JSP	Varies with the vendor	Tight integration with Java/Enterprise JavaBeans. Technical support available from some vendors.	Can be costly, depending on the vendor. Not always open source, depending on the vendors.

Table 1-1 *Comparing PHP with Similar Programming Languages*

What to Take Away

The purpose of this chapter was threefold. The first objective was to welcome you to the book and to explain the book's instructional approach. This is a hands-on, project-oriented book that will provide the intermediate to advanced PHP developer with a well-rounded base of experience from which to draw. The second objective was to examine the development process utilized in the projects featured in the following chapters. And the last objective was to take a brief look at PHP's competition. PHP is not the only tool available for dynamic web site development, but its openness, cost, and short learning curve make it a formidable option against the competition. Now that we have covered these topics, we are ready to dive into the first project.

CHAPTER

2

Developing in PHP

IN THIS CHAPTER:

chapter2_example.php—Simple multiplication table code used in the CVS examples

This chapter introduces you to the concept of source code control. Specifically, we will look at the CVS and WinCVS software packages. You will learn how to check code into the system, check code out of the system, modify and comment the code, and then check the modified code back into the system. We'll also discuss debugging and troubleshooting techniques, and introduce the Zend debugger.

Setting Up Your Environment

One of the most time-consuming tasks that any developer has to perform is setting up an adequate development environment. Before you begin developing an application, you must take into consideration all aspects of your setup and make sure that it satisfactorily represents real-world situations. In small development shops, this environment might serve a dual function by providing a setting for carrying out engineering as well as quality assurance tasks. In larger shops, quality assurance work is often performed on separate computers in a separate environment.

In this section, you will learn about two important elements of setting up a PHP development environment; version control and the Zend integrated development environment (IDE). This section is meant only to introduce you to the subject of version control, and it provides only general guidelines for selecting an editor.

Version Control

The most important purposes of a source code control system are to provide a record of development. This record provides the complete history of changes made to source code along with developer comments and dates. This allows developers to more easily trace the source of any problem that is associated with recent changes. The source code control system also provides a central repository for all code. This repository can be easily backed up to tape or CD-ROM for archival purposes. Since the most valuable asset of any software company is its source code, it is very important to spend the time to set up a system to protect it.

Source code control can be accomplished in many ways. Small development shops with a few developers can get away with implementing few or no formal processes for controlling source code. As a project grows and the development staff increases, the need for source code control becomes more evident.

This section provides a basic version control example in which the Concurrent Versions System (CVS) and Revision Control System (RCS) source code control systems are used. These software packages complement each other and are included with most Linux distributions. Note that this section discusses only the CVS and RCS installation and configuration procedures relevant to demonstrating source code control. For more information, see http://www.cvshome.org.

The setup in our example includes a Red Hat Linux 7.0 system with CVS version 1.10.8-8 and RCS version 5.7-13 installed. It also includes an Apache 1.3.12 web server that is configured with PHP 4.0.3 patch level 1. We will install a WinCVS client, available at http://www.wincvs.org, on a Windows system. We will use this Windows computer as our remote development system, and the Linux computer as our code repository. Additionally, Samba is installed on the Linux computer to provide connectivity from the Linux system to the Windows system. (Setup and configuration of Samba is beyond the scope of this book; please refer to the Samba installation and configuration documentation.) Finally, the W: drive has been mapped to the docroot directory, /var/www, and the V: drive has been mapped to the cvsroot directory, /home/cvsroot.

Setting Up the RCS and CVS Software

Red Hat 7.0 comes with RCS and CVS software. You install these software packages separately, but remember that CVS uses RCS as its base. To begin using CVS, you need to set up the environment variables on your Linux system. It is easiest to set these variables for all users in /etc/profile, but you can add them to your local profile (.bash_profile) in your home directory. These environment variables should be set as shown here:

```
EDITOR=/bin/vi
CVSROOT=/home/cvsroot
CVSREAD=yes
export EDITOR CVSROOT CVSREAD
```

After you change /etc/profile, you must log in again to set the environment variables. The next steps are to make sure that $CVSROOT exists and to assign the following permissions:

```
mkdir $CVSROOT
chmod o-rwx $CVSROOT
chmod ug+rwx $CVSROOT
chgrp users $CVSROOT
```

Next, we need to create a file in the docroot directory of our web server. On our Linux system, this directory is /var/www/html. The file will contain the following code:

chapter2_example.php

```
<HTML>
<HEAD>
<TITLE>Listing 2.1</TITLE>
</HEAD>
<BODY>
<?
print "<TABLE BORDER=1>\n";
for ( $y=1; $y<=12; $y++ )
```

```
    {
    print "<TR>\n";
    for ( $x=1; $x<=12; $x++ )
        {
        print "\t<TD>";
        print ($x*$y);
        print "</TD>\n";
        }
    print "</TR>\n";
    }
print "</TABLE>";
?>
</BODY>
</HTML>
```

This simple PHP script multiplies 1 × 1 through 12 × 12 and prints all the results in a nice, neat table. Figure 2-1 shows the output of this script. We will use this code during our CVS session. We now need to set up the WinCVS client on our remote Windows system. Run the setup.exe program, and install the application on your D: drive in a WinCVS directory.

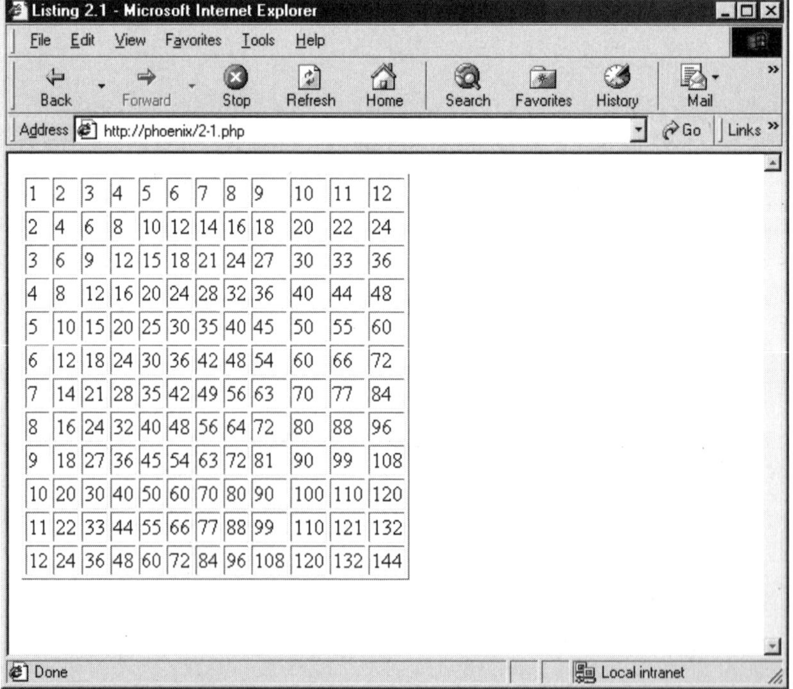

1	2	3	4	5	6	7	8	9	10	11	12
2	4	6	8	10	12	14	16	18	20	22	24
3	6	9	12	15	18	21	24	27	30	33	36
4	8	12	16	20	24	28	32	36	40	44	48
5	10	15	20	25	30	35	40	45	50	55	60
6	12	18	24	30	36	42	48	54	60	66	72
7	14	21	28	35	42	49	56	63	70	77	84
8	16	24	32	40	48	56	64	72	80	88	96
9	18	27	36	45	54	63	72	81	90	99	108
10	20	30	40	50	60	70	80	90	100	110	120
11	22	33	44	55	66	77	88	99	110	121	132
12	24	36	48	60	72	84	96	108	120	132	144

Figure 2-1 *Initial output of our sample script*

Creating a New Repository

Next, we'll create a repository. (First make sure that your CVS Working directory is set. In our example, we'll create the directory D:\CVSWork for this purpose.) Follow these steps:

1. From the Create menu, choose Create A New Repository. In the Init settings dialog box, make sure that the Force using the CVSROOT (-d) check box is not checked. The General tab should be set like it is here:

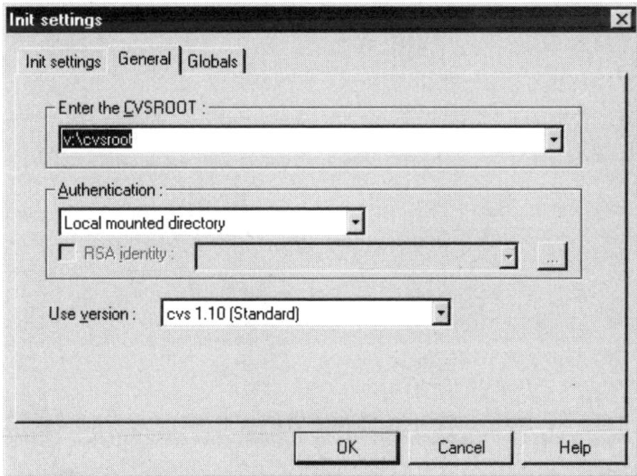

2. Additionally, set the Globals tab as shown here:

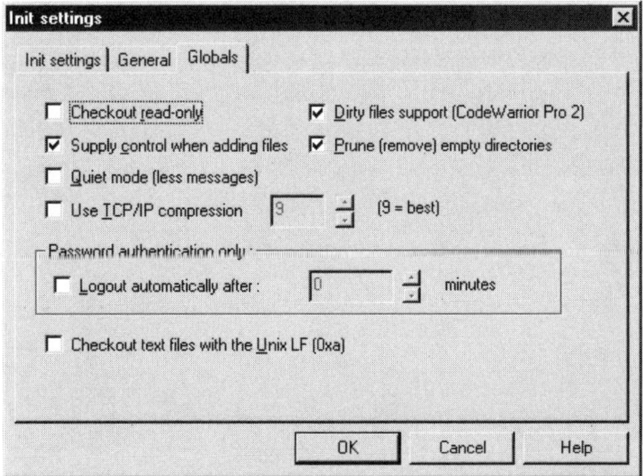

3. Click the OK button, and the status pane will display the following message if the operation is successful:

```
cvs init
*****CVS exited normally with code 0*****
```

Importing a Module

Now that we have created a code repository on our Linux system, we can import code into that repository. To do this, follow these steps:

1. Choose Create | Import Module from the menu bar.
2. You are then prompted to browse to the folder containing the code. Remember that our code is in W:\html, so we will browse to that folder and click OK.
3. In the next dialog box, Import Filter, click Continue to import PHP files.
4. You are next presented with the Import Settings dialog box. Make sure its settings are similar to those shown in Figure 2-2. Once these settings are correct, click OK. You will receive a status message similar to the following if the import operation is successful:

```
Filtering 'W:\html'...
cvs import -I ! -I CVS -m "no message" html instant chapter2 (in directory
W:\html)
N html/2-1.php
No conflicts created by this import
*****CVS exited normally with code 0*****
```

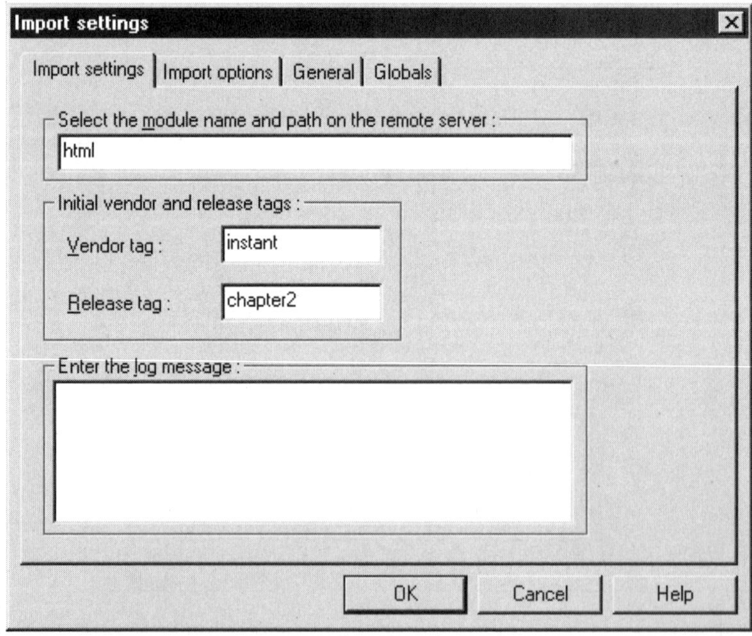

Figure 2-2 *Configuring import settings*

Checking Out a Module

Now that we have created a repository and imported our source code into it, we are ready to check out the code and work on it:

1. From the menu bar, choose Create | Checkout Module.
2. You will then be presented with the Checkout Settings dialog box. Make sure the settings are like those here:

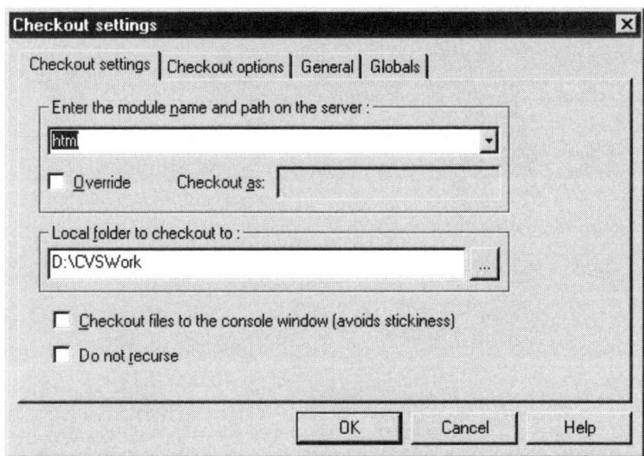

   Once again, if this checkout operation is successful, you will see a message similar to the following in the status pane:

```
cvs checkout -P html (in directory D:\CVSWork)
cvs checkout: Updating html
U html/2-1.php
*****CVS exited normally with code 0*****
```

3. You can refresh the window by pressing F5; the interface will look like the one shown in Figure 2-3.

Our source code is now checked out, and the filename of the file in which it resides is displayed in the user interface along with a version number of 1.1.1.1, a date, and a status.

Editing and Saving the Source Code

The file mentioned in the previous section is now ready for you to edit. To do so, double-click the filename, and WinCVS will launch Notepad, containing your

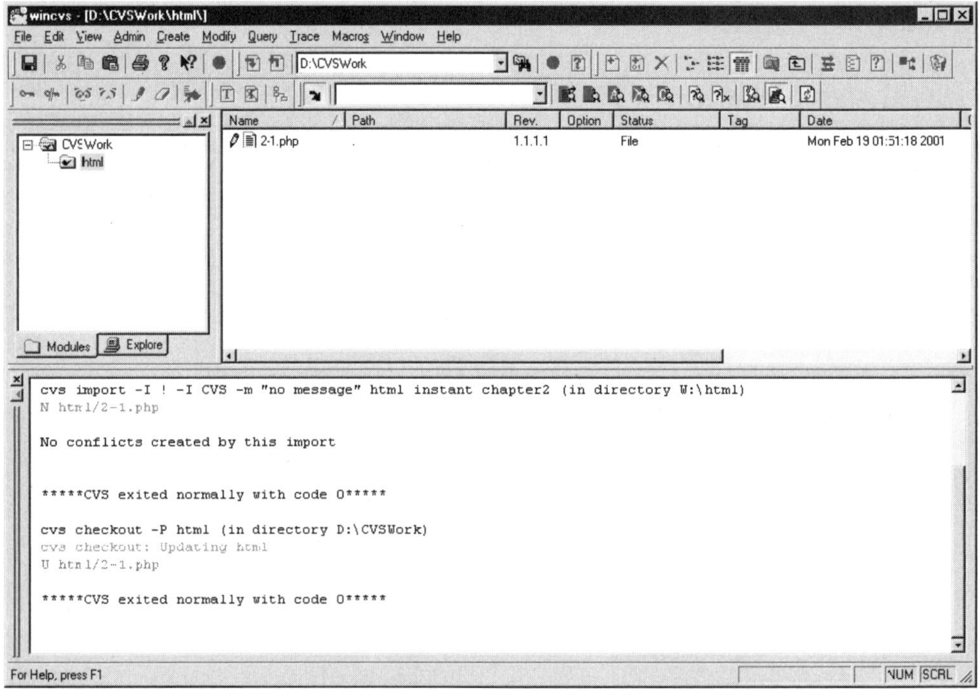

Figure 2-3 *Refreshing the WinCVS interface*

source code. Let's add a header, Multiplication Tables, to the table. To do this, add the following code after line 7, and save the file:

```
print "<TH colspan=12>Multiplication Tables</th>\n";
```

The output will be similar to that shown in Figure 2-4.

Notice that some of the items in the WinCVS interface have changed. The icon to the left of the filename has changed from white to red, and the status has changed to Mod. File, indicating that the file has been modified. Your WinCVS window will look like the one shown in Figure 2-5.

To save your changes back to the repository, or check in the code, select the file, and then, from the menu bar, choose Modify | Commit Selection. A dialog box, shown in Figure 2-6, will appear so that you can comment on the changes you have made. Once you have added your comments, click OK. You will then see the following text in the status pane if the operation is successful:

```
cvs commit -m "Added Header "Multiplication Tables" to the code" 2-1.php (in
directory D:\CVSWork\html\)
Checking in 2-1.php;
v:\cvsroot/html/2-1.php,v  <--  2-1.php
new revision: 1.2; previous revision: 1.1
done
*****CVS exited normally with code 0*****
```

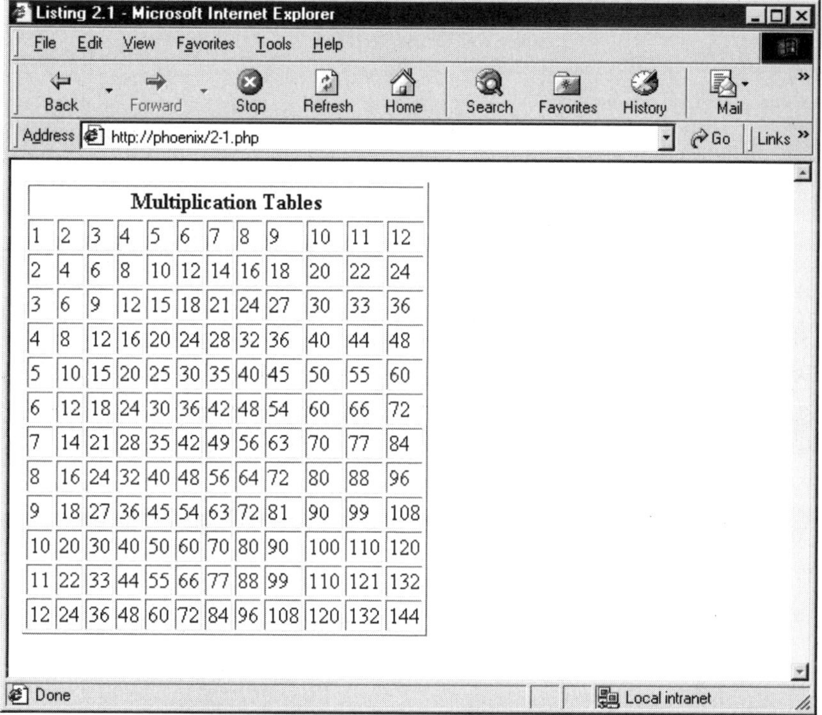

Multiplication Tables											
1	2	3	4	5	6	7	8	9	10	11	12
2	4	6	8	10	12	14	16	18	20	22	24
3	6	9	12	15	18	21	24	27	30	33	36
4	8	12	16	20	24	28	32	36	40	44	48
5	10	15	20	25	30	35	40	45	50	55	60
6	12	18	24	30	36	42	48	54	60	66	72
7	14	21	28	35	42	49	56	63	70	77	84
8	16	24	32	40	48	56	64	72	80	88	96
9	18	27	36	45	54	63	72	81	90	99	108
10	20	30	40	50	60	70	80	90	100	110	120
11	22	33	44	55	66	77	88	99	110	121	132
12	24	36	48	60	72	84	96	108	120	132	144

Figure 2-4 *Revising the sample script*

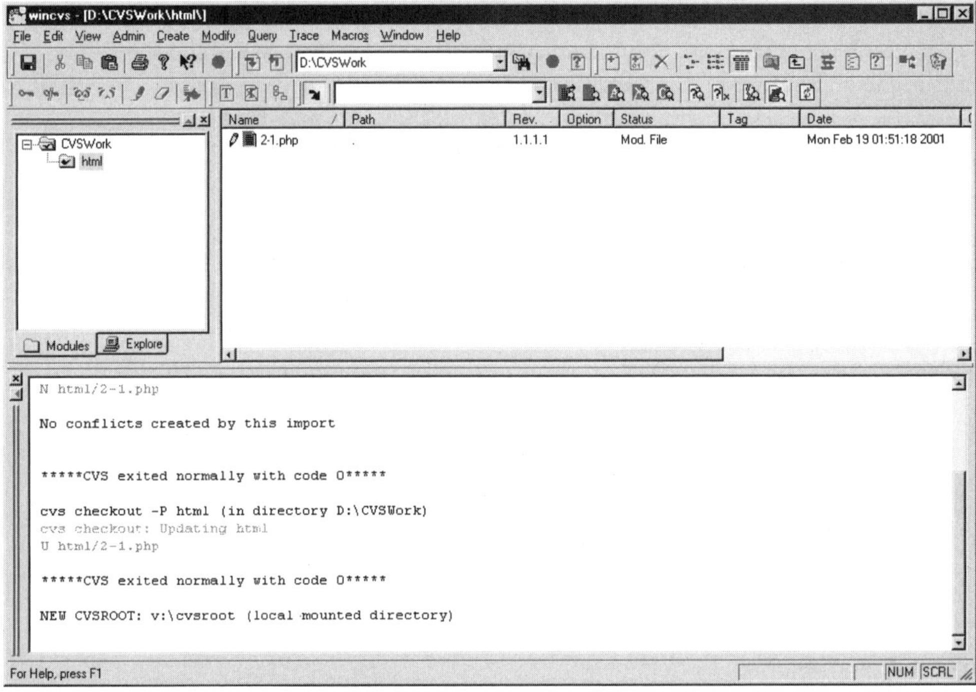

Figure 2-5 *After modifying a file*

Notice that as part of this operation, a new revision number is associated with the file. Figure 2-7 shows how the WinCVS workspace looks after you check in code.

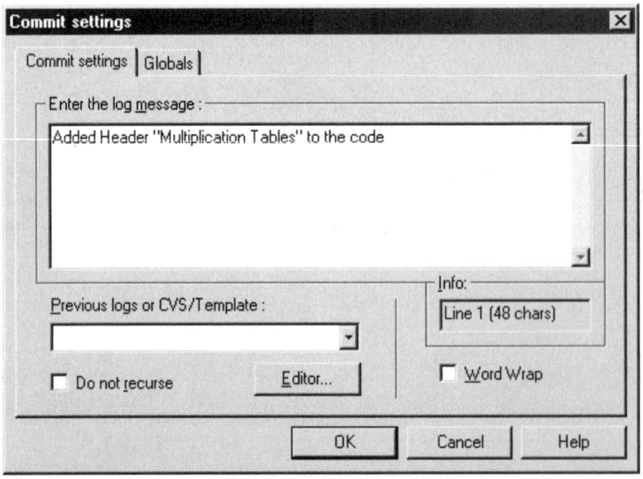

Commit settings
Commit settings | Globals
Enter the log message :
Added Header "Multiplication Tables" to the code
Info:
Line 1 (48 chars)
Previous logs or CVS/Template :
Do not recurse
Editor...
Word Wrap
OK
Cancel
Help

Figure 2-6 *Commenting on code edits in the Commit Settings dialog box*

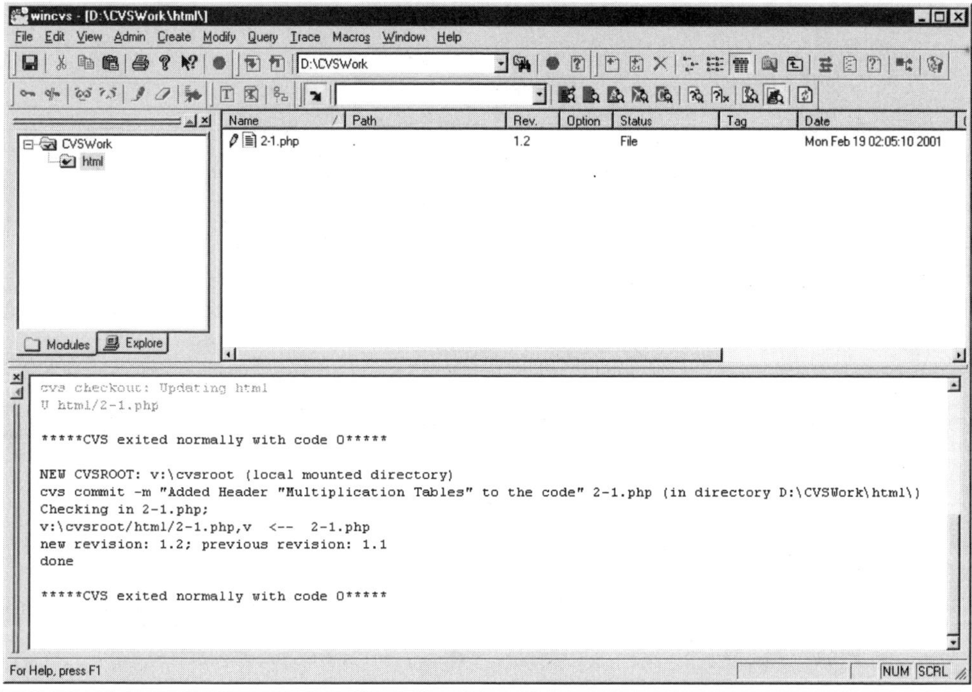

Figure 2-7 *After checking in code*

Now that we have successfully checked out, modified, and checked in code, let's do it one more time. Double-click the file, and change the code as follows:

```
<HTML>
<HEAD>
<TITLE>Listing 2.1</TITLE>
</HEAD>
<BODY>
<?
print "<TABLE BORDER=1>\n";
print "<TH colspan=13>Multiplication Tables</th>\n";
    print "<TR><td></td>\n";
    for ( $x=1; $x<=12; $x++ )
        {
        print "\t<TD>$x *</TD>\n";
        }
    print "</TR>\n";
for ( $y=1; $y<=12; $y++ )
    {
    print "<TR>\n";
print "<td>$y =</td>";
```

```
        for ( $x=1; $x<=12; $x++ )
            {
            print "\t<TD>";
            print ($x*$y);
            print "</TD>\n";
            }
        print "</TR>\n";
        }
print "</TABLE>";
?>
</BODY>
</HTML>
```

These changes direct the script to include a row at the top and a column on the left side of the table as a reference to aid in readability. The sample output is displayed in Figure 2-8. You could also mark the new code in some way, like color coding it or inserting arrows at the beginning of the added lines, to indicate the additions and aid in readability.

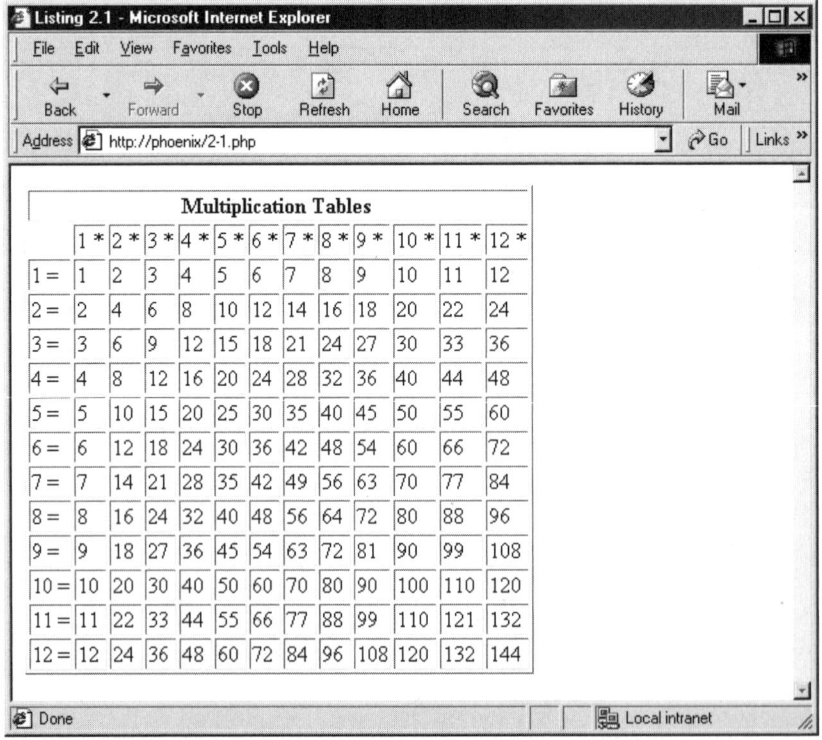

Multiplication Tables												
	1 *	2 *	3 *	4 *	5 *	6 *	7 *	8 *	9 *	10 *	11 *	12 *
1 =	1	2	3	4	5	6	7	8	9	10	11	12
2 =	2	4	6	8	10	12	14	16	18	20	22	24
3 =	3	6	9	12	15	18	21	24	27	30	33	36
4 =	4	8	12	16	20	24	28	32	36	40	44	48
5 =	5	10	15	20	25	30	35	40	45	50	55	60
6 =	6	12	18	24	30	36	42	48	54	60	66	72
7 =	7	14	21	28	35	42	49	56	63	70	77	84
8 =	8	16	24	32	40	48	56	64	72	80	88	96
9 =	9	18	27	36	45	54	63	72	81	90	99	108
10 =	10	20	30	40	50	60	70	80	90	100	110	120
11 =	11	22	33	44	55	66	77	88	99	110	121	132
12 =	12	24	36	48	60	72	84	96	108	120	132	144

Figure 2-8 *Making final revisions to the sample script*

When you commit the source code, add comments similar to those shown here, and click OK.

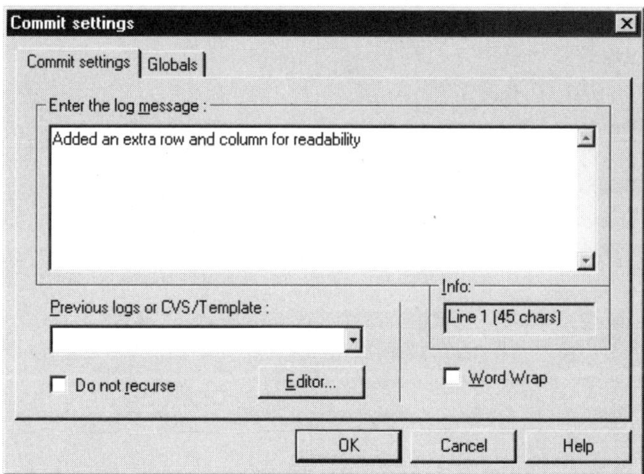

The status pane at the bottom of the WinCVS interface will display the following message, and the file version will be changed from 1.2 to 1.3.

```
cvs commit -m "Added an extra row and column for readability" 2-1.php (in
directory D:\CVSWork\html\)
Checking in 2-1.php;
v:\cvsroot/html/2-1.php,v  <--  2-1.php
new revision: 1.3; previous revision: 1.2
done
*****CVS exited normally with code 0*****
```

Your WinCVS interface will look like the one shown in Figure 2-9.

Viewing a Previous Code Version

Let's say that after you have checked in your final code, version 1.3, someone asks you what features and functionality are included in the 1.2 version. You could either try to remember or get the information from your source code control system. To do this, in WinCVS, select the file, and choose Query | Graph Selection. The entire revision history of the file is displayed, as shown in Figure 2-10.

If you click a box in the upper-right pane, you will receive output summarizing the revision that you chose. For example, if you click the box labeled 2-1.php, you will receive the following output:

```
Rcs file : 'v:\cvsroot/html/2-1.php,v'
Working file : '2-1.php'
```

```
Head revision : 1.3
Branch revision :
Locks : strict
Access :
Symbolic names :
1.1.1.1 : 'chapter2'
1.1.1 : 'instant'
Keyword substitution : 'kv'
Total revisions : 4
Selected revisions : 4
Description :
```

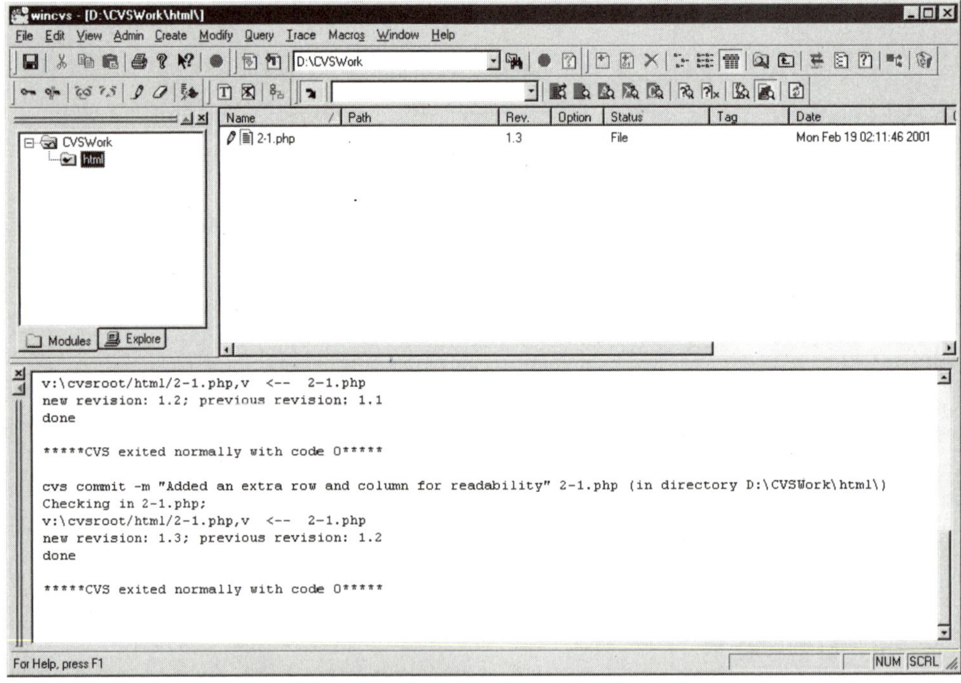

Figure 2-9 *After making final revisions*

Similarly, if you click the box labeled 1.2, you will get information in the status pane about this revision, as follows:

```
Revision : 1.2
Date : 2001/2/19 2:8:33
Author : 'rcox'
State : 'Exp'
Lines : +1 0
Description :
Added Header "Multiplication Tables" to the code
```

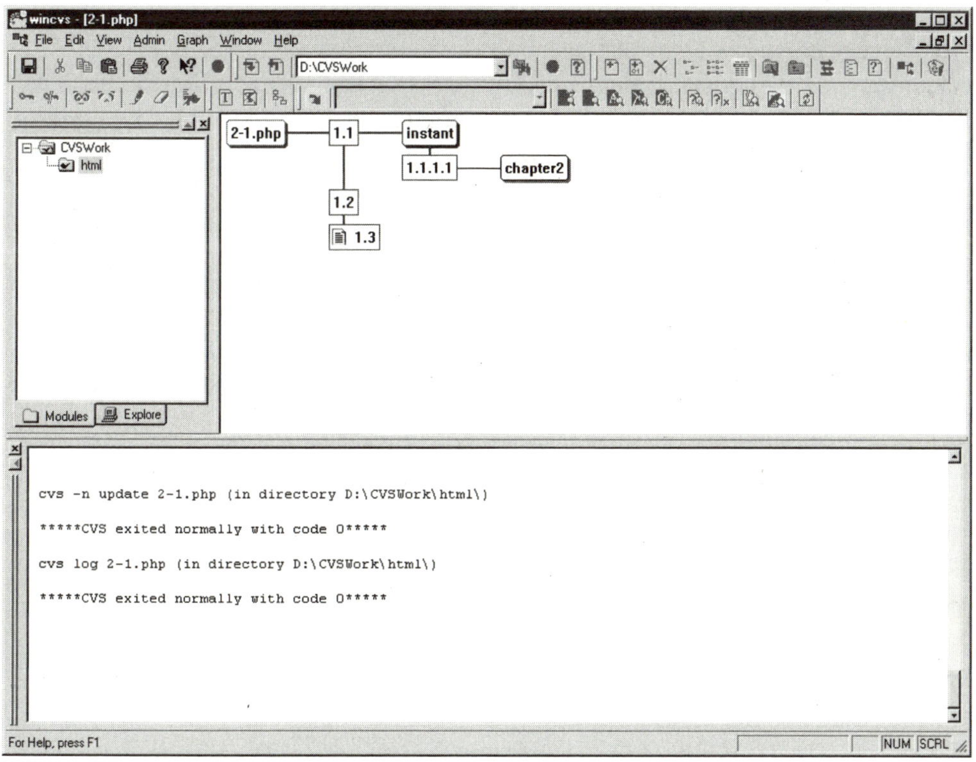

Figure 2-10 *Displaying the file history*

To view the version 1.2 source code, simply select the box labeled 1.2 in the graph pane, and choose Graph | Retrieve Version. A file, named 1-2.php.#.1.2, will be placed in your working directory. This will be version 1.2 of the file. Figure 2-11 shows how your window will look.

You can see that even though this is a simple example scenario of source code control, CVS is a very powerful tool. Coupled with the WinCVS client as in our configuration, you can put together an entire system to safeguard your most valuable asset.

Editors

Ask ten developers which web application editor they prefer, and you are likely to get ten different answers. The features and functionality that are important to each of these developers are likely to vary as wildly as the developers' opinions about editors. One thing is sure: there is a select set of features that every good editor should have. In this section, you'll learn about the characteristics you should look for in an editor. You'll also be introduced to the Zend IDE, which provides an editor as well as other desirable features that are available only in an IDE.

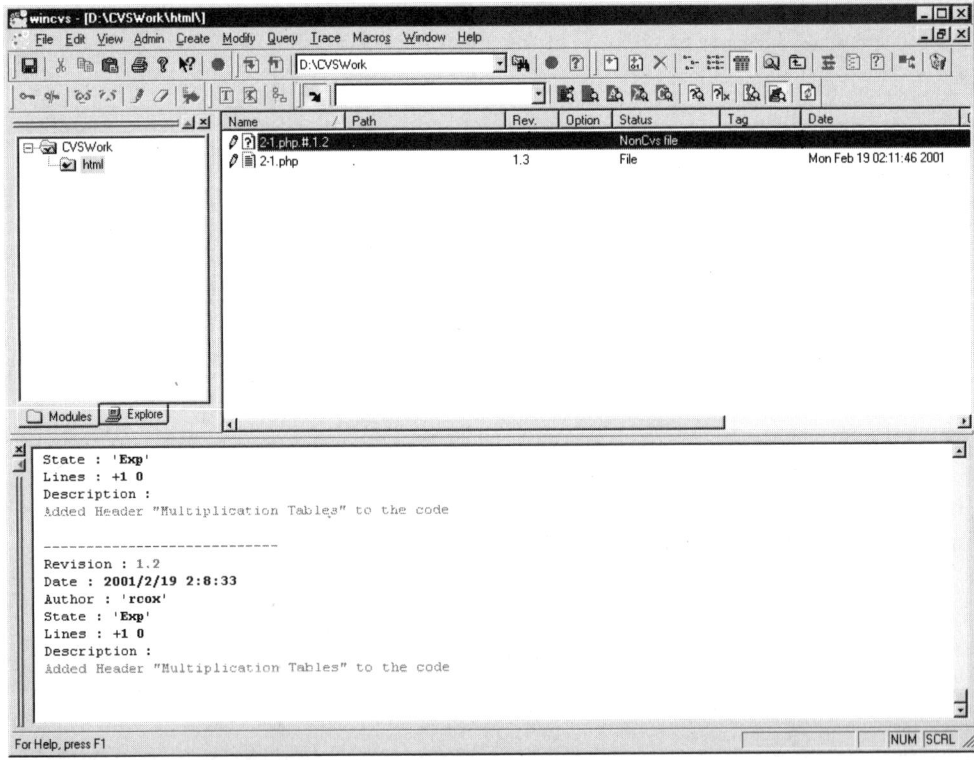

Figure 2-11 *Retrieving version 1.2 of the sample script*

HTML Editors

When choosing an editor, find one that can maintain pure Hypertext Markup Language (HTML)—that is, one that doesn't add characters or control codes. What-You-See-Is-What-You-Get (WYSIWYG) editors, like FrontPage, add code in HTML and PHP files. You should look for an editor that provides some level of syntax highlighting and code completion. These features are available with many commercial editors and open-source editors. An editor should also recognize and highlight the latest web technologies and languages, such as Active Server Pages (ASP); Cascading Style Sheets (CSS); Dynamic HTML (DHTML); JavaServer Pages (JSP); JavaScript; Perl; Visual Basic, Scripting Edition (VBScript); Wireless Markup Language (WML); and Handheld Device Markup Language (HDML).

Some editors include features that enable developers to define custom tags or custom code, features that automatically complete code, features that help with code syntax, and so forth. Still others include software that scans your code for mismatched parentheses, misused tags, or other syntax errors. One very useful feature provides color-coding support for different languages, such as ASP, CSS, HTML, JavaScript, JSP, Perl, PHP, and VBScript.

There are editors that provide assistance when creating image maps, frames, tables, and JavaScript. Some editors even offer integration with File Transfer Protocol (FTP) for deploying files to your web site. There are link verifiers, spell checkers, and CSS editors. The point here is that if you can dream up a feature, you can probably find an editor out there that has it.

The Zend IDE

Because of the excitement surrounding PHP, some companies are beginning to offer support and products for developers using the language. Zend is one such company. Zeev Suraski and Andi Gutmans, two members of the PHP core development team, formally founded Zend in 1997. In 1999, after the Zend Engine was complete, the company was incorporated, and it is currently privately held and is headquartered in Ramat Gan, Israel. Along with creating the Zend Engine, Zend has developed a few exciting new products that can benefit the PHP developer. One of these products is the Zend IDE, a Java-based application that runs on both Windows and Linux and provides some of the major features mentioned in the preceding section.

The Zend IDE provides syntax highlighting for both PHP and HTML code and is fully customizable. The IDE also includes an automatic code completion feature that allows you to choose a tag from a drop-down list when you begin to define a tag or an attribute. This feature also provides syntax help with PHP and HTML tags. There are also multiple docking areas in the IDE that allow you to browse your file system and incorporate some of the built-in debugging features. In the next section, you'll learn more about the debugging aspects of the Zend IDE.

Debugging and Troubleshooting Techniques

Debugging your code can be one of the most frustrating tasks you undertake during the development cycle. Many hours can be spent tracking down bugs and creating sound and stable code. If you don't have the luxury of owning a debugger, you can still quickly track down problems. This section discusses some techniques for doing so. It also describes a very helpful debugging tool offered by Zend. Additionally, this section examines some practices that you can use to prevent bugs in the first place.

Techniques and Practices

When you run into a problem, you should first print out all related variables, return codes, and anything that will help you determine the cause of the problem. The print() function will be your best friend during the troubleshooting process. You can print out variables, return codes, indexes, arrays, and more. This allows you to check data and verify the values. Often, if you are experiencing problems, this technique will expose data or variables that are not what you expected. It doesn't matter if the format of the page is messed up while you are printing out variables during the debugging process—you can go back and fix that later. The important thing is to track down the source of the problem and correct it. Verifying the value of counters and variables can help you do this.

Second, make sure you check the return values for all PHP function calls. This seems so obvious, yet many novice programmers forget to check the return values and trap error codes. Almost every PHP function produces some return value. For instance, if you are establishing a connection to a PostgreSQL database, you will need to check the connection to the database and the return result from the query. If either of the return codes is a zero (0), you can print out an error message to let the user know of the failure. An example of this technique is shown here:

```
$conn = pg_Connect("localhost", "5432", "", "", "ap");
   if (!$conn) {echo "A database connection error occurred.\n"; exit;}
$result = pg_Exec($conn,"SELECT name, idid FROM idea ORDER BY name");
   if (!$result) {echo "A query error occurred.\n"; exit;}
```

Notice that we check the return value of $conn after calling pg_Connect() and the value of $result after calling pg_Exec(). If either of these functions returns a zero (0), the function was unsuccessful. The preceding example captures this result and prints out an appropriate error.

Another common mistake that is often made by novice and expert programmers alike is not taking into account all programmatic circumstances. It is very difficult to think of all the ways users can input data and browsers can behave. You need to consider as many of these possibilities as you can. What happens if a user bookmarks a page in the middle of your application? What happens if a user clicks the Back button and resubmits information? What happens if the database goes down? What happens if foreign characters get submitted to your database? All these questions and many more have to be considered when you are designing your application. If you are the sole developer or are part of a small development shop, you will be required to think of ways to break your application. If you are fortunate enough to have a quality assurance group, they will develop the plans to test your application.

The Zend Debugger

If you have ever developed in a traditional programming language like C or C++, you understand the value of using a debugger to step through your code, set breakpoints, and watch variables. As part of its IDE, Zend has developed a debugger for PHP development. This is a great little tool that can save you many hours tracking down problems.

The Zend debugger comes in two parts: the server component and the client component. The client component, as explained earlier, is part of the Zend IDE. This application is Java based and enables you to set breakpoints, watch variables, and step through the code. The second part of the Zend debugger, the server component, is very easy to install. You just place a few files in the appropriate locations and edit the php.ini file to include the code. In less than 30 minutes, even a novice developer can set up the server and client components and be ready to debug scripts. More information about the Zend IDE, the debugger, and other Zend products is available at http://www.zend.com. Figure 2-12 shows the Zend debugger's interface.

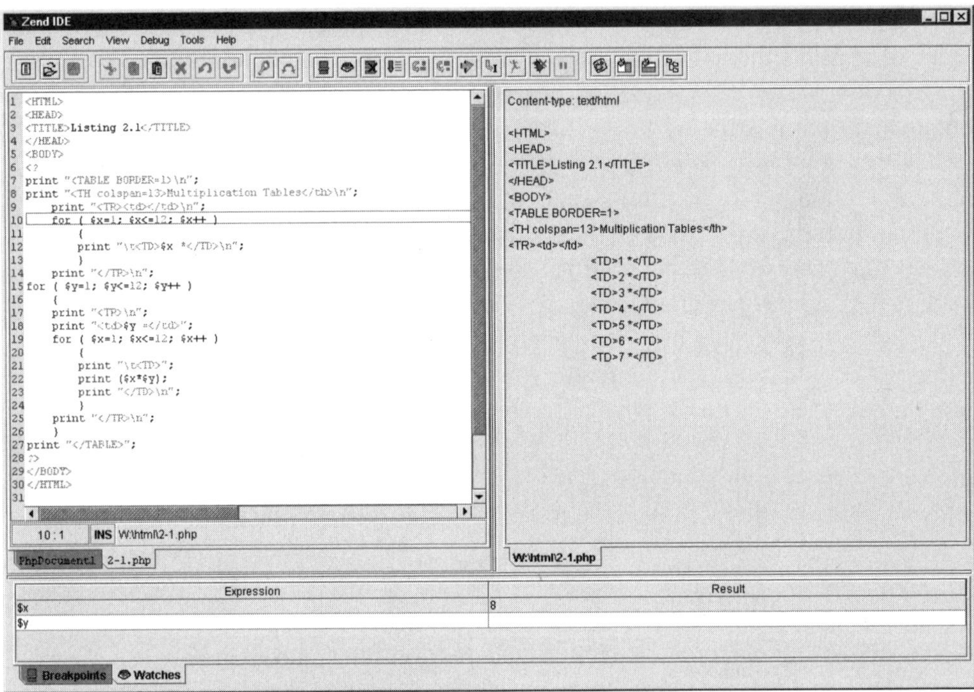

Figure 2-12 *Using the Zend debugger*

What to Take Away

Setting up your environment, which includes your source code control system, your editor, and your debugging environment, can take a significant amount of time. However, the more time you invest in this initial process, the better the quality of your code will be and the less time you'll spend debugging your application. You have learned some techniques in this chapter that will help you debug your code. You have also learned how to set up and administer a source code control system. As you go throughout this book, it is hoped that you will be able to build upon the examples that are presented and use the techniques you have learned in this chapter.

PART II

Basic PHP and Dynamic HTML

OBJECTIVES

- Use readily available functions in PHP to display the current date
- Display a monthly calendar using either the current date or one passed in
- Devise a way to view different months of the year, including preceding and previous years
- Use existing and user-defined functions in PHP to play a game of Connect 4
- Include error checking and game logic

CHAPTER

3

A Simple PHP Calendar

IN THIS CHAPTER:

chapter 3_calendar.php—Contains all the needed PHP code to display a monthly calendar

Our first project will be to design and implement a simple web-based calendar using PHP. We will stick to the basics, using the functions already available to us in PHP. In this chapter, you will learn to use the date() and the checkdate() functions. You will also use the if, while, switch, and case control structures. The finished example will look similar to Figure 3-1.

Calendar Requirements

To keep things simple, you'll use top-down design and keep the features of your calendar to a minimum. You will need to be able to determine and display the current date; display a month (either based on a date being passed in or the current date); and have a way to view other months in the current year, as well as in other years. You will display your calendar inside an HTML table that, when printed out, should look similar to what you see in your web browser.

Designing the Calendar

The first thing to do in this project is to design a simple HTML page with a table, links, and formatting. You can do this on your own. This is a simple HTML exercise and something that most beginning web developers can do in 30 minutes or less. Many HTML editors can produce a simple working table with the characteristics you will need by clicking a few buttons. The conversion from HTML to PHP is just as easy: simply save the file under your web server's document root directory with a .php extension. Assuming that your web server is running, has PHP 4 properly installed, and recognizes the .php extension as a script, you should be able to call the file through a browser and see your non-dynamic calendar.

Converting the static HTML calendar to dynamic PHP will take a little work; but since the format and page design are done, you have already completed a large part of the development. The first few lines of your program don't look much different from the static page. Remember to change all references to your file from .html to .php.

Let's begin your calendar.php script with some standard HTML tags. These tags may already be present if you created a calendar.html with an HTML editor.

Today is: Tuesday, March 06th 2001

March 2001						
Sunday	**Monday**	**Tuesday**	**Wednesday**	**Thursday**	**Friday**	**Saturday**
				1	2	3
4	5	6	7	8	9	10
11	12	13	14	15	16	17
18	19	20	21	22	23	24
25	26	27	28	29	30	31
2000	Jan. | Feb. | Mar. | Apr. | May | Jun. | Jul. | Aug. | Sep. | Oct. | Nov. | Dec.					2002

Figure 3-1 *A simple web-based calendar*

chapter3_calendar.php

```
<html>
<head>
<title>A 'Simple' PHP Calendar</title>
</head>
<body>
```

The first step in your code is to check for two parameters that are optionally passed into the script. They are as follows:

- $Year, in the format of a four-digit year, such as 2001
- $Month, which corresponds to the numerical month, such as 11 for November

If the $Year and $Month values are not passed in or have not been set, your script will use the current year and month, based on the system clock of the machine the script is run on. You can determine what the current year and month are by using the PHP date() function as shown here:

```
<?
/* One of the first things we should do is check for $Year and $Month
   parameters. If they are null then we assume that the year and
   month to displayed will be the current year and month, and
   therefore set the $Year and $Month variables with the PHP date()
   function. Otherwise we will use the values passed in. */
if ($Year=="")
{
   $Year=date("Y");
}
if ($Month=="")
{
   $Month=date("m");
}
?>
```

Now, you want to display today's date. Again, use the date() function provided by PHP. You also want to provide a link back to your script, so that users of the calendar have a place to click to take them back to the current month's calendar, as shown here:

```
<p align="center"><b><a href="./chapter3_calendar.php">Today</a> is:
<?
```

```
/* Display today's date via the PHP date() function */
printf(date("l, F dS Y"));
?>
</b><br><br>
```

Note the formatting strings used in the date() function. For this example, we used the following options:

- **l** Displays the entire day of the week as a text string, such as Friday
- **F** Displays the entire month as a text string, such as January
- **d** Displays the day of the month as two digits with leading zeros, such as 01
- **S** Displays the English ordinal suffix as two characters, such as th or nd
- **Y** Displays the year as four digits, such as 1999

Now that you know how to get the current date, and you know that, optionally, a date can be passed into your script, you can display a visual representation of the month in the form of a calendar. Start by creating an HTML table and displaying the month, which you will get based on your $Month value. You want to make the display of the month a little more user friendly, so you will use the PHP switch() function to print the name of the month. For instance, if $Month = 11, your output is November. Your code will look as follows:

```
<table width="700" border="1" cellspacing="0" cellpadding="4" align="center">
<tr>
<td colspan="7" height="55" align="center" valign="middle"><font size="6">
<?
// Display the month of the calendar we are going to show.
switch($Month)
{
   case "1":
      printf("January");
      break;
   case "2":
      printf("February");
      break;
   case "3":
      printf("March");
      break;
```

```
    case "4":
       printf("April");
       break;
    case "5":
       printf("May");
       break;
    case "6":
       printf("June");
       break;
    case "7":
       printf("July");
       break;
    case "8":
       printf("August");
       break;
    case "9":
       printf("September");
       break;
    case "10":
       printf("October");
       break;
    case "11":
       printf("November");
       break;
    case "12":
       printf("December");
       break;
}
```

Let's also display the year. You can do this by printing out your $Year value, as follows:

```
// Display the year of the calendar we are going to show.
printf(" %d",$Year);
```

Now that you have the year and month displayed, you need to display the days of that month. You'll need to know some things first, so you can properly fill in each cell of the table. Start by determining how many days there are in the month. To do this, you use a counter, a while() loop, and a PHP function, checkdate(). This allows you to pass in a date in the form of month, day, and year, such as 9,11,2001. If this is a valid date, the function returns True; if not, the function returns False. As long as the checkdate() function returns True, you will increment your counter: $DaysInMonth. Once False is returned, you exit your loop, and you have the number of days in the month, stored in the variable $DaysInMonth. Following is the code for the loop we will use:

```
/* Now we need to figure out how many days are in this month, using
   the PHP checkdate() function. We will loop and increment the
   $DaysInMonth counter until we exceed the number of days for the month
   (when the checkdate() function then returns False). */
$DaysInMonth = 1;
while (checkdate($Month,$DaysInMonth,$Year))
   $DaysInMonth++;
endwhile;
```

With that out of the way, you also should determine which day of the week the first day of the month starts on, because not every month begins on a Sunday. To do this, you'll use some basic conditional if() statements, and another wonderful PHP function, mktime(). You will use this function in conjunction with your $Year and $Month values, as follows:

```
/* Now we need to figure out which day of the week the first day of
   the month falls on. */
if ( date("l", mktime(0,0,0,$Month,1,$Year)) == "Sunday" )
{
   $DayOfWeek = 1;
}
if ( date("l", mktime(0,0,0,$Month,1,$Year)) == "Monday" )
{
   $DayOfWeek = 2;
}
if ( date("l", mktime(0,0,0,$Month,1,$Year)) == "Tuesday" )
{
   $DayOfWeek = 3;
}
if ( date("l", mktime(0,0,0,$Month,1,$Year)) == "Wednesday" )
{
   $DayOfWeek = 4;
}
if ( date("l", mktime(0,0,0,$Month,1,$Year)) == "Thursday" )
{
```

```
    $DayOfWeek = 5;
}
if ( date("l", mktime(0,0,0,$Month,1,$Year)) == "Friday" )
{
    $DayOfWeek = 6;
}
if ( date("l", mktime(0,0,0,$Month,1,$Year)) == "Saturday" )
{
    $DayOfWeek = 7;
}
?>
</font></td>
</tr>
```

Let's display a table row with the days of the week at the top of your calendar. The code for this is simple enough, as shown here:

```
<tr>
<td align="center" width="100" height="30" bgcolor="#EFEFEF">
<b>Sunday</b>
</td>
<td align="center" width="100" bgcolor="#EFEFEF"><b>Monday</b></td>
<td align="center" width="100" bgcolor="#EFEFEF"><b>Tuesday</b></td>
<td align="center" width="100" bgcolor="#EFEFEF"><b>Wednesday</b></td>
<td align="center" width="100" bgcolor="#EFEFEF"><b>Thursday</b></td>
<td align="center" width="100" bgcolor="#EFEFEF"><b>Friday</b></td>
<td align="center" width="100" bgcolor="#EFEFEF"><b>Saturday</b></td>
</tr>
```

The next few rows of the table will contain the numerical representation for each of the days. You will use for() loops to go through each row representing the week and each column representing the day of the week. $Row and $Col will be used as counters to keep track of your table rows and columns. Since months don't always start on a Sunday and end on a Saturday, you will "pad" the beginning and ending empty table cells with spaces. The code looks like this:

```
<tr>
<?
/* Let's start off displaying our calendar month by setting some
    starting values. */
```

```
$Row = 1;
$Col = 1;
$DayCounter = 1;
/* Now let's go output our calendar days, week by week. We will use
   some simple for() loops and counters to move through each row and
   column in our table. */
/* If the first day of the month doesn't fall on a Sunday we need to
   pad the table cells for each day with spaces, until we reach the
   day of the week the month starts on. Once we get to that point
   we can start outputting the days of the month. */
if ($DayOfWeek > $DayCounter)
{
   for($Col = 1; $Col < $DayOfWeek; $Col++)
   {
      printf("<td height=\"100\" valign=\"top\"> </td>");
   }
   for($Col = $Col; $Col <= 7; $Col++)
   {
      printf("<td height=\"100\" valign=\"top\"><b>%d</b>", $DayCounter);
      printf("</td>");
      $DayCounter++;
   }
   $Col = 1;
   $Row++;
}
/* If the first day of the month falls on a Sunday we can go right
 into displaying the entire week. */
else
{
   printf("<tr>");
   for($Col = $Col; $Col <= 7; $Col++)
   {
      printf("<td height=\"100\" valign=\"top\"><b>%d</b>", $DayCounter);
      printf("</td>");
      $DayCounter++;
   }
   $Col = 1;
   $Row++;
   printf("</tr>");
}
```

Now that your first week of the month is done, you can continue displaying the remaining days of the month. You will once again use your $Row and $Col values to keep track of where you are in your table, and start new rows where necessary, as follows:

```
/* With our first week of the month out of the way, we can continue
  displaying the rest of the days of the month, starting a new table
  row for each new week. Once the $DayCounter exceeds the number of
  $DaysInMonth, we just pad the remaining table cells with spaces. */
for($Row = $Row; $Row <= 6; $Row++)
{
   printf("<tr>");
   for($Col = $Col; $Col <= 7; $Col++)
   {
      if($DayCounter >= $DaysInMonth)
      {
         printf("<td height=\"100\" valign=\"top\"> ");
      }
      else
      {
         printf("<td height=\"100\" valign=\"top\"><b>%d</b>", $DayCounter);
      }
      printf("</td>");
      $DayCounter++;
   }
   $Col = 1;
   printf("</tr>");
}
?>
</tr>
```

Notice how you increment the $DayCounter as you go through each row and column in the table, and make sure it does not exceed the number of days in the month ($DaysInmonth). If it does, simply pad the remaining table cells with spaces, until your loop is finished.

The last feature of this program will be to provide a way for the user to "jump" forward and backward to other months in the year and to other years. Since you already know the month and year, you can use these values as a starting point, as follows:

```
<tr>
<td align="center" valign="middle" height="30" bgcolor="#EFEFEF">
<?
/* We need to provide the user with a link so they can skip to a
   previous year. To do this we will take our current $Year and
   subtract 1, and assign it to the value $LastYear. */
$LastYear = ($Year-1);
```

```
printf("<a href=\"./chapter3_calendar.php?Year=%d&Month=%d\">%d</a>",
 $LastYear , $Month, $LastYear);
?>
</td>
<td colspan="5" align="center" valign="middle" bgcolor="#EFEFEF">
<?
/* We also need to provide the user with links to all of the months
   of the year. To do this we will use our $Year, and hard-code the
   values for each month. */
printf("<a href=\"./chapter3_calendar.php?Year=%d&Month=1\">Jan.</a> | ", $Year);
printf("<a href=\"./chapter3_calendar.php?Year=%d&Month=2\">Feb.</a> | ", $Year);
printf("<a href=\"./chapter3_calendar.php?Year=%d&Month=3\">Mar.</a> | ", $Year);
printf("<a href=\"./chapter3_calendar.php?Year=%d&Month=4\">Apr.</a> | ", $Year);
printf("<a href=\"./chapter3_calendar.php?Year=%d&Month=5\">May</a> | ", $Year);
printf("<a href=\"./chapter3_calendar.php?Year=%d&Month=6\">Jun.</a> | ", $Year);
printf("<a href=\"./chapter3_calendar.php?Year=%d&Month=7\">Jul.</a> | ", $Year);
printf("<a href=\"./chapter3_calendar.php?Year=%d&Month=8\">Aug.</a> | ", $Year);
printf("<a href=\"./chapter3_calendar.php?Year=%d&Month=9\">Sep.</a> | ", $Year);
printf("<a href=\"./chapter3_calendar.php?Year=%d&Month=10\">Oct.</a> | ", $Year);
printf("<a href=\"./chapter3_calendar.php?Year=%d&Month=11\">Nov.</a> | ", $Year);
printf("<a href=\"./chapter3_calendar.php?Year=%d&Month=12\">Dec.</a>", $Year);
?>
</td>
<td align="center" valign="middle" bgcolor="#EFEFEF">
<?
/* In our last bit of code we need to provide the user with a link so
   they can skip to the next year. To do this we will take our
   current $Year and increment it by 1, and assign it to the value
   $NextYear. */
$NextYear = ($Year+1);
printf("<a href=\"./chapter3_calendar.php?Year=%d&Month=%d\">%d</a>",
$NextYear , $Month, $NextYear);
?>
```

To finish up, close your cell, row, and table, and end the body of your script, as follows:

```
</td>
</tr>
</table>
</body>
</html>
```

Implementing Your Calendar

Assuming your web server is configured correctly to handle PHP scripts, you should be able to place this script in the document-root directory, and make a request by specifying the URL.

Testing the Calendar

When you first view your calendar, you'll notice that no parameters are passed in the query string, like so: http://twoheadedcow/calendar.php. When you click on one of the Month or Year links at the bottom, you'll notice that the $Year and $Month values are being passed in. The calendar should work fairly well, but there are limitations.

Limitations and Additional Features

Experiment with the functionality of this calendar and you will notice that you can change the variables in the query string to jump to any month and year. You will soon notice that if you enter a date before January 1970 or a date after January 2038, the calendar returns warnings from the date() function and tries to print out the calendar but fails. This is due to limitations of the date() function. This function uses a long integer to store the number of seconds since Unix Epoch, or January 1, 1970. This invalidates any date before January 1, 1970. The long integer rolls over after 68 years and thus beyond 2038 the date() function doesn't work.

Knowing this limitation of the date() function, additional logic could be written to check the date and display a more user-friendly error if the date is out of bounds. Other ideas for the expansion of this script would be to design input fields or drop-down list boxes to input the month and year.

What to Take Away

This chapter detailed a simple example in which you learned how to use date and time functions along with some program control structures. Our output was displayed in an HTML table in a way that replicated what most calendars look like. We touched on some of the more commonly used functions, and showed you different ways to implement them. In the next chapters, we will build upon the items that you learned in this chapter.

CHAPTER

4

PHP Connect 4

IN THIS CHAPTER:

chapter4_connect4.php—Contains all the needed PHP code to play a game of Connect 4

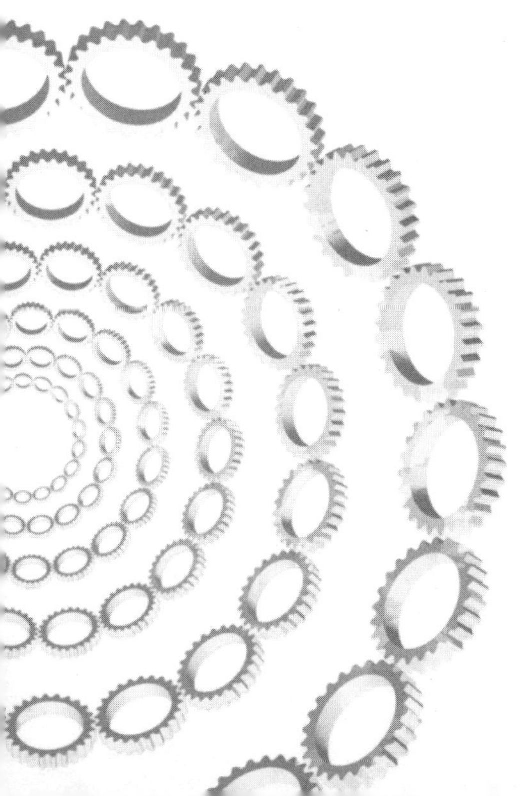

Our next project will be to design and implement a web-based game of Connect 4. The approach this time will be function based. You will use functions in PHP and some that you will design on your own. You will also learn to create multi-dimensional arrays; create a class and its methods; and use the fopen(), fputs(), fgets(), and fclose() functions to read and write data to a file. The finished example will look similar to Figure 4-1.

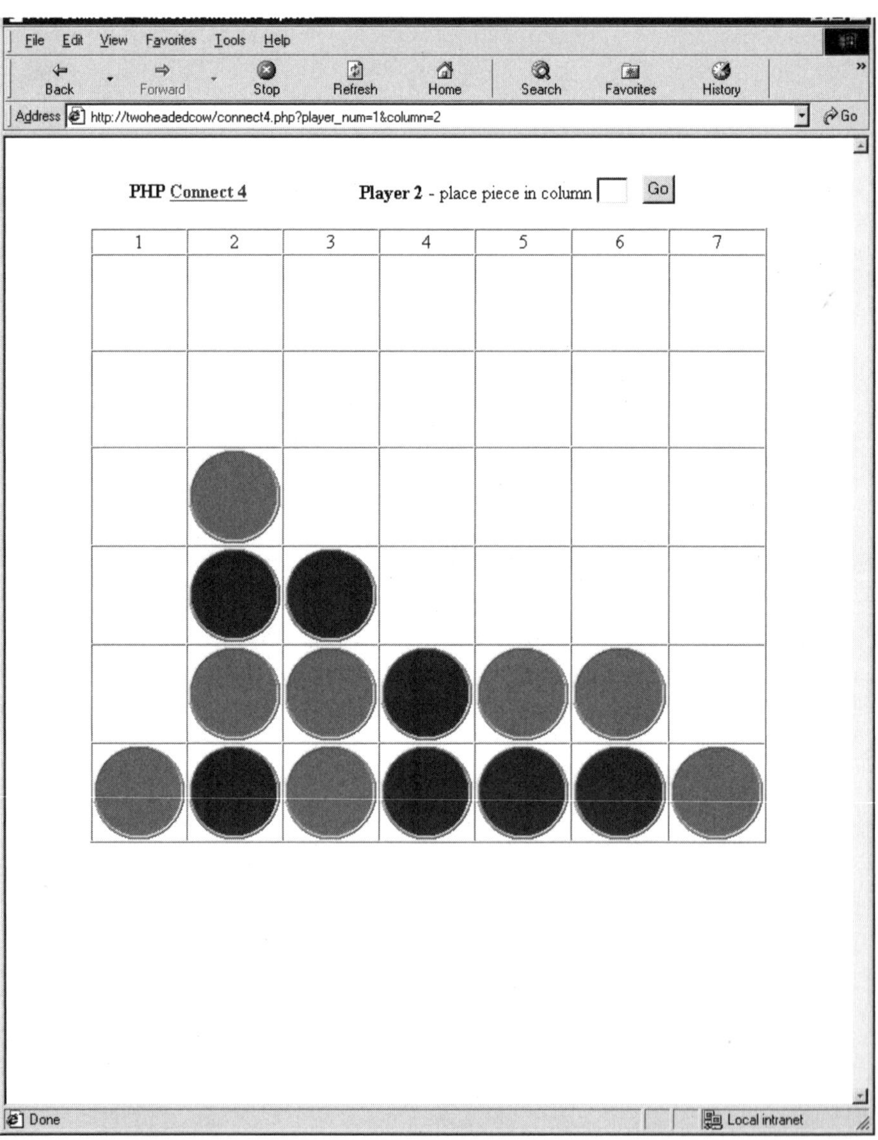

Figure 4-1 *PHP Connect 4*

Connect 4 Requirements

The game will allow two players sitting in front of the same computer to take turns placing their red or black pieces into one of seven columns. When one of the players has four pieces connecting to each other in a horizontal, vertical, or diagonal line, he will win the game. You should also include some error checking in your code to make sure players enter a correct column number, and that the column they choose is not already full.

Designing and Implementing the Game

You'll start by designing some components that you will always use. Since your game is a grid of seven columns and six rows, you can store the information in a multi-dimensional array. You'll need a way to figure out what's in each spot in the array, so you'll create a simple class to hold each player's number. After each player chooses which column to place his piece in, you should check to make sure the column isn't already full, place the piece, and then check to see whether he has four connecting pieces. Since the information in your array will be lost each time the page is reloaded, you want to store the game data in your array to a file, so you will need a way to read and write the file as well.

Since your game will be viewed in a web browser, you'll need to start your PHP script with the basics, as follows:

```
<html>
<head>
<title>PHP Connect 4</title>
</head>
<body>
<p align="center">
```

Now, let's create a class and some methods to hold the player's number in each spot of your array:

```
<?
/* We start by specifying some components we will always use. */
/* Create a class to hold the player's number on each square of the board. */
class square
{
   /* Values in the class */
   var $player;
```

```
    /* Methods in the class*/
    function init($playerNum)
    {
        $this->player = $playerNum;
    }

    function getPlayer()
    {
        return($this->player);
    }

    function setPlayer($player)
    {
        $this->player = $player;
    }
}
```

Your first function will create a blank array that will make up your game board. Note that you put a player number of zero in each spot to start off:

```
function initializeBoard()
{
/* Now we create a multidimensional array which will represent our board. We
    will use the class square as a placeholder for the information about
    which player's piece is where. Let's start off by creating an array with
    no player information: */

    for($rowCounter = 1; $rowCounter  <= 6; $rowCounter++)
    {
        for($colCounter = 1; $colCounter <= 7; $colCounter++)
        {
            $board[$rowCounter][$colCounter] = new square;
            $board[$rowCounter][$colCounter]->init("0");
        }
    }
    return $board;
}
```

Now you need a way to save your game data in the array to a file. Note that if you'll be running this under a *nix-based system, the directory/location of the file you save your data to must have the correct read and write permissions for the user under which your web server is running. In most cases, the web server processes will be running under the "nobody" or "root" user; so for this example, we've created a directory called "webtmp" with the proper permissions. Also, you will store the value of each position in your array on a new line in the data file. It's then just a simple matter of looping through your array and using the fputs() function to write the value out, as you can see here:

```
/* Write our game data to a file. */
function writeData($board)
{
   /* Open the file */
   $dataFile = fopen("/webtmp/connect4.dat","w");

   /* Check to make sure the file open was successful */
   if(!$dataFile)
   {
      echo "Error writing to data file...";
      exit;
   }

   /* Write data to the file */
   for($rowCounter = 1; $rowCounter  <= 6; $rowCounter++)
   {
      for($colCounter = 1; $colCounter <= 7; $colCounter++)
      {
         $player = $board[$rowCounter][$colCounter]->getPlayer();
         fputs($dataFile, $player);
         fputs($dataFile, "\n");
      }
   }

   /* Close the file */
   fclose($dataFile);
}
```

You'll also want to do the opposite—zread in the data from your file and place it into the correct spot in the array, as follows:

```
/* Read our game data from the file. */
function readData($board)
{
   /* Open the file */
   $dataFile = fopen("/webtmp/connect4.dat","r");

   /* Check to make sure the file open was successful */
```

```
    if(!$dataFile)
    {
        echo "Error reading from data file...";
        exit;
    }

    /* Set some starting values for our array positions. */
    $rowCounter = 1;
    $colCounter = 1;

    /* Read in the data from the file */
    while(!feof($dataFile))
    {
        /* Read in each line */
        $dataLine = fgets($dataFile, 255);

        /* Parse the line and get the player. */
        $player = substr($dataLine,0,1);

        /* Set the value into our array */
        $board[$rowCounter][$colCounter]->setPlayer($player);
        if($colCounter == 7)
        {
            $colCounter = 1;
            $rowCounter++;
            if($rowCounter == 7)
            {
                break;
            }
        }
        else
        {
            $colCounter++;
        }
    }

    /* Close the file */
    fclose($dataFile);
    return $board;
}
```

Your next step is to make a function that will go through each position in your array and check for four connecting pieces for a player. You need to check each row, each column, and all the diagonal possibilities, as shown here:

```
/* Check to see if the move made connects four, or if all the columns
 are full. */
function connect_four($board, $playerNum, $row, $column)
{
   /* Check the Rows. */
   for($rowCounter = 1; $rowCounter <= 6; $rowCounter++)
   {
      $connectFour = 0;
      $colCounter = 1;
      while($colCounter <= 7)
      {
         $player = $board[$rowCounter][$colCounter]->getPlayer();
         if($player == $playerNum)
         {
            $connectFour++;
         }
         else
         {
            $connectFour = 0;
         }
         if($connectFour == 4)
         {
            writeData($board);
            $status = "Player $playerNum wins!";
            break;
         }
         $colCounter++;
      }
   }

   /* Check the Columns. */
   for($colCounter = 1; $colCounter <= 7; $colCounter++)
   {
      $connectFour = 0;
      $rowCounter = 1;
      while($rowCounter <= 6)
      {
```

```
            $player = $board[$rowCounter][$colCounter]->getPlayer();
            if($player == $playerNum)
            {
               $connectFour++;
            }
            else
            {
               $connectFour = 0;
            }
            if($connectFour == 4)
            {
               writeData($board);
               $status = "Player $playerNum wins!";
               break;
            }
            $rowCounter++;
         }
      }
```

Checking for four connecting pieces in each of the rows and columns was easy enough. The code you will use to check all of the diagonal possibilities is very similar, but a little more lengthy. Your next block of code will check all of the diagonal possibilities working from left to right and down:

```
/* Check all of the diagonals */
/* Down and to the right. */
$rowCounter = 3;
$colCounter = 1;
$connectFour = 0;
for($diagCounter = 1; $diagCounter <= 4; $diagCounter++)
{
   $player = $board[$rowCounter][$colCounter]->getPlayer();
   if($player == $playerNum)
   {
      $connectFour++;
   }
   else
   {
      $connectFour = 0;
   }
   if($connectFour == 4)
   {
      writeData($board);
```

```
      $status = "Player $playerNum wins!";
      break;
   }
   $rowCounter++;
   $colCounter++;
}

$rowCounter = 2;
$colCounter = 1;
$connectFour = 0;
for($diagCounter = 1; $diagCounter <= 5; $diagCounter++)
{
   $player = $board[$rowCounter][$colCounter]->getPlayer();
   if($player == $playerNum)
   {
      $connectFour++;
   }
   else
   {
      $connectFour = 0;
   }
   if($connectFour == 4)
   {
      writeData($board);
      $status = "Player $playerNum wins!";
      break;
   }
   $rowCounter++;
   $colCounter++;
}

$rowCounter = 1;
$colCounter = 1;
$connectFour = 0;
for($diagCounter = 1; $diagCounter <= 6; $diagCounter++)
{
   $player = $board[$rowCounter][$colCounter]->getPlayer();
   if($player == $playerNum)
   {
         $connectFour++;
   }
   else
   {
      $connectFour = 0;
```

```
        }
        if($connectFour == 4)
        {
            writeData($board);
            $status = "Player $playerNum wins!";
            break;
        }
        $rowCounter++;
        $colCounter++;
    }

    $rowCounter = 1;
    $colCounter = 2;
    $connectFour = 0;
    for($diagCounter = 1; $diagCounter <= 6; $diagCounter++)
    {
        $player = $board[$rowCounter][$colCounter]->getPlayer();
        if($player == $playerNum)
        {
            $connectFour++;
        }
        else
        {
            $connectFour = 0;
        }
        if($connectFour == 4)
        {
            writeData($board);
            $status = "Player $playerNum wins!";
            break;
        }
        $rowCounter++;
        $colCounter++;
    }

    $rowCounter = 1;
    $colCounter = 3;
    $connectFour = 0;
    for($diagCounter = 1; $diagCounter <= 5; $diagCounter++)
    {
        $player = $board[$rowCounter][$colCounter]->getPlayer();
```

```
    if($player == $playerNum)
    {
       $connectFour++;
    }
    else
    {
       $connectFour = 0;
    }
    if($connectFour == 4)
    {
       writeData($board);
       $status = "Player $playerNum wins!";
       break;
    }
    $rowCounter++;
    $colCounter++;
 }

 $rowCounter = 1;
 $colCounter = 4;
 $connectFour = 0;
 for($diagCounter = 1; $diagCounter <= 4; $diagCounter++)
 {
    $player = $board[$rowCounter][$colCounter]->getPlayer();
    if($player == $playerNum)
    {
       $connectFour++;
    }
    else
    {
       $connectFour = 0;
    }
    if($connectFour == 4)
    {
       writeData($board);
       $status = "Player $playerNum wins!";
       break;
    }
    $rowCounter++;
    $colCounter++;

 }
```

You will now repeat the process, checking for four connecting pieces, working from right to left and down:

```
/* Down and to the left. */
$rowCounter = 1;
$colCounter = 4;
$connectFour = 0;
for($diagCounter = 1; $diagCounter <= 4; $diagCounter++)
{
   $player = $board[$rowCounter][$colCounter]->getPlayer();
   if($player == $playerNum)
   {
      $connectFour++;
   }
   else
   {
      $connectFour = 0;
   }
   if($connectFour == 4)
   {
      writeData($board);
      $status = "Player $playerNum wins!";
      break;
   }
   $rowCounter++;
   $colCounter--;
}

$rowCounter = 1;
$colCounter = 5;
$connectFour = 0;
for($diagCounter = 1; $diagCounter <= 5; $diagCounter++)
{
   $player = $board[$rowCounter][$colCounter]->getPlayer();
   if($player == $playerNum)
   {
      $connectFour++;
   }
   else
   {
      $connectFour = 0;
   }
   if($connectFour == 4)
```

```
   {
      writeData($board);
      $status = "Player $playerNum wins!";
      break;
   }
   $rowCounter++;
   $colCounter--;
}

$rowCounter = 1;
$colCounter = 6;
$connectFour = 0;
for($diagCounter = 1; $diagCounter <= 6; $diagCounter++)
{
   $player = $board[$rowCounter][$colCounter]->getPlayer();
   if($player == $playerNum)
   {
      $connectFour++;
   }
   else
   {
      $connectFour = 0;
   }
   if($connectFour == 4)
   {
      writeData($board);
      $status = "Player $playerNum wins!";
      break;
   }
   $rowCounter++;
   $colCounter--;<p align="right"></p>
}

$rowCounter = 1;
$colCounter = 7;
$connectFour = 0;
for($diagCounter = 1; $diagCounter <= 6; $diagCounter++)
{
   $player = $board[$rowCounter][$colCounter]->getPlayer();
   if($player == $playerNum)
   {
      $connectFour++;
   }
```

```
      else
      {
         $connectFour = 0;
      }
      if($connectFour == 4)
      {
         writeData($board);
         $status = "Player $playerNum wins!";
         break;
      }
      $rowCounter++;
      $colCounter--;
   }

   $rowCounter = 2;
   $colCounter = 7;
   $connectFour = 0;
   for($diagCounter = 1; $diagCounter <= 5; $diagCounter++)
   {
      $player = $board[$rowCounter][$colCounter]->getPlayer();
      if($player == $playerNum)
      {
         $connectFour++;
      }
      else
      {
         $connectFour = 0;
      }
      if($connectFour == 4)
      {
         writeData($board);
         $status = "Player $playerNum wins!";
         break;
      }
      $rowCounter++;
      $colCounter--;
   }

   $rowCounter = 3;
   $colCounter = 7;
   $connectFour = 0;
   for($diagCounter = 1; $diagCounter <= 4; $diagCounter++)
   {
```

```
      $player = $board[$rowCounter][$colCounter]->getPlayer();
      if($player == $playerNum)
      {
         $connectFour++;
      }
      else
      {
         $connectFour = 0;
      }
      if($connectFour == 4)
      {
         writeData($board);
         $status = "Player $playerNum wins!";
         break;
      }
      $rowCounter++;
      $colCounter--;
   }
```

While you're at it, let's also check to make sure the column the player chooses isn't full already:

```
   /* Check the top row to see if all the columns are full. */
   if((($board[1][1]->getPlayer() != "0") and ($board[1][2]->getPlayer()
 != "0") and ($board[1][3]->getPlayer() != "0") and ($board[1][4]-
>getPlayer() != "0") and ($board[1][5]->getPlayer() != "0") and
($board[1][6]->getPlayer() != "0") and ($board[1][7]->getPlayer() != "0") and
$status == ""))
   {
      $status = "The game is a stalemate.";
   }
   return $status;
}
```

If you haven't noticed already, this last bit of code was quite lengthy. There are other ways to implement this function. For instance, instead of using brute force and checking each row, column, and diagonal, you could devise a way to start at the location in the array where the piece was just placed. Check each surrounding piece to see whether it corresponds to the player number of the piece just placed. If so, continue checking in that direction for more connecting pieces for that player. Once that is exhausted, start from the initial location and check the other directions. If you find four connecting pieces, return the corresponding message via the $status variable.

All of this won't do you any good if you can't place the piece on the board. Let's design a function that does just that, and do some error checking to make sure the player actually enters a correct column value. We will also call the connect_four() function we just created to see whether the piece the player placed wins the game. The code looks like this:

```
function placePiece($board, $playerNum, $column)
{
   if(($column == "") or ($column <= "0") or ($column >= "8"))
 // Make sure the value they entered for the column is valid.
   {
      $status = "You entered an incorrect column value!";
   }
   elseif($board[1][$column]->getPlayer() != "0")
 // Make sure the column they choose isn't already full.
   {
      $status = "Column $column is all filled up!";
   }
   else // Ok, everything checks out, let's place the piece.
   {
      /* Let's find the first empty row to place the piece in. */
      $row = 1;
      while(($board[$row][$column]->getPlayer() == "0"))
      {
         if($row == 6)
         {
            $row = 7;
            break;
         }
         else
         {
            $row++;
         }
      }
      $row = $row - 1;

      /* Set the piece in the board. */
      $board[$row][$column]->setPlayer($playerNum);

      /* Save the board data to a file */
      writeData($board);
```

```
        /* See if the last piece placed "connects 4". */
        $status = connect_four($board, $playerNum, $row, $column);
    }
    return $status;
}
```

You've got most of your coding done now. You need a way to display the contents of the array in a way the player understands. The displayBoard() function will do just that:

```
/* Display the board */
function displayBoard($board, $playerNum)
{
    echo "<table width=\"560\" border=\"0\" cellspacing=\"0\"
    cellpadding=\"0\" align=\"center\">\n";
    echo "<tr>\n<td height=\"60\" align=\"center\" valign=\"middle\"><b>PHP
    <a href=\"./chapter4_connect4.php\">Connect 4</a></b></td>\n";
    echo "<td align=\"center\" valign=\"bottom\"><form
    action=\"./chapter4_connect4.php\" method=\"get\">\n";
    echo "<input type=\"hidden\" name=\"playerNum\" value=\"$playerNum\">\n";
    if($playerNum == 1)
    {
        echo "<b><font color=\"RED\">Player 1</font></b>";
    }
    else
    {
        echo "<b><font color=\"BLACK\">Player 2</font></b>";
    }
    echo " - place piece in column <input type=\"text\" name=\"column\"
    size=\"2\" maxsize=\"2\">";
    echo "   <input type=\"submit\" value=\"Go\">\n";
    echo "</form>\n";
    echo "</td>\n";
    echo "</tr>\n";
    echo "</table>\n";
    echo "<table width=\"576\" border=\"1\" cellspacing=\"0\"
    cellpadding=\"0\" align=\"center\">\n";
    echo "<tr>\n";
    echo "<td align=\"center\" width=\"80\">1</td>\n";
    echo "<td align=\"center\" width=\"80\">2</td>\n";
    echo "<td align=\"center\" width=\"80\">3</td>\n";
    echo "<td align=\"center\" width=\"80\">4</td>\n";
    echo "<td align=\"center\" width=\"80\">5</td>\n";
    echo "<td align=\"center\" width=\"80\">6</td>\n";
    echo "<td align=\"center\" width=\"80\">7</td>\n";
```

```
    echo "</tr>\n";
    for($rowCounter = 1; $rowCounter  <= 6; $rowCounter++)
    {
        echo "<tr>\n";
        for($colCounter = 1; $colCounter <= 7; $colCounter++)
        {
            echo "<td width=\"80\" height=\"80\" align=\"center\"
            valign=\"middle\">";
            if($board[$rowCounter][$colCounter]->getPlayer() == 0)
            {
                echo " ";
            }
            else
            {
                printf("<img src=\"./p%s.gif\" border=\"0\" width=\"80\"
                height=\"80\">", $board[$rowCounter][$colCounter]->getPlayer());
            }
            echo "</td>";
        }
        echo "</tr>\n";
    }
    echo "</table>\n";
}
```

Okay, so you've got ways to initialize your game array, place pieces in the array, check for errors, check for four connecting pieces, and read and write your data to a file. Now let's put all of these functions to use:

```
/* Now we get into the control of the game. This is where all the action is.
 */
if ($playerNum == "") // Must be starting the game, no one has had a turn yet.
{
    /* Set the Default Player Number since one wasn't passed in. */
    $playerNum = 1;

    /* Initialize our board */
    $board = initializeBoard();

    /* Save the board data to a file */
    writeData($board);

    /* Display the board to the players */
    displayBoard($board, $playerNum);

}
else
```

```
{
   /* Game On!*/
   /* Initialize the board */
   $board = initializeBoard();

   /* Read in the data */
   $board = readData($board);

   /* Let's try and drop the player's piece into the board. */
   $status = placePiece($board, $playerNum, $column);
   if($status == "") // No status is a good status.
   {
      /* Set the next player's turn */
      if($playerNum == "1")
      {
         $playerNum = "2";
      }
      else
      {
         $playerNum = "1";
      }

      /* Read in the updated data */
      $board = readData($board);

      /* Display the updated board */
      displayBoard($board, $playerNum);
   }
   else // We got back a value for $status. Must be an error message or
   someone won the game!
   {
      echo "<b><i>$status</i></b>";

      /* Read in the updated data */
      $board = readData($board);

      /* Display the updated board */
      displayBoard($board, $playerNum);

   }
}
?>
```

To finish up your game, you need to close the body and HTML tags:

```
</body>
</html>
```

Implementing Your Game

Assuming your web server is configured correctly to handle PHP scripts, you should be able to place this script in the document-root directory, and make a request by specifying the URL. Since the script will be run under the same user that the web server is running under, you'll need to make sure you have read and write permissions wherever your data file resides. For this example, we logged in as root on our web server machine, and created a directory called webtmp with the correct permissions. You'll also need to find or create two 80×80 pixel GIF images, one called p1.gif and the other called p2.gif. Place these in the same location as your script, as they will represent the player pieces you see on the game.

Testing and Debugging the Game

When you first start the game, player 1 will go first, entering the number of the column he wishes to place a piece in. If all goes well, the piece will be placed, and then it's player 2's turn. Each player takes turns entering a column number in which they want a piece to fall. The ultimate goal is to get four matching colored pieces connecting in either a horizontal, diagonal, or vertical row.

If you get an error message like "error reading/writing to data file," check to make sure the location of the data file you specified in the PHP fopen() function, within your readData() and writeData() functions, exists, and that the user under which your web server is running has the correct read and write privileges to that location and file.

Limitations and Additional Features

This game is limited to only two players at a time. If you get more than one set of players playing, they will overwrite the game data file, as the name of the file stays the same. You may also find yourself in a position where you are unable to obtain the correct permissions on the web server machine to create the data file in a temporary directory. As an alternative, in this case you could use PHP session variables, but that falls outside the scope of this chapter. Some aspects of the code, such as the connect_four() function, may seem lengthy. In this instance, we used a brute-force approach. There are other, less lengthy, but perhaps more complex ways to check the array.

What to Take Away

This chapter showed you how to create a basic PHP class and implement methods to initialize, set, and retrieve the values stored in it. You also used a multi-dimensional array to represent the game board, and read and write information in that array to a data file. We used control structures and Boolean logic to enforce game rules and determine a winner. In the next chapters, we will build upon the items that you learned here.

PART III

PHP and Databases

OBJECTIVES:

- Develop a web-based interface to administer a MySQL database
- Familiarize yourself with the available PHP MySQL functions
- Examine the use of classes to organize code
- Examine the use of sessions to maintain user data
- Design and set up a simple MySQL database
- Select and update data from a MySQL database
- Loop through a result set and display in an HTML page
- Use simple mathematical functions
- Understand the benefits of persistent database connections
- Build a MySQL database to store contact information
- Use PHP and MySQL functions to manipulate data
- Build a user-friendly web-based interface for your address book

CHAPTER

5

Web-Based Database Administration

IN THIS CHAPTER:

chapter5_common.php—Common set of functions used for connecting to the database and displaying HTML output used throughout the chapter

chapter5_dbAdmin.php—Class with methods for administering a table and submenu to perform database administrative actions

chapter5_dbMonitor.php—Class with methods for monitoring the status of the database and submenu to perform database monitoring actions

chapter5_login.php—Script to handle login/logout of the application

chapter5_mainMenu.php—Presents the main menu of options and verifies that the user is able to log in to the database

chapter5_sql.php—Class with methods to execute SQL queries and report results

chapter5_tableAdmin.php—Class with methods to administer database tables and submenu to perform table administrative actions

chapter5_userAdmin.php—Class with methods to administer users and submenu to perform user administrative actions

The project for this chapter is to develop a web-based database administration application. The code in this chapter is designed to allow a user to administer a MySQL database. When possible, however, the code has been segmented to allow it to be easily adapted to the other databases supported with PHP.

The chapter includes code for many of the basic database operations such as listing databases and their corresponding tables, along with overall database status. It also includes a query interface for running queries on demand that don't fall within the predefined administration options.

Application Requirements

The general requirement for this application is to allow a user to easily administer a MySQL database from a web browser. This would allow a user to work with the database from remote locations, regardless of whether they have a MySQL client installed on their machine. The core requirement of the application is to allow users to connect to the database through a web browser. Once connected, the operations a user can perform can be grouped into the following categories: database administration, table administration, database monitoring, user administration, and SQL query execution.

The application described by these requirements does not cover all possible administrative tasks, but meets many of the common needs for a user who wants to have control over their database regardless of what machine and location they are currently working from.

Connection Requirements

The connection is established by prompting the user for their username, password, and the hostname that the user is authorized to access the MySQL server from. Due to the stateless nature of the Internet, an open connection cannot be maintained between the browser and the database; therefore, once the user has connected successfully, the application keeps track of who the user is and which database within the MySQL server they are currently working with.

Database Administration Requirements

The next requirement of the application is to allow the user to perform overall database administration duties. The first duty is to provide a listing of which databases are available on the server that the user may access. Second, a user may select which database they would like to work with for subsequent requests that access a specific database, such as table administration or SQL queries. Finally, the user is allowed to create and drop databases as long as their user permissions allow such actions.

Table Administration Requirements

Similar requirements are necessary for table administration. The user can list all of the tables available within a selected database, as well as view a description of the columns that make up a particular table. In addition to these requirements, a user may create and drop a table from a database. Finally, the user can display contents of a table.

Server Monitoring Requirements

The database monitoring requirements are designed to allow the user to view the overall status of the MySQL server. A user may view the server status, the version of the MySQL software, and its current variable settings. Finally, a listing of the server processes are available for the user to examine.

User Administration Requirements

In the case of user administration, the application provides a listing of all users who are allowed to log in to the database. Second, the facility to add and remove users is available. Finally, the ability to alter a user's information or to log in to the server as an entirely different user is possible.

SQL Execution

The last requirement of the application is to let users execute raw SQL queries. This provides a mechanism for the user to do other administrative functions that are not part of the point-and-click requirements of the application. With the inclusion of a query interface, the functionality of the application is greatly expanded to include almost all of the actions that a user could perform if they had a direct client connection to the MySQL database.

Application Design

The next phase in development of this project is to divide the application into discrete components and plan their functionality.

User Logins

The first major design consideration stems from the requirement that the application knows who the user is, whether they have access to the server, and what database they are working with at all times. One method to accomplish this is to store the user's login criteria and database selection at the server. This can be accomplished by creating a session in PHP that stores the user's data in a temporary file, which is accessible through session variables during the execution of each PHP script. Session variables are chosen, to provide a better level of security to the application, as opposed to putting all of the login information into a cookie and returning it to the browser. By not placing the user's password in the cookie, it is more difficult for an unauthorized user to obtain a user's credentials. Also, using session data means that the information only exists while the user is accessing the application, and it is destroyed automatically at the end of a user's session. PHP's session-handling functions provide an easy-to-implement, secure mechanism for managing a user's access to the server.

Since the first step in using the application is to validate the user against the MySQL server, a screen needs to be developed for the user to input their login credentials. This screen prompts the user for their login name, password, and hostname they are expected to access the server from. Note that normally in MySQL terms, this is the actual machine the user is working on; but for this application, this will be whatever the user enters, to allow for remote administration from any machine. This method is inherently not as secure as the normal MySQL server login verification process. The login screen can also have a dual role in that it can be used not only to validate a new application user, but also to change which username the application user is currently accessing the server as. A corresponding requirement to the login screen is one that provides an exit message when the user leaves the application and offers a link for the user to re-login to the application.

Once the user has logged in to the application, they are presented with a high-level menu of available database administration tasks. As defined in the requirements, the menu of available options includes table administration, database administration, database status monitoring, user administration, and SQL query execution.

Table Administration

Activating the table administration menu selection brings up a submenu of available options. These options include listing all tables in the selected database, describing a table, displaying the contents of the table, altering a table's structure, creating a new table, and dropping an existing table. When a user selects the List-Tables option, an HTML table is generated with the heading Tables, and then a vertical listing of all of the tables within the selected database. In the case of describing a table, the user first needs to select a particular table, and then the columns and their characteristics will be returned as an HTML table. Displaying the contents of a table requires that the user first select a table and then a **select *** query is run against the table with all of the rows being returned within an HTML table. The option to drop a table prompts the user for the table name, and then reports the success or failure of the operation. All of these table operations can be incorporated into a single class, referred to as the tableAdmin class. Any operation that operates on a table is implemented as a method of this class.

Database Administration

Selection of the Database Administration option from the main menu results in the display of a submenu of available options that include listing all the databases available to the user, selecting a particular database for subsequent actions, dropping an existing database, and creating a new one. If the user selects listing the databases, an HTML table is generated providing a vertical list of the databases. If the user selects a particular database, the user's session variable for the database is altered to reflect that selection, along with providing the user with a success or failure indication for the selection, If the user chooses to drop a database, they will be prompted for which database they would like to drop, and after the drop is executed, the user is informed about the success or failure of the drop. Likewise, for database creation, the user will be prompted for the name of the new database and then informed if the database creation action was successful. All of these database administration tasks can be incorporated into a PHP class referred to as the dbAdmin class. Any operation that involves an entire database (not server) is implemented as a method of this class.

Database Monitoring

The selection of database status monitoring prompts the user with a submenu of available options to perform the following tasks: show database status, show the version of MySQL that is running, display a list of current processes, and show the current server variable settings. All of these menu selections result in an HTML table being generated with the corresponding information displayed, such as a single column table with the heading Version and a row containing the MySQL server version number. All of these operations are implemented as methods of a dbMonitor class.

User Administration

Selecting User Administration from the application's main menu prompts the user with the following options: Add User, Remove User, Update User, Change User, and List Users. The Add User option queries the user for the new user's login name, password, hostname, and database name they will be allowed to access. The statement is executed at the server, and the user is given an indication of success or failure. In the case of Remove User, the application prompts for the same fields as mentioned in the Add User screen. If the application user selects Update User, they are prompted for the new password they wish to set for themselves. If they select Change User from the submenu, they are effectively taken to the application's main login screen, logged out, and asked to log back in to the application. Finally, the List Users option displays in an HTML table all of the users along with the host associated with each user. All of these operations are implemented as methods of the userAdmin class.

SQL Query Execution

Finally, selecting the SQL option from the main menu brings up a large text area for the user to input a raw SQL query that will be executed at the server. If the query is a **select** statement, the number of rows returned is indicated and the actual rows in the result set are displayed. If the query is not a **select** or **show** statement, the number of rows impacted by the operation is indicated. In either case, if an error resulted from the query, the user is informed of that as well. The methods that allow a user to execute a query against a database and display the results are implemented as part of the SQL class in PHP.

Implementation

Now that we have finished designing the components that will make up the application, we may implement them as PHP scripts.

Common Functions

We will begin the implementation of this application by creating a set of functions that will prove useful throughout the application. These include displaying both one- and two-dimensional arrays as HTML tables. The two-dimensional arrays will typically be the result sets of SQL queries. The one-dimensional arrays will typically represent a list of items returned from a query. Another function needed several times in the application is the ability to query the user for a single field of data. To accomplish this, a generic form can be created that accepts parameters such as field name and action. Finally, a class will be created that represents a connection to the database. This class is utilized throughout the application, as all of the actions in the application require a connection to the database. These functions, along with the connection class, are collected together in the chapter5_common.php file.

User Session Data

Since the chapter5_common.php file will be included with all subsequent scripts in the application, we will also include the necessary code to establish a session for the user.

chapter5_common.php

```
<?php
session_start();
session_register("sessiondata");
```

This tells the PHP engine to issue a session cookie to the user if they don't already have one, and then register the sessiondata variable, which is actually an array containing multiple user-related fields.

Database Connection

The next section of code defines the database connection class that is used throughout the application to establish a connection to the database and then hold the corresponding connection details:

```
//####################################################################
//##    Class:          DBConnection                               ##
//##    Description:    Establishes a connection to the database ##
//##                    given a host, username, and password     ##
//####################################################################
class DBConnection
   {
   //member variables
   var $database;
```

```
    var $linkid;
    var $sqlstmt;
    var $rc;

    //Constructor
    function DBConnection($hostname,$username,$password)
        {
        $this->linkid =
        mysql_pconnect ($hostname,$username, $password);
        if (!$this->linkid)
            {
            $this->linkid =
            mysql_connect ($hostname,$username,$password);
            }
        }
    }
```

The constructor is a function that is called whenever a new instance of the class is created. Within the constructor, you first attempt to establish a persistent connection to the database, and if that fails, you then attempt to establish a nonpersistent connection. The advantage of the persistent connection is that it takes fewer machine resources to reuse an existing connection than it does to establish a new connection each time. Persistent connections are available with most relational databases and should be used whenever possible. Note that if PHP is run as a web server CGI program, the connection will be destroyed, regardless of whether a persistent call is made or not.

Display Two-Dimensional Arrays

Next we will examine the function that displays a two-dimensional array. As mentioned previously, this function will most often be called when the application needs to display the result set of a particular query. It is important to point out that the parameter to the function must be a two-dimensional associative array. If the array has both keys and numerical indixes, the function will not operate properly. The first part of the function iterates through the keys in the array and outputs an HTML table with the header row as the keys from the array, as shown here:

```
//###################################################################
//##        Function:           displayResultSet                  ##
//##      Parameters:           2D associative array              ##
//##     Description:     Outputs a 2 dimensional array in an HTML ##
//##                      table. The first row contains the        ##
//##                      column names.                            ##
//###################################################################
```

```
function displayResultSet($resultset)
   {
   //Indicate if the resultset is empty
   if (empty($resultset))
      {
      echo "<CENTER>\n";
      echo "<BR>\n";
      echo "Action Returned No Rows!";
      echo "</CENTER>\n";
      return ;
      }

   echo "<BR>\n";
   echo "<CENTER>\n";
   echo "<TABLE CELLSPACING=5 CELLPADDING=5 BORDER=3 ";
   echo "BORDERCOLOR=\"0000FF\" >\n";
   echo "<THEAD>\n";
   echo "<TR>\n";

   $keycount = 0;
   //Output each key as a column heading
   while (list ($key,$value) = each($resultset[0]))
      {
      $keycount++;
      echo "<TH>";
      echo $key;
      echo "</TH>\n";
      }
   echo "</TR>\n";
   echo "</THEAD>\n";
```

The second part of the function steps through the values in the array, displaying one row of data into a table at a time. Notice that the sizeof() function returns the number of rows in the associative array and not the total number of elements, as you might expect:

```
//Output each value as elements of a table starting a new row
//each time the key number of columns is reached
   $rowcount = sizeof ($resultset);

   for($rowCounter = 0;$rowCounter  < $rowcount;
      $rowCounter++)
```

```
        {
        $valuesarray = array_values($resultset[$rowCounter]);
        echo "<TR>\n";
        for($colCounter = 0; $colCounter < $keycount; $colCounter++)
           {
           echo "<TD>\n";
           echo " ";
           echo $valuesarray[$colCounter];
           echo " ";
           echo "</TD>\n";
           }
        }
   echo "</TR>\n";
   echo "</TABLE>\n";
   echo "</CENTER>\n";
   echo "<BR>\n";
   }
```

Display One-Dimensional Array

The next function in chapter5_common.php displays a one-dimensional array. This function is simpler than the two-dimensional in that it doesn't have to output multiple elements per row in the table. Each element is its own row, which makes it much easier to iterate through the array. The code used to do this is as follows:

```
//#####################################################################
//##        Function:           displayArray                        ##
//##      Parameters:           1D array                            ##
//##     Description:     Outputs a 1 dimensional array as an HTML  ##
//##                      table. The first row is the heading for   ##
//##                      the array.                                ##
//#####################################################################
function displayArray($heading,$resultset)
   {
   //Indicate if the resultset is empty
   if (empty($resultset))
      {
      echo "<CENTER>\n";
      echo "<BR>\n";
      echo "Action Returned No Rows!";
      echo "</CENTER>\n";
      return ;
      }
```

```
//The first row names the results
echo "<BR>\n";
echo "<CENTER>\n";
echo "<TABLE CELLSPACING=5 CELLPADDING=5 BORDER=3 ";
echo "BORDERCOLOR=\"0000FF\" >\n";
echo "<THEAD>\n";
echo "<TR>\n";
echo "<TH>";
echo $heading;
echo "</TH>\n";
echo "</TR>\n";
echo "</THEAD>\n";

//Display a new row for each element of the input array
$itemcount = sizeof ($resultset);
for($rowCounter = 0; $rowCounter  < $itemcount; $rowCounter++)
   {
   echo "<TR>\n";
   echo "<TD>\n";
   echo " ";
   echo $resultset[$rowCounter];
   echo " ";
   echo "</TD>\n";
   }
echo "</TR>\n";
echo "</TABLE>\n";
echo "</CENTER>\n";
echo "<BR>\n";
}
```

Single Line Form

Now that you can display both one- and two-dimensional arrays, let's move on to displaying a form to retrieve the user's input into the application. This code is a template for a single line form that takes the user's input and passes it along to another portion of the application:

```
//#################################################################
//##       Function:    displayOneLineForm                       ##
//##     Parameters:    formaction,caption,inputname,action      ##
//##                    submitvalue                              ##
//##    Description:    Outputs a single entry HTML form for     ##
//##                    gathering input                          ##
//#################################################################
```

```
function displayOneLineForm
($formaction,$caption,$inputname,$action,$submitvalue)
   {
   echo "<CENTER>\n";
   echo "<FORM ACTION=\"$formaction\"";
   echo "METHOD=\"POST\">\n";
   echo $caption." <INPUT TYPE=\"TEXT\"";
   echo "NAME=\"".$inputname."\" SIZE=\"30\">\n";
   echo "<INPUT TYPE=\"HIDDEN\" NAME=\"action\" VALUE=\"";
   echo $action."\" SIZE=\"30\">\n";
   echo "<INPUT TYPE=\"SUBMIT\" VALUE=\"".$submitvalue."\">\n";
   echo "</FORM>\n";
   echo "<CENTER>\n";
   }
?>
```

The code for displayOneLineForm() is fairly straightforward. It outputs a form with a single text input box. The key to utilizing this code is getting the parameters correct when calling the function. Of course, this function could be readily expanded to include things such as field size, spacing, and so on. For now it is left as a very generic bit of code, which allows it to be used throughout the application.

Managing the Login

The next section of code we are going to examine covers the user's logging in to and out of the application. This code is contained in the chapter5_login.php file. The code starts out by starting a session for the user if they don't already have one. Next, it establishes sessiondata as the variable that should be tracked. Before prompting the user for login information, it invalidates any previous login that may exist by setting the login name to NULL. This prevents the user from going directly to a page in the application and bypassing the entry page.

chapter5_login.php

```
<?php
session_start();
session_register("sessiondata");
$sessiondata[username] = NULL;
```

After you have established the user's session data, you then check to see whether this script was called with a logout action, such as chapter5_login.php?action=logout.

When the application directs the user to this screen, it passes the logout action to indicate that the user plans to exit the application, as shown here:

```
//Retrieve input variables from HTTP get or post
$userinfo = strtolower($REQUEST_METHOD) == 'get'
   ? $HTTP_GET_VARS : $HTTP_POST_VARS;

if ($userinfo[action] == 'logout')
   {
   echo "<CENTER>\n";
   echo "<BR><BR><BR>\n";
   echo "You have been logged out of the MySQL Database\n";
   echo "<BR><BR><BR>\n";
   echo "<A HREF=\"chapter5_login.php\">Click Here To Log ";
   echo "In Again</A>\n";
   echo "</CENTER>\n";
   }
```

If the action of logout is not included in the page request, the user will be prompted to log in to the application, as follows:

```
else
   {
   echo "<!doctype html public \"";
   echo "-//W3C//DTD HTML 4.0 //EN\">\n";
   echo "<HTML>\n";
   echo "<HEAD>";
   echo "<TITLE>Instant PHP4 Chapter5 - ";
   echo "Database Administration</TITLE>\n";
   echo "</HEAD>\n";
   echo "<CENTER>\n";
   echo "<BODY>\n";
   echo "Chapter5 - Database Administration - Login\n";
   echo "<BR><BR><BR>\n";
   echo "<FORM ACTION=\"chapter5_dbMonitor.php\"\n";
   echo "METHOD=\"POST\">\n";
   echo "<TABLE CELLSPACING=5 CELLPADDING=5 BORDER=3 ";
   echo "BORDERCOLOR=\"0000FF\" >\n";
   echo "<TR><TD>\n";
   echo "Username</TD><TD><INPUT TYPE=\"TEXT\" NAME=\"";
   echo "in_username\" SIZE=\"30\" MAXLENGTH=\"16\" ";
   echo "SELECTED=TRUE><BR>\n";
   echo "</TD></TR>\n";
```

```
    echo "<TR><TD>\n";
    echo "Password</TD><TD><input type=\"password\" name=\"";
    echo "in_password\" SIZE=\"30\"><BR>\n";
    echo "</TD></TR>\n";
    echo "<TR><TD>\n";
    echo "Hostname</TD><TD><input type=\"text\" name=\"";
    echo "in_hostname\" SIZE=\"30\"><BR>\n";
    echo "</TD></TR>\n";
    echo "</TABLE>\n";
    echo "<BR><BR>\n";
    echo "<INPUT TYPE=\"SUBMIT\" VALUE=\"Login\">\n";
    echo "   \n";
    echo "<INPUT TYPE=\"RESET\" VALUE=\"Reset\">\n";
    echo "</FORM>\n";
    echo "</CENTER>\n";
    echo "</BODY>\n";
    echo "</HTML>\n";
    }
?>
```

Database Monitoring

Once the user fills in their login credentials and clicks Submit, they are directed to a page within the application. The user is brought to the chapter5_dbMonitor.php page, although having this as an entry page to the application is not a requirement. The first action in this script is to bring in the common functions we defined earlier in chapter5_common.php.

chapter5_dbMonitor.php

```
<?php
include ('chapter5_common.php');
```

Next, the dbMonitor class is defined. The class contains variables and methods that allow the user to monitor and report on the overall status of the database server. When you create an instance of this class, you supply the link ID you obtained from the database connection that was established during the chapter5_common.php portion of this script. The code is as follows:

```
//##################################################################
//##    Class:          dbMonitor                                ##
//##    Description:    Manage a db connection                   ##
//##################################################################
```

```
class dbMonitor
   {
   //member variables
   var $database;
   var $linkid;
   var $resultid;
   var $sqlstmt;
   var $rc;

    //constructor
   function dbMonitor($alinkid)
      {
      $this->linkid = $alinkid;
      }
```

The first method in the dbMonitor class we'll look at is displayStatus(). The purpose of this method is to let the user view the current state of the database. Information such as the number of clients and the number of open tables is returned to the user, as follows:

```
//###################################################################
//##    Method:           displayStatus                             ##
//##    Parameters:       none                                      ##
//##    Return value:     array of status variables                 ##
//###################################################################
   function displayStatus()
      {
      $this->sqlstmt = "show status";
      $this->resultid = mysql_query ($this->sqlstmt,$this->linkid);
      $count =  mysql_numrows($this->resultid);
      for ($i=0;$i < $count;$i++)
         {
         $statuslist[$i] =
         mysql_fetch_array ($this->resultid, MYSQL_ASSOC);
         }
      return $statuslist;
      }
```

As you can see, the displayStatus() method executes the "show status" command on the server and places the results of this command into an associative array. The actual display of the status values is handled at the point in the code where the method is called.

Next, let's look at the displayVersion() method of the dbMonitor class. The purpose of this method is to query the server to find out what version of the software is running:

```
//###############################################################
//##    Method:         displayVersion                        ##
//##    Parameters:     none                                  ##
//##    Return value:   the version number                    ##
//###############################################################
   function displayVersion()
      {
      $this->sqlstmt = "select version() as Version";
      $queryid = mysql_query ($this->sqlstmt,$this->linkid);
      $versionnumber[0] = mysql_fetch_array ($queryid, MYSQL_ASSOC);
      return $versionnumber;
      }
```

The version number is returned as an associative array to allow it to be displayed with the displayResultSet() function of the chapter5_common.php file. It could have just as easily been returned as a single value.

The next method of the dbMonitor class to examine is displayProcessList(). This method requests a list of active processes from the server and returns the result set as an associative array:

```
//###############################################################
//##    Method:         displayProcessList                    ##
//##    Parameters:     none                                  ##
//##    Return value:   array of active processes             ##
//###############################################################
   function displayProcessList()
      {
      $this->sqlstmt = "show processlist";
      $this->resultid = mysql_query ($this->sqlstmt,$this->linkid);
      $count =  mysql_numrows($this->resultid);
      for ($i=0;$i < $count;$i++)
         {
         $processlist[$i] =
         mysql_fetch_array ($this->resultid, MYSQL_ASSOC);
         }
      return $processlist;
      }
```

The last method in the dbMonitor class that we will examine is the displayVariables() method. This method returns all of the configurable server variables and what they are currently set to. This method executes the show variables command on the server and returns the result set as an associative array:

```
//####################################################################
//##    Method:          displayVariables                           ##
//##    Parameters:      none                                       ##
//##    Return value:    array of MySQL variables                   ##
//####################################################################
   function displayVariables()
      {
      $this->sqlstmt = "show variables";
      $this->resultid = mysql_query ($this->sqlstmt,$this->linkid);
      $count =  mysql_numrows($this->resultid);
      for ($i=0;$i < $count;$i++)
         {
         $variables[$i] = mysql_fetch_array ($this->resultid, MYSQL_ASSOC);
         }
      return $variables;
      }
   }

include ('chapter5_checklogin.php');
```

You have probably noticed by now the similarities between the methods in this class. Each of these methods involves executing a command on the server and then returning the result set as an associative array. Implementing each of these methods separately as part of the dbMonitor class as opposed to calling a method to execute the command directly has some definite advantages. The first advantage is that the code is modularized so that each method can be updated or improved without impacting other methods. Second, if you make several calls to this or subsequent applications that need this functionality, you will only need to change the code in one place. Finally, although this chapter focuses on MySQL administration, you may want to implement the application, for another database, and separating out the actual command to do the action from the overall code makes that easier to accomplish. Note that throughout the application, PHP MySQL functions are used when available; but for many actions, no function exists and you must execute raw commands.

The next step in this script (chapter5_dbMonitor.php) is to verify that the user is actually logged in to the application. If they are not logged in, they are prompted to return to the login page. The functionality to verify that they are logged in to the page is in the chapter5_checklogin.php file. The first portion of this file actually just presents the main menu to the user. The user will see this whether they are logged in to the application or not.

chapter5_checklogin.php

```
<?php
echo "<!doctype html public \"-//W3C//DTD HTML 4.0 //EN\">\n";
echo "<HTML>\n";
echo "<HEAD>\n";
echo "<TITLE>Instant PHP4 Chapter5 - Database Administration";
echo "</TITLE>\n";
echo "</HEAD>\n";
echo "<BODY>\n";
echo "<CENTER>Chapter5 - Database Administration</CENTER>\n";
echo "<BR><BR>\n";
echo "<CENTER>\n";
echo "<TABLE BORDER=5 BORDERCOLOR=\"0000FF\" CELLPADDING=2 ";
echo "CELLSPACING=5 >\n";
echo "<TR>\n";
echo "<TD><A HREF=\"chapter5_login.php\">Login</A></TD>\n";
echo "<TD><A HREF=\"chapter5_userAdmin.php\">User Admin</A></TD>\n";
echo "<TD><A HREF=\"chapter5_dbAdmin.php\">DB Admin</A></TD>\n";
echo "<TD><A HREF=\"chapter5_dbMonitor.php\">DB Monitor</A></TD>\n";
echo "<TD><A HREF=\"chapter5_tableAdmin.php\">Table Admin</A>";
echo "</TD>\n";
echo "<TD><A HREF=\"chapter5_sql.php\">SQL Admin</A></TD>\n";
echo "<TD><A HREF=\"chapter5_login.php?action=logout\">Logout</A></TD>\n";
echo "</TR>\n";
echo "</TABLE>\n";
echo "</CENTER>\n";
echo " <TR>\n";
echo "<BR><BR>\n";
```

Once the main menu is displayed, you then check to verify that the user logged in and should be allowed to perform one of the actions indicated on the menu. You start the check by examining the session variable username. If it is empty, they are definitely not logged in yet. The following code uses the form variables to determine whether the user is logged in:

```
//Retrieve input variables from HTTP get or post
$userinfo = strtolower($REQUEST_METHOD) == 'get'
   ? $HTTP_GET_VARS : $HTTP_POST_VARS;

$loggedin = TRUE;

//If no username in sessiondata or form data then they are not
//logged in and are not trying to
if ($userinfo[in_username] == NULL && empty($sessiondata[username]))
   {
   echo "<CENTER>\n";
   echo "<BR><BR><BR>\n";
   echo "You are not logged in\n";
   echo "<BR>\n";
   echo "<A HREF=\"chapter5_login.php\">Click Here To Log In</A>\n";
   echo "</CENTER>\n";
   $loggedin = FALSE;
   }
```

If username is empty and there is a post or get variable that includes a login name, the user may have just come from the login screen. If they are just logging in, you take all of the login data and store that in a session variable to be used throughout the application to establish a database connection for the user, as follows:

```
//If they are logging in, set the session data
else if (empty($sessiondata[username]))
   {
       $sessiondata[username] = $uscrinfo[in_username];
       $sessiondata[password] = $userinfo[in_password];
       $sessiondata[hostname] = $userinfo[in_hostname];
   }
```

Now that you have the user's connection information, either from the session variables or from the login screen, try to establish a connection with the database:

```
$myDBConn =
new DBConnection($sessiondata[hostname],$sessiondata[username],
$sessiondata[password]);
```

The connection is attempted by creating a new DBConnection object. If the connection fails, indicate that to the user and ask them to log in again:

```
//If their connection fails, ask them to try logging in again
if (empty($myDBConn->linkid) && $loggedin)
   {
   echo "<CENTER>\n";
   echo "<BR><BR><BR>\n";
   echo "Login Failed!\n";
   echo "<BR>\n";
   echo "<A HREF=\"chapter5_login.php\">Click Here To Try Again</A>\n";
   echo "</CENTER>\n";
   $loggedin = FALSE;
   }
?>
```

At this point in the chapter5_dbMonitor.php script, the user is logged in and you can present them with the submenu of available options to choose from:

```
if ($loggedin == TRUE)
   {
   echo "<CENTER>\n";
   echo "<A HREF=\"chapter5_dbMonitor.php?action=status\"");
   echo ">Show Status</A>\n";
   echo "<A HREF=\"chapter5_dbMonitor.php?action=version\"");
   echo ">Show Version</A>\n";
   echo "<A HREF=\"chapter5_dbMonitor.php?action=processlist\">");
   echo "Show Process List</A>\n";
   echo "<A HREF=\"chapter5_dbMonitor.php?action=variables\"");
   echo ">Show Variables</A>\n";
   echo "</CENTER>\n";
   }
```

You'll notice that each of these links in the menu call the same page the links are coming from. This time, however, the page will be called with the appropriate action variable as a get variable. The next step is to examine the action variable and execute the corresponding method of the dbMonitor class:

```
$myDBMonitor = new dbMonitor($myDBConn->linkid);
switch($userinfo[action])
   {
   case 'status':
      {
      $statusarray = $myDBMonitor->displayStatus();
      displayResultSet($statusarray);
      break;
      }
   case 'processlist':
      {
      $processarray = $myDBMonitor->displayProcessList();
      displayResultSet($processarray);
      break;
      }
   case 'variables':
      {
      $variablearray = $myDBMonitor->displayVariables();
      displayResultSet($variablearray);
      break;
      }
   case 'version':
      {
      $versionarray = $myDBMonitor->displayVersion();
      displayResultSet($versionarray);
      break;
      }
   }
?>
</BODY>
</HTML>
```

For each action, you call the appropriate method of the dbMonitor class and then display the result set returned from the method to the user. That completes the chapter5_dbMonitor.php script, which handles all actions relating to the overall status of the MySQL server.

Database Administration

The next item we will look at on the main menu is the Database Administration option. The code that handles this set of operations is contained in the chapter5_dbAdmin.php file. The first step in this script is to include the common functions that we have described previously.

chapter5_dbAdmin.php

```
<?php

include ('chapter5_common.php');
```

The next step is to define the dbAdmin class, which contains all the member variables and methods that handle actions related to the individual databases within MySQL:

```
//#################################################################
//##    Class:          dbAdmin                                 ##
//##    Description:    Class for administering a database.     ##
//##                    Requires a link identifier              ##
//#################################################################
class dbAdmin
   {
   //member variables
   var $linkid;
   var $database;
   var $rc;

   //constructor
   function dbAdmin ($linkidentifier)
      {
      $this->linkid = $linkidentifier;
      }
```

A dbAdmin class is instantiated by creating a new dbAdmin object with a link identifier supplied by the dbConnection class. The first method we will look at in the dbAdmin class is listDBs():

```
//#################################################################
//##    Method:         listDBs                                 ##
//##    Parameters:     None                                    ##
//##    Return value:   array of database names available to user ##
//#################################################################
```

```
function listDBs()
   {
   $list = mysql_list_dbs();
   $count = mysql_num_rows($list);

   for ($i=0;$i < $count;$i++)
      {
      $dblist[$i] = mysql_db_name ($list,$i);
      }
   return $dblist;
   }
```

This method executes the PHP function for listing the available databases in a MySQL database and returns the results as an associative array. The next method we examine is selectDB():

```
//####################################################################
//##    Method:          selectDB                                  ##
//##    Parameters:      db                                        ##
//##    Return value:    return code (TRUE = success)              ##
//####################################################################
   function selectDB($db)
      {
      $this->rc = mysql_select_db($db,$this->linkid);
      if ($this->rc)
         {
      $this->database = $db;
         }

      return $this->rc;
      }
```

This method executes the PHP function that sets which database the connected user is accessing. Subsequent SQL statements will bc made against the database selected by this method.

The next two methods are very straightforward in their design. They simply take a database name as their lone parameter and either drop or create the database as indicated:

```
//####################################################################
//##    Method:          dropDB                                    ##
//##    Parameters:      db                                        ##
//##    Return value:    return code (TRUE = success)              ##
//####################################################################
```

```
   function dropDB($db)
      {
      $this->rc = mysql_drop_db ($db,$this->linkid);
      return $this->rc;
      }

//#####################################################################
//##    Method:          createDB                                     ##
//##    Parameters:      db                                           ##
//##    Return value:    return code (TRUE = success)                 ##
//#####################################################################
   function createDB($db)
      {
      $this->rc = mysql_create_db ($db,$this->linkid);
      return $this->rc;
      }

   }//end of dbAdmin class
```

The next step is to include the chapter5_checklogin.php script to get the user's login credentials or ask them to log in if they have not already done so:

```
include ('chapter5_checklogin.php');
```

Once the user is logged in, you present them with a list of available submenu choices to choose from:

```
//If logged in, give list of dbAdmin actions
if ($loggedin == TRUE)
   {
echo "<CENTER>\n";
echo "<A HREF=\"chapter5_dbAdmin.php?action=list\"";
echo ">List Databases</A>\n";
echo "<A HREF=\"chapter5_dbAdmin.php?action=select1\"";
echo ">Select Database</A>\n";
echo "<A HREF=\"chapter5_dbAdmin.php?action=drop1\"";
echo ">Drop Database</A>\n";
echo "<A HREF=\"chapter5_dbAdmin.php?action=create1\"";
echo ">Create Database</A>\n";
echo "</CENTER>\n";
   }
```

Similar to chapter5_dbMonitor.php code, the links direct the user back to this page with a particular action specified. For each of the actions, you are going to need to call a method of the dbAdmin class, so you next create a dbAdmin object:

```
$myDBAdmin = new dbAdmin($myDBConn->linkid);
```

Then you call the appropriate method based on the passed-in action value:

```
switch($userinfo[action])
   {
   case 'list':
      {
      $dblistarray = $myDBAdmin->listDBs();
      displayArray("Databases",$dblistarray);
      break;
      }
```

If the user needs to select a database, you'll need to ask more information—namely, what database they want to select—before you can invoke the selectDB() method of the dbAdmin class. To do this, output a single line form and direct the user back to this page with an action of **select2** indicating that the database to select has been named, and now you are ready to call the selectDB() method, as shown here:

```
   case 'select1':
      {
      echo "<CENTER>\n";
      echo "<FORM ACTION=\"chapter5_dbAdmin.php\"";
      echo "METHOD=\"POST\">\n";
      echo "DB Name <INPUT TYPE=\"TEXT\"";
      echo "NAME=\"in_database\"";
      echo "SIZE=\"30\">\n";
      echo "<INPUT TYPE=\"hidden\" NAME=\"action\" VALUE=\"";
      echo "select2\" SIZE=\"30\">\n";
      echo "<INPUT TYPE=\"submit\" VALUE=\"Select DB\">\n";
      echo "</FORM>\n";
      echo "</CENTER>\n";
      break;
      }
   case 'select2':
      {
```

```
$rc = $myDBAdmin->selectDB($userinfo[in_database]);
echo "<BR><BR>\n";
echo "<CENTER>\n";
if  ($rc ==TRUE)
   {
   echo "Database changed to ".$userinfo[in_database].".";
   $sessiondata[database] = $userinfo[in_database];
   }
else
   {
   echo "Database could not be changed to ";
   echo $userinfo[in_database].".";
   }
echo "</CENTER>\n";
break;
}
```

A similar situation occurs for both Drop and Create Database. You must first identify which database the user wants to create or drop and then call the appropriate dbAdmin method, as follows:

```
case 'drop1':
      {
      echo "<CENTER>\n";
      echo "<FORM ACTION=\"chapter5_dbAdmin.php\"";
      echo "METHOD=\"POST\">\n";
      echo "DB Name <INPUT TYPE=\"text\" NAME=\"";
      echo "in_dropdatabase\" SIZE=\"30\">\n";
      echo "<INPUT TYPE=\"hidden\" NAME=\"action\" VALUE=\"drop2\"";
      echo "SIZE=\"30\">\n";
      echo "<INPUT TYPE=\"submit\" VALUE=\"Drop DB\">\n";
      echo "</FORM>\n";
      echo "<CENTER>\n";
      break;
      }
   case 'drop2':
      {
      $rc = $myDBAdmin->dropDB($userinfo[in_dropdatabase]);
      echo "<BR><BR>\n";
      echo "<CENTER>\n";
      if  ($rc ==TRUE)
         {
         echo "Database ".$userinfo[in_dropdatabase]." was dropped.";
```

```
            }
         else
            {
            echo "Database ".$userinfo[in_dropdatabase]." could not be dropped.";
            }
         echo "</CENTER>\n";
         break;
         }
      case 'create1':
         {
         echo "<CENTER>\n";
         echo "<FORM ACTION=\"chapter5_dbAdmin.php\" METHOD=\"POST\">\n";
         echo "DB Name <INPUT TYPE=\"text\" NAME=\"";
         echo "in_createdatabase\" SIZE=\"30\">\n";
         echo "<INPUT TYPE=\"hidden\" NAME=\"action\" VALUE=\"";
         echo "create2\" SIZE=\"30\">\n";
         echo "<INPUT TYPE=\"submit\" VALUE=\"Create DB\">\n";
         echo "</FORM>\n";
         echo "<CENTER>\n";
         break;
         }
      case 'create2':
         {
         $rc = $myDBAdmin->createDB($userinfo[in_createdatabase]);
         echo "<BR><BR>\n";
         echo "<CENTER>\n";
         if  ($rc ==TRUE)
            {
            echo "Database ".$userinfo[in_createdatabase];
            echo " was created.";
            }
         else
            {
            echo "Database ".$userinfo[in_createdatabase];
            echo " could not be created.";
            }
         echo "</CENTER>\n";
         break;
      }
}
?>
</BODY>
</HTML>
```

Table Administration

Once a user has selected a particular database to work with using the dbAdmin class's selectDB() method, they can work with individual tables within the selected database. The actions associated with table administration are contained in the chapter5_tableAdmin.php file. The script starts out as usual by including the common functions and defining the tableAdmin class.

chapter5_tableAdmin.php

```
<?php

include ('chapter5_common.php');

//#####################################################################
//##    Class:          tableAdmin                                 ##
//##    Description:    Methods to administer a table              ##
//#####################################################################
class tableAdmin
   {
   //member variables
   var $database;
   var $linkid;
   var $sqlstmt;
   var $rc;

   //constructor
   function tableAdmin ($database,$linkid)
      {
      $this->database = $database;
      $this->linkid = $linkid;
      }
```

The first method in the tableAdmin class is the listTables() method, which uses the PHP MySQL function to query what tables are in the selected database:

```
//#####################################################################
//##    Method:         listTables                                 ##
//##    Parameters:     none                                       ##
//##    Return value:   array of table names                       ##
//#####################################################################
```

```
    function listTables()
       {
       $list = mysql_list_tables ($this->database,$this->linkid);
       $count = mysql_num_rows($list);
       $tablelist = array ($count);
       for ($i=0;$i < $count;$i++)
          {
          $tablelist[$i] = mysql_tablename ($list,$i);
          }
       return $tablelist;
       }
```

The next method is describeTable(), which details the column descriptions that make up the table:

```
//####################################################################
//##    Method:         describeTable                              ##
//##    Parameters:     table                                      ##
//##    Return value:   array of table detail                      ##
//####################################################################
    function describeTable($table)
       {
       $this->sqlstmt = "describe ".$table;
       $queryid =
       mysql_db_query
       ($this->database,$this->sqlstmt,$this->linkid);
       if (empty($queryid))
         {
         echo "empty";
         return 0;
         }
       $count = mysql_num_rows($queryid);
       for ($i=0;$i < $count;$i++)
          {
          $describeresults[$i] =
          mysql_fetch_array ($queryid,MYSQL_ASSOC);
          }
       return $describeresults;
       }
```

The dropTable() method simply takes a table name to be dropped and returns a result code indicating success or failure:

```
//####################################################################
//##    Method:          dropTable                                 ##
//##    Parameters:      tablename                                 ##
//##    Return value:    return code (TRUE = success)              ##
//####################################################################
   function dropTable($tablename)
      {
      $this->sqlstmt = "drop table ".$tablename;
      $this->rc = mysql_db_query ($this->database,$this->sqlstmt,$this->linkid);
      return $this->rc;
      }
```

The displayTable() method executes a **select * from <table>** command and returns all of the rows in an associative array:

```
//####################################################################
//##    Method:          displayTable                              ##
//##    Parameters:      tablename                                 ##
//##    Return value:    array of records in table                 ##
//####################################################################
   function displayTable($table)
      {
      $this->sqlstmt = "select * from ".$table;
      $queryid =
      mysql_db_query($this->database,$this->sqlstmt,$this->linkid);
      if (empty($queryid))
         {
         return 0;
         }
      $count = mysql_num_rows($queryid);
      for ($i=0;$i < $count;$i++)
         {
         $tableresults[$i] =
         mysql_fetch_array ($queryid,MYSQL_ASSOC);
         }
      return $tableresults;
      }

   }//end of tableAdmin class
```

After defining the methods of the tableAdmin class, check that the user is able to establish a connection to the server and that they have selected a database to work with before administering any tables:

```
include ('chapter5_checklogin.php');

if ($sessiondata[database]  ==  NULL )
   {
   echo "<CENTER>\n";
   echo "<BR><BR>\n";
   echo "You must use dbAdmin to select a database to work with.";
   echo "</CENTER>\n";;
   $nodatabase = TRUE;
   }
```

Next, present the user with the submenu of available table administration options:

```
if ($loggedin == TRUE && !$nodatabase)
   {
   echo "<CENTER>\n";
   echo "<A HREF=\"chapter5_tableAdmin.php?action=list\"";
   echo ">List Tables</A>\n";
   echo "<A HREF=\"chapter5_tableAdmin.php?action=describe1\"";
   echo ">Describe Table</A>\n";
   echo "<A HREF=\"chapter5_tableAdmin.php?action=drop1\"";
   echo ">Drop Table</A>\n";
   echo "<A HREF=\"chapter5_tableAdmin.php?action=display1\"";
   echo ">Display Table</A>\n";
   echo "</CENTER>\n";
   }
```

You then create a tableAdmin object that you will use to execute any table administration methods:

```
 $myTableAdmin =
new tableAdmin($sessiondata[database],$myDBConn->linkid);
```

We examine the action variable to determine which method to call:

```
switch($userinfo[action])
   {
```

If the action is list, you display a single-column listing of all the tables in the database:

```
case 'list':
   {
   $tablelistarray = $myTableAdmin->listTables();
   displayArray("Tables",$tablelistarray);
   break;
   }
```

If the action is describe, you first ask which table you want to describe, and then call the describe method of your tableAdmin object:

```
case 'describe1':
   {
   displayOneLineForm('chapter5_tableAdmin.php','Table Name',
                        'in_table','describe2','Describe Table');
   break;
   }
case 'describe2':
   {
   $descriptionlist =
   $myTableAdmin->describeTable($userinfo[in_table]);
   displayResultSet($descriptionlist);
   break;
   }
```

We used the displayOneLineForm() function from the chapter5_common.php file to simplify this script.

In the case of dropTable() and displayTable(), you again prompt for the table name and then call the corresponding method of the tableAdmin object:

```
case 'drop1':
   {
   displayOneLineForm('chapter5_tableAdmin.php','Table Name',
                        'in_table','drop2','Drop Table');
   break;
   }
case 'drop2':
   {
   $rc = $myTableAdmin->dropTable($userinfo[in_table]);
   echo "<BR><BR>\n";
   echo "<CENTER>\n";
```

```
        if  ($rc ==TRUE)
          {
          echo "Table ".$userinfo[in_table]." was dropped.";
          }
          else
          {
          echo "Table ".$userinfo[in_table]." could not be dropped.";
          }
          echo "</CENTER>\n";
          break;
        }
    case 'display1':
        {
        displayOneLineForm('chapter5_tableAdmin.php','Table Name',
                             'in_table','display2','Display Table');
        break;
        }
    case 'display2':
        {
        $tableresults =
        $myTableAdmin->displayTable($userinfo[in_table]);
        displayResultSet($tableresults);
        break;
        }
    }
?>
</BODY>
</HTML>
```

User Administration

The chapter5_userAdmin.php file contains the userAdmin class, which contains methods that allow the application's user to administer database users. This script starts off by including the common functions and then defining the class structure for a userAdmin object.

chapter5_userAdmin.php

```
<?php

include ('chapter5_common.php');
```

```
//##################################################################
//##    Class:          userAdmin                               ##
//##    Description:    Class for administering database users  ##
//##                    requires a link identifier              ##
//##################################################################
class userAdmin
   {
   //member variables
   var $userName;
   var $database;
   var $linkid;
   var $sqlstmt;
   var $rc;

   //constructor
     function userAdmin ($linkid)
      {
      $this->linkid = $linkid;
      }
```

The first method of this class is the addUser() method, which takes as parameters the necessary information about a new user and attempts to give them rights to all of the tables in the database indicated. The code is as follows:

```
//##################################################################
//##    Method:         addUser                                 ##
//##    Parameters:     dbname,username,hostname, password      ##
//##    Return VALUE:   return code (TRUE = success)            ##
//##################################################################
   function addUser
   ($au_dbname,$au_username,$au_hostname =  "%",$au_password)
      {
      $this->sqlstmt = "GRANT ALL PRIVILEGES ";
      $this->sqlstmt = $this->sqlstmt . "ON $au_dbname.* ";
      $this->sqlstmt = $this->sqlstmt . "TO $au_username";
      if ($au_hostname == "%")
         {
         $this->sqlstmt = $this->sqlstmt . "@'%' ";
         }
      else
         {
         $this->sqlstmt = $this->sqlstmt . "@$au_hostname ";
         }
      $this->sqlstmt = $this->sqlstmt . "IDENTIFIED BY ";
```

```
    $this->sqlstmt = $this->sqlstmt . "'$au_password' ";
    $this->sqlstmt = $this->sqlstmt . "WITH GRANT OPTION";

    $this->rc = mysql_query ($this->sqlstmt,$this->linkid);
    return $this->sqlstmt;
    }
```

The next method in the userAdmin class is listUsers(), which displays all of the users registered in the MySQL database:

```
//###################################################################
//##     Method:              listUsers                            ##
//##     Parameters:          username                             ##
//##     Return VALUE:        array which contains a list          ##
//##                          of current users                     ##
//###################################################################
       function listUsers ()
          {
          //must have access rights to the user table to see this list

          $this->sqlstmt = "select host,user from user";
          $queryid =
          mysql_db_query ("mysql",$this->sqlstmt,$this->linkid);
          $count = mysql_num_rows($queryid);
          for ($i=0;$i < $count;$i++)
             {
             $userlist[$i] = mysql_fetch_array ($queryid,MYSQL_ASSOC);
             }
          return $userlist;
          }
   }//end of userAdmin class
```

Once the methods of the userAdmin class have been defined, you then check to make sure the user is logged in and present them with the submenu items for user administration:

```
if ($loggedin == TRUE)
   {
   echo "<CENTER>\n";
   echo "<A HREF=\"chapter5_userAdmin.php?action=addUser1\"";
   echo ">Add User</A>\n";
   echo "<A HREF=\"chapter5_userAdmin.php?action=removeUser1\"";
   echo ">Remove User</A>\n";
   echo "<A HREF=\"chapter5_userAdmin.php?action=updateUser1\"";
```

```
echo ">Update User</A>\n";
echo "<A HREF=\"chapter5_login.php\">Change User</A>\n";
echo "<A HREF=\"chapter5_userAdmin.php?action=listUsers\"";
echo ">List Users</A>\n";
echo "</CENTER>\n";
}
```

In the case of addUser(), you first prompt for the user criteria and then call the addUser() method to add the user to the specified database:

```
switch($userinfo[action])
   {
   case 'addUser1':
      {
      echo "<CENTER>\n";
      echo "<FORM ACTION=\"chapter5_userAdmin.php\" METHOD=\"";
      echo "POST\">\n";
      echo "<TABLE CELLSPACING=5 CELLPADDING=5 BORDER=3 ";
      echo "BORDERCOLOR=\"0000FF\" >\n";
      echo "<TR><TD>\n";
      echo "UserName</TD><TD><INPUT TYPE=\"TEXT\" NAME=\"au_username\"";
      echo "SIZE=\"30\" MAXLENGTH=\"16\"><BR>\n";
      echo "</TD></TR>\n";
      echo "<TR><TD>\n";
      echo "Password</TD><TD><INPUT TYPE=\"password\" NAME=\"";
      echo "au_password\" SIZE=\"30\"><BR>\n";
      echo "</TD></TR>\n";
      echo "<TR><TD>\n";
      echo "HostName</TD><TD><INPUT TYPE=\"TEXT\" NAME=\"au_hostname\"";
      echo "SIZE=\"30\"><BR>\n";
      echo "</TD></TR>\n";
      echo "<TR><TD>\n";
      echo "DB Name</TD><TD><INPUT TYPE=\"TEXT\" NAME=\"au_dbname\"";
      echo "SIZE=\"30\"><BR>\n";
      echo "</TD></TR>\n";
      echo "</TABLE>\n";
      echo "<BR><BR>\n";
      echo "<INPUT TYPE=\"SUBMIT\" VALUE=\"add User\">\n";
      echo "<INPUT TYPE=\"HIDDEN\" NAME=\"action\" VALUE=\"";
      echo "addUser2\" SIZE=\"30\"><BR>\n";
      echo "</FORM>\n";
      echo "<CENTER>\n";
```

```
        break;
        }
    case 'addUser2':
        {
        $auinfo = strtolower($REQUEST_METHOD) == 'get'
        ? $HTTP_GET_VARS : $HTTP_POST_VARS;
        $myuserAdmin = new userAdmin($myDBConn->linkid);
        $stmt = $myuserAdmin->addUser($auinfo[au_dbname],
        $auinfo[au_username],$auinfo[au_hostname],
        $auinfo[au_password]);
        echo "<CENTER>\n";
        echo "<BR>";
        echo $stmt;
        echo "<BR>";
        echo "</CENTER>\n";
        break;
        }
```

For the listUser menu option, you simply call the listUser() method of the userAdmin object and then display the array of users as an HTML table, as follows:

```
        case 'listUsers':
        {
        $myuserAdmin = new userAdmin($myDBConn->linkid);
        $userarray = $myuserAdmin->listUsers();
        displayResultSet($userarray);
        break;
        }
    }
?>
</BODY>
</HTML>
```

SQL Query Execution

The last PHP script we are going to look at is the chapter5_sql.php file. This contains the class and methods to execute raw SQL statements against the database.

You start off by defining the SQL class based on the SQL statement that you want to execute.

chapter5_sql.php

```
<?php

include ('chapter5_common.php');

//####################################################################
//##    Class:          SQL                                         ##
//##    Description:    A SQL for execution against db              ##
//####################################################################
class SQL
   {
   var $stmt;
   var $linkid;
   var $queryid;

   function SQL($database,$stmt,$linkid)
      {
      $this->stmt = $stmt;
      $this->linkid = $linkid;
      $this->database = $database;
      }
```

Then you define a method to take a **select** or **show** query and execute it against the database:

```
//####################################################################
//##    Method:       executeSQLSelect                              ##
//##    Parameters: SQLStmt                                         ##
//##    Return value:  return code (0 = success)                    ##
//####################################################################
   function executeSQLSelect()
      {
      $this->queryid =
      mysql_db_query ($this->database,$this->stmt,$this->linkid);
      if (empty($this->queryid))
         {
         return  0;
         }

      $count = mysql_num_rows($this->queryid);
      for ($i=0;$i < $count;$i++)
         {
```

```
        $results[$i] = mysql_fetch_array ($this->queryid,MYSQL_ASSOC);
        }

     return $results;
     }
```

The method returns the result set from the SQL query or 0 if the query was not successful. The next method takes a query that doesn't start with **select** or **show** and executes it against the database:

```
//####################################################################
//##    Method:      executeSQL                                     ##
//##    Parameters: none                                            ##
//##    Return value:  return code (0 = success)                    ##
//####################################################################
   function executeSQL()
      {
      $this->resultid = mysql_query ($this->stmt,$this->linkid);
      return $rc;
      }
```

The class also contains a couple of extra utility methods to further define the results of the query:

```
//####################################################################
//##    Method:          affectedRows                               ##
//##    Parameters:      none                                       ##
//##    Return value:    number of affected rows                    ##
//##    Note:            valid for insert,update,delete statements ##
//####################################################################
   function affectedRows()
      {
      $rowcount = mysql_affected_rows ($this->linkid);
      return $rowcount;
      }

//####################################################################
//##    Method:          numRows                                    ##
//##    Parameters:      none                                       ##
//##    Return value:    number of affected rows                    ##
//##    Note:            valid for select statement only            ##
//####################################################################
```

```
    function numRows()
        {
        $rowcount = mysql_num_rows ($this->queryid);
        return $rowcount;
        }

//####################################################################
//##    Method:           numFields                                 ##
//##    Parameters:       none                                      ##
//##    Return value:     number of fields in result set            ##
//####################################################################
    function numFields()
        {
        $fieldcount = mysql_num_fields ($this->queryid);
        return $fieldcount;
        }

//####################################################################
//##    Method:           fetchRow                                  ##
//##    Parameters:       none                                      ##
//##    Return value:     enumerated array containing row of        ##
//##                      result set                                ##
//####################################################################
    function fetchRow()
        {
        return mysql_fetch_row($this-resultid);
        }

    }//end of SQL class
```

After the methods are defined, the script continues on, and it either executes the passed-in statement or provides the user with a text area to input the SQL statement:

```
include ('chapter5_checklogin.php');


if ($loggedin == TRUE)
    {
    if($userinfo[action]=="query2")
        {
```

```
    $mySQL  = new
    SQL($sessiondata[database],$userinfo[in_query],$myDBConn->linkid);

    if (stristr($userinfo[in_query],'select') ||
        stristr($userinfo[in_query],'show'))
       {
       $sqlResults = $mySQL->executeSQLSelect();
       $numrows = $mySQL->numRows();
       echo "<CENTER>";
       echo $numrows." rows were returned.";
       echo "</CENTER>";
       echo "<BR><BR><BR>";
       displayResultSet($sqlResults);
       }
    else
       {
       $sqlResults = $mySQL->executeSQL();
       $affectedrows = $mySQL->affectedRows();
       echo "<CENTER>";
       echo $affectedrows." rows were affected by the query.";
       echo "</CENTER>";
       }
    }
  else
    {
    echo "<CENTER>\n";
    echo "<FORM ACTION=\"chapter5_sql.php\" METHOD=\"POST\">\n";
    echo "<TEXTAREA NAME=\"in_query\" ";
    echo "ROWS=\"8\" COLS=\"60\"></TEXTAREA>\n";
    echo "<INPUT TYPE=\"HIDDEN\" NAME=\"action\" VALUE=\"";
    echo "query2\" SIZE\"30\"><BR><BR><BR>\n";
    echo "<INPUT TYPE=\"SUBMIT\" VALUE=\"Execute Query\">\n";
    echo "<INPUT TYPE=\"RESET\" VALUE=\"Reset\">\n";
    echo "</FORM>\n";
    echo "</CENTER>\n";
    }
  }

?>
</BODY>
</HTML>
```

Notice that if the query was a **select** or **show** statement, the number of rows in the result set are indicated. If the query was not a **select** statement, the number of rows impacted by the query are indicated.

That completes the code portion of the application. This code should have demonstrated to you the advantage of organizing your code into classes to keep logical functionality together. Also, when possible, code is reused in the application, which results in more streamlined code as well as code that is easier to debug.

Next Steps

This application is a good start toward providing a mechanism for remote database administration. Of course, not all possible actions have been incorporated into the application. By providing a mechanism for executing raw SQL commands, the user should be capable of doing most of the necessary day-to-day administration tasks. However, the application could be improved by offering more point-and-click interfaces to other actions that are possible, such as a visual query builder in which you can select the names of columns and tables from drop-down boxes.

Additionally, the application is designed using minimalist HTML, as this is a book focused on PHP and not HTML. With that said, there is definitely an opportunity to dress up the look and feel of the application.

Finally, a very powerful next step for the application would be to make it entirely independent by utilizing a database abstraction layer. ODBC can provide this, but that would require you to obtain ODBC drivers for each database you want to work with. You may be better served by creating classes, which translate a generic database command into the appropriate format for whatever database you are working with. There is already considerable work done in this area, so you are advised to check out the latest on http://www.php.net.

What to Take Away

This chapter presented an application for administering a MySQL database from a web browser. Not every possible action was implemented within the application, but a framework was developed, which will allow you to easily expand the application to include whatever functionality you feel is necessary. By utilizing classes, we were able to subdivide the application into a handful of smaller modules, which in general makes the application easier to develop and easier to debug. This chapter exemplified how a good framework and careful planning can simplify the development process.

CHAPTER

6

Interactive Visitor Poll

IN THIS CHAPTER:

chapter6_bar.html—Sample used to create the bar graph
chapter6_test.php—Test script to verify database connectivity
chapter6_vpoll.php—Entire code listing for this chapter

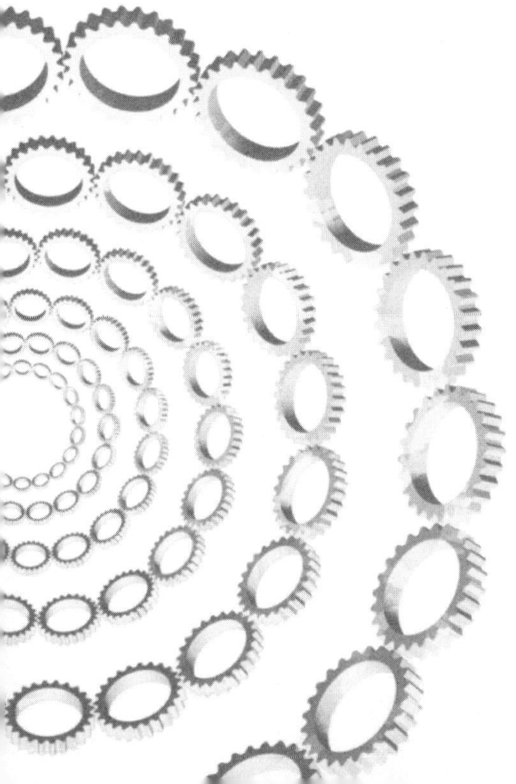

The overall objective of this chapter is to create an interactive visitor poll. These polls can be found on many web sites and usually ask questions that are relevant to their specific user base. For instance, a financial site might ask when the NASDAQ will finally bottom out; a sports news site might poll their users to find out who the best basketball or baseball player is. Political sites could ask for feedback on how public officials are performing; technical sites would be interested in the best new technology of the year. The point is that this simple application has a specific use, but can fill many needs. When designing this application, keep in mind requirements such as configurability, expandability, and ease of use.

Application Requirements

The requirements for this project include connecting the visitor poll to a database to store and retrieve the data that will be displayed. The details of the visitor poll requirements are detailed in the following items.

Store, Increment, and Read Data

The database should be designed for MySQL, and all data should be stored in the database. This means that the initial question should be retrieved from the database along with the valid voting options for the visitor poll. When the user selects an option, the user's vote will increment the overall count and then be stored in the database.

Handling Multiple-Visitor Poll Data

The database design should have the capability to store multiple voting topics and data. The voting question, choices, and other relative information should be stored and retrieved from the database when the script is run. Changing the poll should be as simple as possible and based on a single variable placed at the front of the script. This polling key will be used to select all the appropriate data from the database and then display it in the poll.

Show Voting Options and Results

The visitor poll functionality should initially show the polling question and the voting options. The user should have the ability to pick one option and then click the Submit button. After the user submits the vote, the results of the visitor poll will be displayed. These results are to be displayed graphically along with the voting percentages.

Bar Graph Results Display

The graph on the results screen should not contain any graphical images. This means that the results must be dynamically generated and then displayed using HTML only. This is not necessarily a function of PHP or database design, but often the requirements of a project don't deal with a single topic or group of topics. We will present a design that will fulfill this requirement even though you would find this in an HTML or web design book.

Application Design

Now that you have the requirements for this project, you can start some of your visitor poll design. Let's first look at your database design. MySQL should already be installed on your system. The first thing to do is create a user that will have access to read and write to your database. To do this, connect to the mysql database and insert the following row into the user table. The SQL statement looks like this.

```
INSERT INTO user
VALUES('localhost','webuser',PASSWORD('abc123'),'Y','Y','Y',
'Y','Y','Y','Y','Y','Y','Y','Y','Y','Y','Y');
```

It is important to note that versions of MySQL prior to 3.22.11 had fewer privilege columns. This INSERT statement will fail if used on a MySQL database prior to 3.22.11. For this example, please note that we are using MySQL version 2.23.32.

This command sets up a MySQL superuser to which you will later grant privileges. The output of this command should look something like the following:

```
[root@rambo mysql]# mysql mysql
Reading table information for completion of table and column names
You can turn off this feature to get a quicker startup with -A

Welcome to the MySQL monitor.  Commands end with ; or \g.
Your MySQL connection id is 13 to server version: 3.23.32

Type 'help;' or '\h' for help. Type '\c' to clear the buffer

mysql> INSERT INTO user
VALUES('localhost','webuser',PASSWORD('abc123'),'Y','Y','Y','Y'
,'Y','Y','Y','Y','Y','Y','Y','Y','Y','Y');
Query OK, 1 row affected (0.02 sec)
```

Next, you will create a database called vpoll. This will be the database you will use to store all the information for your visitor poll. At the command prompt, type the following:

```
[root@rambo mysql]# /usr/bin/mysqladmin create vpoll
```

Now you have a user called webuser and a database called vpoll; you next need to grant privileges to this user allowing the ability to read and write data to the database. You do this using the GRANT statement in MySQL. Using this statement you can be as specific or broad with your privileges as you would like. The syntax of the command looks like this:

```
GRANT priv_type [(column_list)] [, priv_type [(column_list)] ...]
    ON {tbl_name | * | *.* | db_name.*}
    TO user_name [IDENTIFIED BY 'password']
        [, user_name [IDENTIFIED BY 'password'] ...]
    [WITH GRANT OPTION]
```

There are several options available to you when granting privileges. We will not go into depth on all the different options, but just remember that you can grant privileges on a global, database, table, or column level.

Depending on whether you are granting privileges globally, on databases, on tables, or on columns, some of the priv_type options listed next are not valid for the GRANT statement. Please refer to the MySQL documentation for further information.

```
ALL PRIVILEGES      FILE            RELOAD
ALTER               INDEX           SELECT
CREATE              INSERT          SHUTDOWN
DELETE              PROCESS         UPDATE
DROP
```

The syntax of the command you will use is simple. You want to grant all privileges to the webuser user specifically on the vpoll database. The command will look something like this:

```
mysql> GRANT ALL PRIVILEGES ON vpoll TO webuser@localhost;
Query OK, 0 rows affected (0.01 sec)
mysql> flush privileges;
Query OK, 0 rows affected (0.02 sec)
```

Notice a new command, flush privileges, is used after the GRANT statement. The flush command clears some of the internal caches MySQL uses. When used in conjunction with the privileges option, the command is used to reload the grant tables from the mysql database. The user issuing the command must have the RELOAD privilege for the command to be successful.

Currently, you have an empty vpoll database and a user called webuser who has all rights to that database. You now need to connect to the database and create the tables you will use in your interactive visitor poll code. To connect to the database, enter the following at the command prompt:

```
[root@rambo mysql]# /usr/bin/mysql vpoll
Welcome to the MySQL monitor.  Commands end with ; or \g.
Your MySQL connection id is 16 to server version: 3.23.32
Type 'help;' or '\h' for help. Type '\c' to clear the buffer
mysql>
```

Your database will consist of two tables, one named topic and one named data. The topic table will contain question and header information that will ultimately be displayed in the visitor poll. The columns in this table are defined here.

- **tid** An auto-incremented integer that has to have a value. This column has to be unique and will be the primary key.
- **question** A variable-length character that has to have a value.
- **header** A variable-length character.

The data table will contain all the options and the total number of votes for each option. These options and data will be associated with the question and header through the tid value. The tid for the question in the topic table has a one-to-many relationship to the options contained in the data table. This means that one question can have one or more options. The columns in the data table are defined here.

- **tid** An integer that has to have value.
- **name** A variable length character that has to contain a value. This column has to be unique and will be the primary key.
- **votes** An integer.

You can use a simple SQL statement to create the tables. The CREATE TABLE for the data table will look like this:

```
CREATE TABLE data (
    tid SMALLINT UNSIGNED NOT NULL,
```

```
    name varchar(30) DEFAULT '0' NOT NULL,
    votes int(5),
    PRIMARY KEY (name)
);
```

If you are new to SQL, this syntax may look strange. Let's take a few moments and look at this query line by line. The first line is creating a table in your database named data. The attributes of this table are defined within the beginning and ending parentheses. The first column in the table is tid. We have previously defined what tid is and why it is important. This query tells the database to make tid a small unsigned integer and make it required. A small unsigned integer, as defined in MySQL, can hold values from 0 to 65535.

The next line defines the column name. This is defined as a variable-length string that can be from 1 to 30 characters in length. In MySQL, trailing spaces are removed from the string being inserted into the database when the value is stored.

Next, you define the column name votes. This column is given the attribute int(5). int is defined as a normal-size integer. The signed range of an integer is –2147483648 to 2147483647. The unsigned range is 0 to 4294967295. The (5) indicates a maximum display size of 5 for this column.

You will also notice the very last line before the ending parenthesis has a PRIMARY KEY statement. The primary key is a unique field and must not be NULL. There can only be one primary key per table; and if a primary key is not defined, MySQL will use the first column that has the UNIQUE attribute set.

Now that you understand the command, let's use it. When entered at the MySQL command line, the command and its output will look like this:

```
mysql> CREATE TABLE data (
    ->     tid SMALLINT UNSIGNED NOT NULL,
    ->     name varchar(30) DEFAULT '0' NOT NULL,
    ->     votes int(5),
    ->     PRIMARY KEY (name)
    -> );
Query OK, 0 rows affected (0.03 sec)
```

The SQL statement you will use to create the topic table is similar to the script you used previously except for the AUTO_INCREMENT attribute on the tid column and a few other minor differences. Let's talk about the AUTO_INCREMENT attribute. The AUTO_INCREMENT column is an integer column. When a value of NULL or 0 is inserted into an AUTO_INCREMENT column, the value is set to the largest value + 1. You will notice that all AUTO_INCREMENT sequences begin with 1.

We will illustrate this later in this section. There can be only one AUTO_ INCREMENT column per table and this column must be indexed.

The CREATE TABLE script looks like this:

```
CREATE TABLE topic (
    tid SMALLINT UNSIGNED NOT NULL AUTO_INCREMENT,
    question varchar(100) DEFAULT '0' NOT NULL,
    header varchar(15),
    PRIMARY KEY (tid)
);
```

The output of this command is the same as previously shown:

```
mysql> CREATE TABLE topic (
    ->     tid SMALLINT UNSIGNED NOT NULL AUTO_INCREMENT,
    ->     question varchar(100) DEFAULT '0' NOT NULL,
    ->     header varchar(15),
    ->     PRIMARY KEY (tid)
    -> );
Query OK, 0 rows affected (0.00 sec)
```

Now let's look at your newly formed tables in the database. To do this, you will use the SHOW command at the MySQL command prompt. The SHOW command can be used to provide information about databases, tables, columns, or even status information about the server. Valid commands are listed next; for details on each of these commands, please refer to the MySQL documentation.

```
SHOW DATABASES [LIKE wild]
SHOW TABLES [FROM db_name] [LIKE wild]
SHOW COLUMNS FROM tbl_name [FROM db_name] [LIKE wild]
SHOW INDEX FROM tbl_name [FROM db_name]
SHOW TABLE STATUS [FROM db_name] [LIKE wild]
SHOW STATUS [LIKE wild]
SHOW VARIABLES [LIKE wild]
SHOW [FULL] PROCESSLIST
SHOW GRANTS FOR user
```

For this example, you will use the SHOW TABLES command. The output should look something like the following.

```
mysql> show tables;
+-----------------+
| Tables_in_vpoll |
+-----------------+
| data            |
| topic           |
+-----------------+
3 rows in set (0.01 sec)
```

You now have a database and tables ready to receive data. All you need to do now is come up with a poll you would like to display and enter the data into the database.

Let's assume you are running a sports site and the question of the day has to do with baseball. The oft-argued question of the best baseball player ever to play the game is always a good poll subject, and maybe your visitors will vote and then debate the subject in your threaded discussion group.

A simple illustration of the data in the poll would look like this:

```
Who is the best baseball player of all time?
     Player Name
     Mickey Mantle
     Reggie Jackson
     Joe DiMaggio
     Lou Gehrig
     Pete Rose
     Ted Williams
     Willie Mays
```

The simple INSERT queries that need to be used are shown next. These queries will insert the value of the baseball player's name, along with the ID for the poll in which it is to be used. In this case, the ID for the poll is 1. The last entry is for the vote tally. When a vote is submitted for a player, this number is incremented by one.

```
INSERT INTO data VALUES (1,'Mickey Mantle', '0');
INSERT INTO data VALUES (1,'Reggie Jackson', '0');
INSERT INTO data VALUES (1,'Joe DiMaggio', '0');
INSERT INTO data VALUES (1,'Lou Gehrig', '0');
INSERT INTO data VALUES (1,'Pete Rose', '0');
INSERT INTO data VALUES (1,'Ted Williams', '0');
INSERT INTO data VALUES (1,'Willie Mays', '0');
```

The output of these commands as they are put into MySQL looks like this:

```
mysql> INSERT INTO data VALUES (1,'Mickey Mantle', '0');
Query OK, 1 row affected (0.00 sec)
```

```
mysql> INSERT INTO data VALUES (1,'Reggie Jackson', '0');
Query OK, 1 row affected (0.00 sec)
mysql> INSERT INTO data VALUES (1,'Joe DiMaggio', '0');
Query OK, 1 row affected (0.00 sec)
mysql> INSERT INTO data VALUES (1,'Lou Gehrig', '0');
Query OK, 1 row affected (0.00 sec)
mysql> INSERT INTO data VALUES (1,'Pete Rose', '0');
Query OK, 1 row affected (0.00 sec)
mysql> INSERT INTO data VALUES (1,'Ted Williams', '0');
Query OK, 1 row affected (0.00 sec)
mysql> INSERT INTO data VALUES (1,'Willie Mays', '0');
Query OK, 1 row affected (0.00 sec)
```

Next, you will use another INSERT query to enter the polling question and the header information. You define the header information so that when you change a poll—say, to query users about their favorite operating system—the header on the poll doesn't say "Player Name." You can change it to say "Operating System."

Notice that the first data item in this query is 0, but your poll ID is 1. We have done this to illustrate that the AUTO_INCREMENT attribute you defined previously will begin counting at 1 and continue sequentially. Even though the query explicitly inserts a 0 into the table, the data will be changed to reflect the automatically incremented integer value.

The query looks like this:

```
INSERT INTO topic VALUES (0,'Who is the best baseball player of all
time?','Player Name');
```

The output of the command is successful and looks like this:

```
mysql> INSERT INTO topic VALUES (0,'Who is the best baseball player
of all time?','Player Name');
Query OK, 1 row affected (0.00 sec)
```

Let's take a look at the data you have entered into your database. You can simply output the data from a specific table by using a simple SELECT query. The command for viewing values from the data table and output from that table would look like the following:

```
mysql> select * from data;
+-----+----------------+-------+
| tid | name           | votes |
+-----+----------------+-------+
|   1 | Mickey Mantle  |     0 |
```

```
|    1 | Reggie Jackson |      0 |
|    1 | Joe DiMaggio   |      0 |
|    1 | Lou Gehrig     |      0 |
|    1 | Pete Rose      |      0 |
|    1 | Ted Williams   |      0 |
|    1 | Willie Mays    |      0 |
+-----+----------------+-------+
7 rows in set (0.07 sec)
```

A similar command and output from the topic table would look like the following:

```
mysql> select * from topic;
+-----+--------------------------------------------+-------------+
| tid | question                                   | header      |
+-----+--------------------------------------------+-------------+
|   1 | Who is the best baseball player of all time? | Player Name |
+-----+--------------------------------------------+-------------+
1 row in set (0.00 sec)
```

You now have a database that is entirely designed, configured, set up, and ready to go. Often when integrating PHP and MySQL, there are configuration items that need to be resolved before the PHP can successfully speak to the MySQL database.

For instance, let's create a simple PHP script that will connect to the database, query for data, and display the data in a browser. The PHP script looks like this:

chapter6_test.php

```
<?
    $link =  mysql_connect( "localhost", "admin", "admin"  );
    if ( ! $link )
        die( "Couldn't connect to MySQL" );
    mysql_select_db( "vpoll", $link )
        or die ( "Couldn't open VPOLL database: ".mysql_error() );

    $qid=mysql_db_query("vpoll","select * from data where tid=1
order by votes DESC");
    if ( ! $qid )
        die ( "Query fatal error: ".mysql_error() );

    while($row=mysql_fetch_row($qid)) {
print "$row[1]<br>";
    }
?>
```

This script is very simple: it first opens a connection to the MySQL database and then selects the vpoll database. If either of these commands fails, an error message will be displayed. Next, data is selected from the data table and placed in descending order. The data is then displayed row by row. If this exercise is successful, your browser should look like Figure 6-1 and you have successfully integrated MySQL and PHP.

On occasion you may get errors. If there are errors, first make sure that you have PHP compiled with the --with-mysql option and that the compilation was successful. Also verify the names of your database, table, users, and so on.

If you happen to see an error that looks like the following, there are a couple of things you can check:

```
Warning: MySQL Connection Failed: Can't connect to local MySQL server
through socket '/tmp/mysql.sock' (111) in /var/www/html/chapter6/vpoll.php
on line 11
Couldn't connect to MySQL with admin
```

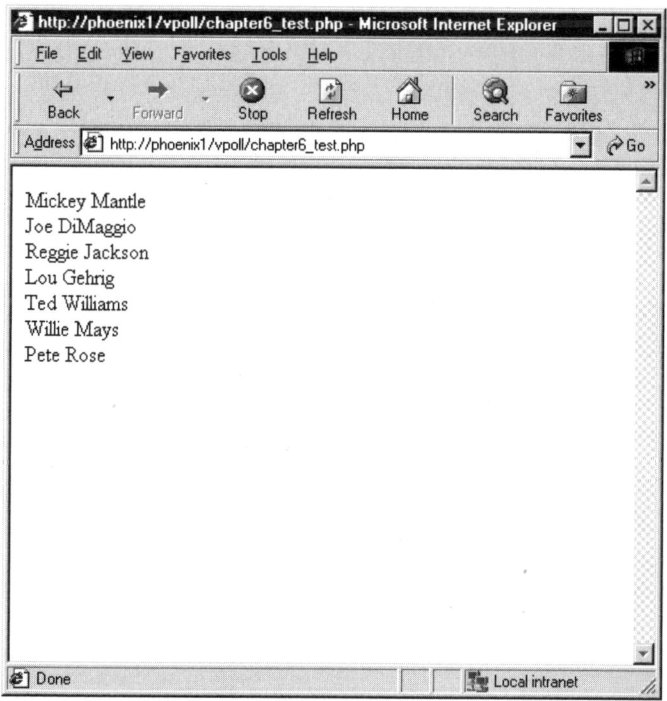

Figure 6-1 *Testing PHP and MySQL integration*

The first thing to do is check the MySQL version and settings. You can do this by using the mysqladmin command along with the version option like this:

```
[root@rambo bin]# mysqladmin version
mysqladmin  Ver 8.14 Distrib 3.23.32, for pc-linux-gnu on i686
Copyright (C) 2000 MySQL AB & MySQL Finland AB & TCX DataKonsult AB
This software comes with ABSOLUTELY NO WARRANTY. This is free software,
and you are welcome to modify and redistribute it under the GPL license

Server version          3.23.32
Protocol version        10
Connection              Localhost via UNIX socket
UNIX socket             /var/lib/mysql/mysql.sock
Uptime:                 5 days 5 hours 30 min 22 sec

Threads: 1  Questions: 47  Slow queries: 0  Opens: 16  Flush tables: 1  Open
tables: 8 Queries per second avg: 0.000
```

This command shows the version of MySQL that is installed, the connection, and how long the MySQL daemon has been running. The option you are looking for, however, is the Unix socket setting. MySQL's Unix sockets connect through a file in the file system. By default, this is configured to /tmp/mysqld.sock. The other connection option that is available is TCP/IP, which connects through a port number. Unix sockets are approximately 7.5 percent faster than TCP/IP, but can only be used when connecting to a server on the same computer.

The problem detailed in the preceding concerns MySQL communicating on one socket and using one file, and PHP using another socket and file. You have two options to correct this error. The first is to reconfigure MySQL and set the --with-unix-socket-path set to wherever you have it set within the php.ini file. The command would look like this:

```
[root@rambo mysql]# ./configure —with-unix-socket-path=/path/to/socket
```

The simpler option is to change the path that PHP uses for the default socket. This setting is located in the php.ini file under the MySQL section. Since /var/lib/mysql/mysql.sock is used by MySQL, in the following example the mysql.default_socket setting should be set to /var/lib/mysql/mysql.sock. Restart the web server and the error situation will have been corrected, as follows:

```
[MySQL]
mysql.allow_persistent                  = On
mysql.max_persistent                    = -1
mysql.max_links                         = -1
mysql.default_port                      =
mysql.default_socket                    = /tmp/mysql.sock
```

```
mysql.default_host                  =
mysql.default_user                  =
mysql.default_password              =
```

Implementation

Looking at the requirements, it is fairly obvious that one of the items that may be difficult to achieve is to be able to display a graph of the votes without using any images. To accomplish this, you will have to rely on what you have available through HTML, style sheets, and tables. We have included an example of how to accomplish this requirement.

chapter6_bar.html

```
<html>
<head>
   <title>Untitled</title>
</head>
   <style type=text/css>
      body             { margin: 10px; background-color:#FFFFFF;
 font-family: Verdana; }
      table            { background-color:#E2E2E2; }
      td.background    { background-color: #000000; border:0px; }
      td.barcolor      { background-color: #FFFF00; border:0px; }
      table.barcolor   { background-color: #FFFF00; border:0px; }
      td.text          { font-size:8pt; }
      td.question      { font-size:10pt; color:#FFFFFF;
font-weight:bold; text-align:center; background-color: #000000;}
   </style>
<body>
<table border=0 width=150 class="background"><tr><td colspan="3"></td></tr>
   <tr><td></td><td>
      <table align=center border=0 cellspacing=0 cellpadding=1
width="80%" height="10">
      <tr><td class="background">
         <table align=left border=0 cellspacing=0 cellpadding=0
width="50%" height="100%">
         <tr><td class="barcolor">
            <table class="barcolor"><tr><td></td></tr></table>
         </td></tr>
         </table>
      </td></tr>
      </table>
   </td><td></td></tr>
   <tr><td class="text" colspan="3" align="center"></td></tr>
</table>
```

```
</body>
</html>
```

Notice that you first define a style sheet that defines colors and other attributes for the table components you will be using. The style sheet is a set of instructions that suggests how to draw a page. The style sheet does not force the browser to display a page in a particular way, it merely suggests to the browser how the page should be displayed. This is an important distinction to remember.

The style sheet contains a series of instructions called *statements*, which identify elements and set attributes for those elements. The statement that identifies page elements is called a *selector*. The definition of how these statements should be displayed is called the *declaration*. The declaration can contain a variety of items, and these items are called *properties*.

Using the prceding example, here is how this works:

```
<style type=text/css>
   body             { margin: 10px; background-color:#FFFFFF;
font-family: Verdana; }
   table            { background-color:#E2E2E2; }
   td.background    { background-color: #000000; border:0px; }
   td.barcolor      { background-color: #FFFF00; border:0px; }
   table.barcolor   { background-color: #FFFF00; border:0px; }
   td.text          { font-size:8pt; }
   td.question      { font-size:10pt; color:#FFFFFF; font-weight:bold;
 text-align:center; background-color: #000000;}
</style>
```

The selectors are body, table, td.background, td.barcolor, table.barcolor, and so on. These statements will affect any of the elements on the page that use these selectors.

Take the body selector, for example. The declaration has three properties: margin, background color, and font family. In this particular page, the body tag will have the margin set to 10 pixels, the background color set to white, and the font family set to Verdana.

For reference, the colors used in this example are gray (#E2E2E2), yellow (#FFFF00), black (#000000), and white (#FFFFFF).

The second part of this example uses four nested tables to draw the bar graph. Since this is only a mock-up, we have set the bar length at 50 percent. You will notice that the attributes that we defined in our style sheet are used in these table definitions. This is done through the class statement, as in class="background" and class="barcolor".

The output from this code should look like Figure 6-2.

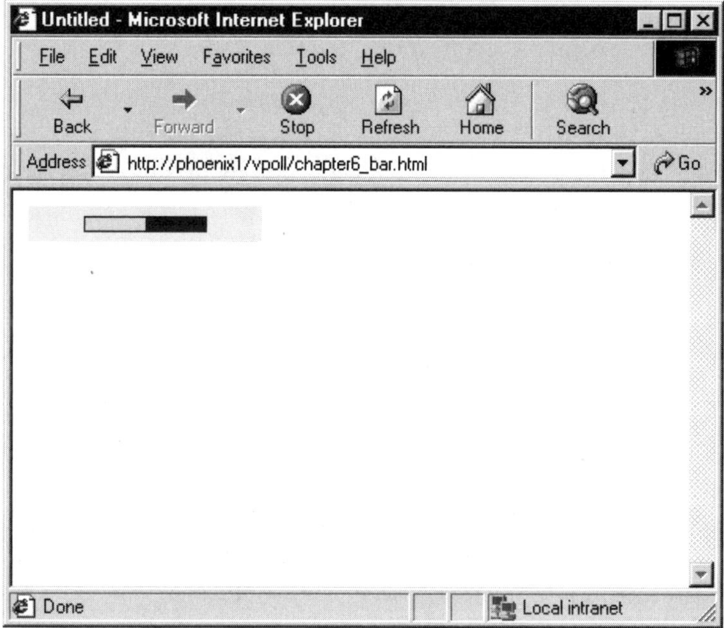

Figure 6-2 *Output of chapter6_bar.html*

Let's now take a line-by-line look at the code for the interactive visitor poll. The first section of the code is shown here:

```
// Set the poll selection for this script.
$poll=1;

// Check for Post variables and transfer them to a script variable.
if (isset($HTTP_POST_VARS[vote]) )
   $vote = $HTTP_POST_VARS[vote];
else
   $vote=NULL;
```

The first thing this script does is set a variable. This variable tells the script what polling data to use. In this case, since you only have a single set of polling data, this is set to 1. You will see later in this chapter how to add additional data and set this variable to display another set of data.

Next, you look for the existence of a POST variable. This variable would be present when the user selects a player and submits the form. This variable, called vote, would contain the name of the player the user chose and would be used to increment the total vote count. To check the existence of this variable, we use the isset() function. The usage for isset() looks like this:

```
int isset(mixed var);
```

where var is the variable you are checking for. The function returns True or 1 if the variable exists, False or 0 if it does not.

To check for this variable, you must tell PHP what kind of variable it is. To do this, you can use the HTTP_POST_VARS[] array. Whenever a form is submitted, whether it be through the POST or the GET method, an associative array is passed containing the variables that are submitted. In this case, the array is HTTP _POST _ VARS[]. If you had used the GET method, the array would be called HTTP_ GET_VARS.

Using these functions and arrays, you check for the vote variable using the HTTP_ GET_VARS array and the isset() function. If the variable is present, you assign that value to the PHP variable $vote. If the variable is not present, you assign the PHP variable $vote a NULL value. This variable is now ready to be used throughout your PHP script.

Moving on, you will now connect to your vpoll database:

```
// Connect to MySql and select the proper database
$link = mysql_pconnect( "localhost", "webuser", "abc123" );
    if ( ! $link )
        die( "Couldn't connect to MySQL" );
    mysql_select_db( "vpoll", $link )
        or die ( "Couldn't open Visitor Poll: ".mysql_error($link) );
```

To connect to your MySQL database, use the mysql_pconnect() function. This function has the following usage:

```
int mysql_pconnect(string [hostname [:port] [:/path/to/socket] ] ,
string [username] , string [password] );
```

where hostname is the hostname of the MySQL server. Note that this string can also include the hostname and port of the server, or the path to the socket if MySQL is on the local host. The second argument is the username with which you want to connect to the server. The last argument is this user's password. If the function is successful, an integer file handle is returned. If the function is not successful, False or 0 is returned.

We could have used the mysql_connect() function here and decided not to because of the performance factors. The mysql_pconnect() function opens a persistent connection to the MySQL database. This means that once the connection is established, it is continuously available. This connection establishment requires communication overhead each time it is called. The mysql_connect() function does not use persistent connections; so each time the database is accessed, there is a significant performance hit associated with the action. This overhead can be anywhere from 50 to 80 percent, depending on the format and set of instructions that are passed to the database.

If the call to open a persistent connection to the database is not successful, the script prints out an error and ends. If the script is successful, you select the MySQL database you want to use. This is done with the mysql_select_db() function. This function's usage looks like this:

```
int mysql_select_db(string database_name, int [link_identifier] );
```

where database_name is the name of the MySQL database you are using and link_identifier is the file handle that was returned by your msql_pconnect() function. The link_identifier function is optional, and if it is not present, mysql_select_db() will attempt to use the last opened file handle. However, we recommend always calling either mysql_connect() or mysql_pconnect() to ensure that the proper database is accessed. The mysql_select_db() function returns True or 1 if the function is successful, and False or 0 if it is not. In this example, if the function is not successful, you print out a message along with the results from the mysql_error() function. This function takes one argument that is the MySQL file handle and returns the text of the last error returned from the MySQL server process. This function will not display warnings.

The next thing this script does is check for the $vote variable. If it exists, it increments the count for votes in the database:

```
// If a vote has been registered update the count in the database
if ($vote) {
   $qid = mysql_db_query("vpoll","update data set votes=votes+1 where
   name='$vote' and tid='$poll'");
   if ( ! $qid )
      die ( "getPoll fatal error: ".mysql_error($link) );
}
```

To increment the counts, you first have to query the database. Use the mysql_db_query() function for this. The usage for this function is as follows:

```
int mysql_db_query(string database, string query, int [link_identifier] );
```

This function takes three arguments. The first is the database, in this case vpoll. The second is the query that is to be preformed on the database. The third is the optional link_identifier argument. If this argument is not present, the last link_identifier or file handle will be used. If the function is successful, the result identifier will be returned. If the function is not successful, False or 0 is returned.

Let's look at the query that you perform:

```
update data set votes=votes+1 where name='$vote' and tid='$poll'
```

This query updates the data table and increments the votes field depending on which player's name is passed in and which poll is selected. For instance, if you select Mickey Mantle and poll number 1, the query will look like this:

```
update data set votes=votes+1 where name='Mickey Mantle' and tid='1'
```

So, for the Mickey Mantle record, the total number of votes will be incremented by one.

Next are the <html>, <head>, <title> and <body> tags, along with your style sheet definition. They look like this:

```
<html>
 <head>
  <title>Interactive Visitor Poll</title>
  <style type=text/css>
    body               { margin: 10px; background-color:#FFFFFF;
 font-family: Verdana; }
    table           { background-color:#E2E2E2; }
    td.background   { background-color: #000000; border:0px; }
    td.barcolor   { background-color: #FFFF00; border:0px; }
    table.barcolor      { background-color: #FFFF00; border:0px; }
    td.text       { font-size:8pt; }
    td.question   { font-size:10pt; color:#FFFFFF; font-weight:bold;
 text-align:center; background-color: #000000;}
  </style>
</head>
<body>
```

We have already discussed your style sheet, and the rest of the tags are basic to any HTML page. We will not go into the tags, their definitions, and why they are used in this book. If you need information on these items, please refer to an HTML reference or other web programming guide.

The next part of your script involves selecting data from the topic and data tables to display in the interactive visitor poll. The code looks like this:

```
$qid=mysql_db_query("vpoll","select * from topic where tid=$poll");
if ( ! $qid )
   die ( "getPoll fatal error: ".mysql_error($link) );
else{
   $text=mysql_fetch_row($qid);
```

```
    mysql_free_result($qid);
}
```

Again, you use the mysql_db_query() function to select the appropriate columns from the topic table. These columns will be the poll's question and the header information. If the database query is successful, the mysql_fetch_row() function is called. This function has the following usage:

```
array mysql_fetch_row(int result_identifier);
```

This function takes the result_identifier that was returned from the mysql_ db_ query() function and returns an array of the results. In your code, the results will be returned in an array called text and will have two elements, $text[1], and $text[2]. The $text[1] element will contain the poll's question and the $text[2] element contains the header row. You will use these later in the script. The last function you use in this section is called mysql_free_result(). This function frees the memory for the specified result identifier.

Next, your script will perform two queries: the first to tally all the votes in the database for the specified poll, the second to select the valid options for the interactive visitor poll:

```
$qid=mysql_db_query("vpoll","select sum(votes) as sum from data where tid=$poll");
if ( ! $qid )
    die ( "getPoll fatal error: ".mysql_error($link) );
else{
    $sum = mysql_result($qid,0,"sum");
    mysql_free_result($qid);
}
$qid=mysql_db_query("vpoll","select * from data where tid=$poll order by votes
DESC") or die("Database Query Error");
```

The first query selects the votes field from the data table in the database and produces a sum of all the votes. This is done with the following query. We have replaced the variables with actual values:

```
select sum(votes) as sum from data where tid=1
```

This query produces a result called sum that contains the sum of all the votes submitted thus far. If the query is successful, the results are placed in a PHP variable called sum. If it is not successful, the script ends.

The second query looks like this:

```
select * from data where tid=1 order by votes DESC
```

This query returns all the columns in the data table and orders them in descending order. If the query is successful, the value of $qid will contain the results identifier. If the query is not successful, $qid will contain False or 0. Later in this script, you will loop through the values identified by $qid and place them into PHP variables.

The next portion of this script handles the logic if a vote is submitted. If the $vote variable contains any value other than NULL, you start to draw the table that will be your graph. The beginning of the code is shown here:

```
if($vote){
   print "<table border=0 width=150 class=\"background\"><tr>
   <td class=\"question\" colspan=\"3\">$text[1]<br><br></td></tr>
   <tr><td class=\"text\">$text[2]</td><td class=\"text\">Results</td>
   <td class=\"text\">%</td></tr>\n";
```

Notice that you are using your style sheet that has been previously defined. This is done by using the class= property of the <table> or <td> tag. In the preceding small script portion, you use three different styles: background, question, and text. You also print the values of $text[1] and $text[2] out in this table. Remember, these variables contain the polling question, "Who is the best baseball player of all time?" and the header, "Player Name."

The next section loops through the rows that were retrieved through the last query. Remember that you have results that are identified by the $qid variable that hold the values of the following query:

```
select * from data where tid=1 order by votes DESC
```

If you were to query the database through the mysql command line, your result set might look something like this:

```
mysql> select * from data where tid=1 order by votes DESC;
+-----+----------------+-------+
| tid | name           | votes |
+-----+----------------+-------+
|   1 | Joe DiMaggio   |    63 |
|   1 | Mickey Mantle  |    42 |
|   1 | Willie Mays    |    31 |
|   1 | Lou Gehrig     |    13 |
|   1 | Ted Williams   |    11 |
|   1 | Reggie Jackson |    10 |
|   1 | Pete Rose      |     1 |
+-----+----------------+-------+
7 rows in set (0.36 sec)
```

Knowing this information is useful when looking at the following section of code. You will have to remember that $row[1] is equal to the name of the baseball player and $row[2] is equal to the total number of votes for that player.

```
   while($row=mysql_fetch_row($qid)) {
      print "<tr><td align=center></td>";
      print "<td class=\"text\" colspan=\"2\"></td></tr><tr>
      <td class=\"text\" align=\"left\">".$row[1]."</td>
<td class=\"text\">";
      if($sum && $row[2]) {
          $per = (int)(100 * $row[2]/$sum);
          print "<table align=center border=0 cellspacing=0
 cellpadding=1 width=\"80%\" height=\"10\">\n";
          print " <tr>\n";
          print "  <td class=\"background\">\n";
          print "   <table align=left border=0 cellspacing=0
 cellpadding=0 width=\"$per%\" height=\"100%\">\n";
          print "    <tr>\n";
          print "     <td class=\"barcolor\">\n";
          print "       <table
class=\"barcolor\"><tr><td></td></tr></table>\n";
          print "     </td>\n";
          print "    </tr>\n";
          print "   </table>\n";
          print "  </td>\n";
          print " </tr>\n";
          print "</table>\n";
          print"</td><td class=\"text\">$per</td>";
      }
   print "</tr>\n";
   }
print "<tr><td class=\"text\" colspan=\"3\" align=\"center\"></td></tr>";
print "</table>\n";
}
```

In the preceding section of code, the first thing you do is enter a while loop, and you don't exit until all the elements pointed to by $qid are exhausted. You call the mysql_fetch_row() function that we discussed earlier in this chapter, and transfer those results to the $row variable. Remember, these results are in array form. Next, you display the contents of $row[1], or the player's name, and then check the presence of $sum, which is the sum of all the votes, and $row[2], or the player's individual votes. If either of these variables do not exist, you don't perform the contents of the if statement. This is because the very next statement calculates the percentage of the total votes that the player has. If either the $sum or the $row[2] variable is 0, either the result will be 0 or you will get a divide by zero error. Neither of these conditions is desirable.

If the contents of $sum and $row[2] contain values other than 0 or NULL, you will calculate the percentage of the total vote for that player. You also use the calculated percentage, contained in the $per variable, to adjust the width of the table that controls the yellow bar. The $per variable is also printed out at the end as a definition of the percentage and for reference to the user.

If the value of the $vote variable is NULL, that means the user has not submitted a vote and the options should be displayed. The following section of code does just that:

```
else{
   print "<form action=\"chapter6_vpoll.php\" method=\"POST\">";
   print "<table border=0 width=150><tr><td class=\"question\"
 colspan=\"3\">$text[1]<br><br></td></tr><tr><td class=\"text\"
 align=\"center\">Select</td><td class=\"text\">$text[2]</td>
<td class=\"text\"></td></tr>\n";
   while($row=mysql_fetch_row($qid)) {
      print "<tr><td align=center><input type=radio name=vote
 value=\"$row[1]\"></td>";
      print "<td class=\"text\" colspan=\"2\">" .$row[1]."</td></tr><tr>
             <td class=\"text\" align=\"center\"></td><td class=\"text\">";
      print "</tr>\n";
   }
   print "<tr><td class=\"text\" colspan=\"3\" align=\"center\"><input
   type=submit value=\"Submit\"></form></td></tr>";
   print "</table>\n";
}
print "</body></html>";
```

The first part of this code section creates the form that is to be submitted. The action is set to call the same page and the method is set to POST. Just like the previous section of code, the polling question and header are displayed by using the $text[1] and $text[2] variables, respectively. The players' names are displayed, again through using a while loop and the mysql_fetch_row() function. The <input> tag is used with the type set to radio and the name set to vote. The value is set to the baseball player's name. Remember that when this form is submitted, this value is passed again to the script in the form of the HTTP_POST_VARS array. You use this variable to increment the count and figure the percentage at that instant.

When you put all these sections together, the final script looks like this:

chapter6_vpoll.php

```
<?
// Set the poll selection for this script.
$poll=1;

// Check for Post variables and transfer them to a script variable.
if (isset($HTTP_POST_VARS[vote]) )
   $vote = $HTTP_POST_VARS[vote];
else
   $vote=NULL;

// Connect to MySql and select the proper database
$link = mysql_pconnect( "localhost", "webuser", "abc123" );
    if ( ! $link )
        die( "Couldn't connect to MySQL" );
    mysql_select_db( "vpoll", $link )
        or die ( "Couldn't open Visitor Poll: ".mysql_error($link) );

// If a vote has been registered update the count in the database
if ($vote) {
   $qid = mysql_db_query("vpoll","update data set votes=votes+1
where name='$vote' and tid='$poll'");
   if ( ! $qid )
      die ( "getPoll fatal error: ".mysql_error($link) );
}
?>

<html>
 <head>
  <title>Interactive Visitor Poll</title>
  <style type=text/css>
    body     { margin: 10px; background-color:#FFFFFF; font-family: Verdana; }
    table           { background-color:#E2E2E2; }
    td.background   { background-color: #000000; border:0px; }
    td.barcolor { background-color: #FFFF00; border:0px; }
    table.barcolor { background-color: #FFFF00; border:0px; }
    td.text     { font-size:8pt; }
    td.question { font-size:10pt; color:#FFFFFF; font-weight:bold;
text-align:center; background-color: #000000;}
  </style>
</head>
<body>

<?
```

```
$qid=mysql_db_query("vpoll","select * from topic where tid=$poll");
if ( ! $qid )
   die ( "getPoll fatal error: ".mysql_error($link) );
else{
   $text=mysql_fetch_row($qid);
   mysql_free_result($qid);
}
$qid=mysql_db_query("vpoll","select sum(votes) as sum from data where tid=$poll");
if ( ! $qid )
   die ( "getPoll fatal error: ".mysql_error($link) );
else{
   $sum = mysql_result($qid,0,"sum");
   mysql_free_result($qid);
}
$qid=mysql_db_query("vpoll","select * from data where tid=$poll
order by votes DESC") or die("Database Query Error");
   while($row=mysql_fetch_row($qid)) {
      print "<tr><td align=center></td>";
      print "<td class=\"text\" colspan=\"2\"></td></tr><tr>
      <td class=\"text\" align=\"left\">".$row[1]."</td><td class=\"text\">";
      if($sum && $row[2]) {
          $per = (int)(100 * $row[2]/$sum);
          print "<table align=center border=0 cellspacing=0
cellpadding=1 width=\"80%\" height=\"10\">\n";
          print " <tr>\n";
          print "  <td class=\"background\">\n";
          print "   <table align=left border=0 cellspacing=0
cellpadding=0 width=\"$per%\" height=\"100%\">\n";
         print "    <tr>\n";
         print "     <td class=\"barcolor\">\n";
         print "        <table class=\"barcolor\"><tr><td></td></tr></table>\n";
         print "     </td>\n";
         print "    </tr>\n";
         print "   </table>\n";
         print "  </td>\n";
         print " </tr>\n";
         print "</table>\n";
         print"</td><td class=\"text\">$per</td>";
      }
   print "</tr>\n";
   }
print "<tr><td class=\"text\" colspan=\"3\" align=\"center\"></td></tr>";
print "</table>\n";
}
else{
   print "<form action=\"chapter6_vpoll.php\" method=\"POST\">";
   print "<table border=0 width=150><tr><td class=\"question\"
```

```
 colspan=\"3\">$text[1]<br><br></td></tr><tr><td class=\"text\"
align=\"center\">Select</td><td class=\"text\">$text[2]</td>
<td class=\"text\"></td></tr>\n";
   while($row=mysql_fetch_row($qid)) {
      print "<tr><td align=center><input type=radio name=vote
 value=\"$row[1]\"></td>";
      print "<td class=\"text\" colspan=\"2\">" .$row[1]."</td></tr><tr>
             <td class=\"text\" align=\"center\"></td><td class=\"text\">";
      print "</tr>\n";
   }
   print "<tr><td class=\"text\" colspan=\"3\" align=\"center\">
<input type=submit value=\"Submit\"></form></td></tr>";
   print "</table>\n";
}
print "</body></html>";
?>
```

The initial screen from this script should look like Figure 6-3.

Once the user chooses a baseball player and clicks the Submit button, the final output should look like Figure 6-4.

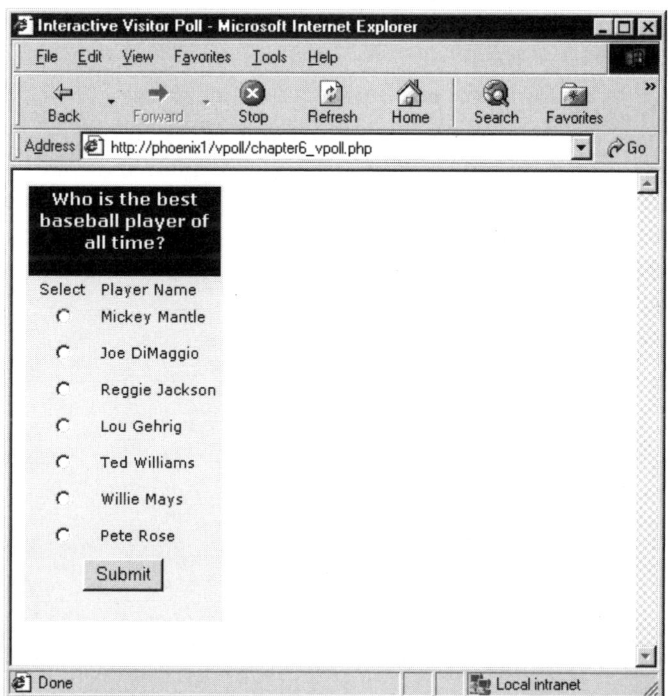

Figure 6-3 *Initial interactive visitor poll output*

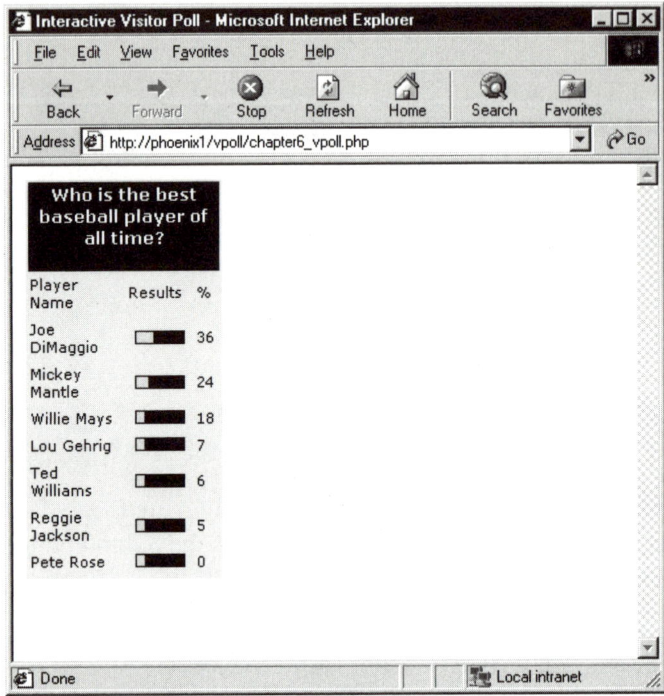

Figure 6-4 *Final interactive visitor poll output*

We mentioned that it is possible to use multiple sets of polling data in this script. Let's create another question for your poll, along with another set of possible answers, just to show how easy it is. First, you will use a mock-up as you did at the beginning of this chapter. This mock-up should look like this.

```
What is your favorite operating system?
     OS Name
     Linux
     Windows 2000
     Windows NT
     MacOS
     Solaris
```

You will now have to form some additional INSERT queries in the following format. By now you should be familiar with this process. The queries will look like this:

```
INSERT INTO data VALUES (2,'Linux', '0');
INSERT INTO data VALUES (2,'Windows 2000', '0');
```

```
INSERT INTO data VALUES (2,'Windows NT', '0');
INSERT INTO data VALUES (2,'MacOS', '0');
INSERT INTO data VALUES (2,'Solaris', '0');
```

When these queries are placed into the MySQL command line, the output will be similar to the following:

```
mysql> INSERT INTO data VALUES (2,'Linux', '0');
Query OK, 1 row affected (0.00 sec)
mysql> INSERT INTO data VALUES (2,'Windows 2000', '0');
Query OK, 1 row affected (0.00 sec)
mysql> INSERT INTO data VALUES (2,'Windows NT', '0');
Query OK, 1 row affected (0.00 sec)
mysql> INSERT INTO data VALUES (2,'MacOS', '0');
Query OK, 1 row affected (0.00 sec)
mysql> INSERT INTO data VALUES (2,'Solaris', '0');
Query OK, 1 row affected (0.00 sec)
```

Next, you will do the same with the values in the topic table. This query should look like this:

```
INSERT INTO topic VALUES (2,'What is your favorite operating system?','OS Name');
```

The output of this query should be similar to the following:

```
mysql> INSERT INTO topic VALUES (2,'What is your favorite operating system?','OS Name');
Query OK, 1 row affected (0.00 sec)
```

You can now check the contents of both the data and the topic tables by performing the following SELECT queries:

```
mysql> select * from data;
+-----+----------------+-------+
| tid | name           | votes |
+-----+----------------+-------+
|   1 | Mickey Mantle  |    42 |
|   1 | Reggie Jackson |    10 |
|   1 | Joe DiMaggio   |    63 |
|   1 | Lou Gehrig     |    13 |
|   1 | Pete Rose      |     1 |
|   1 | Ted Williams   |    11 |
|   1 | Willie Mays    |    31 |
|   2 | MacOS          |     0 |
|   2 | Windows 2000   |     0 |
|   2 | Solaris        |     0 |
|   2 | Windows NT     |     0 |
```

```
|   2 | Linux          |      0 |
+-----+----------------+-------+
12 rows in set (0.00 sec)
mysql> select * from topic;
+-----+-----------------------------------------------+-----------------+
| tid | question                                      | header          |
+-----+-----------------------------------------------+-----------------+
|   1 | Who is the best baseball player of all time? | Player Name     |
|   2 | What is your favorite operating system?      | OS Name         |
+-----+-----------------------------------------------+-----------------+
2 rows in set (0.00 sec)
```

Now, with this new data in the database, changing the poll is as simple as changing the following line of the script to look like this:

```
$poll=2;
```

You can now see that the initial screen for the new interactive visitor poll will look like Figure 6-5.

If the user chooses Linux, the visitor poll output will look like Figure 6-6.

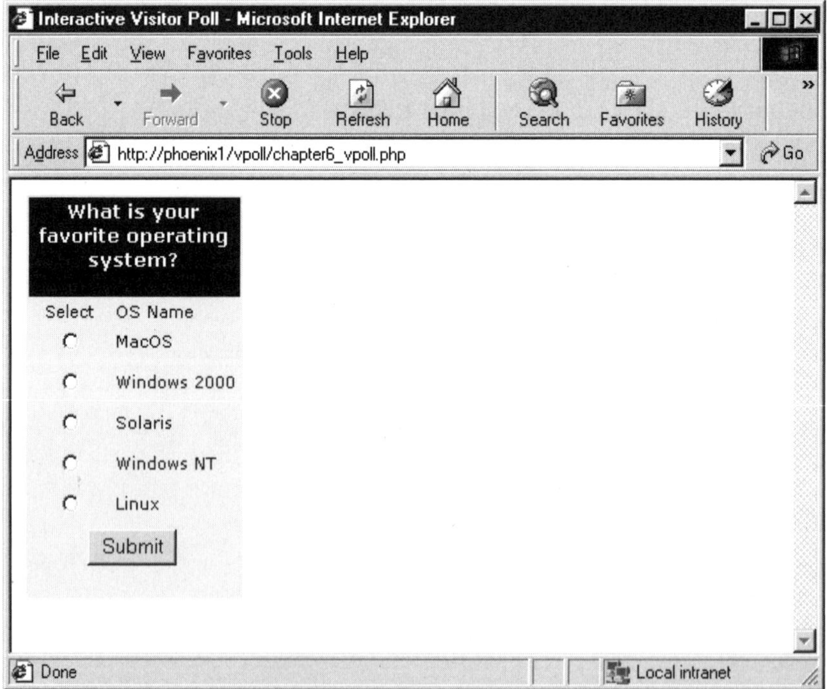

Figure 6-5 *New interactive visitor poll output*

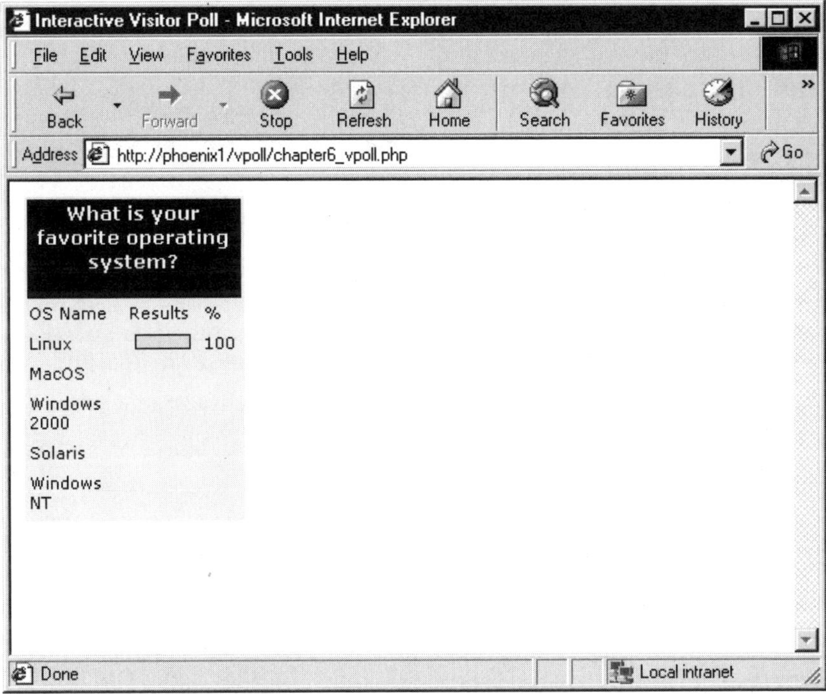

Figure 6-6 *After the user chooses Linux in the new poll*

This proves to be a very easy change from one script to another. In the next section, we will discuss limitations of this script and some improvements that can be made.

Next Steps

The visitor poll script described in this chapter will serve you well, but there are some upgrades you might want to consider as your site grows. These upgrades will increase the functionality of this script and provide a good programming exercise for you.

Don't Let Users Vote More Than Once

One of the limitations of this script is that a user can vote once, click the Back button, and vote again. The user can do this over and over again, thus somewhat invalidating the results.

To correct this, you can set a cookie when the user submits a vote. You will want to associate this cookie with a single poll. When you create another poll, the cookied user will be allowed to submit a vote for this second poll.

Dynamically Change the Poll

Another nice feature to add to this script would be the ability to dynamically change the poll. This could be based on date, user, IP address, operating system, and so forth. The logic could be that at midnight, the $poll variable is given another value, thus changing the poll for the new day. This functionality could be expanded so that if a user has already voted on a particular poll, another poll is displayed.

The $poll variable can be passed from one page to another so that when a user hits your financial page, one poll is displayed, for instance; and when the user goes to the sports page, a different poll is displayed.

Dynamically Change Colors

Since some of your pages could have different color schemes, or the color scheme that we have designed might not look good on your web site, this script might not fit with your site. One of the enhancements you could consider is the ability to expand the database schema to include colors. When the script queries the database to pull in data for the poll, the query could pull in colors as well.

Administration Interface

If this script is to be used extensively, you may want to consider an administration interface. This interface will be used to insert new poll data through a web page, rather than through handwritten SQL queries and the MySQL command line. This would make administration of the poll easier, and eliminate the need for access to the MySQL interface to change the polling data. With this interface, you could allow nontechnical personnel to add polling information to the database with very limited knowledge of databases or web pages.

Build a Profile

Through these polls, you are collecting valuable information about your users. If you are cookieing your users and tracking them through a unique ID, you can begin to build a database of the users' likes and dislikes. For instance, you could have polls that ask the users about their favorite team, ice cream, car, operating system, city, shoe manufacturer, and so forth. This information would be valuable for advertising purposes. Your web site could then sell ad space based on users' likes and dislikes. You could approach advertisers claiming, for instance, that 50 percent of your polled user base likes Reebok shoes or have three children under the age of ten.

What to Take Away

In this chapter, you should have learned how to design a simple MySQL database. You should know how to integrate MySQL into your web page to build dynamic content. You have been given methods to access the data and loop through the result set. You are able to select, insert, and update data in the MySQL database. We also used simple mathematical expressions and functions.

Another skill you should have learned in this chapter is how to set up and test a MySQL database. We spent quite some time explaining how to perform queries and test connectivity, and we even discussed some debugging techniques if the tests are not successful. Hopefully,- this chapter has built a sufficient foundation that you can build upon as you expand your skills.

CHAPTER 7

PHP Online Address Book

IN THIS CHAPTER:

myoabsql.txt—Contains all the needed SQL commands to create your database

chapter7_dbconnect.php—Connects you to the database

chapter7_dbdisconnect.php—Disconnects you from the database

chapter7_oab.php—The main file that controls the program logic and flow of your address book

chapter7_oabAdd.php—Contains all of the code needed to add a contact into your address book

chapter7_oabDelete.php—Contains all of the code needed to delete a contact from your address book

chapter7_oabEdit.php—Contains all of the code necessary to edit a contact's information

chapter7_oabList.php—Allows you to list contacts based on the first letter of their last name

chapter7_oabSearch.php—Allows you to search for contacts by first or last name

chapter7_oabView.php—The code needed to view a contact's home and work information

In this chapter, you'll build a simple online address book using readily available functions in PHP. The information for each contact will be stored in a small table inside a MySQL database. The layout and presentation of this information will replicate the look and feel of a traditional (hard copy) address book. The finished example will look similar to Figure 7-1.

Online Address Book Requirements

Your address book will have the capability to store information about contacts, such as first and last name, middle initial, mailing address, phone, e-mail, and web site, for both at home and at work. You will also want to have the ability to add, edit, delete, and search this information in an easy fashion. Hence, you'll need access to a web server with PHP and MySQL installed, and the ability to log in and create a database and table.

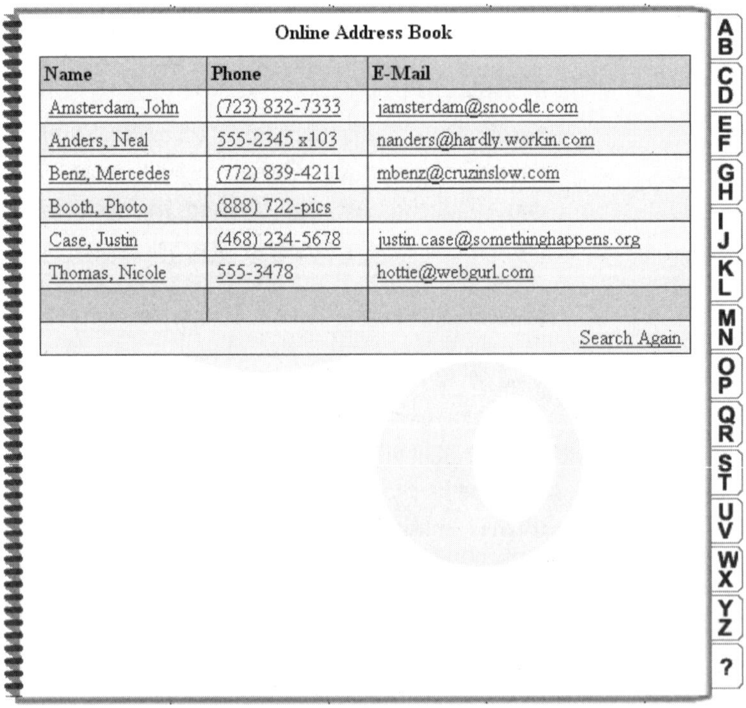

Online Address Book

Name	Phone	E-Mail
Amsterdam, John	(723) 832-7333	jamsterdam@snoodle.com
Anders, Neal	555-2345 x103	nanders@hardly.workin.com
Benz, Mercedes	(772) 839-4211	mbenz@cruzinslow.com
Booth, Photo	(888) 722-pics	
Case, Justin	(468) 234-5678	justin.case@somethinghappens.org
Thomas, Nicole	555-3478	hottie@webgurl.com
		Search Again.

AB CD EF GH IJ KL MN OP QR ST UV WX YZ ?

Figure 7-1 *PHP online address book*

Designing and Implementing the Address Book

You'll start by creating a database and table to store the information in your address book. All of the components of the address book will be modular in the sense that the code for connecting to the database, adding, editing, deleting, viewing, and searching on your contact information will be contained in separate PHP files. All of the files will be called upon in a master PHP file that controls which modules are processed.

Let's begin by creating a database and table for your information. These commands can also be found in the myoabsql.txt file. While there are many tools available to do this, the direct command-line approach is taken here:

myoabsql.txt file

```
[root@twoheadedcow oab]# mysql
mysql> create database oab;
Query OK, 0 rows affected (0.00 sec)

mysql>use oab
Database changed

mysql> create table oabContact (contactID int primary key auto_increment,
lastName varchar(30), firstName varchar(20), midName varchar(3), primaryInfo
varchar(1), homeAddr1 varchar(50), homeAddr2 varchar(50), homeCity
varchar(30), homeState varchar(3), homeZip varchar(12), homePhone
varchar(20), homeCellular varchar(20), homePager varchar(20), homeEmail
varchar(50), homeWeb varchar(50), workAddr1 varchar(50), workAddr2
varchar(50), workCity varchar (30), workState varchar(3), workZip
varchar(12), workPhone varchar(20), workCellular varchar(20), workPager
varchar(20), workEmail varchar(50), workWeb varchar(50));
Query OK, 0 rows affected (0.00 sec)
mysql>
```

You've connected to MYSQL, created a database called oab, selected that database for use, and then created a table called oabContact in which to store the needed information. For reference, here are the fields in your oabContact table:

```
Mysql> desc oabContact;
+--------------+-------------+------+-----+---------+----------------+
| Field        | Type        | Null | Key | Default | Extra          |
+--------------+-------------+------+-----+---------+----------------+
| contactID    | int(11)     |      | PRI | NULL    | auto_increment |
| lastName     | varchar(30) | YES  |     | NULL    |                |
| firstName    | varchar(20) | YES  |     | NULL    |                |
```

```
| midName       | char(3)     | YES  |     | NULL    |                |
| primaryInfo   | char(1)     | YES  |     | NULL    |                |
| homeAddr1     | varchar(50) | YES  |     | NULL    |                |
| homeAddr2     | varchar(50) | YES  |     | NULL    |                |
| homeCity      | varchar(30) | YES  |     | NULL    |                |
| homeState     | char(3)     | YES  |     | NULL    |                |
| homeZip       | varchar(12) | YES  |     | NULL    |                |
| homePhone     | varchar(20) | YES  |     | NULL    |                |
| homeCellular  | varchar(20) | YES  |     | NULL    |                |
| homePager     | varchar(20) | YES  |     | NULL    |                |
| homeEmail     | varchar(50) | YES  |     | NULL    |                |
| homeWeb       | varchar(50) | YES  |     | NULL    |                |
| workAddr1     | varchar(50) | YES  |     | NULL    |                |
| workAddr2     | varchar(50) | YES  |     | NULL    |                |
| workCity      | varchar(30) | YES  |     | NULL    |                |
| workState     | char(3)     | YES  |     | NULL    |                |
| workZip       | varchar(12) | YES  |     | NULL    |                |
| workPhone     | varchar(20) | YES  |     | NULL    |                |
| workCellular  | varchar(20) | YES  |     | NULL    |                |
| workPager     | varchar(20) | YES  |     | NULL    |                |
| workEmail     | varchar(50) | YES  |     | NULL    |                |
| workWeb       | varchar(50) | YES  |     | NULL    |                |
+---------------+-------------+------+-----+---------+----------------+
```

As you can see, there are provisions for the contact's name, home, and work information. Note also the inclusion of the primaryInfo field. This will be explained later in the chapter and plays an important role in which information is displayed when contact information is listed.

Now that you have a place to keep all of the contact information, let's begin actually coding in PHP. In keeping with modular design, you'll need a file that connects you to the oab database and selects which table you wish to interact with. Following is the code listing that performs this operation. The file can be saved as chapter7_dbconnect.php:

chapter7_dbconnect.php

```
<?
// chapter7_dbconnect.php
   $mysql_link = mysql_connect("localhost", "root", "") or die ("<p>Could not
   connect to the database!");
   mysql_select_db("oab", $mysql_link) or die ("<p>Could not select the
   database!");
?>
```

As you can see, you are using the MySQL functions already available in PHP to connect to your database. In using the mysql_connect() function, you specify the host, user name, and password for your database, and also check to see whether the connection goes through. If it does not, you display an error message. You also use the mysql_ select_db() function to select the table inside your database that you wish to use, and make provisions in case there is an error. To quickly summarize, in the preceding code, you connected to the database and selected the table you'll be using.

While you are at it, make a PHP file called chapter7_dbdisconnect.php. This will store the code that closes the connection to your database when you are through performing operations. Here is the listing:

chapter7_dbdisconnect.php

```
<?
// chapter7_dbdisconnect.php
   mysql_close($mysql_link);
?>
```

Could it get any easier than that? You call the mysql_close() function and free up the connection to the database now that it is no longer needed.

Now that you have a way to connect and disconnect from your database, let's move on and work on adding contact information into the database. Following is the listing for chapter7_oabAdd.php. This will contain the code needed to add a contact into the oabContact table.

To start things off, let's look at this code in two parts. The first section of code contains everything you need to insert the contact information into the database. However, this code is not executed until after you have gathered such information, which is where the second section of code comes into play. The second section contains the needed code to generate an HTML form, which will allow a user to enter the actual information.

chapter7_oabAdd.php

```
<?
// chapter7_oabAdd.php
if($submit)
{
   if((!$firstName) or (!$lastName))
   {
      print ("<p>Whoops! You forgot to enter the first <i>and</i> last name
      for the contact.");
   }
```

```
else
{
    include("./chapter7_dbconnect.php");
    $query = "insert into oabContact (lastName, firstName, midName,
    primaryInfo, ";
    $query .= "homeAddr1, homeAddr2, homeCity, homeState, homeZip,
    homePhone, homeCellular, homePager, homeEmail, homeWeb, ";
    $query .= "workAddr1, workAddr2, workCity, workState, workZip,
    workPhone, workCellular, workPager, workEmail, workWeb) ";
    $query .= "values ('$lastName', '$firstName', '$midName',
    '$primaryInfo', ";
    $query .= "'$homeAddr1', '$homeAddr2', '$homeCity', '$homeState',
    '$homeZip', '$homePhone', '$homeCellular', '$homePager', '$homeEmail',
    '$homeWeb', ";
    $query .= "'$workAddr1', '$workAddr2', '$workCity', '$workState',
    '$workZip', '$workPhone', '$workCellular', '$workPager', '$workEmail',
    '$workWeb')";
    $mysql_result = mysql_query($query, $mysql_link);
    include("./chapter7_dbdisconnect.php");
```

Wow! So much is happening already, but do not fret! What you've done thus far is check to see whether the user actually passed in a first and last name. If they did not, you really don't have a way to keep track of this contact. Note also how you used the PHP include() function to include the code needed to connect and disconnect from your database. Much easier than typing in those extra lines of code each time! You also go about developing a SQL query that will insert into the oabContact table the information that will be passed in. Since this SQL query is so long, we will break it up into separate lines. You use the mysql_query() function to execute your query, and you'll store the results of that query in $mysql_result.

Let's continue on and display what the user passed in for your contact information. This is the continuation for the code:

```
    print ("<table width=\"525\" cellspacing=\"1\" cellpadding=\"3\"
    border=\"0\" bgcolor=\"#123456\">\n");
    print ("<tr>\n");
    print ("<td colspan=\"2\" bgcolor=\"#DFFFDF\"><b>The following Contact
    has been added into your Address Book..</b></td>\n");
    print ("</tr>\n");
    print ("<tr>\n");
    print ("<td colspan=\"2\" bgcolor=\"#ffffff\">\n");
    print ("<table width=\"100%\" cellspacing=\"0\" cellpadding=\"0\"
    border=\"0\">\n");
    print ("<tr>\n");
    print ("<td> <u>First Name</u></td>\n");
    print ("<td><u>M.I.</u></td>\n");
    print ("<td><u>Last Name</u></td>\n");
```

```
print ("</tr>\n");
print ("<tr>\n");
printf ("<td> <i>%s</i></td>\n", $firstName);
printf ("<td><i>%s</i></td>\n", $midName);
printf ("<td><i>%s</i></td>\n", $lastName);
print ("</tr>\n");
print ("</table>\n");
print ("</td>\n");
print ("</tr>\n");
print ("<tr>\n");
print ("<td bgcolor=\"#EEFFEE\" width=\"50%\" colspan=\"2\">\n");
print ("<b>Home</b>");
  if($primaryInfo == 1){ print ("<i>(Primary)</i>"); }
  print ("</td>\n");
print ("</tr>\n");
print ("<tr>\n");
print ("<td colspan=\"2\"
bgcolor=\"#ffffff\"> <u>Address</u><br>");
printf (" <i>%s</i><br>\n", $homeAddr1);
printf (" <i>%s</i><br>\n", $homeAddr2);
print ("<table width=\"75%\" cellspacing=\"0\" cellpadding=\"0\"
border=\"0\">\n");
print ("<tr>\n");
print ("<td> <u>City</u></td>\n");
print ("<td> <u>State</u></td>\n");
print ("<td> <u>Zip-Code</u></td>\n");
print ("</tr>\n");
print ("<tr>\n");
printf ("<td> <i>%s</i></td>\n", $homeCity);
printf ("<td> <i>%s</i></td>\n", $homeState);
printf ("<td> <i>%s</i></td>\n", $homeZip);
print ("</tr>\n");
print ("</table>\n");
print ("<table width=\"75%\" cellspacing=\"0\" cellpadding=\"0\"
border=\"0\">\n");
print ("<tr>\n");
print ("<td> <u>Phone</u></td>\n");
print ("<td> <u>Cellular</u></td>\n");
print ("<td> <u>Pager</u></td>\n");
print ("</tr>\n");
print ("<tr>\n");
printf ("<td> <i>%s</i></td>\n", $homePhone);
printf ("<td> <i>%s</i></td>\n", $homeCellular);
printf ("<td> <i>%s</i></td>\n", $homePager);
print ("</tr>\n");
print ("</table>\n");
printf (" <u>E-Mail Address</u><br> <i>%s</i><br>",
$homeEmail);
```

```
printf (" <u>Web Site URL</u><br> <i>%s</i>", $homeWeb);
print ("</td>\n");
print ("</tr>\n");
print ("<tr>\n");
print ("<td bgcolor=\"#EEFFEE\" width=\"50%\" colspan=\"2\">\n");
print ("<b>Work</b>");
if($primaryInfo == 2){ print ("<i>(Primary)</i>"); }
print ("</td>\n");
print ("</tr>\n");
print ("<tr>\n");
print ("<td colspan=\"2\"
bgcolor=\"#ffffff\"> <u>Address</u><br>");
printf (" <i>%s</i><br>\n", $workAddr1);
printf (" <i>%s</i><br>\n", $workAddr2);
print ("<table width=\"75%\" cellspacing=\"0\" cellpadding=\"0\"
border=\"0\">\n");
print ("<tr>\n");
print ("<td> <u>City</u></td>\n");
print ("<td> <u>State</u></td>\n");
print ("<td> <u>Zip-Code</u></td>\n");
print ("</tr>\n");
print ("<tr>\n");
printf ("<td> <i>%s</i></td>\n", $workCity);
printf ("<td> <i>%s</i></td>\n", $workState);
printf ("<td> <i>%s</i></td>\n", $workZip);
print ("</tr>\n");
print ("</table>\n");
print ("<table width=\"75%\" cellspacing=\"0\" cellpadding=\"0\"
border=\"0\">\n");
print ("<tr>\n");
print ("<td> <u>Phone</u></td>\n");
print ("<td> <u>Cellular</u></td>\n");
print ("<td> <u>Pager</u></td>\n");
print ("</tr>\n");
print ("<tr>\n");
printf ("<td> <i>%s</i></td>\n", $workPhone);
printf ("<td> <i>%s</i></td>\n", $workCellular);
printf ("<td> <i>%s</i></td>\n", $workPager);
print ("</tr>\n");
print ("</table>\n");
printf (" <u>E-Mail Address</u><br> %s<br>", $workEmail);
printf (" <u>Web Site URL</u><br> %s", $workWeb);
print ("</td>\n");
print ("</tr>\n");
print ("<tr>\n");
print ("<td colspan=\"2\" align=\"right\" bgcolor=\"#DFFFDF\">\n");
print ("<a href=\"./chapter7_oab.php?tab=add\">Add another
```

```
Contact</a>.");
        print ("</td>\n");
        print ("</tr>\n");
        print ("</table>\n");
    }
}
```

There are several HTML tables that went into that part of the code, however, the end result displays the information quite nicely. Continuing on with the code, you'll need an HTML form with text fields so the user can enter the information about the contact. Once they have finished entering the information and click Submit, the data will be passed back to the preceding code and inserted into the database. The code for the form is as follows:

```
Else
{
    print ("<form action=\"./chapter7_oab.php\" method=\"get\">\n");
    print ("<table width=\"525\" cellspacing=\"1\" cellpadding=\"3\"
    border=\"0\" bgcolor=\"#123456\">\n");
    print ("<tr>\n");
    print ("<td colspan=\"2\" bgcolor=\"#DFFFDF\"><b>Contact Information</b>
    <font color=\"red\">(Required fields are in red.)</font></td>\n");
    print ("</tr>\n");
    print ("<tr>\n");
    print ("<td colspan=\"2\" bgcolor=\"#ffffff\">\n");
    print ("<table width=\"100%\" cellspacing=\"0\" cellpadding=\"0\"
    border=\"0\">\n");
    print ("<tr>\n");
    print ("<td> <font color=\"red\">First Name</font></td>\n");
    print ("<td>M.I.</td>\n");
    print ("<td><font color=\"red\">Last Name</font></td>\n");
    print ("</tr>\n");
    print ("<tr>\n");
    print ("<td> <input type=\"text\" name=\"firstName\" size=\"20\"
    maxsize=\"20\"></td>\n");
    print ("<td><input type=\"text\" name=\"midName\" size=\"3\"
    maxsize=\"3\"></td>\n");
    print ("<td><input type=\"text\" name=\"lastName\" size=\"30\"
    maxsize=\"30\"></td>\n");
    print ("</tr>\n");
    print ("</table>\n");
    print ("</td>\n");
    print ("</tr>\n");
    print ("<tr>\n");
    print ("<td bgcolor=\"#EEFFEE\" width=\"50%\" colspan=\"2\">\n");
    print ("<input type=\"radio\" name=\"primaryInfo\" value=\"1\" checked>");
    print ("<b>Home</b></td>\n");
```

```
print ("</tr>\n");
print ("<tr>\n");
print ("<td colspan=\"2\" bgcolor=\"#ffffff\"> Address<br>");
print (" <input type=\"text\" name=\"homeAddr1\" size=\"50\"
maxsize=\"50\"><br>");
print (" <input type=\"text\" name=\"homeAddr2\" size=\"50\"
maxsize=\"50\"><br>");
print ("<table width=\"75%\" cellspacing=\"0\" cellpadding=\"0\"
border=\"0\">\n");
print ("<tr>\n");
print ("<td> City</td>\n");
print ("<td> State</td>\n");
print ("<td> Zip-Code</td>\n");
print ("</tr>\n");
print ("<tr>\n");
print ("<td> <input type=\"text\" name=\"homeCity\" size=\"30\"
maxsize=\"30\"></td>\n");
print ("<td> <input type=\"text\" name=\"homeState\" size=\"3\"
maxsize=\"3\"></td>\n");
print ("<td> <input type=\"text\" name=\"homeZip\" size=\"12\"
maxsize\"12\"></td>\n");
print ("</tr>\n");
print ("</table>\n");
print ("<table width=\"75%\" cellspacing=\"0\" cellpadding=\"0\"
border=\"0\">\n");
print ("<tr>\n");
print ("<td> Phone</td>\n");
print ("<td> Cellular</td>\n");
print ("<td> Pager</td>\n");
print ("</tr>\n");
print ("<tr>\n");
print ("<td> <input type=\"text\" name=\"homePhone\" size=\"20\"
maxsize=\"20\"></td>\n");
print ("<td> <input type=\"text\" name=\"homeCellular\" size=\"20\"
maxsize=\"20\"></td>\n");
print ("<td> <input type=\"text\" name=\"homePager\" size=\"20\"
maxsize\"20\"></td>\n");
print ("</tr>\n");
print ("</table>\n");
print (" E-Mail Address<br> <input type=\"text\"
name=\"homeEmail\" size=\"50\" maxsize=\"50\"><br>");
print (" Web Site URL<br> <input type=\"text\" name=\"homeWeb\"
size=\"50\" maxsize=\"50\">");
print ("</td>\n");
print ("</tr>\n");
print ("<tr>\n");
print ("<td bgcolor=\"#EEFFEE\" width=\"50%\" colspan=\"2\">\n");
print ("<input type=\"radio\" name=\"primaryInfo\" value=\"2\">");
```

```
print ("<b>Work</b></td>\n");
print ("</td>\n");
print ("</tr>\n");
print ("<tr>\n");
print ("<td colspan=\"2\" bgcolor=\"#ffffff\"> Address<br>");
print (" <input type=\"text\" name=\"workAddr1\" size=\"50\"
maxsize=\"50\"><br>");
print (" <input type=\"text\" name=\"workAddr2\" size=\"50\"
maxsize=\"50\"><br>");
print ("<table width=\"75%\" cellspacing=\"0\" cellpadding=\"0\"
border=\"0\">\n");
print ("<tr>\n");
print ("<td> City</td>\n");
print ("<td> State</td>\n");
print ("<td> Zip-Code</td>\n");
print ("</tr>\n");
print ("<tr>\n");
print ("<td> <input type=\"text\" name=\"workCity\" size=\"30\"
maxsize=\"30\"></td>\n");
print ("<td> <input type=\"text\" name=\"workState\" size=\"3\"
maxsize=\"3\"></td>\n");
print ("<td> <input type=\"text\" name=\"workZip\" size=\"12\"
maxsize\"12\"></td>\n");
print ("</tr>\n");
print ("</table>\n");
print ("<table width=\"75%\" cellspacing=\"0\" cellpadding=\"0\"
border=\"0\">\n");
print ("<tr>\n");
print ("<td> Phone</td>\n");
print ("<td> Cellular</td>\n");
print ("<td> Pager</td>\n");
print ("</tr>\n");
print ("<tr>\n");
print ("<td> <input type=\"text\" name=\"workPhone\" size=\"20\"
maxsize=\"20\"></td>\n");
print ("<td> <input type=\"text\" name=\"workCellular\" size=\"20\"
maxsize=\"20\"></td>\n");
print ("<td> <input type=\"text\" name=\"workPager\" size=\"20\"
maxsize\"20\"></td>\n");
print ("</tr>\n");
print ("</table>\n");
print (" E-Mail Address<br> <input type=\"text\"
name=\"workEmail\" size=\"50\" maxsize=\"50\"><br>");
print (" Web Site URL<br> <input type=\"text\" name=\"workWeb\"
size=\"50\" maxsize=\"50\">");
print ("</td>\n");
print ("</tr>\n");
print ("<tr>\n");
```

```
    print ("<td colspan=\"2\" align=\"right\" bgcolor=\"#DFFFDF\">\n");
    print ("<input type=\"hidden\" name=\"tab\" value=\"Add\">");
    print ("<input type=\"submit\" name=\"submit\" value=\"Add
    Contact\"> ");
    print ("</td>\n");
    print ("</tr>\n");
    print ("</table>\n");
    print ("</form>\n");
}
?>
```

This finishes up your code for adding a contact. While it may seem a bit confusing with all the HTML tables, rows, and cells, the end result is very visually appealing. You'll want to maintain this style throughout your address book. The end result should look similar to Figures 7-2 and 7-3.

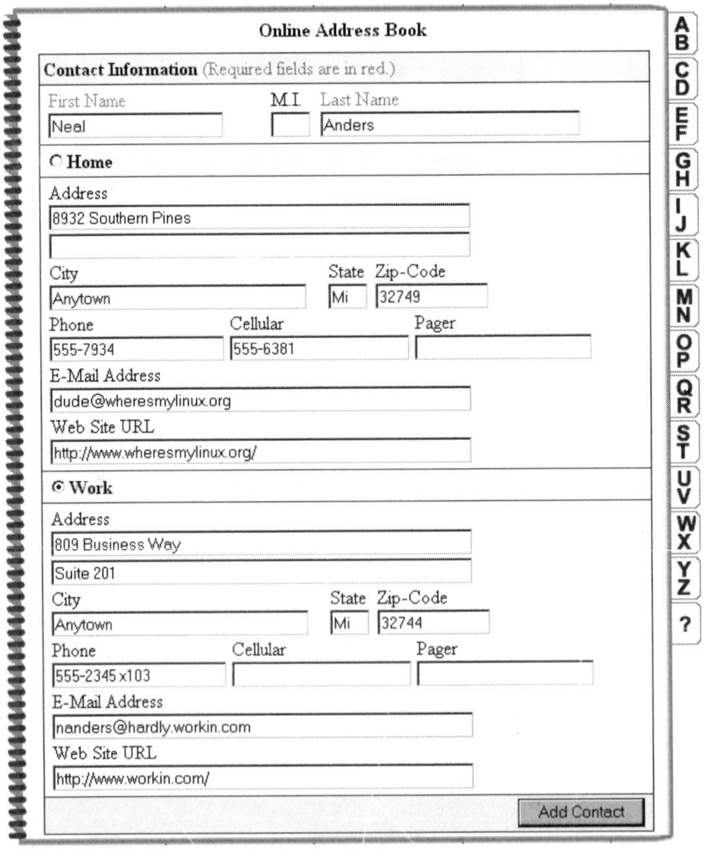

Figure 7-2 *PHP online address book: adding a contact*

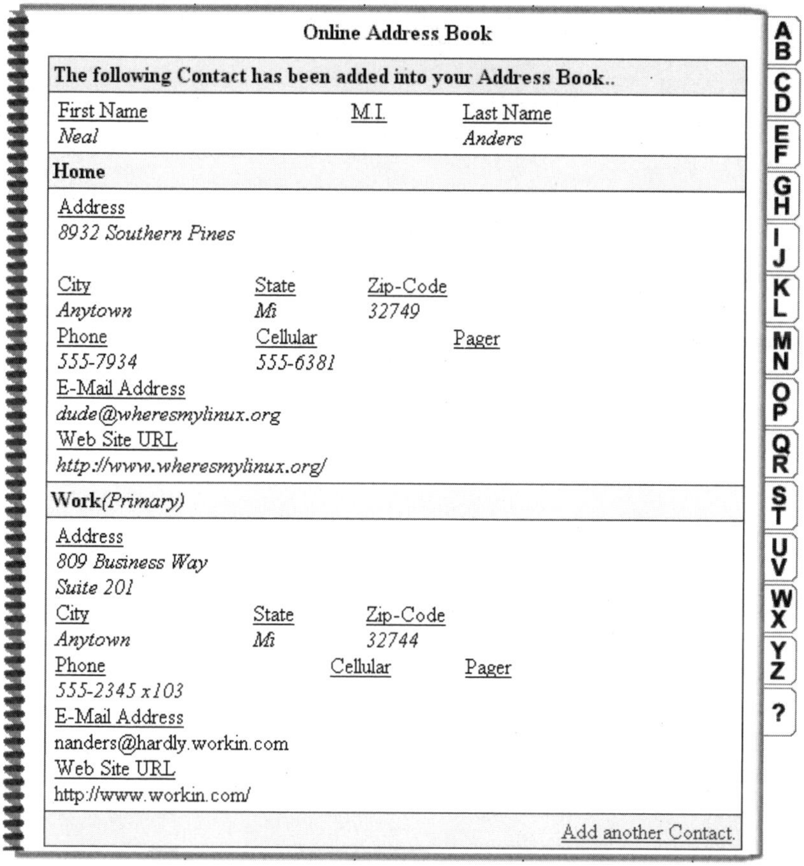

Online Address Book

The following Contact has been added into your Address Book..

First Name M.I. Last Name
Neal Anders

Home

Address
8932 Southern Pines

City State Zip-Code
Anytown Mi 32749
Phone Cellular Pager
555-7934 555-6381
E-Mail Address
dude@wheresmylinux.org
Web Site URL
http://www.wheresmylinux.org/

Work(Primary)

Address
809 Business Way
Suite 201
City State Zip-Code
Anytown Mi 32744
Phone Cellular Pager
555-2345 x103
E-Mail Address
nanders@hardly.workin.com
Web Site URL
http://www.workin.com/

Add another Contact.

A B C D E F G H I J K L M N O P Q R S T U V W X Y Z ?

Figure 7-3 *PHP online address book: adding a contact (submit)*

Now you'll want to implement a way to edit this contact information. The code for this follows along the same lines as adding a contact. Here is the listing for chapter7_oabEdit.php:

chapter7_oabEdit.php

```
<?
// chapter7_oabEdit.php
if($submit)
{
   if((!$firstName) or (!$lastName))
   {
      print ("<p>Whoops! You forgot to enter the first <i>and</i> last name for
the contact.");
```

```
}
else
{
   include("./chapter7_dbconnect.php");
   $query = "update oabContact set lastName = '$lastName', firstName =
   '$firstName', midName = '$midName', primaryInfo = '$primaryInfo', ";
   $query .= "homeAddr1 = '$homeAddr1', homeAddr2 = '$homeAddr2', homeCity =
   '$homeCity', homeState = '$homeState', homeZip = '$homeZip', ";
   $query .= "homePhone = '$homePhone', homeCellular = '$homeCellular',
   homePager = '$homePager', homeEmail = '$homeEmail', homeWeb = '$homeWeb', ";
   $query .= "workAddr1 = '$workAddr1', workAddr2 = '$workAddr2', workCity =
   '$workCity', workState = '$workState', workZip = '$workZip', ";
   $query .= "workPhone = '$workPhone', workCellular = '$workCellular',
   workPager = '$workPager', workEmail = '$workEmail', workWeb = '$workWeb'";
   $query .= " where contactID = $contactID";
   $mysql_result = mysql_query($query, $mysql_link);
   include("./chapter7_dbdisconnect.php");
   print ("<table width=\"525\" cellspacing=\"1\" cellpadding=\"3\"
   border=\"0\" bgcolor=\"#123456\">\n");
   print ("<tr>\n");
   print ("<td colspan=\"2\" bgcolor=\"#DFFFDF\"><b>The following Contact has
   been Updated..</b></td>\n");
   print ("</tr>\n");
   print ("<tr>\n");
   print ("<td colspan=\"2\" bgcolor=\"#ffffff\">\n");
   print ("<table width=\"100%\" cellspacing=\"0\" cellpadding=\"0\"
   border=\"0\">\n");
   print ("<tr>\n");
   print ("<td> <u>First Name</u></td>\n");
   print ("<td><u>M.I.</u></td>\n");
   print ("<td><u>Last Name</u></td>\n");
   print ("</tr>\n");
   print ("<tr>\n");
   printf ("<td> <i>%s</i></td>\n", $firstName);
   printf ("<td><i>%s</i></td>\n", $midName);
   printf ("<td><i>%s</i></td>\n", $lastName);
   print ("</tr>\n");
   print ("</table>\n");
   print ("</td>\n");
   print ("</tr>\n");
   print ("<tr>\n");
   print ("<td bgcolor=\"#EEFFEE\" width=\"50%\" colspan=\"2\">\n");
   print ("<b>Home</b>");
   if($primaryInfo == 1){ print ("<i>(Primary)</i>"); }
   print ("</td>\n");
   print ("</tr>\n");
   print ("<tr>\n");
```

```
print ("<td colspan=\"2\" bgcolor=\"#ffffff\"> <u>Address</u><br>");
printf (" <i>%s</i><br>\n", $homeAddr1);
printf (" <i>%s</i><br>\n", $homeAddr2);
print ("<table width=\"75%\" cellspacing=\"0\" cellpadding=\"0\"
border=\"0\">\n");
print ("<tr>\n");
print ("<td> <u>City</u></td>\n");
print ("<td> <u>State</u></td>\n");
print ("<td> <u>Zip-Code</u></td>\n");
print ("</tr>\n");
print ("<tr>\n");
printf ("<td> <i>%s</i></td>\n", $homeCity);
printf ("<td> <i>%s</i></td>\n", $homeState);
printf ("<td> <i>%s</i></td>\n", $homeZip);
print ("</tr>\n");
print ("</table>\n");
print ("<table width=\"75%\" cellspacing=\"0\" cellpadding=\"0\"
border=\"0\">\n");
print ("<tr>\n");
print ("<td> <u>Phone</u></td>\n");
print ("<td> <u>Cellular</u></td>\n");
print ("<td> <u>Pager</u></td>\n");
print ("</tr>\n");
print ("<tr>\n");
printf ("<td> <i>%s</i></td>\n", $homePhone);
printf ("<td> <i>%s</i></td>\n", $homeCellular);
printf ("<td> <i>%s</i></td>\n", $homePager);
print ("</tr>\n");
print ("</table>\n");
printf (" <u>E-Mail Address</u><br> <i>%s</i><br>", $homeEmail);
printf (" <u>Web Site URL</u><br> <i>%s</i>", $homeWeb);
print ("</td>\n");
print ("</tr>\n");
print ("<tr>\n");
print ("<td bgcolor=\"#EEFFEE\" width=\"50%\" colspan=\"2\">\n");
print ("<b>Work</b>");
if($primaryInfo == 2){ print ("<i>(Primary)</i>"); }
print ("</td>\n");
print ("</tr>\n");
print ("<tr>\n");
print ("<td colspan=\"2\" bgcolor=\"#ffffff\"> <u>Address</u><br>");
printf (" <i>%s</i><br>\n", $workAddr1);
printf (" <i>%s</i><br>\n", $workAddr2);
print ("<table width=\"75%\" cellspacing=\"0\" cellpadding=\"0\"
border=\"0\">\n");
print ("<tr>\n");
print ("<td> <u>City</u></td>\n");
```

```
        print ("<td> <u>State</u></td>\n");
        print ("<td> <u>Zip-Code</u></td>\n");
        print ("</tr>\n");
        print ("<tr>\n");
        printf ("<td> <i>%s</i></td>\n", $workCity);
        printf ("<td> <i>%s</i></td>\n", $workState);
        printf ("<td> <i>%s</i></td>\n", $workZip);
        print ("</tr>\n");
        print ("</table>\n");
        print ("<table width=\"75%\" cellspacing=\"0\" cellpadding=\"0\"
        border=\"0\">\n");
        print ("<tr>\n");
        print ("<td> <u>Phone</u></td>\n");
        print ("<td> <u>Cellular</u></td>\n");
        print ("<td> <u>Pager</u></td>\n");
        print ("</tr>\n");
        print ("<tr>\n");
        printf ("<td> <i>%s</i></td>\n", $workPhone);
        printf ("<td> <i>%s</i></td>\n", $workCellular);
        printf ("<td> <i>%s</i></td>\n", $workPager);
        print ("</tr>\n");
        print ("</table>\n");
        printf (" <u>E-Mail Address</u><br> %s<br>", $workEmail);
        printf (" <u>Web Site URL</u><br> %s", $workWeb);
        print ("</td>\n");
        print ("</tr>\n");
        print ("<tr>\n");
        print ("<td colspan=\"2\" align=\"right\" bgcolor=\"#DFFFDF\">\n");
        print ("<a href=\"./chapter7_oab.php?\">Return to your address
        book</a>.");
        print ("</td>\n");
        print ("</tr>\n");
        print ("</table>\n");
    }
}
else
{
    include("./chapter7_dbconnect.php");
    $query = "select * from oabContact where oabContact.contactID = $contactID";
    $mysql_result = mysql_query($query, $mysql_link);
    while($row = mysql_fetch_row($mysql_result))
    {
    print ("<form action=\"./chapter7_oab.php\" method=\"get\">\n");
    print ("<table width=\"525\" cellspacing=\"1\" cellpadding=\"3\" border=\"0\"
    bgcolor=\"#123456\">\n");
    print ("<tr>\n");
    print ("<td colspan=\"2\" bgcolor=\"#DFFFDF\"><b>Edit Contact Information</b>
    <font color=\"red\">(Required fields are in red.)</font></td>\n");
```

```
print ("</tr>\n");
print ("<tr>\n");
print ("<td colspan=\"2\" bgcolor=\"#ffffff\">\n");
print ("<table width=\"100%\" cellspacing=\"0\" cellpadding=\"0\"
border=\"0\">\n");
print ("<tr>\n");
print ("<td> <font color=\"red\">First Name</font></td>\n");
print ("<td>M.I.</td>\n");
print ("<td><font color=\"red\">Last Name</font></td>\n");
print ("</tr>\n");
print ("<tr>\n");
printf ("<td> <input type=\"text\" name=\"firstName\" size=\"20\"
maxsize=\"20\" value=\"%s\"></td>\n", $row[2]);
printf ("<td><input type=\"text\" name=\"midName\" size=\"3\" maxsize=\"3\"
value=\"%s\"></td>\n", $row[3]);
printf ("<td><input type=\"text\" name=\"lastName\" size=\"30\" maxsize=\"30\"
value=\"%s\"></td>\n", $row[1]);
print ("</tr>\n");
print ("</table>\n");
print ("</td>\n");
print ("</tr>\n");
print ("<tr>\n");
print ("<td bgcolor=\"#EEFFEE\" width=\"50%\" colspan=\"2\">\n");
if($row[4] == 1)
{
   print ("<input type=\"radio\" name=\"primaryInfo\" value=\"1\" checked>");
}
else
{
   print ("<input type=\"radio\" name=\"primaryInfo\" value=\"1\">");
}
print ("<b>Home</b></td>\n");
print ("</tr>\n");
print ("<tr>\n");
print ("<td colspan=\"2\" bgcolor=\"#ffffff\"> Address<br>");
printf (" <input type=\"text\" name=\"homeAddr1\" size=\"50\"
maxsize=\"50\" value=\"%s\"><br>", $row[5]);
printf (" <input type=\"text\" name=\"homeAddr2\" size=\"50\"
maxsize=\"50\" value=\"%s\"><br>", $row[6]);
print ("<table width=\"75%\" cellspacing=\"0\" cellpadding=\"0\"
border=\"0\">\n");
print ("<tr>\n");
print ("<td> City</td>\n");
print ("<td> State</td>\n");
print ("<td> Zip-Code</td>\n");
print ("</tr>\n");
```

```
print ("<tr>\n");
printf ("<td> <input type=\"text\" name=\"homeCity\" size=\"30\"
maxsize=\"30\" value=\"%s\"></td>\n", $row[7]);
printf ("<td> <input type=\"text\" name=\"homeState\" size=\"3\"
maxsize=\"3\" value=\"%s\"></td>\n", $row[8]);
printf ("<td> <input type=\"text\" name=\"homeZip\" size=\"12\"
maxsize\"12\" value=\"%s\"></td>\n", $row[9]);
print ("</tr>\n");
print ("</table>\n");
print ("<table width=\"75%\" cellspacing=\"0\" cellpadding=\"0\"
border=\"0\">\n");
print ("<tr>\n");
print ("<td> Phone</td>\n");
print ("<td> Cellular</td>\n");
print ("<td> Pager</td>\n");
print ("</tr>\n");
print ("<tr>\n");
printf ("<td> <input type=\"text\" name=\"homePhone\" size=\"20\"
maxsize=\"20\" value=\"%s\"></td>\n", $row[10]);
printf ("<td> <input type=\"text\" name=\"homeCellular\" size=\"20\"
maxsize=\"20\" value=\"%s\"></td>\n", $row[11]);
printf ("<td> <input type=\"text\" name=\"homePager\" size=\"20\"
maxsize\"20\" value=\"%s\"></td>\n", $row[12]);
print ("</tr>\n");
print ("</table>\n");
printf (" E-Mail Address<br> <input type=\"text\" name=\"homeEmail\"
size=\"50\" maxsize=\"50\" value=\"%s\"><br>", $row[13]);
printf (" Web Site URL<br> <input type=\"text\" name=\"homeWeb\"
size=\"50\" maxsize=\"50\" value=\"%s\">", $row[14]);
print ("</td>\n");
print ("</tr>\n");
print ("<tr>\n");
print ("<td bgcolor=\"#EEFFEE\" width=\"50%\" colspan=\"2\">\n");
if($row[4] == 2)
{
   print ("<input type=\"radio\" name=\"primaryInfo\" value=\"2\" checked>");
}
else
{
   print ("<input type=\"radio\" name=\"primaryInfo\" value=\"2\">");
}
print ("<b>Work</b></td>\n");
print ("</td>\n");
print ("</tr>\n");
print ("<tr>\n");
print ("<td colspan=\"2\" bgcolor=\"#ffffff\"> Address<br>");
printf (" <input type=\"text\" name=\"workAddr1\" size=\"50\"
maxsize=\"50\" value=\"%s\"><br>", $row[15]);
```

```
printf (" <input type=\"text\" name=\"workAddr2\" size=\"50\"
maxsize=\"50\" value=\"%s\"><br>", $row[16]);
print ("<table width=\"75%\" cellspacing=\"0\" cellpadding=\"0\"
border=\"0\">\n");
print ("<tr>\n");
print ("<td> City</td>\n");
print ("<td> State</td>\n");
print ("<td> Zip-Code</td>\n");
print ("</tr>\n");
print ("<tr>\n");
printf ("<td> <input type=\"text\" name=\"workCity\" size=\"30\"
maxsize=\"30\" value=\"%s\"></td>\n", $row[17]);
printf ("<td> <input type=\"text\" name=\"workState\" size=\"3\"
maxsize=\"3\" value=\"%s\"></td>\n", $row[18]);
printf ("<td> <input type=\"text\" name=\"workZip\" size=\"12\"
maxsize\"12\" value=\"%s\"></td>\n", $row[19]);
print ("</tr>\n");
print ("</table>\n");
print ("<table width=\"75%\" cellspacing=\"0\" cellpadding=\"0\"
border=\"0\">\n");
print ("<tr>\n");
print ("<td> Phone</td>\n");
print ("<td> Cellular</td>\n");
print ("<td> Pager</td>\n");
print ("</tr>\n");
print ("<tr>\n");
printf ("<td> <input type=\"text\" name=\"workPhone\" size=\"20\"
maxsize=\"20\" value=\"%s\"></td>\n", $row[20]);
printf ("<td> <input type=\"text\" name=\"workCellular\" size=\"20\"
maxsize=\"20\" value=\"%s\"></td>\n", $row[21]);
printf ("<td> <input type=\"text\" name=\"workPager\" size=\"20\"
maxsize\"20\" value=\"%s\"></td>\n", $row[22]);
print ("</tr>\n");
print ("</table>\n");
printf (" E-Mail Address<br> <input type=\"text\" name=\"workEmail\"
size=\"50\" maxsize=\"50\" value=\"%s\"><br>", $row[23]);
printf (" Web Site URL<br> <input type=\"text\" name=\"workWeb\"
size=\"50\" maxsize=\"50\" value=\"%s\">", $row[24]);
print ("</td>\n");
print ("</tr>\n");
print ("<tr>\n");
print ("<td colspan=\"2\" align=\"right\" bgcolor=\"#DFFFDF\">\n");
print ("<input type=\"hidden\" name=\"tab\" value=\"Edit\">");
print ("<input type=\"hidden\" name=\"contactID\" value=\"$contactID\">");
print ("<input type=\"submit\" name=\"submit\" value=\"Update
Contact\"> ");
```

```
    print ("</td>\n");
    print ("</tr>\n");
    print ("</table>\n");
    print ("</form>\n");
    include("./chapter7_dbdisconnect.php");
    }
}
?>
```

The resulting code should produce output like that pictured in Figures 7-4 and 7-5. Now that you have a way to add and edit contact information, you might also want to delete a contact from your address book. Moving right along, here is the code listing for chapter7_oabDelete.php, which performs such an operation:

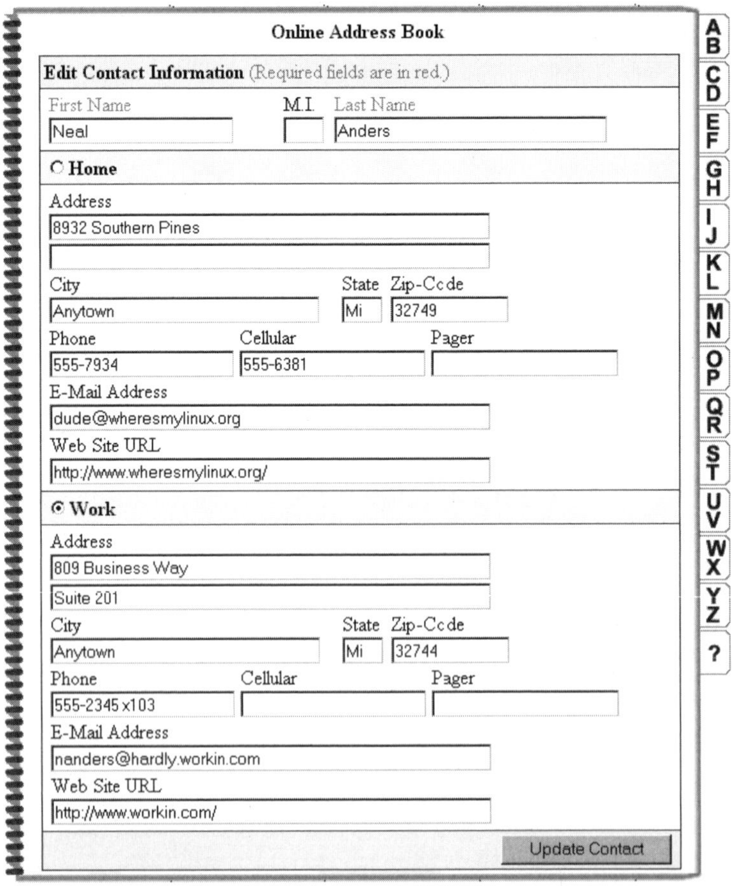

Figure 7-4 *PHP online address book: editing a contact*

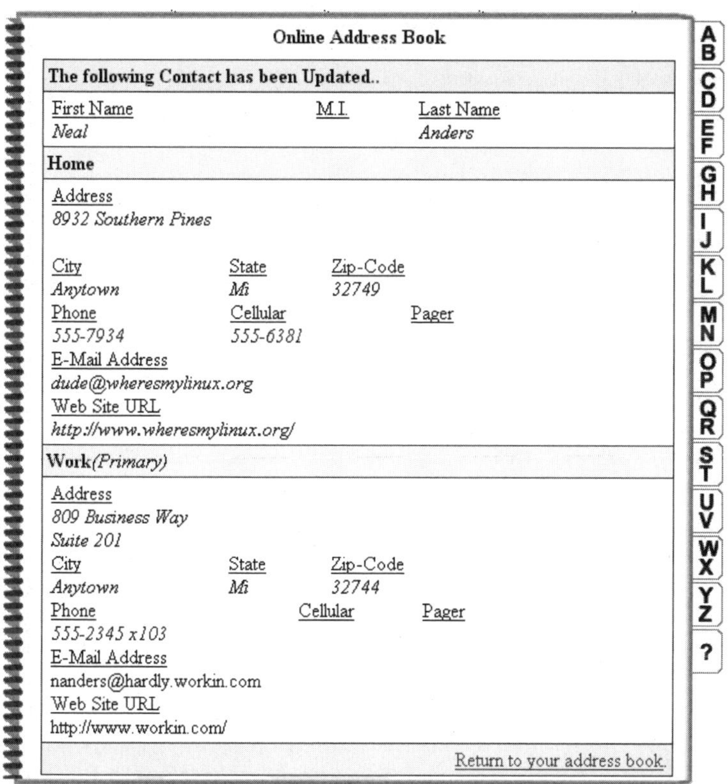

Figure 7-5 *PHP online address book: editing a contact (submit)*

chapter7_oabDelete.php

```
<?
// chapter7_oabDelete.php
if($submit)
{
   if((!$firstName) or (!$lastName))
   {
      print ("<p>Whoops! You forgot to enter the first <i>and</i> last name for
the contact.");
   }
   else
   {
      include("./chapter7_dbconnect.php");
      $query = "delete from oabContact where contactID = $contactID";
        $mysql_result = mysql_query($query, $mysql_link);
```

```
        include("./chapter7_dbdisconnect.php");
        print ("<table width=\"525\" cellspacing=\"1\" cellpadding=\"3\"
        border=\"0\" bgcolor=\"#123456\">\n");
        print ("<tr>\n");
        print ("<td colspan=\"2\" bgcolor=\"#DFFFDF\"><b>The following contact has
        been deleted:</b></td>\n");
        print ("</tr>\n");
        print ("<tr>\n");
        print ("<td colspan=\"2\" bgcolor=\"#ffffff\">\n");
        print ("<table width=\"100%\" cellspacing=\"0\" cellpadding=\"0\"
        border=\"0\">\n");
        print ("<tr>\n");
        print ("<td> <u>First Name</u></td>\n");
        print ("<td><u>M.I.</u></td>\n");
        print ("<td><u>Last Name</u></td>\n");
        print ("</tr>\n");
        print ("<tr>\n");
        printf ("<td> <i>%s</i></td>\n", $firstName);
        printf ("<td><i>%s</i></td>\n", $midName);
        printf ("<td><i>%s</i></td>\n", $lastName);
        print ("</tr>\n");
        print ("</table>\n");
        print ("</td>\n");
        print ("</tr>\n");
        print ("<tr>\n");
        print ("<td colspan=\"2\" align=\"right\" bgcolor=\"#DFFFDF\">\n");
        print ("<a href=\"./chapter7_oab.php?\">Return to your address
        book</a>.");
        print ("</td>\n");
        print ("</tr>\n");
        print ("</table>\n");
    }
}
else
{
    include("./chapter7_dbconnect.php");
    $query = "select * from oabContact where oabContact.contactID = $contactID";
    $mysql_result = mysql_query($query, $mysql_link);
    while($row = mysql_fetch_row($mysql_result))
    {
    print ("<form action=\"./chapter7_oab.php\" method=\"get\">\n");
    print ("<table width=\"525\" cellspacing=\"1\" cellpadding=\"3\" border=\"0\"
    bgcolor=\"#123456\">\n");
    print ("<tr>\n");
    print ("<td colspan=\"2\" bgcolor=\"#DFFFDF\"><b>Are you sure you want to
    delete:</b></td>\n");
    print ("</tr>\n");
```

```
    print ("<tr>\n");
    print ("<td colspan=\"2\" bgcolor=\"#ffffff\">\n");
    print ("<table width=\"100%\" cellspacing=\"0\" cellpadding=\"0\"
    border=\"0\">\n");
    print ("<tr>\n");
    print ("<td> <u>First Name</u></td>\n");
    print ("<td><u>M.I.</u></td>\n");
    print ("<td><u>Last Name</u></td>\n");
    print ("</tr>\n");
    print ("<tr>\n");
    printf ("<td> <i>%s</i></td>\n", $row[2]);
    printf ("<td><i>%s</i></td>\n", $row[3]);
    printf ("<td><i>%s</i></td>\n", $row[1]);
    print ("</tr>\n");
    print ("</table>\n");
    print ("</td>\n");
    print ("</tr>\n");
    print ("<tr>\n");
    print ("<td colspan=\"2\" align=\"right\" bgcolor=\"#DFFFDF\">\n");
    print ("<input type=\"hidden\" name=\"lastName\" value=\"$row[1]\">");
    print ("<input type=\"hidden\" name=\"midName\" value=\"$row[3]\">");
    print ("<input type=\"hidden\" name=\"firstName\" value=\"$row[1]\">");
    print ("<input type=\"hidden\" name=\"tab\" value=\"Delete\">");
    print ("<input type=\"hidden\" name=\"contactID\" value=\"$contactID\">");
    print ("<input type=\"submit\" name=\"submit\" value=\"Delete
    Contact\"> ");
    print ("</td>\n");
    print ("</tr>\n");
    print ("</table>\n");
    print ("</form>\n");
    include("./chapter7_dbdisconnect.php");
    }
}
?>
```

As you'll note in the preceding code, all you really needed to delete a contact from the database is the contact's $contactID. However, to be more user friendly, you displayed the contact's name as well, assuring the user that this is the contact that was deleted. Figures 7-6 and 7-7 show you the expected results.

Now that you are able to add, edit, and delete contact information, what good is it if there is no way to list your contacts? In comes chapter7_oabList.php. This should allow you to list your contacts. Since you're trying to replicate an actual address book, your code will only display your contacts based on the first letter of their last name, and only in alphabetical groups of two. Hence, contacts will only be displayed based on last name where their last name begins with A or B, C or D, E or F, and so on.

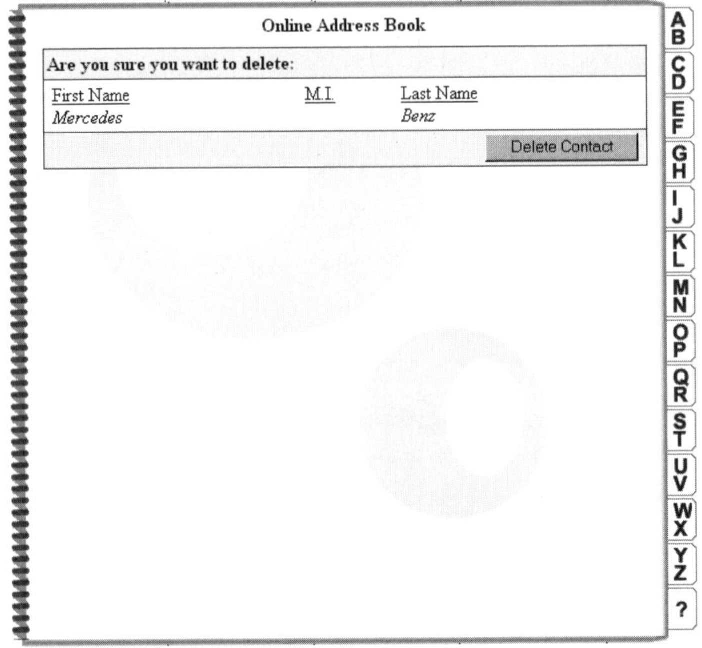

Figure 7-6 *PHP online address book: deleting a contact*

This will be simplified later on in the main part of your code, with the letter tabs. For now, here is the code you'll use:

chapter7_oabList.php

```
<?
// chapter7_oabList.php
   include("./chapter7_dbconnect.php");
   $firstLetter = substr ($tab, 0, 1);
   $lastLetter = substr ($tab, 2, 1);
   $query = "select * from oabContact where lastName like '$firstLetter%' or
   lastName like '$lastLetter%' order by lastName, firstName";
   $mysql_result = mysql_query($query, $mysql_link);
   print ("<table width=\"525\" cellspacing=\"1\" cellpadding=\"3\" border=\"0\"
   bgcolor=\"#123456\">");
   print ("<tr>");
   print ("<td bgcolor=\"#dfdfdf\"><b>Name</b></td>");
   print ("<td bgcolor=\"#dfdfdf\"><b>Phone</b></td>");
   print ("<td bgcolor=\"#dfdfdf\"><b>E-Mail</b></td>");
   print ("</tr>");
```

```
    while($row = mysql_fetch_row($mysql_result))
    {
       $rowcolor = AltCellColor();
       if(($row[4] == 1) or ($row[4] == ""))
       {
          $primaryPhone = $row[10];
          $primaryEmail = $row[13];
       }
       if($row[4] == 2)
       {
          $primaryPhone = $row[20];
          $primaryEmail = $row[23];
       }
       print("<tr>\n");
       printf("<td bgcolor=\"%s\"> <a
       href=\"./chapter7_oab.php?contactID=%s\">%s, %s</a></td>\n", $rowcolor,
       $row[0], $row[1], $row[2]);
       printf("<td bgcolor=\"%s\"> <a
       href=\"./chapter7_oab.php?contactID=%s\">%s</a></td>\n", $rowcolor,
       $row[0], $primaryPhone);
       printf("<td bgcolor=\"%s\"> <a
       href=\"./chapter7_oab.php?contactID=%s\">%s</a></td>\n", $rowcolor,
       $row[0], $primaryEmail);
       print("</tr>\n");
    }
    print ("<tr>");
    print ("<th bgcolor=\"#dfdfdf\"> </th>");
    print ("<th bgcolor=\"#dfdfdf\"> </th>");
    print ("<th bgcolor=\"#dfdfdf\"> </th>");
    print ("</tr>");
    print ("<tr>\n");
    print ("<td colspan=\"3\" align=\"right\" bgcolor=\"#DFFFDF\">\n");
    print ("<a href=\"./chapter7_oab.php?tab=add\">Add a new Contact</a>.");
    print ("</td>\n");
    print ("</tr>\n");
    print ("</table>");
    include("./chapter7_dbdisconnect.php");
?>
```

This code listing was a lot shorter than your previous ones. Toward the beginning of the code, you are looking for a variable called $tab. This contains the letter groups that you will search on. You take the two letters and design your query to search the oabContact table for last names that begin with either of the two letters. The results are displayed in a nice HTML table that has alternating background colors. You may have also noted that there is a function you call that performs this color swap, and

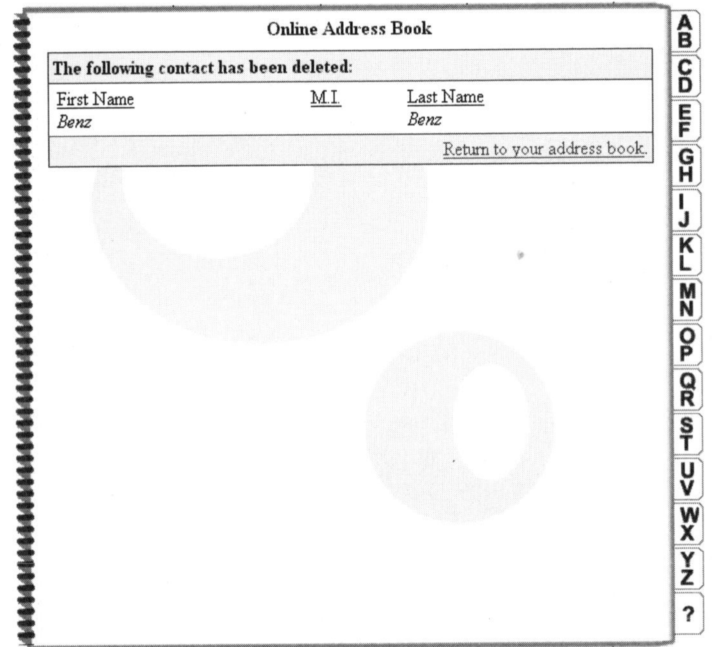

Figure 7-7 *PHP online address book: deleting a contact (submit)*

that the code for this function is not in this code listing. Fear not! You'll get to the specifics of this in a later code listing. There is also some code that looks at the $primaryInfo field for this contact. If you selected Home or Work when you added the contact, the phone number and e-mail address are displayed as a quick way to access this information. Also note that you provide a link in your code that will allow the user to add a contact to their address book. The output from this should look like Figure 7-8.

Moving on, now that you have a way to list the contacts in your address book, you need a way to view each individual contact. Upon viewing this contact, perhaps you

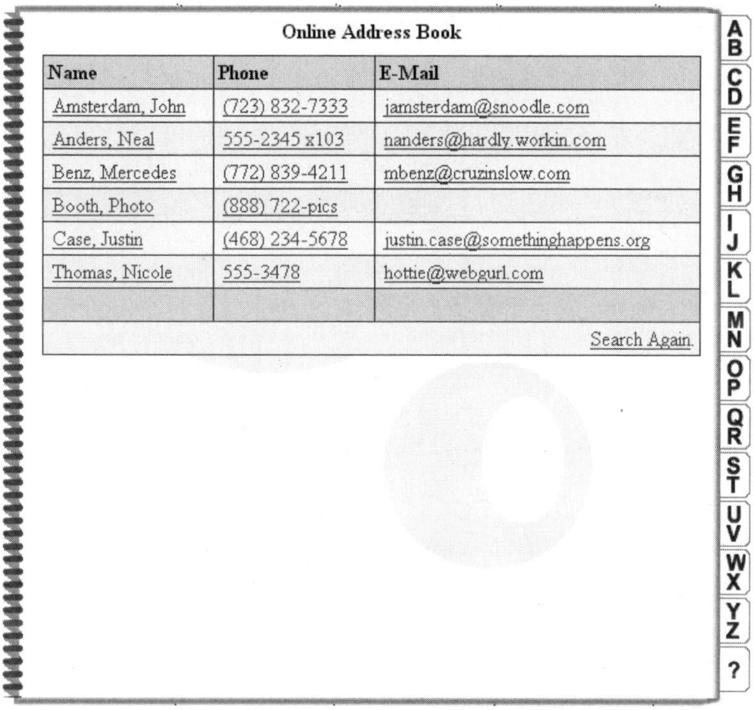

Online Address Book

Name	Phone	E-Mail
Amsterdam, John	(723) 832-7333	jamsterdam@snoodle.com
Anders, Neal	555-2345 x103	nanders@hardly.workin.com
Benz, Mercedes	(772) 839-4211	mbenz@cruzinslow.com
Booth, Photo	(888) 722-pics	
Case, Justin	(468) 234-5678	justin.case@somethinghappens.org
Thomas, Nicole	555-3478	hottie@webgurl.com
		Search Again.

A B C D E F G H I J K L M N O P Q R S T U V W X Y Z ?

Figure 7-8 *PHP online address book: listing contacts*

will want to edit or delete the information. The code needed for this is contained in chapter7_oabView.php:

chapter7_oabView.php

```
<?
// chapter7_oabView.php
include("./chapter7_dbconnect.php");
$query = "select * from oabContact where oabContact.contactID = $contactID";
```

```
$mysql_result = mysql_query($query, $mysql_link);
while($row = mysql_fetch_row($mysql_result))
{
   print ("<table width=\"525\" cellspacing=\"1\" cellpadding=\"3\"
   border=\"0\" bgcolor=\"#123456\">\n");
   print ("<tr>\n");
   print ("<td colspan=\"2\" bgcolor=\"#DFFFDF\"><b>Here is the contact
   information for...</b></td>\n");
   print ("</tr>\n");
   print ("<tr>\n");
   print ("<td colspan=\"2\" bgcolor=\"#ffffff\">\n");
   print ("<table width=\"100%\" cellspacing=\"0\" cellpadding=\"0\"
   border=\"0\">\n");
   print ("<tr>\n");
   print ("<td> <u>First Name</u></td>\n");
   print ("<td><u>M.I.</u></td>\n");
   print ("<td><u>Last Name</u></td>\n");
   print ("</tr>\n");
   print ("<tr>\n");
   printf ("<td> <i>%s</i></td>\n", $row[2]);
   printf ("<td><i>%s</i></td>\n", $row[3]);
   printf ("<td><i>%s</i></td>\n", $row[1]);
   print ("</tr>\n");
   print ("</table>\n");
   print ("</td>\n");
   print ("</tr>\n");
   print ("<tr>\n");
   print ("<td bgcolor=\"#EEFFEE\" width=\"50%\" colspan=\"2\">\n");
   print ("<b>Home</b>");
   if($row[4] == 1){ print ("<i>(Primary)</i>"); }
   print ("</td>\n");
   print ("</tr>\n");
   print ("<tr>\n");
   print ("<td colspan=\"2\" bgcolor=\"#ffffff\"> <u>Address</u><br>");
   printf (" <i>%s</i><br>\n", $row[5]);
   printf (" <i>%s</i><br>\n", $row[6]);
   print ("<table width=\"75%\" cellspacing=\"0\" cellpadding=\"0\"
   border=\"0\">\n");
   print ("<tr>\n");
   print ("<td> <u>City</u></td>\n");
   print ("<td> <u>State</u></td>\n");
   print ("<td> <u>Zip-Code</u></td>\n");
   print ("</tr>\n");
   print ("<tr>\n");
   printf ("<td> <i>%s</i></td>\n", $row[7]);
   printf ("<td> <i>%s</i></td>\n", $row[8]);
   printf ("<td> <i>%s</i></td>\n", $row[9]);
```

```
print ("</tr>\n");
print ("</table>\n");
print ("<table width=\"75%\" cellspacing=\"0\" cellpadding=\"0\"
border=\"0\">\n");
print ("<tr>\n");
print ("<td> <u>Phone</u></td>\n");
print ("<td> <u>Cellular</u></td>\n");
print ("<td> <u>Pager</u></td>\n");
print ("</tr>\n");
print ("<tr>\n");
printf ("<td> <i>%s</i></td>\n", $row[10]);
printf ("<td> <i>%s</i></td>\n", $row[11]);
printf ("<td> <i>%s</i></td>\n", $row[12]);
print ("</tr>\n");
print ("</table>\n");
printf (" <u>E-Mail Address</u><br> <i>%s</i><br>", $row[13]);
printf (" <u>Web Site URL</u><br> <i>%s</i>", $row[14]);
print ("</td>\n");
print ("</tr>\n");
print ("<tr>\n");
print ("<td bgcolor=\"#EEFFEE\" width=\"50%\" colspan=\"2\">\n");
print ("<b>Work</b>");
if($row[4] == 2){ print ("<i>(Primary)</i>"); }
print ("</td>\n");
print ("</tr>\n");
print ("<tr>\n");
print ("<td colspan=\"2\" bgcolor=\"#ffffff\"> <u>Address</u><br>");
printf (" <i>%s</i><br>\n", $row[15]);
printf (" <i>%s</i><br>\n", $row[16]);
print ("<table width=\"75%\" cellspacing=\"0\" cellpadding=\"0\"
border=\"0\">\n");
print ("<tr>\n");
print ("<td> <u>City</u></td>\n");
print ("<td> <u>State</u></td>\n");
print ("<td> <u>Zip-Code</u></td>\n");
print ("</tr>\n");
print ("<tr>\n");
printf ("<td> <i>%s</i></td>\n", $row[17]);
printf ("<td> <i>%s</i></td>\n", $row[18]);
printf ("<td> <i>%s</i></td>\n", $row[19]);
print ("</tr>\n");
print ("</table>\n");
print ("<table width=\"75%\" cellspacing=\"0\" cellpadding=\"0\"
border=\"0\">\n");
print ("<tr>\n");
print ("<td> <u>Phone</u></td>\n");
print ("<td> <u>Cellular</u></td>\n");
```

```
    print ("<td> <u>Pager</u></td>\n");
    print ("</tr>\n");
    print ("<tr>\n");
    printf ("<td> <i>%s</i></td>\n", $row[20]);
    printf ("<td> <i>%s</i></td>\n", $row[21]);
    printf ("<td> <i>%s</i></td>\n", $row[22]);
    print ("</tr>\n");
    print ("</table>\n");
    printf (" <u>E-Mail Address</u><br> %s<br>", $row[23]);
    printf (" <u>Web Site URL</u><br> %s", $row[24]);
    print ("</td>\n");
    print ("</tr>\n");
    print ("<tr>\n");
    print ("<td colspan=\"2\" align=\"right\" bgcolor=\"#DFFFDF\">You can \n");
    print ("<a
    href=\"./chapter7_oab.php?tab=edit&contactID=$contactID\">Edit</a> or ");
    print ("<a
    href=\"./chapter7_oab.php?tab=delete&contactID=$contactID\">Delete</a> or ");
    print (" this Contact.");
    print ("</td>\n");
    print ("</tr>\n");
    print ("</table>\n");
    include("./chapter7_dbdisconnect.php");
}
?>
```

If you dread typing endless lines of code (any other COBOL programmers out there?), you may have noticed the return of our heavy use of HTML tables. Again, it's all to be aesthetically pleasing. The core of your PHP code is concentrated at the beginning of the listing, where you get a $contactID passed in from your code in chapter7_oabList.php. You take this number and query your oabContacts table for the specific information on the contact and display the result. You also provide links at the end of your code that call upon the editing and deleting features you implemented earlier in the chapter. The eventual output should look similar to Figure 7-9. Is the big picture starting to form?

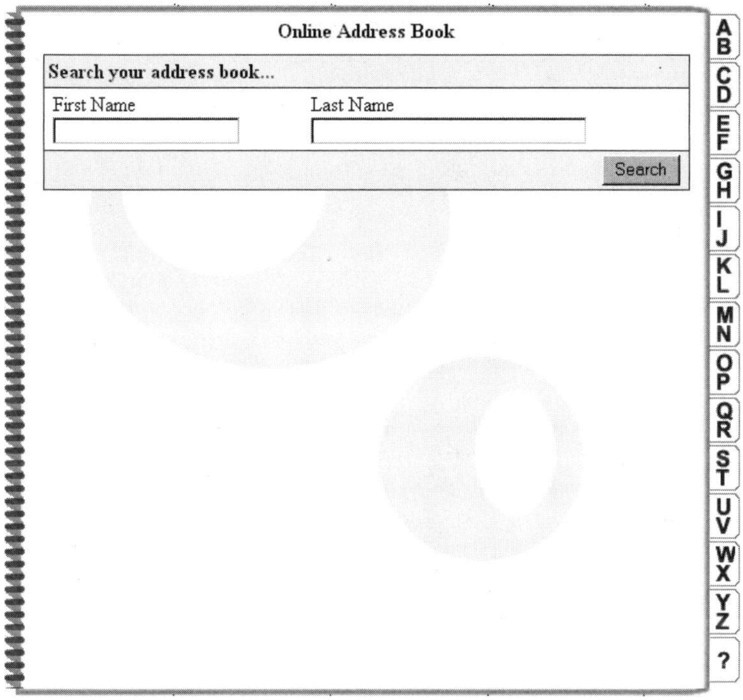

Online Address Book

Search your address book...

First Name Last Name

Search

A B C D E F G H I J K L M N O P Q R S T U V W X Y Z ?

Figure 7-9 *PHP online address book: viewing a contact*

We have one last bit of code to finish up before everything falls in place. You'll want the ability to search your address book to find contacts. Sometimes an exact name just escapes you! Here is the listing for chapter7_oabSearch.php:

chapter7_oabSearch.php

```
<?
// chapter7_oabSearch.php
if($submit)
{
```

```
include("./chapter7_dbconnect.php");
$query = "select * from oabContact where ";
if(($lastName == "") and ($firstName == ""))
{
   $query .= "lastName like '$lastName%' and firstName like '$firstName%'";
}
if(($lastName != "") and ($firstName != ""))
{
   $query .= "lastName like '$lastName%' and firstName like '$firstName%'";
}
if(($lastName != "") and ($firstName == ""))
{
   $query .= "lastName like '$lastName%'";
}
if(($lastName == "") and ($firstName != ""))
{
   $query .= "firstName like '$firstName%'";
}
$query .= " order by lastName, firstName";
$mysql_result = mysql_query($query, $mysql_link);
print ("<table width=\"525\" cellspacing=\"1\" cellpadding=\"3\"
border=\"0\" bgcolor=\"#123456\">");
print ("<tr>");
print ("<td bgcolor=\"#dfdfdf\"><b>Name</b></td>");
print ("<td bgcolor=\"#dfdfdf\"><b>Phone</b></td>");
print ("<td bgcolor=\"#dfdfdf\"><b>E-Mail</b></td>");
print ("</tr>");
while($row = mysql_fetch_row($mysql_result))
{
   $rowcolor = AltCellColor();
   if(($row[4] == 1) or ($row[4] == ""))
   {
      $primaryPhone = $row[10];
      $primaryEmail = $row[13];
   }
   if($row[4] == 2)
   {
      $primaryPhone = $row[20];
      $primaryEmail = $row[23];
   }
   print("<tr>\n");
   printf("<td bgcolor=\"%s\"> <a
   href=\"./chapter7_oab.php?contactID=%s\">%s, %s</a></td>\n", $rowcolor,
   $row[0], $row[1], $row[2]);
   printf("<td bgcolor=\"%s\"> <a
   href=\"./chapter7_oab.php?contactID=%s\">%s</a></td>\n", $rowcolor,
   $row[0], $primaryPhone);
```

```
        printf("<td bgcolor=\"%s\"> <a
        href=\"./chapter7_oab.php?contactID=%s\">%s</a></td>\n", $rowcolor,
        $row[0], $primaryEmail);
        print("</tr>\n");
    }
    print ("<tr>");
    print ("<th bgcolor=\"#dfdfdf\"> </th>");
    print ("<th bgcolor=\"#dfdfdf\"> </th>");
    print ("<th bgcolor=\"#dfdfdf\"> </th>");
    print ("</tr>");
    print ("<tr>\n");
    print ("<td colspan=\"3\" align=\"right\" bgcolor=\"#DFFFDF\">\n");
    print ("<a href=\"./chapter7_oab.php?tab=?\">Search Again</a>.");
    print ("</td>\n");
    print ("</tr>\n");
    print ("</table>");
    include("./chapter7_dbdisconnect.php");
}
```

This first section of your code deals with the name parameters that will be passed in. It builds the needed query and displays any results that may have come back. The user can then click a contact and view their information. Let's continue on and code a simple search form to use:

```
else
{
    print ("<form action=\"./chapter7_oab.php\" method=\"get\">\n");
    print ("<table width=\"525\" cellspacing=\"1\" cellpadding=\"3\"
    border=\"0\" bgcolor=\"#123456\">\n");
    print ("<tr>\n");
    print ("<td colspan=\"2\" bgcolor=\"#DFFFDF\"><b>Search your address
    book...</b></td>\n");
    print ("</tr>\n");
    print ("<tr>\n");
    print ("<td colspan=\"2\" bgcolor=\"#ffffff\">\n");
    print ("<table width=\"100%\" cellspacing=\"0\" cellpadding=\"0\"
    border=\"0\">\n");
    print ("<tr>\n");
    print ("<td> First Name</td>\n");
    print ("<td>Last Name</td>\n");
    print ("</tr>\n");
    print ("<tr>\n");
    print ("<td> <input type=\"text\" name=\"firstName\" size=\"20\"
    maxsize=\"20\"></td>\n");
    print ("<td><input type=\"text\" name=\"lastName\" size=\"30\"
    maxsize=\"30\"></td>\n");
```

```
    print ("</tr>\n");
    print ("</table>\n");
    print ("</td>");
    print ("</tr>");
    print ("<tr>\n");
    print ("<td colspan=\"2\" align=\"right\" bgcolor=\"#DFFFDF\">\n");
    print ("<input type=\"hidden\" name=\"tab\" value=\"?\">");
    print ("<input type=\"submit\" name=\"submit\" value=\"Search\"> ");
    print ("</td>\n");
    print ("</tr>\n");
    print ("</table>\n");
    print ("</form>\n");
}
?>
```

And that is that. To summarize this code, you implement a search form and then display any results that are found, as well as allow the user to view the contact or perform another search. The end result is pictured in Figures 7-10 and 7-11.

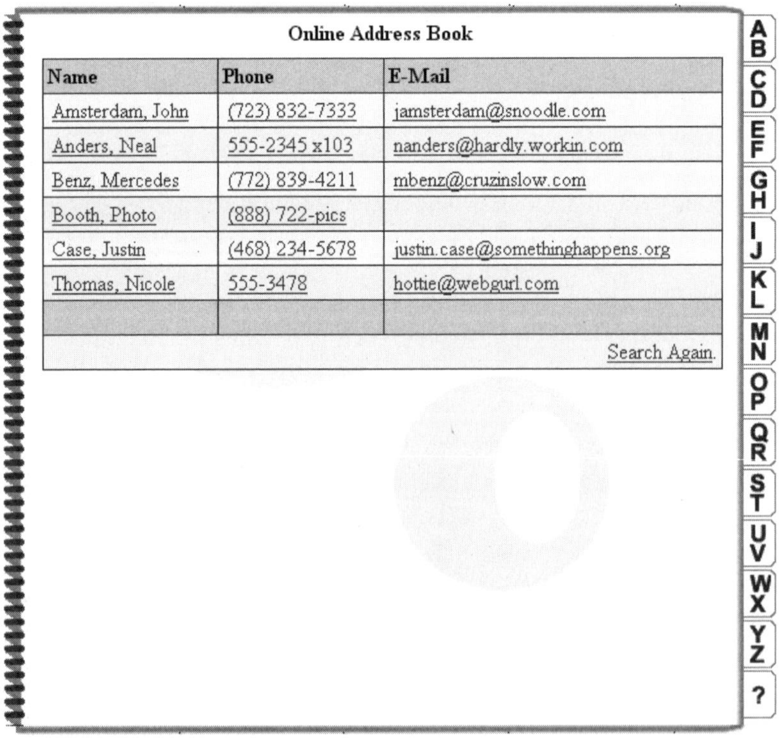

Online Address Book

Name	Phone	E-Mail
Amsterdam, John	(723) 832-7333	jamsterdam@snoodle.com
Anders, Neal	555-2345 x103	nanders@hardly.workin.com
Benz, Mercedes	(772) 839-4211	mbenz@cruzinslow.com
Booth, Photo	(888) 722-pics	
Case, Justin	(468) 234-5678	justin.case@somethinghappens.org
Thomas, Nicole	555-3478	hottie@webgurl.com
		Search Again.

AB CD EF GH IJ KL MN OP QR ST UV WX YZ ?

Figure 7-10 *PHP online address book: searching*

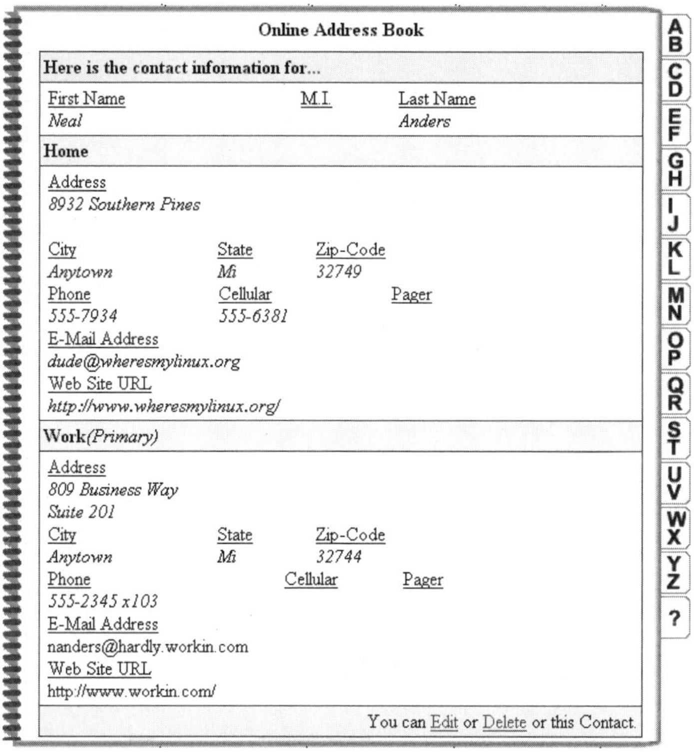

Online Address Book

Here is the contact information for...

First Name M.I. Last Name
Neal Anders

Home

Address
8932 Southern Pines

City State Zip-Code
Anytown Mi 32749
Phone Cellular Pager
555-7934 555-6381
E-Mail Address
dude@wheresmylinux.org
Web Site URL
http://www.wheresmylinux.org/

Work(Primary)

Address
809 Business Way
Suite 201
City State Zip-Code
Anytown Mi 32744
Phone Cellular Pager
555-2345 x103
E-Mail Address
nanders@hardly.workin.com
Web Site URL
http://www.workin.com/

You can Edit or Delete or this Contact.

A B C D E F G H I J K L M N O P Q R S T U V W X Y Z ?

Figure 7-11 *PHP online address book: search results*

And thus concludes the coding of all of the individual modules. We have a few more things to take care of before we wrap this up. You'll want to pull all of the features of your address book into one spot. As you may have picked up on, all of these features rely on either a $contactID, $tab, or $submit value to be passed in. If you know these values already, you could just type them into the address bar in your browser and get actual results. But let us make things much easier and provide a means by which to click your way through the address book. The final code listing is chapter7_oab.php. Let's step through this code section by section to make things clear:

chapter7_oab.php

```
<!-- chapter7_oab.php -->
<html>
<head>
<title>Online Address Book</title>
```

```
</head>
<body>
<table width="600" height="540" border="0" cellspacing="0" cellpadding="0">
<tr><td colspan="3"><img src="./oab_topborder.gif" border="0"></td></tr>
<tr>
   <td background="./oab_bind.gif" width="20"> </td>
   <td valign="top" align="center" background="./oabbg.gif">
      <table width="550" height="535" border="0" cellspacing="0"
      cellpadding="3">
      <tr>
         <td height="30" align="center">
            <b>Online Address Book</b>
         </td>
      </tr>
      <tr>
         <td height="505" valign="top" align="center">
            <!-- Start of tab content -->
```

We start off simply enough. We begin with some standard HTML tags, and a table that will contain our information and tabs. Now it's time for some PHP code.

```
<?
   static $cellcolor = "#DFFFDF";
   function AltCellColor() // Alternates the cell background colors
   {
      static $cellcolor = "#DFFFDF";
      if($cellcolor == "#DFFFDF")
      {
         $cellcolor = "#EEFFEE";
       }
       else
       {
          $cellcolor = "#DFFFDF";
       }
       return($cellcolor);
   }
```

Ah-ha! The missing code for the function you called in your View and Search modules! By placing the code here, you eliminate the need to type it twice. As an alternative, you could have placed the code in a separate PHP file and included them, as shown here:

```
if($tab)
 {
    $tab = strtoupper($tab);
```

```
switch ($tab)
{
    case "A-B":
       include("./chapter7_oabList.php");
       break;
   case "C-D":
       include("./chapter7_oabList.php");
       break;
   case "E-F":
       include("./chapter7_oabList.php");
       break;
   case "G-H":
       include("./chapter7_oabList.php");
       break;
   case "I-J":
       include("./chapter7_oabList.php");
       break;
   case "K-L":
       include("./chapter7_oabList.php");
       break;
   case "M-N":
       include("./chapter7_oabList.php");
       break;
   case "O-P":
       include("./chapter7_oabList.php");
       break;
   case "Q-R":
       include("./chapter7_oabList.php");
       break;
   case "S-T":
       include("./chapter7_oabList.php");
       break;
   case "U-V":
       include("./chapter7_oabList.php");
       break;
   case "W-X":
       include("./chapter7_oabList.php");
       break;
   case "Y-Z":
       include("./chapter7_oabList.php");
       break;
   case "?":
       include("./chapter7_oabSearch.php");
       break;
```

```
            case "ADD":
               include("./chapter7_oabAdd.php");
               break;
            case "EDIT":
               include("./chapter7_oabEdit.php");
               break;
            case "DELETE":
               include("./chapter7_oabDelete.php");
               break;
         }
   }
```

The preceding code uses the PHP switch() function to handle the $tab and optional $contactID parameters that may be passed in. You have case statements for all of the letters of the alphabet; a question mark, which represents your need to display the search form; and add, edit, and delete, which call upon the code you did earlier that handles the adding, editing, and deleting of contacts and their information. But what happens if you don't pass in a value for $tab? In that case, you either passed in no parameters at all—for instance, when you first accessed your address book—or you passed in a $contactID so you can view the contact, as shown here:

```
  else
   {
      if($contactID)
      {
         include("./chapter7_oabView.php");
      }
      else
      {
         include("./chapter7_oabSearch.php");
      }
   }
?>
               <!-- End of tab content -->
```

And this rounds out our PHP code. There is a small portion of HTML at the end of your file and then you're through. You want to provide a means for the user to click tabs and view groups of contacts based on a letter. You can do this by having separate images that are linked back to your PHP code and passing in a value for $tab. Here's how you'll do it:

```
</td>
      </tr>
      </table>
   </td>
   <td width="25" bgcolor="#ffffff" valign="top">
      <!-- Start tab listing -->
      <a href="./chapter7_oab.php?tab=a-b"><img src="./ab_tab.gif" border="0"></a><br>
      <a href="./chapter7_oab.php?tab=c-d"><img src="./cd_tab.gif" border="0"></a><br>
      <a href="./chapter7_oab.php?tab=e-f"><img src="./ef_tab.gif" border="0"></a><br>
      <a href="./chapter7_oab.php?tab=g-h"><img src="./gh_tab.gif" border="0"></a><br>
      <a href="./chapter7_oab.php?tab=i-j"><img src="./ij_tab.gif" border="0"></a><br>
      <a href="./chapter7_oab.php?tab=k-l"><img src="./kl_tab.gif" border="0"></a><br>
      <a href="./chapter7_oab.php?tab=m-n"><img src="./mn_tab.gif" border="0"></a><br>
      <a href="./chapter7_oab.php?tab=o-p"><img src="./op_tab.gif" border="0"></a><br>
      <a href="./chapter7_oab.php?tab=q-r"><img src="./qr_tab.gif" border="0"></a><br>
      <a href="./chapter7_oab.php?tab=s-t"><img src="./st_tab.gif" border="0"></a><br>
      <a href="./chapter7_oab.php?tab=u-v"><img src="./uv_tab.gif" border="0"></a><br>
      <a href="./chapter7_oab.php?tab=w-x"><img src="./wx_tab.gif" border="0"></a><br>
      <a href="./chapter7_oab.php?tab=y-z"><img src="./yz_tab.gif" border="0"></a><br>
      <a href="./chapter7_oab.php?tab=?"><img src="./search_tab.gif" border="0"></a>
      <!-- End tab listing -->
   </td>
</tr>
<tr><td colspan="3"><img src="./oab_bottomborder.gif" border="0"></td></tr>
</table>
</body>
</html>
```

As you'll note, you finish closing up your table and end your HTML document. You should now be able to fully test your online address book!

Implementing Your Online Address Book

Assuming your web server is configured correctly to handle PHP scripts, and you've set up your MySQL database and created the needed table correctly, it should be a simple matter of placing all of the PHP scripts in a directory under your web server document root directory, and calling the main PHP script (chapter7_oab.php) from a web browser. In the screen shots in the example, we logged in to our host machine, created our database and table, and then placed all of our files in a directory under our document root, /www/htdocs/oab/, and subsequently called these scripts via our web browser like so: http://twoheadedcow/oab/chapter7_oab.php.

Testing and Debugging the Address Book

When you first call your online address book, you don't need to specify any parameters. The code is designed to start by displaying the search form. From there, you can either search for a contact or click one of the tabs to the right to display your contacts. The error checking in the code is very simplistic. For the most part, it merely checks to make sure you connected to the database, and that when you add or edit a contact, a first and last name are specified.

Limitations and Additional Features

While the type of information and functionality of the online address book is very simple, there is plenty of room to add or change the fields and type of information you keep on each contact. If nothing else, you've built a nice groundwork that you can expand upon.

What to Take Away

This chapter showed you how to create a basic database in MySQL and add, edit, and delete information from it via PHP. With the exception of the custom function that alternated the cell backgrounds on contact listings, you used functions that were readily available, both from PHP directly and from some of the MySQL PHP database functions. You should have a general idea of what it takes to interact with a database and display the information it contains on the Web.

PART

IV

PHP Sessions and Authentication

OBJECTIVES

- Design a database for your store
- Build web-based forms to manage your products
- Create a menu system to navigate your store administration
- Create a web-based front for your store
- Implement a way to show your products
- Design a shopping cart for your customers

CHAPTER

8

PHP Online Store Administration

IN THIS CHAPTER:

chapter8_dbconnect.php—Connects you to the database
chapter8_dbdisconnect.php—Disconnects you from the database
chapter8_storeAdminAuth.php—Logs the store owner into the store
chapter8_storeAdminHome.php—The Admin Menu home page
chapter8_storeAdminMenu.php—The main file that contains all of your menu and component controls
chapter8_storeAdminOrdersDelete.php—The code to cancel or delete an order
chapter8_storeAdminOrdersView.php—All of the code needed to view and process orders
chapter8_storeAdminProdCatAdd.php—Adds a product category
chapter8_storeAdminProdCatDelete.php—Deletes a product category
chapter8_storeAdminProdCatEdit.php—Allows you to edit a product category
chapter8_storeAdminProductsAdd.php—Adds a product
chapter8_storeAdminProductsDelete.php—Deletes a product
chapter8_storeAdminProductsEdit.php—Allows you to edit a product

In Chapters 8 and 9, you'll build a very basic online store. We will cover some of the concepts and considerations surrounding setting up and running a store. For simplicity's sake, we will exclude the actual credit card processing and secure server setup, as this varies widely in the realm of e-commerce, and the topics can take up entire books. This exercise is merely intended to give you a general idea of what might go into an online store.

In this chapter, you will cover the administrative side of the store. You'll create a simple database to house the needed information, create forms to handle the management of products and product categories, and set a framework in place to view and process orders received on the site. The end result will look similar to that shown in Figure 8-1.

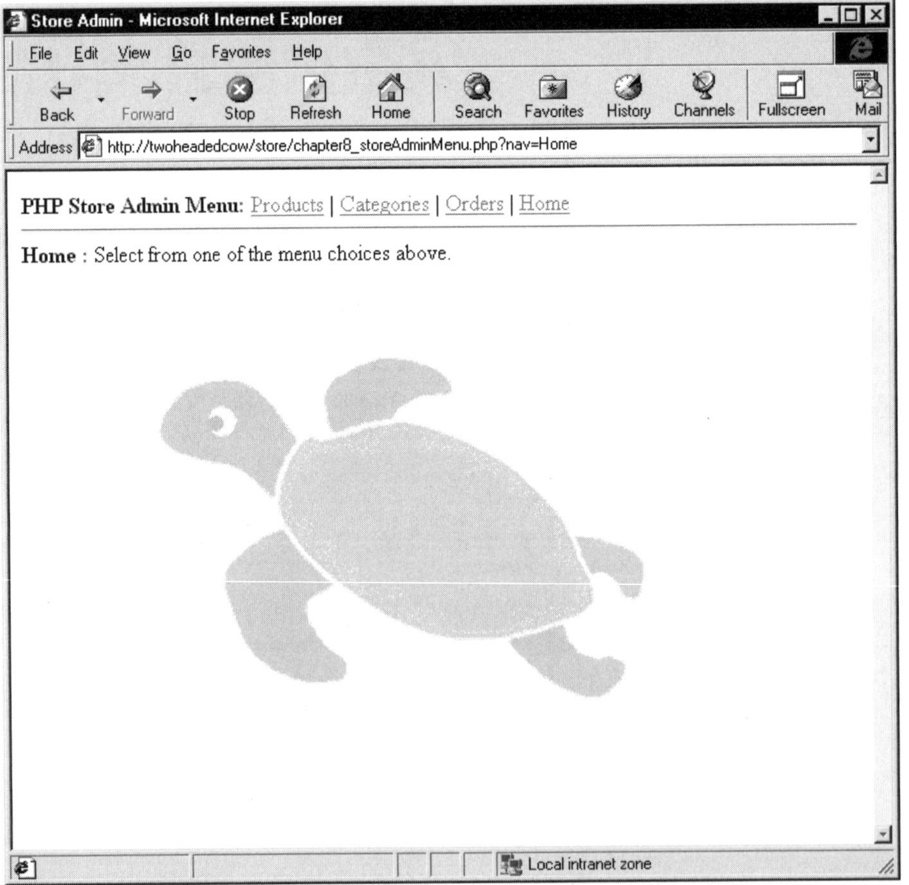

Figure 8-1 *PHP online store administration*

Online Store Administration Requirements

Your online store will have the capability to store information about the different products you plan to sell and their categories, as well as keep track of orders from people who purchase these products. To keep things simple, a secure web server and a third-party credit card processor will not be needed. You will need access to an Apache web server with PHP and MySQL installed, and you'll need the ability to log in and create a database and table.

Designing and Implementing the Online Store Administration

You'll want to start off by creating a database and table to store the information about your products and orders. All of the components of the store administration will be modular, in the sense that the code for connecting to the database, adding, editing, deleting, viewing, and searching on your products and orders will be contained in separate PHP files. All of the files will be called upon in a master PHP file that controls which modules are processed.

If you are already logged into the machine and at a shell prompt, you can begin as follows:

```
create database store;
use store;
```

Now that your database is created, create the needed tables to store the information. Begin with your product table, as follows:

```
create table storeProduct
(
productID int primary key auto_increment,
productName varchar(50),
productCategory int,
productDescription varchar(200),
productImage varchar(100),
productPrice varchar(10),
productInventory varchar(10)
);
```

Next on our list is a product category table. This will allow you to group your products into relevant categories. The code is as follows:

```
create table storeProductCategory(
productcategoryID int primary key auto_increment,
productcategoryName varchar(50)
);
```

Now you need to make room for some basic customer information. In a real-world situation, the information you keep on each customer would be far more expansive, but let's keep it simple:

```
create table storeCustomer(
customerID int primary key auto_increment,
customerUserID  varchar(20),
customerPassword varchar(20),
customerName varchar(50),
customerAddress1 varchar(50),
customerAddress2 varchar(50),
customerCity varchar(30),
customerState varchar(3),
customerZip varchar(12),
customerEmail varchar(50),
customerPhone varchar(20),
customerCardNumber varchar(50),
customerCardType varchar(10),
customerCardExpire varchar(8)
);
```

Now let's create a table to keep track of orders. Each order item will get a unique ID, along with an order number, customer ID, product ID, and quantity. The code is as follows:

```
create table storeOrders(
orderID int primary key auto_increment,
orderNumber varchar(10),
orderStatus varchar(20),
orderCustomerID int,
orderProductID int,
orderQuantity int
);
```

And last but not least, you need to store the administrator's user name and password. You will use this table to make sure the person accessing the site is the store owner. Here's the code:

```
create table storeAdmin(
adminID int primary key auto_increment,
adminUserID varchar(20),
adminPassword varchar(20)
);
```

With your tables out of the way, let's go ahead and populate two of the tables with some default information to get things started:

```
insert into storeAdmin(adminUserID, adminPassword)
values
('admin', 'mystore');
insert into storeProductCategory(productcategoryName)
 values
('Other');
```

Note that we created a default product category and admin user name and password. This will allow you to get started running your store once you finish the coding in this chapter.

To begin your coding, let's make provisions for connecting and disconnecting from the database, as shown here:

chapter8_dbconnect.php

```
<?
   $mysql_link = mysql_connect("localhost", "root", "")
 or die
("<p>Could not connect to the database!");
   mysql_select_db("store", $mysql_link)
or die
("<p>Could not select the database!");
?>
```

You will need to be able to disconnect from the database as well, like so:

chapter8_dbdisconnect.php

```
<?
   mysql_close($mysql_link);
?>
```

Now that talking to your database is out of the way, you can begin to develop a framework for the store administration. One of the most important parts of this is being able to authenticate a user, as you wouldn't want just anyone controlling your store. For this you will use one of the many wonderful features of the Apache Web Server, and prompt a user for the administrator name and password. If correct, they can continue; if incorrect, an error is displayed. The code follows along the lines listed here:

chapter8_storeAdminAuth.php

```
<?
$AdminPage = "./chapter8_storeAdminMenu.php";
if (!isset($PHP_AUTH_USER) || $unauthorized)
{
   $realm = "MyPHPStore_".time();
   Header("WWW-Authenticate: Basic realm=\"$realm\"");
   Header("Status: HTTP/1.0 401 Unauthorized");
   print "<h1>401 Unauthorized</h1>Unable to authorize you. Please <a
   href=\"$AdminPage\">click here</a> to try again.";
   exit;
}
else
{
   include("./chapter8_dbconnect.php");
   $query = "select * from storeAdmin
where
adminUserID = '$PHP_AUTH_USER'
 and
adminPassword = '$PHP_AUTH_PW'";
   $mysql_result = mysql_query($query, $mysql_link);

   if(mysql_affected_rows() == 0)
   {
      header("Location: ".$AdminPage."?unauthorized=1");
      exit();
   }
   else
   {
   }
   include("./chapter8_dbdisconnect.php");
}
?>
```

Note how you take the name and password entered, and compare it to what is contained in your storeAdmin table. If you find a match, you continue on, otherwise you'll display an error message. Now that you have a means to verify an administrative user, you'll need a menu system to control access to the store administration features. Since this will be the brains of your operation, let's step through each section of code:

chapter8_storeAdminMenu.php

```
<?
include("./chapter8_storeAdminAuth.php");
print("<html>\n");
print("<head>\n");
print("<title>Store Admin</title>\n");
print("</head>\n");
print("<body background=\"./turtle_bg_admin.gif\" text=\"#000000\"
bgcolor=\"#ffffff\" link=\"#2FB472\" alink=\"#2FB472\"
vlink=\"#2FB472\">\n");
```

You begin simply enough, just your basic beginning HTML tags to start off. Next you will need to provide links for the user to click to access the features of the store:

```
print("<p><b>PHP Store Admin Menu:</b>
 <a href=\"./chapter8_storeAdminMenu.php?nav=Products\">Products</a> |
 <a href=\"./chapter8_storeAdminMenu.php?nav=Category\">Categories</a> |
 <a href=\"./chapter8_storeAdminMenu.php?nav=Orders\">Orders</a> |
 <a href=\"./chapter8_storeAdminMenu.php?nav=Home\">Home</a>");
print("<hr>\n");
```

As you can see, you now have links to products, categories, orders, and the beginning home page. Note how in the query string you pass in a value for the variable $nav. You'll use this to include various PHP code files that handle these features. One of the easiest ways to do this is with the PHP switch() function, as follows:

```
if($nav == '')
{
 $nav = "Home";
}
printf("<b>%s : </b>", $nav);

switch ($nav)
{
```

```
case "Home":
   include("./chapter8_storeAdminHome.php");
   break;
```

In case the user requests the home page, you're including the PHP file chapter8_storeAdminHome.php, which contains the code for the home page. We will get to this file and others after we complete the menu system. The menu system code continues:

```
case "Products":
   print("<a
href=\"./chapter8_storeAdminMenu.php?nav=Products&action=Add\">Add</a> | ");
     print("<a href=\"./
     chapter8_storeAdminMenu.php?nav=Products&action=Edit\">Edit</a> | ");
     print("<a href=\"./
     chapter8_storeAdminMenu.php?nav=Products&action=Delete\">Delete</a>");
     if($action == ''){$action = "Edit"; }
   switch ($action)
   {
        case "Add":
      include("./chapter8_storeAdminProductsAdd.php");
          break;
        case "Edit":
      include("./chapter8_storeAdminProductsEdit.php");
          break;
        case "Delete":
      include("./chapter8_storeAdminProductsDelete.php");
          break;
     }
   break;
```

The preceding code includes the PHP scripts for adding, editing, and deleting products. Note that you're now also checking for a second parameter in the query string called $action. This method will be used through this particular PHP script for the other administrative menu features.

Your next snip of code covers the adding, editing, and deleting of categories:

```
case "Category":
   print("<a href=\"./
   chapter8_storeAdminMenu.php?nav=Category&action=Add\">Add</a> | ");
   print("<a href=\"./
   chapter8_storeAdminMenu.php?nav=Category&action=Edit\">Edit</a> | ");
```

```
    print("<a href=\"./
    chapter8_storeAdminMenu.php?nav=Category&action=Delete\">Delete</a>");
    if($action == ''){$action = "Edit"; }
  switch ($action)
  {
       case "Add":
     include("./chapter8_storeAdminProdCatAdd.php");
         break;
       case "Edit":
     include("./chapter8_storeAdminProdCatEdit.php");
         break;
       case "Delete":
     include("./chapter8_storeAdminProdCatDelete.php");
         break;
    }
  break;
```

Your last menu feature is order processing. Here is the code that will handle this:

```
case "Orders":
   print("<a href=\"./
   chapter8_storeAdminMenu.php?nav=Orders&action=View\">View -
   Process</a>");
     if($action == ''){$action = "View"; }
   switch ($action)
   {
        case "View":
      include("./chapter8_storeAdminOrdersView.php");
          break;
     }
   switch ($action)
   {
        case "Delete":
      include("./chapter8_storeAdminOrdersDelete.php");
          break;
     }
   break;
}
```

To finish out the menu code, you close your HTML document as follows:

```
print("\n</body>\n");
print("</html>");
?>
```

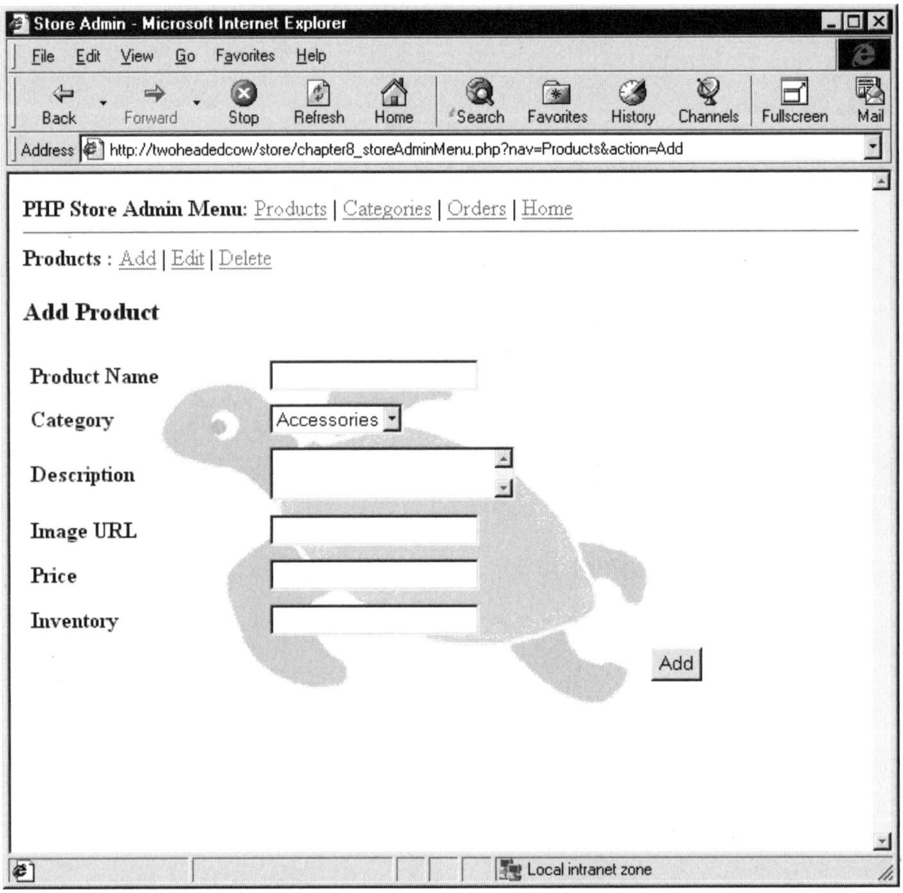

Figure 8-2 *PHP online store administration—adding products*

Now that you have a basic framework in place, let's cover each feature in more detail. We begin with the addition of products. The end result will look like Figure 8-2. The code for this is as follows:

chapter8_storeAdminProductsAdd.php

```
<?
if($submit)
{
   print("<h3>Adding Product...</h3>");
   printf("Product: <b>%s</b><br>\n", $productName);
```

```
    printf("Category: <b>%s</b><br>\n", $productCategory);
    printf("Description: <b>%s</b><br>\n", $productDescription);
    printf("Image: <br><img src=\"%s\"><br>\n", $productImage);
    printf("Price: <b>%s</b><br>\n", $productPrice);
    printf("Inventory: <b>%s</b>\n", $productInventory);
    include("./chapter8_dbconnect.php");
    $query = "insert into storeProduct (
productName,
productCategory,
productDescription,
productImage,
productPrice,
productInventory
) values (
'$productName',
'$productCategory',
'$productDescription',
'$productImage',
'$productPrice',
'$productInventory'
)";
    $mysql_result = mysql_query($query, $mysql_link);
    include("./chapter8_dbdisconnect.php");
}
else
{
    print("<h3>Add Product</h3>");
    print("<form action=\"./chapter8_storeAdminMenu.php\">");
    print("<table width=\"500\" border=\"0\" cellpadding=\"3\">\n");
    print("<tr><td><b>Product Name</b></td>
    <td><input type=\"text\" name=\"productName\"></td></tr>\n");
    print("<tr><td><b>Category</b></td><td>\n");
    print("<select name=\"productCategory\">");
    include("./chapter8_dbconnect.php");
    $query = "select * from storeProductCategory order by
    productcategoryName";
    $mysql_result = mysql_query($query, $mysql_link);
    while($row = mysql_fetch_row($mysql_result))
    {
       printf("<option value=\"%s\">%s", $row[0], $row[1]);
    }
    include("./chapter8_dbdisconnect.php");
    print("</select>\n");
```

```
    print("</td></tr>\n");
    print("<tr><td><b>Description</b></td>
    <td><textarea name=\"productDescription\"></textarea></td></tr>\n");
    print("<tr><td><b>Image URL</b></td><td><input type=\"text\"
    name=\"productImage\"></td></tr>\n");
    print("<tr><td><b>Price</b></td><td><input type=\"text\"
    name=\"productPrice\"></td></tr>\n");
    print("<tr><td><b>Inventory</b></td><td><input type=\"text\"
    name=\"productInventory\"></td></tr>\n");
    print("<input type=\"hidden\" name=\"nav\" value=\"Products\">");
    print("<input type=\"hidden\" name=\"action\" value=\"Add\">");
    print("<tr><td colspan=\"2\" align=\"right\"><input
    type=\"submit\" name=\"submit\" value=\"Add\"></td></tr>");
    print("</table>");
    print("</form>");
}
?>
```

As you can see, you have a simple HTML form to handle input of product information and insert the data into the database. Note that you pass back the $nav and $action values as well, so in your menu code the proper PHP file gets included. The end result will look like Figure 8-3. The next piece of code is for editing that product information, as follows:

chapter8_storeAdminProductsEdit.php

```
<?
if($submit)
{
    print("<h3>Updating Product...</h3>");
    printf("Product: <b>%s</b><br>\n", $productName);
    printf("Category: <b>%s</b><br>\n", $productCategory);
    printf("Description: <b>%s</b><br>\n", $productDescription);
    printf("Image: <br><img src=\"%s\"><br>\n", $productImage);
    printf("Price: <b>%s</b><br>\n", $productPrice);
    printf("Inventory: <b>%s</b>\n", $productInventory);
    include("./chapter8_dbconnect.php");
    $query = "update storeProduct set
productName = '$productName',
productCategory = '$productCategory',
productDescription = '$productDescription', ";
```

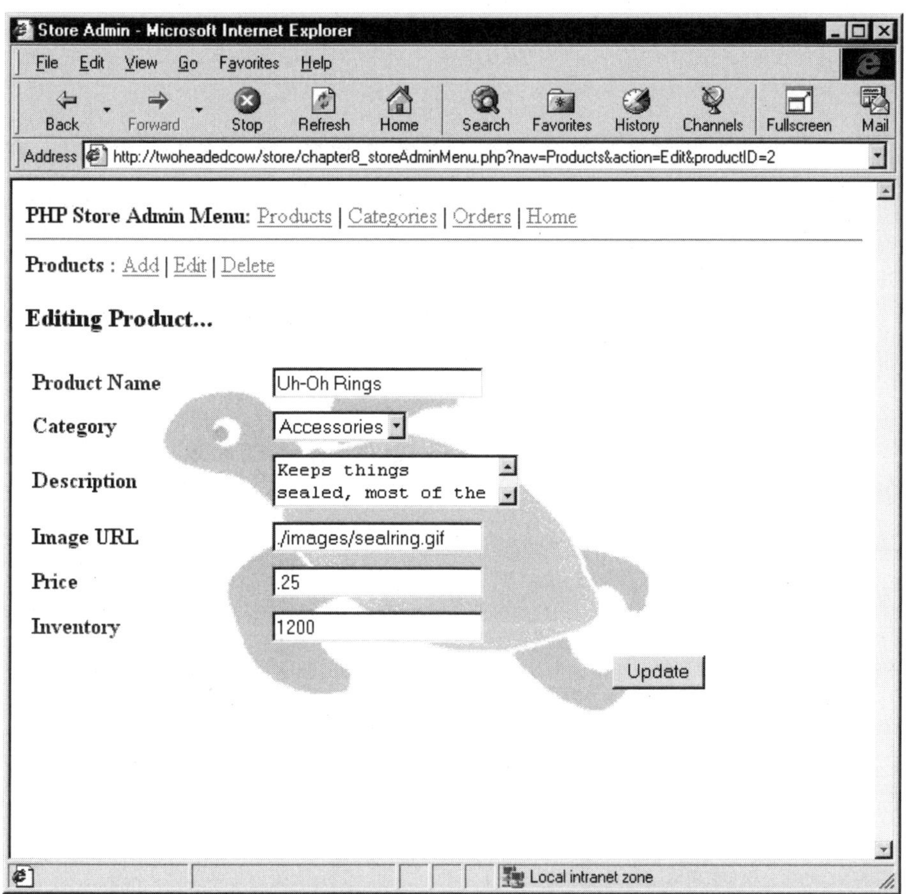

Figure 8-3 *PHP online store administration—editing products*

```
   $query .= "productImage = '$productImage',
 productPrice = '$productPrice',
productInventory = '$productInventory'
where productID = '$productID'";
   $mysql_result = mysql_query($query, $mysql_link);
   include("./chapter8_dbdisconnect.php");
}
else
{
   if($productID)
```

```
{
   include("./chapter8_dbconnect.php");
   $query = "select * from storeProduct
   where storeProduct.productID  = '$productID'";
   $queryCat = "select * from storeProductCategory
   order by productcategoryName";
   $mysql_result = mysql_query($query, $mysql_link);
   $mysql_resultCat = mysql_query($queryCat, $mysql_link);
   while($row = mysql_fetch_row($mysql_result))
   {
      print("<h3>Editing Product...</h3>");
      print("<form action=\"./chapter8_storeAdminMenu.php\">");
      print("<table width=\"500\" border=\"0\"
      cellpadding=\"3\">\n");
      printf("<tr><td><b>Product Name</b></td>
      <td><input type=\"text\" name=\"productName\"
      value=\"%s\"></td></tr>\n", $row[1]);
      print("<tr><td><b>Category</b></td><td>\n");
      print("<select name=\"productCategory\">");
      while($rowCat = mysql_fetch_row($mysql_resultCat))
      {
             if($row[2] == $rowCat[0])
               {
            printf("<option value=\"%s\" selected>%s", $rowCat[0],
            $rowCat[1]);
               }
               else
               {
            printf("<option value=\"%s\">%s", $rowCat[0],
            $rowCat[1]);
               }
      }
      print("</select>\n");
      print("</td></tr>\n");
      printf("<tr><td><b>Description</b></td><td><textarea
      name=\"productDescription\">%s</textarea></td></tr>\n", $row[3]);
      printf("<tr><td><b>Image URL</b></td><td><input
      type=\"text\" name=\"productImage\" value=\"%s\"></td></tr>\n",
      $row[4]);
      printf("<tr><td><b>Price</b></td><td><input type=\"text\"
      name=\"productPrice\" value=\"%s\"></td></tr>\n", $row[5]);
      printf("<tr><td><b>Inventory</b></td><td><input
```

```
        type=\"text\" name=\"productInventory\" value=\"%s\"></td></tr>\n",
        $row[6]);
        print("<input type=\"hidden\" name=\"nav\"
        value=\"Products\">");
        print("<input type=\"hidden\" name=\"action\"
        value=\"Edit\">");
        printf("<input type=\"hidden\" name=\"productID\"
        value=\"%s\">", $productID);
        print("<tr><td colspan=\"2\" align=\"right\"><input
        type=\"submit\" name=\"submit\" value=\"Update\"></td></tr>");
        print("</table>");
        print("</form>");
    }
    include("./chapter8_dbdisconnect.php");
  }
  else
  {
    print("<h3>Edit Product</h3>");
      include("./chapter8_dbconnect.php");
    $query = "select * from storeProduct,
storeProductCategory
where storeProduct.productCategory = storeProductCategory.
productcategoryID order by productcategoryName";
    $mysql_result = mysql_query($query, $mysql_link);
      print("<ul>\n");
    while($row = mysql_fetch_row($mysql_result))
    {
        printf("<li><a
 href=\"chapter8_storeAdminMenu.php?nav=Products&action=Edit&productID
=%s\">[%s] - %s</a>", $row[0], $row[8], $row[1]);
    }
      print("</ul>\n");
    include("./chapter8_dbdisconnect.php");
  }
}
?>
```

As you can see, there are three aspects of editing product information. You had to list all of the products, and then select a specific product and use its $productID to pull the specific information from the database. You also included your $nav and $action values for the menu system. The end result will look like Figure 8-4. Last but not least for product-related code is deletion, as follows:

chapter8_storeAdminProductsDelete.php

```
<?
if($submit)
{
   print("<h3>Deleting Product...</h3>");
   printf("Product: <b>%s</b><br>\n", $productName);
   include("./chapter8_dbconnect.php");
   $query = "delete from storeProduct where productID = '$productID'";
   $mysql_result = mysql_query($query, $mysql_link);
```

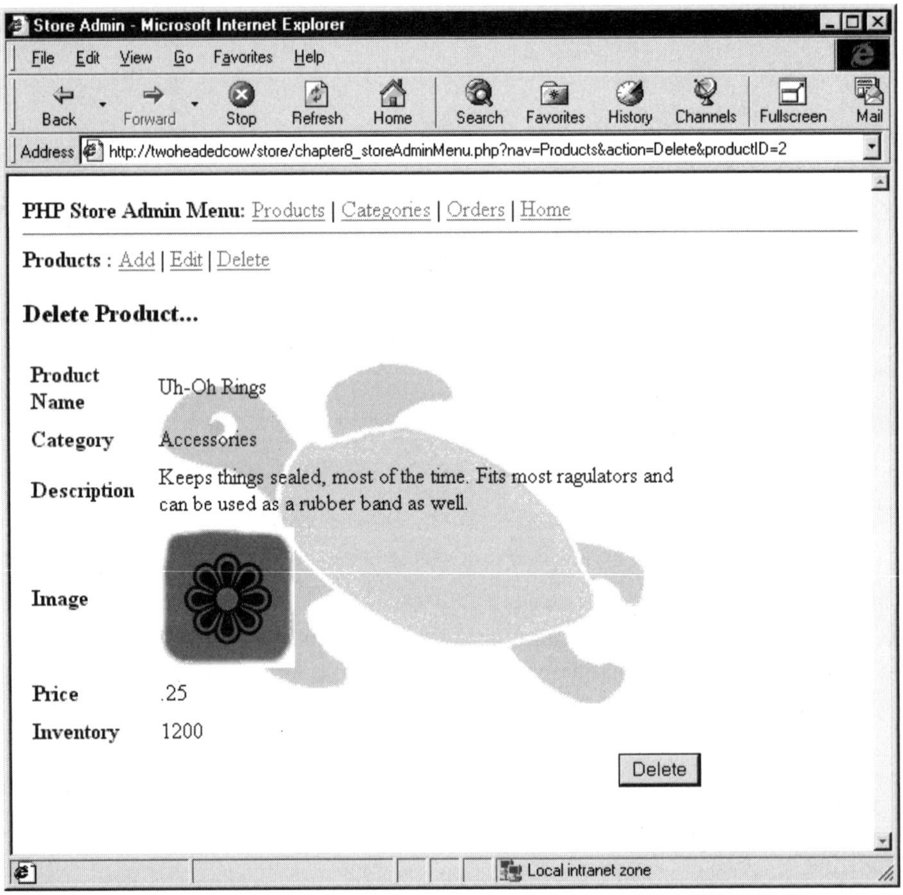

Figure 8-4 *PHP online store administration—deleting products*

```
   include("./chapter8_dbdisconnect.php");
}
else
{
   if($productID)
   {
      include("./chapter8_dbconnect.php");
      $query = "select * from storeProduct, storeProductCategory where
      storeProduct.productID  = '$productID' and
      storeProductCategory.productcategoryID = storeProduct.productCategory";
      $mysql_result = mysql_query($query, $mysql_link);
      while($row = mysql_fetch_row($mysql_result))
      {
         print("<h3>Delete Product...</h3>");
         print("<form action=\"./chapter8_storeAdminMenu.php\">");
         print("<table width=\"500\" border=\"0\" cellpadding=\"3\">\n");
         printf("<tr><td><b>Product Name</b></td><td>%s</td></tr>\n",
         $row[1]);
         printf("<tr><td><b>Category</b></td><td>%s</td></tr>\n",
         $row[8]);
         printf("<tr><td><b>Description</b></td><td>%s</td></tr>\n",
         $row[3]);
         printf("<tr><td><b>Image</b></td><td><img
         src=\"%s\"></td></tr>\n", $row[4]);
         printf("<tr><td><b>Price</b></td><td>%s</td></tr>\n", $row[5]);
         printf("<tr><td><b>Inventory</b></td><td>%s</td></tr>\n",
         $row[6]);
         print("<input type=\"hidden\" name=\"nav\"
         value=\"Products\">");
         print("<input type=\"hidden\" name=\"action\"
         value=\"Delete\">");
         printf("<input type=\"hidden\" name=\"productID\"
         value=\"%s\">", $productID);
         printf("<input type=\"hidden\" name=\"productName\"
         value=\"%s\">", $row[1]);
         print("<tr><td colspan=\"2\" align=\"right\"><input
         type=\"submit\" name=\"submit\" value=\"Delete\"></td></tr>");
         print("</table>");
         print("</form>");
      }
      include("./chapter8_dbdisconnect.php");
   }
   else
   {
```

```
      print("<h3>Delete Product</h3>");
        include("./chapter8_dbconnect.php");
      $query = "select * from storeProduct,
storeProductCategory where storeProduct.
productCategory = storeProductCategory.productcategoryID
order by productcategoryName";
      $mysql_result = mysql_query($query, $mysql_link);
        print("<ul>\n");
      while($row = mysql_fetch_row($mysql_result))
      {
         printf("<li><ahref=\"
         chapter8_storeAdminMenu.php?nav=Products&action=Delete&productID=%
         s\">[%s] - %s</a>", $row[0], $row[8], $row[1]);
      }
        print("</ul>\n");
      include("./chapter8_dbdisconnect.php");
   }
}
?>
```

Again, there are three parts to this code: listing the products, the selection of a specific product, and the deletion from the database. It's also possible that a fourth block of code could be developed for this, to prompt the user to confirm deletion before actually doing it.

With products out of the way, we'll move on to the product categories. You may have noticed we associate categories with each particular product. The end result will look like Figure 8-5. Let's begin this code with the capability to add a category, as follows:

chapter8_storeAdminProdCatAdd.php

```
<?
if($submit)
{
   print("<h3>Adding Product Category...</h3>");
   printf("Category: <b>%s</b><br>\n", $productcategoryName);
   include("./chapter8_dbconnect.php");
   $query = "insert into storeProductCategory (productcategoryName)
 values ('$productcategoryName')";
   $mysql_result = mysql_query($query, $mysql_link);
   include("./chapter8_dbdisconnect.php");
}
else
{
```

```
    print("<h3>Add Product Category</h3>");
    print("<form action=\"./chapter8_storeAdminMenu.php\">");
    print("<table width=\"500\" border=\"0\" cellpadding=\"3\">\n");
    print("<tr><td><b>Product Category</b></td>
    <td><input type=\"text\" name=\"productcategoryName\"></td></tr>\n");
    print("<input type=\"hidden\" name=\"nav\" value=\"Category\">");
    print("<input type=\"hidden\" name=\"action\" value=\"Add\">");
    print("<tr><td colspan=\"2\" align=\"right\"><input
    type=\"submit\" name=\"submit\" value=\"Add\"></td></tr>");
    print("</table>");
    print("</form>");
}
?>
```

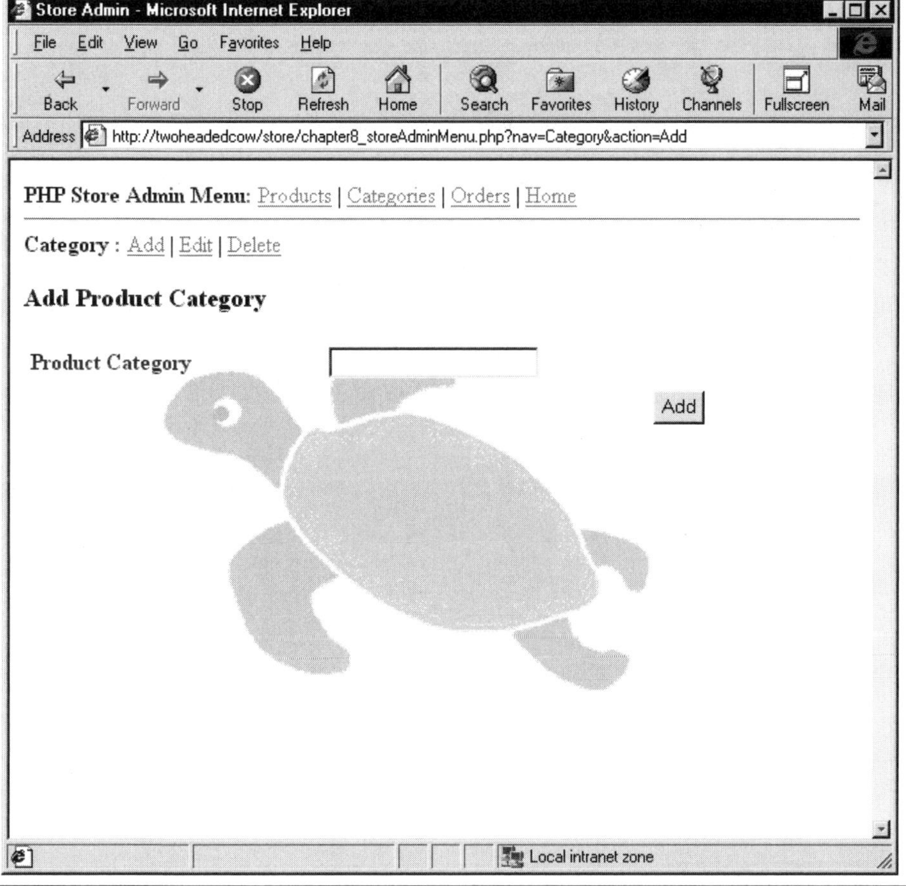

Figure 8-5 *PHP online store administration—adding a category*

That was fairly simple—just a basic form to prompt for values, and then code to insert the data into the database. Next, you need to be able to edit that category. The end result will look like Figure 8-6. The code is as follows:

chapter8_storeAdminProdCatEdit.php

```
<?
if($submit)
{
   print("<h3>Updating Product Category...</h3>");
   printf("Category: <b>%s</b><br>\n", $productcategoryName);
   include("./chapter8_dbconnect.php");
   $query = "update storeProductCategory set productcategoryName =
   '$productcategoryName' where productcategoryID =
```

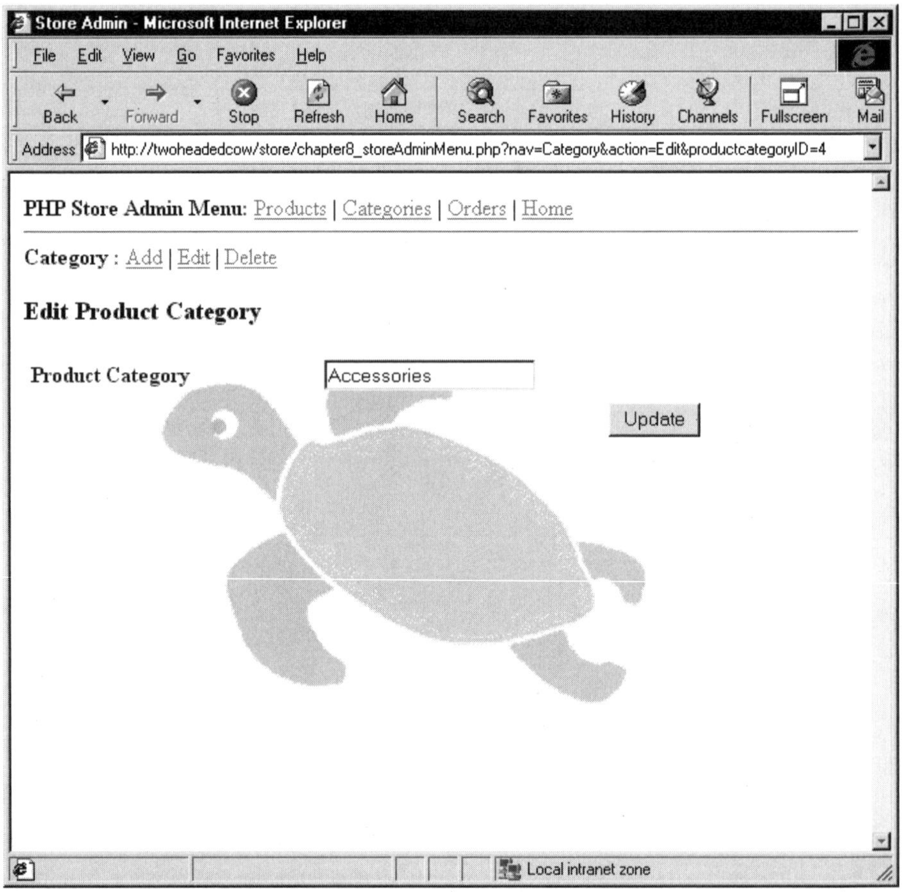

Figure 8-6 *PHP online store administration—editing a category*

```
      '$productcategoryID'";
      $mysql_result = mysql_query($query, $mysql_link);
      include("./chapter8_dbdisconnect.php");
   }
   else
   {
      if($productcategoryID)
      {
         include("./chapter8_dbconnect.php");
         $query = "select * from storeProductCategory
         where productcategoryID = '$productcategoryID'";
         $mysql_result = mysql_query($query, $mysql_link);
         while($row = mysql_fetch_row($mysql_result))
         {
         print("<h3>Edit Product Category</h3>");
         print("<form action=\"./chapter8_storeAdminMenu.php\">");
         print("<table width=\"500\" border=\"0\"
         cellpadding=\"3\">\n");
         printf("<tr><td><b>Product Category</b></td><td><input
         type=\"text\" name=\"productcategoryName\"
         value=\"%s\"></td></tr>\n", $row[1]);
         print("<input type=\"hidden\" name=\"nav\"
         value=\"Category\">");
         print("<input type=\"hidden\" name=\"action\"
         value=\"Edit\">");
         printf("<input type=\"hidden\" name=\"productcategoryID\"
         value=\"%s\">", $productcategoryID);
         print("<tr><td colspan=\"2\" align=\"right\"><input
         type=\"submit\" name=\"submit\" value=\"Update\"></td></tr>");
         print("</table>");
         print("</form>");
         }
         include("./chapter8_dbdisconnect.php");
      }
      else
      {
         print("<h3>Edit Product Category</h3>");
           include("./chapter8_dbconnect.php");
         $query = "select * from storeProductCategory
         order by productcategoryName";
         $mysql_result = mysql_query($query, $mysql_link);
           print("<ul>\n");
         while($row = mysql_fetch_row($mysql_result))
         {
```

```
            printf("<li><a
            href=\"chapter8_storeAdminMenu.php?nav=Category&action=Edit&
            productcategoryID=%s\">%s</a>", $row[0], $row[1]);
        }
          print("</ul>\n");
        include("./chapter8_dbdisconnect.php");
    }
}
?>
```

Just like editing products, product categories have three blocks of code: listing, selecting and editing the category, and updating the database. The end result will look like Figure 8-7. Last for the categories is deletion, as shown next.

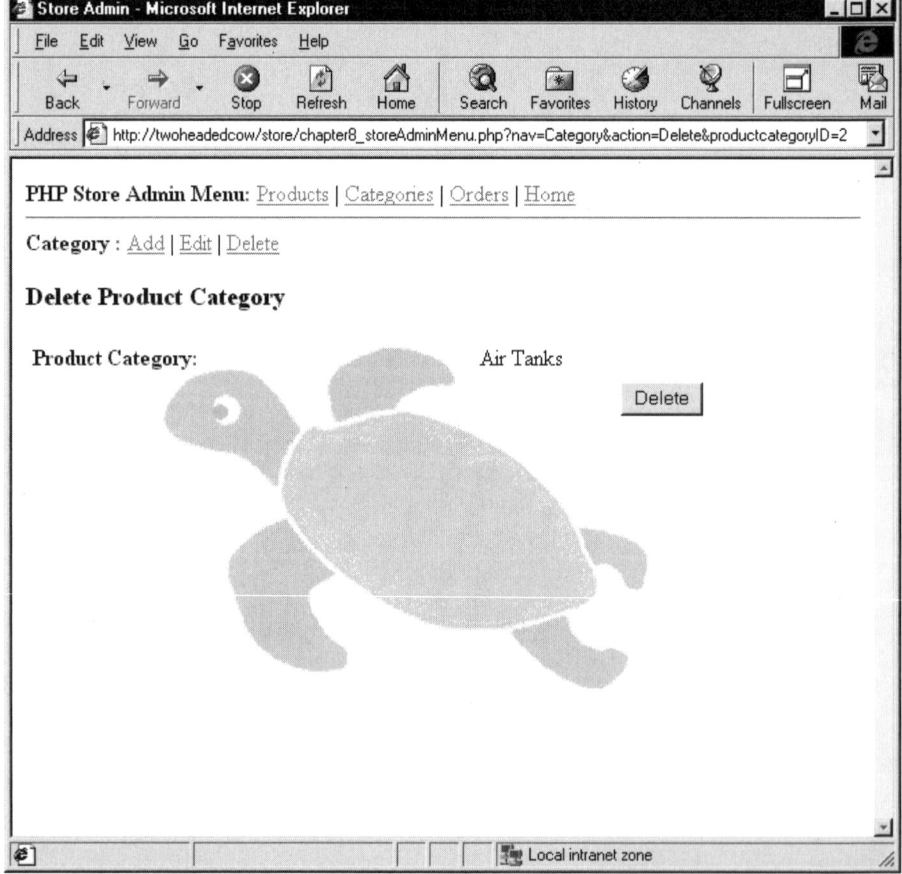

Figure 8-7 *PHP online store administration—deleting a category*

chapter8_storeAdminProCatDelete.php

```
<?
if($submit)
{
   print("<h3>Deleting Product...</h3>");
   printf("Product: <b>%s</b><br>\n", $productName);
   include("./chapter8_dbconnect.php");
   $query = "delete from storeProduct where productID = '$productID'";
   $mysql_result = mysql_query($query, $mysql_link);
   include("./chapter8_dbdisconnect.php");
}
else
{
   if($productID)
   {
      include("./chapter8_dbconnect.php");
      $query = "select * from storeProduct, storeProductCategory
      where storeProduct.productID  = '$productID' and
      storeProductCategory.productcategoryID =
      storeProduct.productCategory";
      $mysql_result = mysql_query($query, $mysql_link);
      while($row = mysql_fetch_row($mysql_result))
      {
         print("<h3>Delete Product...</h3>");
         print("<form action=\"./chapter8_storeAdminMenu.php\">");
         print("<table width=\"500\" border=\"0\"
         cellpadding=\"3\">\n");
         printf("<tr><td><b>Product Name</b></td><td>%s</td></tr>\n",
         $row[1]);
         printf("<tr><td><b>Category</b></td><td>%s</td></tr>\n",
         $row[8]);
         printf("<tr><td><b>Description</b></td><td>%s</td></tr>\n",
         $row[3]);
         printf("<tr><td><b>Image</b></td><td><img
         src=\"%s\"></td></tr>\n", $row[4]);
         printf("<tr><td><b>Price</b></td><td>%s</td></tr>\n",
         $row[5]);
         printf("<tr><td><b>Inventory</b></td><td>%s</td></tr>\n",
         $row[6]);
         print("<input type=\"hidden\" name=\"nav\"
         value=\"Products\">");
```

```
            print("<input type=\"hidden\" name=\"action\"
            value=\"Delete\">");
            printf("<input type=\"hidden\" name=\"productID\"
            value=\"%s\">", $productID);
            printf("<input type=\"hidden\" name=\"productName\"
            value=\"%s\">", $row[1]);
            print("<tr><td colspan=\"2\" align=\"right\"><input
            type=\"submit\" name=\"submit\" value=\"Delete\"></td></tr>");
            print("</table>");
            print("</form>");
        }
        include("./chapter8_dbdisconnect.php");
    }
    else
    {
        print("<h3>Delete Product</h3>");
          include("./chapter8_dbconnect.php");
        $query = "select * from storeProduct, storeProductCategory
        where storeProduct.productCategory = storeProductCategory.productcategoryID
        order by productcategoryName";
        $mysql_result = mysql_query($query, $mysql_link);
          print("<ul>\n");
        while($row = mysql_fetch_row($mysql_result))
        {
            printf("<li><a
            href=\"chapter8_storeAdminMenu.php?nav=Products&action=Delete&product
            ID=%s\">[%s] - %s</a>", $row[0], $row[8], $row[1]);
        }
          print("</ul>\n");
        include("./chapter8_dbdisconnect.php");
    }
}
?>
```

With products and their categories out of the way, we are more than halfway there. Next is the capability to view and process orders, as well as delete them. Some of this code may seem foreign, and we don't really get into creating actual orders and handling customer information until Chapter 9, but just bear with us. The end result will look like Figure 8-8. This code will allow you to view and process orders.

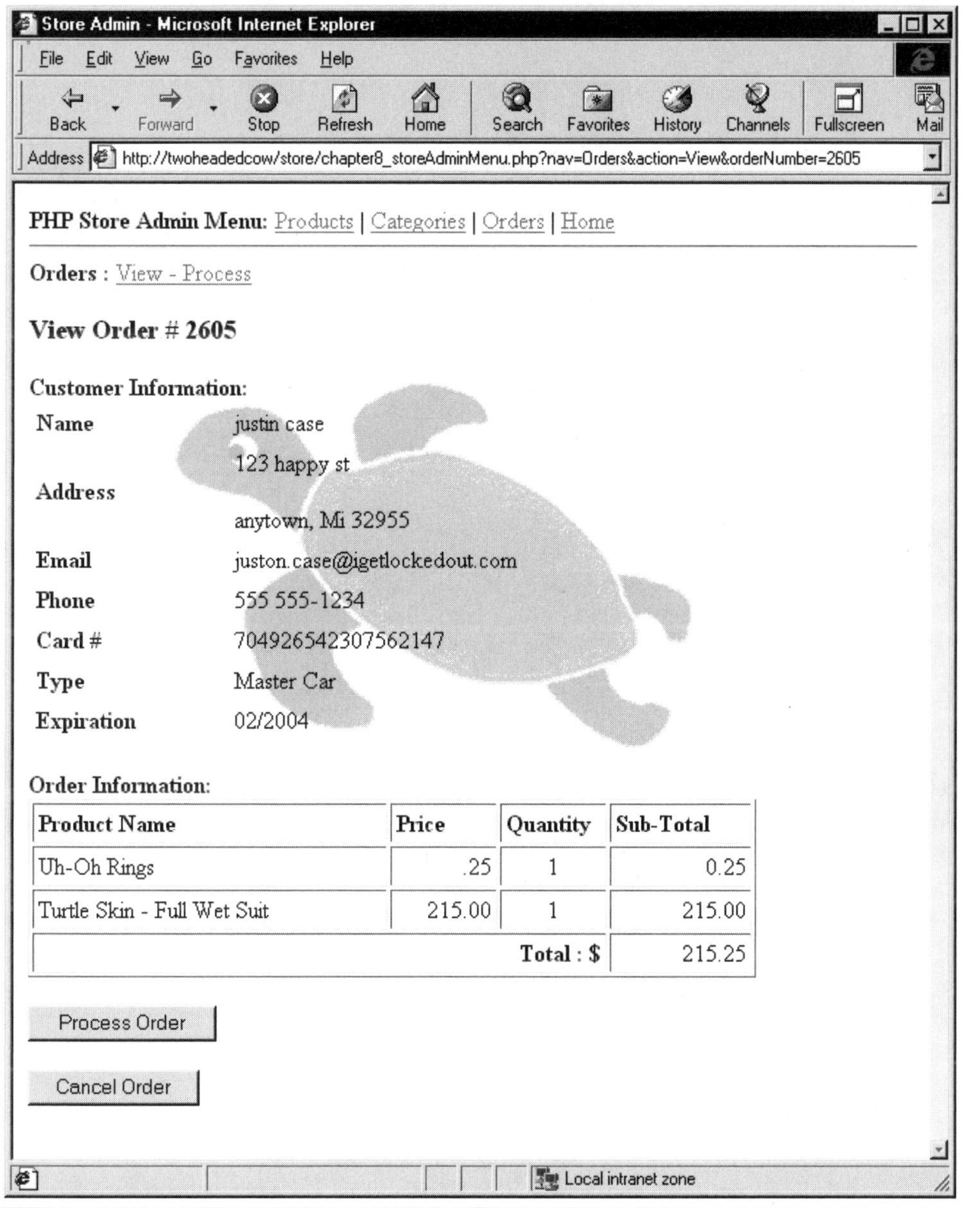

Figure 8-8 *PHP online store administration—processing orders*

chapter8_storeAdminOrdersView.php

```
<?
if($submit)
{
   print("<h3>3rd Party Credit Card Order Processing Goes
   Here...</h3>");
   /* Depending on how you process the order, you would
   more than likely get a confirmation back with whether
   or not the charges were applied. If they are not you'll
   need to display some sort of error message. If the
   charge is approved you can go ahead and notify the
   customer via e-mail about the order, and update
   your database to reflect the order has been processed.
   */
   include("./chapter8_dbconnect.php");
   $query = "update storeOrders set orderStatus = 'Closed' where
   orderNumber = '$orderNumber'";
   $mysql_result = mysql_query($query, $mysql_link);
   print("Order Confimred!");
   include("./chapter8_dbdisconnect.php");
}
```

As noted at the beginning of the chapter, the actual processing and verification of a charge to a credit card can take many forms. The end result will look like Figure 8-9. For this exercise, we will simply pretend the verification went through and move on:

```
else
{
   if($orderNumber)
   {
      $orderTotal = 0;
     printf("<h3>View Order # %s</h3>", $orderNumber);
      print("<b>Customer Information:</b>");
      include("./chapter8_dbconnect.php");
      $query = "select * from storeOrders, storeCustomer where
      storeOrders.orderNumber = '$orderNumber' ";
      $query .= " and storeOrders.orderCustomerID =
      storeCustomer.customerID";
      $mysql_result = mysql_query($query, $mysql_link);
      $row = mysql_fetch_row($mysql_result);
      print("<table width=\"500\" border=\"0\"
      cellpadding=\"3\">\n");
```

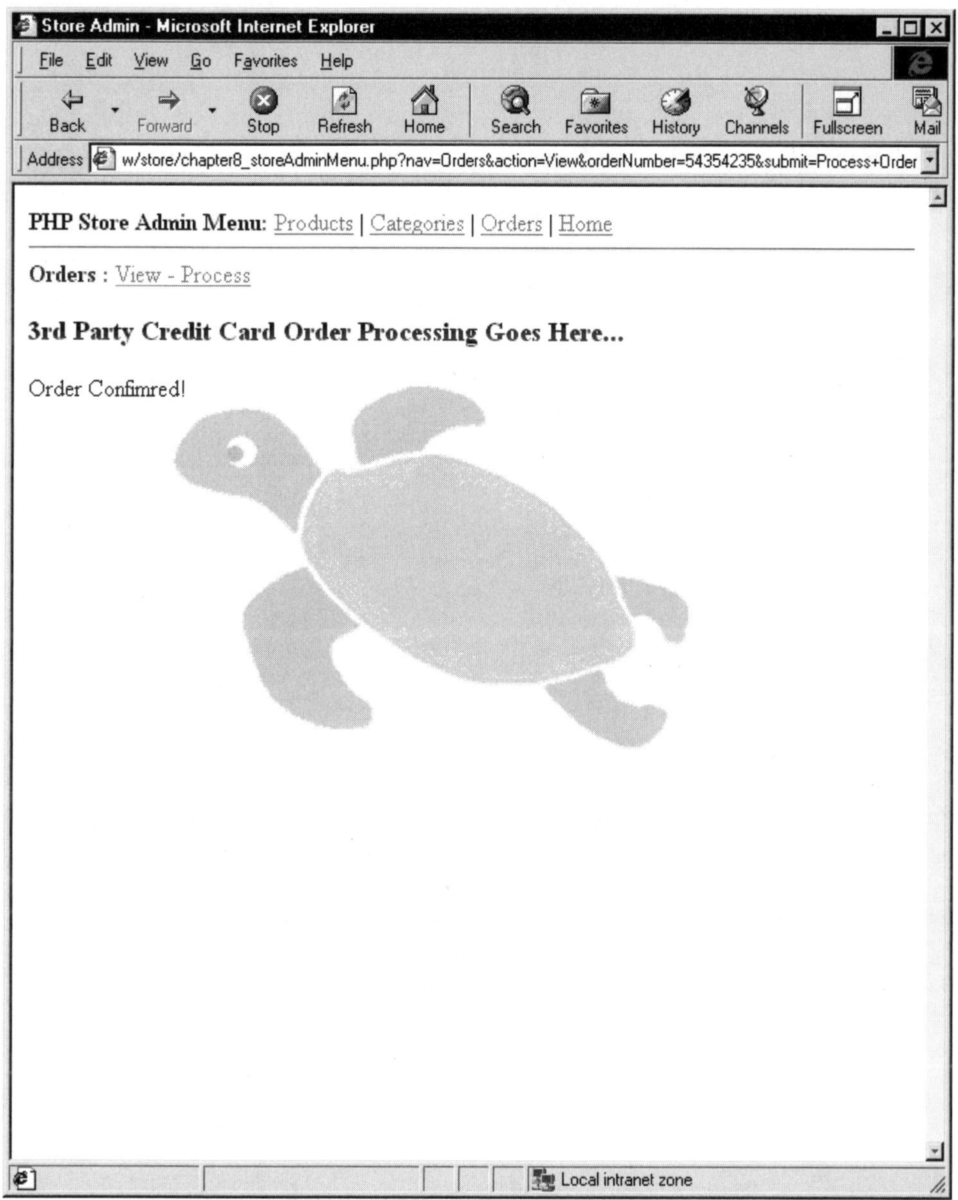

Figure 8-9 *PHP online store administration—viewing orders*

```
printf("<tr><td><b>Name</b></td><td>%s</td></tr>", $row[9]);
printf("<tr><td><b>Address</b></td><td>%s<br>%s<br>%s, %s
%s</td></tr>", $row[10], $row[11], $row[12], $row[13],$row[14]);
printf("<tr><td><b>Email</b></td><td>%s</td></tr>", $row[15]);
printf("<tr><td><b>Phone</b></td><td>%s</td></tr>", $row[16]);
printf("<tr><td><b>Card #</b></td><td>%s</td></tr>", $row[17]);
printf("<tr><td><b>Type</b></td><td>%s</td></tr>", $row[18]);
printf("<tr><td><b>Expiration</b></td><td>%s</td></tr>",
$row[19]);
print("</table>\n");

 print("<p><b>Order Information:</b>");
 $query = "select * from storeOrders, storeProduct where
 storeOrders.orderNumber = '$orderNumber' ";
 $query .= " and storeOrders.orderProductID =
 storeProduct.productID";
 $mysql_result = mysql_query($query, $mysql_link);
 print("<table width=\"500\" border=\"1\"
 cellpadding=\"3\">\n");
 print("<tr><td width=\"50%\"><b>Product Name</b></td>
 <td width=\"15%\"><b>Price</b></td><td
 width=\"15%\"><b>Quantity</b></td>
 <td width=\"20%\"><b>Sub-Total</b></td></tr>\n");
 while($row = mysql_fetch_row($mysql_result))
 {
  $itemSubTotal = ($row[11] * $row[5]);
  $itemSubTotal = number_format($itemSubTotal, 2, '.', '');
  $orderTotal = ($orderTotal + $itemSubTotal);
  $orderTotal = number_format($orderTotal, 2, '.', '');
  print("<tr>\n");
  printf("<td>%s</td><td align=\"right\">%s</td><td
  align=\"center\">%s</td><td align=\"right\">%s</td>", $row[7],
  $row[11], $row[5], $itemSubTotal);
  print("</tr>\n");
 }
 printf("<tr><td colspan=\"3\" align=\"right\"><b>Total :
 $</b></td><td align=\"right\">%s</td></tr>", $orderTotal);
 print("</table>\n");
 include("./chapter8_dbdisconnect.php");
 print("<form action=\"./chapter8_storeAdminMenu.php\">");
```

```
        print("<input type=\"hidden\" name=\"nav\" value=\"Orders\">");
        print("<input type=\"hidden\" name=\"action\"
        value=\"View\">");
        printf("<input type=\"hidden\" name=\"orderNumber\"
        value=\"%s\">",$orderNumber);
        print("<input type=\"submit\" name=\"submit\" value=\"Process
        Order\">");
        print("</form>");
        print("<form action=\"./chapter8_storeAdminMenu.php\">");
        print("<input type=\"hidden\" name=\"nav\" value=\"Orders\">");
        print("<input type=\"hidden\" name=\"action\"
        value=\"Delete\">");
        printf("<input type=\"hidden\" name=\"orderNumber\"
        value=\"%s\">", $orderNumber);
        print("<input type=\"submit\" name=\"submit\" value=\"Cancel
        Order\">");

    }
```

As you can see, you pull the information from the storeOders table, along with customer information from storeCustomer, and calculate the totals for each line item and then the order total. Note the exclusion of any taxes. This could be a good addition to the project once you're done if you'd like to take your store to the next level.

The next piece of code will actually list all of the outstanding orders. You will also generate a total for the orders still being built, and a total for the orders already processed, as follows:

```
    else
    {
        print("<h3>View Orders</h3>");
        include("./chapter8_dbconnect.php");
        $query = "select distinct orderNumber, orderCustomerID,
        orderStatus from storeOrders
        where orderStatus = 'Open'";
        $query .= "order by orderID, orderCustomerID";
        $mysql_result = mysql_query($query, $mysql_link);
        print("<table width=\"500\" border=\"0\"
        cellpadding=\"3\">\n");
        print("<tr><td colspan=\"3\"><b>Open Orders:</b></tr>\n");
        print("<tr><td width=\"34%\"><b>Order Number</b></td><td
```

```
width=\"33%\"><b>Customer ID</b></td><td
width=\"33%\"><b>Status<b></td></tr>\n");
      while($row = mysql_fetch_row($mysql_result))
      {
         print("<tr>\n");
       printf("<td><a
       href=\"./chapter8_storeAdminMenu.php?nav=Orders&action=View&
       orderNumber=%s\">%s</a></td>", $row[0], $row[0]);
       printf("<td>%s</td><td>%s</td>", $row[1], $row[2]);
       print("</tr>\n");
      }
      print("</table>\n");
      $query = "select distinct orderNumber, orderCustomerID,
      orderStatus from storeOrders where orderStatus = 'Pending'";
      $mysql_result = mysql_query($query, $mysql_link);
      $recordCount = 0;
      $recordCount = mysql_affected_rows ($mysql_link);
      print("<p><table width=\"500\" border=\"0\"
      cellpadding=\"3\">\n");
      printf("<tr><td><b>Pending Orders: %s</b></tr>\n",
      $recordCount);
      print("</table>\n");
      $query = "select distinct orderNumber, orderCustomerID,
      orderStatus from storeOrders where orderStatus = 'Closed'";
      $mysql_result = mysql_query($query, $mysql_link);
      $recordCount = 0;
      $recordCount = mysql_affected_rows ($mysql_link);
      print("<table width=\"500\" border=\"0\"
      cellpadding=\"3\">\n");
      printf("<tr><td><b>Filled Orders: %s</b></tr>\n",
      $recordCount);
      print("</table>\n");
      include("./chapter8_dbdisconnect.php");
   }
}
?>
```

With the viewing and processing of orders out of the way, you'll also want the capability to delete the order. The end result will look like Figure 8-10. You may have noticed some code previously that alluded to this. Here's the listing:

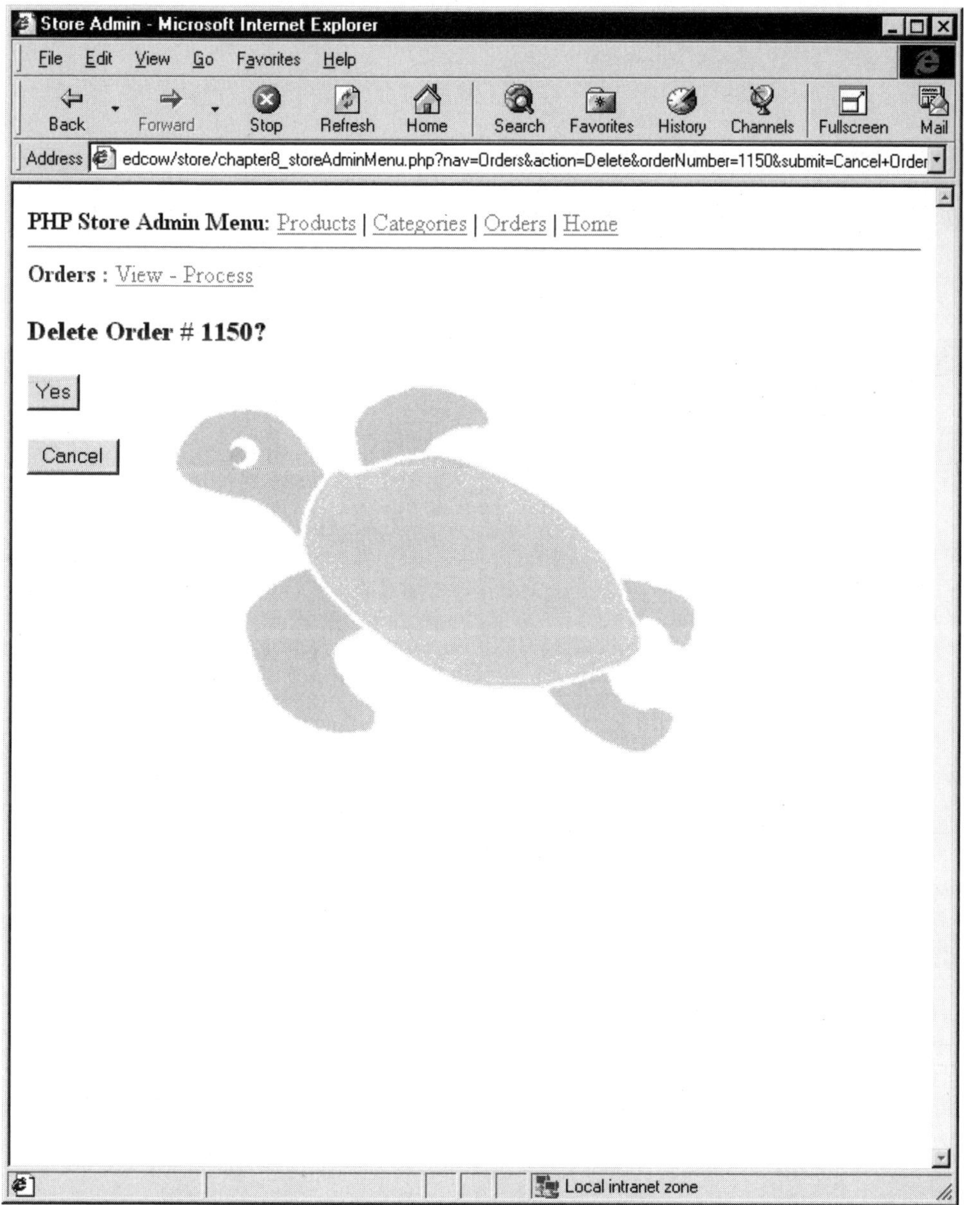

Figure 8-10 *PHP online store administration—deleting orders*

chapter8_storeAdminOrdersDelete.php

```
<?
if($submit == "Yes")
{
   print("<h3>Deleting Order...</h3>");
   /* Depending on how you process the order, you would
   more than likely get a confirmation back with whether
   or not the charges were applied. If they are not you'll
   need to display some sort of error message. If the
   charge is approved you can go ahead and notify the
   customer via e-mail about the order, and update
   your database to reflect the order has been processed.
   */
   include("./chapter8_dbconnect.php");
   $query = "delete from storeOrders where orderNumber =
   '$orderNumber'";
   $mysql_result = mysql_query($query, $mysql_link);
   print("Order Canceled!");
   include("./chapter8_dbdisconnect.php");
}
else
{
   printf("<h3>Delete Order # %s?</h3>", $orderNumber);
   print("<form action=\"./chapter8_storeAdminMenu.php\">");
   print("<input type=\"hidden\" name=\"nav\" value=\"Orders\">");
   print("<input type=\"hidden\" name=\"action\" value=\"Delete\">");
   printf("<input type=\"hidden\" name=\"orderNumber\"
   value=\"%s\">", $orderNumber);
   print("<input type=\"submit\" name=\"submit\" value=\"Yes\">");
   print("</form>");
   print("<form action=\"./chapter8_storeAdminMenu.php\">");
   print("<input type=\"hidden\" name=\"nav\" value=\"Orders\">");
   print("<input type=\"hidden\" name=\"action\" value=\"View\">");
   print("<input type=\"submit\" name=\"cancel\" value=\"Cancel\">");
   print("</form>");
}
?>
```

As you can see, you simply take the passed-in order number, and prompt the user before you actually delete the order. There is one last snip of code before we finish up. The easiest is saved for last, as all this code does is display a little message stating that the user is at the administrative home page and asking them to choose from one of the menu options. Here is the listing:

chapter8_storeAdminHome.php

```
<?
print("Select from one of the menu choices above.");
?>
```

Thus ends the coding of your store administration. Your next step is to implement all of this crazy stuff!

Implementing Your Store Administration

Once your database is completed, you should be able to take all of the PHP files and place them into a directory under your web server document root, and call upon the store menu like so: http://twoheadedcow/store/chapter8_storeAdminMenu.php. Right away you'll be prompted for a name and password. (Hint: These are the default values you inserted into the storeAdmin table when you created your database.) In this case, admin and mystore let you in. You should now be able to manage the aspects of your small, but growing online store.

Testing and Debugging the Address Book

You should be able to place the PHP scripts you just created into the document root of your web server and access the administrative features of your online store. For the example in this chapter, we created a sub-directory called 'store' and referenced the application via the following:

http://twoheadedcow/store/chapter8_storeAdminMenu.php

You can then access the various menu choices and manage your online store. There are several changes you can make to this application to expand and improve your online store; these are discussed in the next section of this chapter.

Limitations and Additional Features

There are many additional features you can tailor to your exact wants and needs. As you may have noticed, there was no additional code in place to check for errors in any of the inputs for adding and editing your store information. We attempted to keep things simple to get you started. You can go back at your leisure and make modifications and additions as you see fit. An additional step you could add to this project would be to run this application via a web server using SSL (Secure Socket Layers) to improve security for your online store.

What to Take Away

You should be able to walk away from this chapter with a high-level overview of what it takes to set up the back-end processing and running of an online store. There are many aspects that go beyond this simple information, and entire books are devoted to the subject of online stores and e-commerce. If nothing else, you've seen examples of basic form input and manipulation of data in a database, as well as the ability to verify a user before letting them have access to private data. In the next chapter, you'll learn the basics of setting up the front end of an online store, and how customers interact with your back-end administration of the store.

CHAPTER

9

PHP Online Store Shopping Cart

IN THIS CHAPTER:

chapter8_dbconnect.php—Connects you to the database
chapter8_dbdisconnect.php—Disconnects you from the database
chapter9_store.php—The main file that contains your menu components
chapter9_storeAccountAdd.php—Creates a new account
chapter9_storeAccountEdit.php—Allows you to edit your account
chapter9_storeCartAdd.php—Allows you to add products to your shopping cart
chapter9_storeCartCheckOut.php—Checks out your order
chapter9_storeCartView.php—Allows you to view your shopping cart
chapter9_storeLogin.php—Logs a user into the store
chapter9_storeProductList.php—Allows you to list products for a category
chapter9_storeProductView.php—Allows you to view a product in the store

In this chapter, you'll build a front end to your online store. We will use the existing database that was created in Chapter 8. You'll also be reusing the code to connect and disconnect from the database. For learning purposes, the store functions have been greatly simplified. A real-life online store would require quite a lot of additional functionality. Nonetheless, we'll cover the basic ability to specify account information, view products, add them to your shopping cart, and check out. You'll also be following a theme of sorts for this store: Turtle's Dive Shop, specializing in the sale of scuba gear.

Online Store Shopping Cart Requirements

Your online store will have the capability to allow potential customers to view all of your products, and if they wish to purchase anything, to create an account and shop your store. The requirements for this example will be similar to those in Chapter 8. You will need access to a Apache web server with PHP and MySQL installed. You should have your database created, and populated with some initial product and category information.

Designing and Implementing the Online Store Shopping Cart

You'll begin the design of your storefront with a way to present all of your product offerings. For this you will need a PHP file that will present menu choices to your customers. As in the previous chapter, the components of your store will be modular. You'll include each PHP file as needed based on menu choices made by the user. By lumping each operational component into a separate file, if you need to debug or make changes to any aspects of your program, it will be much easier.

Let's start off by designing that menu system we mentioned. This will contain all the logic and control needed to allow the customer to navigate your store and for the correct modules of code to be processed as needed. Your eventual store will look similar to Figure 9-1.

To begin, you'll need to check whether the user is attempting to access their shopping cart. In this case, shopping cart and gear bag are interchangeable terms, as it fits into the theme of your store.

chapter9_store.php

```
<? if($gearBag=='Login'){include("./chapter9_storeLogin.php");} ?>
<html>
```

```
<head>
<title>Turtle's Dive Shop</title>
</head>
<body background="./turtle_bg.gif" text="#000000" bgcolor="#ffffff"
 marginwidth="0" marginheight="0" leftmargin="0" topmargin="0"
 link="#2FB472" alink="#2FB472" vlink="#2FB472">
<table width="700" height="600" border="0" cellpadding="0" cellspacing="0">
<tr>
<td colspan="2" height="85"><img src="./turtle_logo_nav.gif"></td>
</tr>
<tr>
<td width="175" valign="top">
<p align="center"><b>Turtle Gear..</b><br>
```

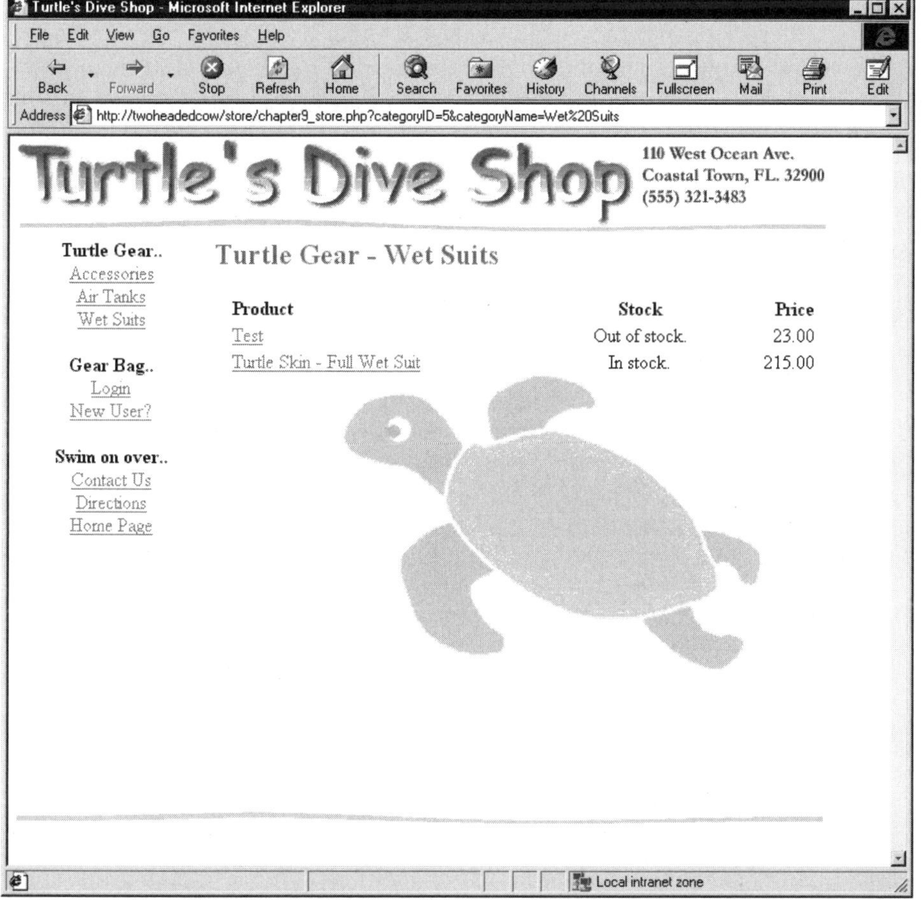

Figure 9-1 *PHP online store shopping cart*

So far, the coding has been easy. Let's dip our coding fingers into a little PHP and implement a way to list all of the product categories you have:

```
<?
include("./chapter8_dbconnect.php");
$query = "select * from storeProductCategory order by productcategoryName";
$mysql_result = mysql_query($query, $mysql_link);
while($row = mysql_fetch_row($mysql_result))
{
   printf("<a
 href=\"./chapter9_store.php?categoryID=%s&categoryName=%s\">%s</a><br>\n",
 $row[0], $row[1], $row[1]);
}
include("./chapter8_dbdisconnect.php");
?>
```

The next step is to determine whether the customer has logged into your store yet. For this you will build upon some of the functionality in Chapter 8. If the user is logged in, you will show them links to their shopping cart (gear bag), and give them the ability to edit their account information and check out. If the user is not logged in, you will provide a means for them to log in or to create an account if they are a new customer. The code is as follows:

```
<p align="center"><b>Gear Bag..</b><br>
<?
if (!isset($PHP_AUTH_USER) || $unauthorized)
{
   print("<a href=\"./chapter9_store.php?gearBag=Login\">Login</a><br>\n");
   print("<a href=\"./chapter9_store.php?gearBag=New+User\">New User?</a>\n");
}
else
{
   include("./chapter9_storeLogin.php");
   printf("<!-- Customer ID: %s -->\n", $custID);
   print("<a href=\"./chapter9_store.php?gearBag=My+Gear\">
   My Gear</a><br>\n");
   print("<a href=\"./chapter9_store.php?gearBag=Account+Info\">
   Account Info</a><br>\n");
   print("<a href=\"./chapter9_store.php?gearBag=Check+Out\">
   Check Out</a><br>\n");
}
?>
<br>
<p align="center"><b>Swim on over..</b><br>
<a href="./chapter9_store.php">Contact Us</a><br>
<a href="./chapter9_store.php">Directions</a><br>
<a href="./chapter9_store.php">Home Page</a><br>
```

```
</td>
<td width="525" valign="top">
```

Now that we have the ability to give the user of your store menu choices, let's begin handling some of the menu choices that a customer might select. In this next bit of code, you determine whether a category ID has been passed in; if so, the user is browsing the product categories. The PHP file needed to handle that request is included, as follows:

```
<?
if($categoryID) // viewing stuff
{
   include("./chapter8_dbconnect.php");
   if($productID)
   {
      include("./chapter9_storeProductView.php");
   }
   else
   {
      include("./chapter9_storeProductList.php");
   }
   include("./chapter8_dbdisconnect.php");
}
```

Next, you need to determine whether the user is accessing a feature of their shopping cart and handle those requests. If no other menu choices have been made, you can assume the user wishes to see the store's home page. The code is as follows:

```
else
{   // home page or shopping cart (Gear Bag)
   if($gearBag)
   {
      printf("<h2><font color=\"#2FB472\">Turtle Gear - %s</font></h2>", $gearBag);
      switch ($gearBag)
      {
         case "Add Gear":
            include("./chapter9_storeCartAdd.php");
            break;
         case "My Gear":
            include("./chapter9_storeCartView.php");
            break;
         case "Check Out":
            include("./chapter9_storeCartCheckOut.php");
            break;
         case "New User":
            include("./chapter9_storeAccountAdd.php");
            break;
```

```
            case "Account Info":
               include("./chapter9_storeAccountEdit.php");
               break;
         }
      }
      else
      {
         print("<h2><font color=\"#2FB472\">Turtle Gear - Home Page</font></h2>");
      }
}
?>
```

Rounding out your menu system, you close up the table cells you've opened and the HTML document itself:

```
</td>
</tr>
<tr>
<td colspan="2" height="50">
<img src="./turtle_bar.gif"><br>
 
</td>
</tr>
</table>
</body>
</html>
```

Now that you have a means in place to handle your customers' requests, let's begin work on those features. You'll want to code the ability to allow customers to create an account for your store. The code for this is chapter9_storeAccountAdd.php, and the end result will look similar to Figure 9-2.

chapter9_storeAccountAdd.php

```
<?
include("./chapter8_dbconnect.php");
if($submit)
{
   print("Creating Account...");
   $query = "insert into storeCustomer (customerUserID, customerPassword,
   customerName,";
   $query .= " customerAddress1, customerAddress2, customerCity,
   customerState, customerZip,";
   $query .= " customerEmail, customerPhone, customerCardNumber,
   customerCardType, customerCardExpire)";
   $query .= " values ('$customerUserID', '$customerPassword',
   '$customerName', '$customerAddress1',";
```

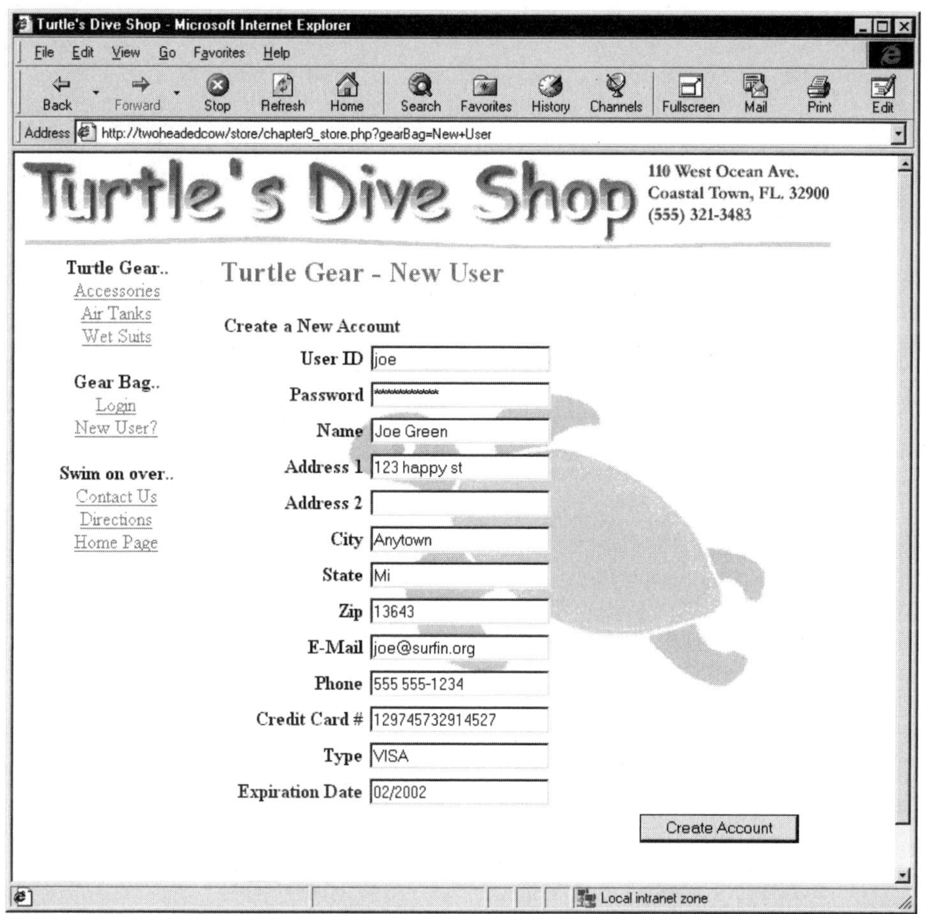

Figure 9-2 *PHP online store shopping cart—creating an account*

```
    $query .= " '$customerAddress2', '$customerCity', '$customerState',
    '$customerZip', '$customerEmail',";
    $query .= " '$customerPhone', '$customerCardNumber', '$customerCardType',
    '$customerCardExpire')";
    $mysql_result = mysql_query($query, $mysql_link);
    print("Done.");
}
else
{
    print("<table border=\"0\" width=\"500\"
    cellspacing=\"0\" cellpadding=\"3\">\n");
    print("<tr>\n");
    print("<td colspan=\"2\"><b>Create a New Account</b>");
    print("<form action=\"./chapter9_store.php\" method=\"get\"></td>\n");
```

```
print("</tr>\n");
print("<tr>\n");
print("<td align=\"right\" width=\"25%\"><b>User ID</b></td>");
print("<td><input type=\"textd\" name=\"customerUserID\"></td>");
print("</tr>\n");
print("<tr>\n");
print("<td align=\"right\"><b>Password</b></td>");
print("<td><input type=\"password\" name=\"customerPassword\"></td>");
print("</tr>\n");
print("<tr>\n");
print("<td align=\"right\"><b>Name</b></td>");
print("<td><input type=\"text\" name=\"customerName\"></td>");
print("</tr>\n");
print("<tr>\n");
print("<td align=\"right\"><b>Address 1</b></td>");
print("<td><input type=\"text\" name=\"customerAddress1\"></td>");
print("</tr>\n");
print("<tr>\n");
print("<td align=\"right\"><b>Address 2</b></td>");
print("<td><input type=\"text\" name=\"customerAddress2\"></td>");
print("</tr>\n");
print("<tr>\n");
print("<td align=\"right\"><b>City</b></td>");
print("<td><input type=\"text\" name=\"customerCity\"></td>");
print("</tr>\n");
print("<tr>\n");
print("<td align=\"right\"><b>State</b></td>");
print("<td><input type=\"text\" name=\"customerState\"></td>");
print("</tr>\n");
print("<tr>\n");
print("<td align=\"right\"><b>Zip</b></td>");
print("<td><input type=\"text\" name=\"customerZip\"></td>");
print("</tr>\n");
print("<tr>\n");
print("<td align=\"right\"><b>E-Mail</b></td>");
print("<td><input type=\"text\" name=\"customerEmail\"></td>");
print("</tr>\n");
print("<tr>\n");
print("<td align=\"right\"><b>Phone</b></td>");
print("<td><input type=\"text\" name=\"customerPhone\"></td>");
print("</tr>\n");
print("<tr>\n");
print("<td align=\"right\"><b>Credit Card #</b></td>");
print("<td><input type=\"text\" name=\"customerCardNumber\"></td>");
print("</tr>\n");
print("<tr>\n");
print("<td align=\"right\"><b>Type</b></td>");
print("<td><input type=\"text\" name=\"customerCardType\"></td>");
print("</tr>\n");
```

```
    print("<tr>\n");
    print("<td align=\"right\"><b>Expiration Date</b></td>");
    print("<td><input type=\"text\" name=\"customerCardExpire\"></td>");
    print("</tr>\n");
    print("<input type=\"hidden\" name=\"gearBag\" value=\"New User\">");
    print("<tr>\n");
    print("<td colspan=\"2\" align=\"right\"><input type=\"submit\"
    name=\"submit\" value=\"Create Account\"> </form></td>\n");
    print("</tr>\n");
    print("</table>\n");
}
include("./chapter8_dbdisconnect.php");
?>
```

As with the code used in Chapter 8, you simply prompted the user for information from a form and then submitted it to the database. While the customer information you collect is still fresh on your mind, let's go ahead and code the ability to edit the information the user entered. The end result will look like Figure 9-3.

chapter9_storeAccountEdit.php

```
<?
include("./chapter8_dbconnect.php");
if($submit)
{
    print("Updating Account...");
    $query = "update storeCustomer set
  customerPassword = '$customerPassword',
  customerName = '$customerName',
  customerAddress1 = '$customerAddress1', ";
    $query .= "customerAddress2 = '$customerAddress2',
  customerCity = '$customerCity',
  customerState = '$customerState',
  customerZip = '$customerZip', ";
    $query .= "customerEmail = '$customerEmail',
  customerPhone = '$customerPhone',
  customerCardNumber = '$customerCardNumber', ";
    $query .= "customerCardType = '$customerCardType',
  customerCardExpire = '$customerCardExpire' ";
    $query .= " where customerID = '$custID'";
    $mysql_result = mysql_query($query, $mysql_link);
    print("Done.");
}
else
{
    $query = "select * from storeCustomer where customerID = '$custID'";
    $mysql_result = mysql_query($query, $mysql_link);
    while($row = mysql_fetch_row($mysql_result))
```

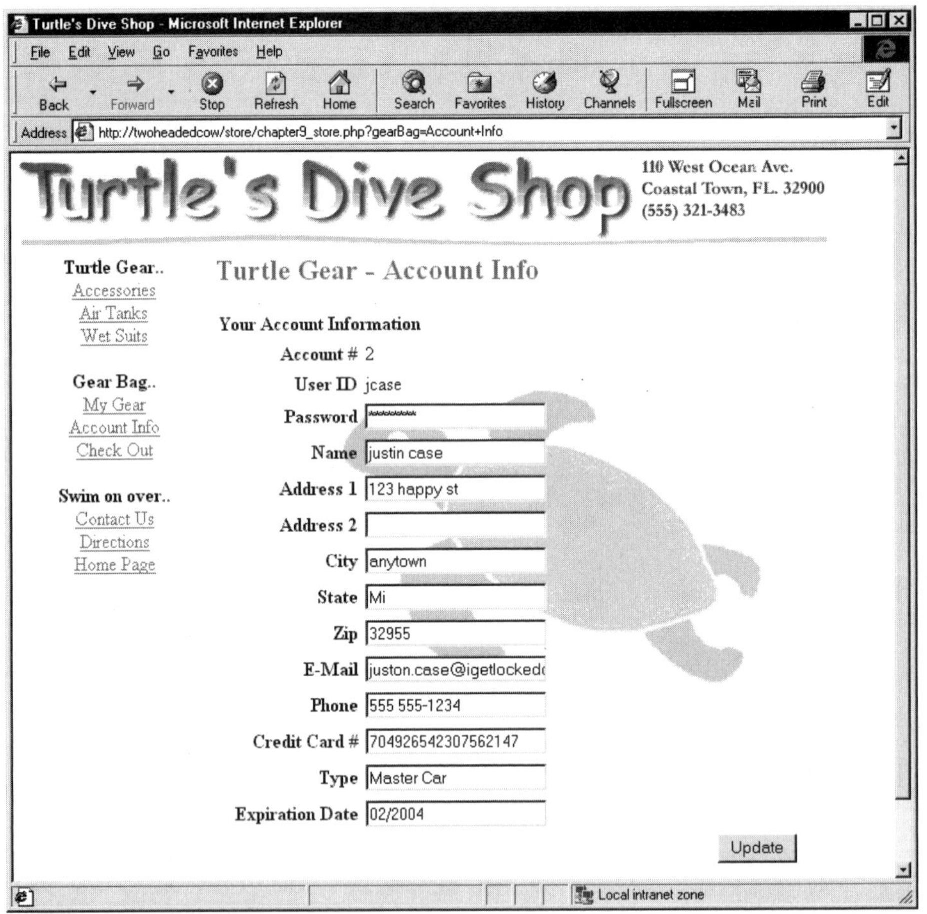

Figure 9-3 *PHP online store shopping cart—editing an account*

```
{
  print("<table border=\"0\" width=\"500\" cellspacing=\"0\"
  cellpadding=\"3\">\n");
  print("<tr>\n");
  print("<td colspan=\"2\"><b>Your Account Information</b>");
  print("<form action=\"./chapter9_store.php\" method=\"get\"></td>\n");
  print("</tr>\n");
  print("<tr>\n");
  print("<td align=\"right\"><b>Account #</b></td>");
  printf("<td>%s</td>", $row[0]);
  print("</tr>\n");
  print("<tr>\n");
  print("<td align=\"right\" width=\"25%\"><b>User ID</b></td>");
  printf("<td>%s</td>", $row[1]);
```

```
print("</tr>\n");
print("<tr>\n");
print("<td align=\"right\"><b>Password</b></td>");
printf("<td><input type=\"password\" name=\"customerPassword\"
value=\"%s\"></td>", $row[2]);
print("</tr>\n");
print("<tr>\n");
print("<td align=\"right\"><b>Name</b></td>");
printf("<td><input type=\"text\" name=\"customerName\"
value=\"%s\"></td>", $row[3]);
print("</tr>\n");
print("<tr>\n");
print("<td align=\"right\"><b>Address 1</b></td>");
printf("<td><input type=\"text\" name=\"customerAddress1\"
value=\"%s\"></td>", $row[4]);
print("</tr>\n");
print("<tr>\n");
print("<td align=\"right\"><b>Address 2</b></td>");
printf("<td><input type=\"text\" name=\"customerAddress2\"
value=\"%s\"></td>", $row[5]);
print("</tr>\n");
print("<tr>\n");
print("<td align=\"right\"><b>City</b></td>");
printf("<td><input type=\"text\" name=\"customerCity\"
value=\"%s\"></td>", $row[6]);
print("</tr>\n");
print("<tr>\n");
print("<td align=\"right\"><b>State</b></td>");
printf("<td><input type=\"text\" name=\"customerState\"
value=\"%s\"></td>", $row[7]);
print("</tr>\n");
print("<tr>\n");
print("<td align=\"right\"><b>Zip</b></td>");
printf("<td><input type=\"text\" name=\"customerZip\"
value=\"%s\"></td>", $row[8]);
print("</tr>\n");
print("<tr>\n");
print("<td align=\"right\"><b>E-Mail</b></td>");
printf("<td><input type=\"text\" name=\"customerEmail\"
value=\"%s\"></td>", $row[9]);
print("</tr>\n");
print("<tr>\n");
print("<td align=\"right\"><b>Phone</b></td>");
printf("<td><input type=\"text\" name=\"customerPhone\"
value=\"%s\"></td>", $row[10]);
print("</tr>\n");
print("<tr>\n");
print("<td align=\"right\"><b>Credit Card #</b></td>");
printf("<td><input type=\"text\" name=\"customerCardNumber\"
```

```
        value=\"%s\"></td>", $row[11]);
        print("</tr>\n");
        print("<tr>\n");
        print("<td align=\"right\"><b>Type</b></td>");
        printf("<td><input type=\"text\" name=\"customerCardType\"
        value=\"%s\"></td>", $row[12]);
        print("</tr>\n");
        print("<tr>\n");
        print("<td align=\"right\"><b>Expiration Date</b></td>");
        printf("<td><input type=\"text\" name=\"customerCardExpire\"
        value=\"%s\"></td>", $row[13]);
        print("</tr>\n");
        print("<input type=\"hidden\" name=\"gearBag\" value=\"Account Info\">");
        printf("<input type=\"hidden\" name=\"customerID\" value=\"%s\">",
        $row[0]);
        print("<tr>\n");
        print("<td colspan=\"2\" align=\"right\"><input type=\"submit\"
        name=\"submit\" value=\"Update\"> </form></td>\n");
        print("</tr>\n");
        print("</table>\n");
    }
}
include("./chapter8_dbdisconnect.php");
?>
```

Now that users have the ability to create an account and edit their information, let's move on to the next logical step: logging into your store. For this, you'll use the code contained in chapter9_storeLogin.php. This will prompt a user for the user name and password they made up when they created an account. The resulting output will look like Figure 9-4.

chapter9_storeLogin.php

```
<?
$loginPage = "./chapter9_store.php?gearBag=Login";
if (!isset($PHP_AUTH_USER) || $unauthorized)
{
   $realm = "MyPHPStore_".time();
   Header("WWW-Authenticate: Basic realm=\"$realm\"");
   Header("Status: HTTP/1.0 401 Unauthorized");
   print "<h1>401 Unauthorized</h1>Unable to authorize you.
 Please <a href=\"$loginPage\">click here</a> to try again.";
   exit;
}
else
{
   include("./chapter8_dbconnect.php");
```

Figure 9-4 *PHP online store shopping cart—login*

```
$query = "select * from storeCustomer where
customerUserID = '$PHP_AUTH_USER' and
customerPassword = '$PHP_AUTH_PW'";
$mysql_result = mysql_query($query, $mysql_link);

if(mysql_affected_rows() == 0)
{
   header("Location: ".$loginPage."&unauthorized=1");
  exit();
}
else
{
   while($row = mysql_fetch_row($mysql_result))
```

```
        {
            $custID = $row[0];
        }
    }
    include("./chapter8_dbdisconnect.php");
}
?>
```

With the ability to create an account, edit it, and log in to your store out of the way, let's devise a way to list the products you're going to offer in your store. The results should display all of the products for the category your customer selected, as pictured in Figure 9-5.

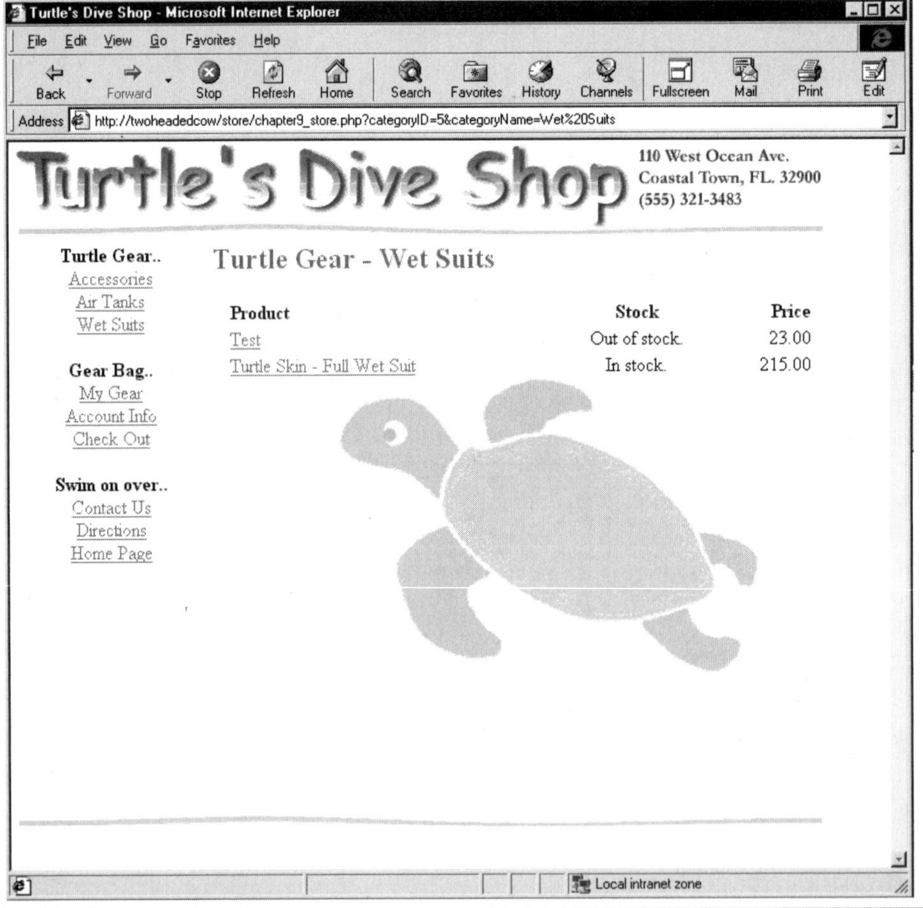

Figure 9-5 *PHP online store shopping cart—listing products*

chapter9_storeProductList.php

```
<?
$query = "select * from storeProduct where storeProduct.productCategory =
'$categoryID' order by productName";
$mysql_result = mysql_query($query, $mysql_link);
printf("<h2><font color=\"#2FB472\">Turtle Gear - %s</font></h2>",
$categoryName);
print("<table width=\"500\" align=\"center\" border=\"0\" cellpadding=\"0\"
cellspacing=\"3\">");
print("<tr><td><b>Product</b></td><td align=\"center\"><b>Stock</b></td><td
align=\"right\"><b>Price</b></td></tr>");
while($row = mysql_fetch_row($mysql_result))
{
   print("<tr>\n");
   printf("<td><a
href=\"./chapter9_store.php?categoryID=%s&categoryName=%s&productID=%s\">%s</a
></td>\n", $row[2], $categoryName, $row[0], $row[1]);
   print("<td align=\"center\">");
   if($row[6] <= 0)
   {
      print("Out of stock.");
   }
   else
   {
      print("In stock.");
   }
   print("</td>\n");
   printf("<td align=\"right\">%s</td>\n", $row[5]);
   print("</tr>");
   }
print("</table>\n");
?>
```

As you may have noticed, the code to list products is fairly simple. Next, you'll want to be able to select an individual product and view it. The results will look like Figure 9-6.

chapter9_storeProductView.php

```
<?
   $query = "select * from storeProduct where storeProduct.productID =
   '$productID'";
   $mysql_result = mysql_query($query, $mysql_link);
   while($row = mysql_fetch_row($mysql_result))
   {
```

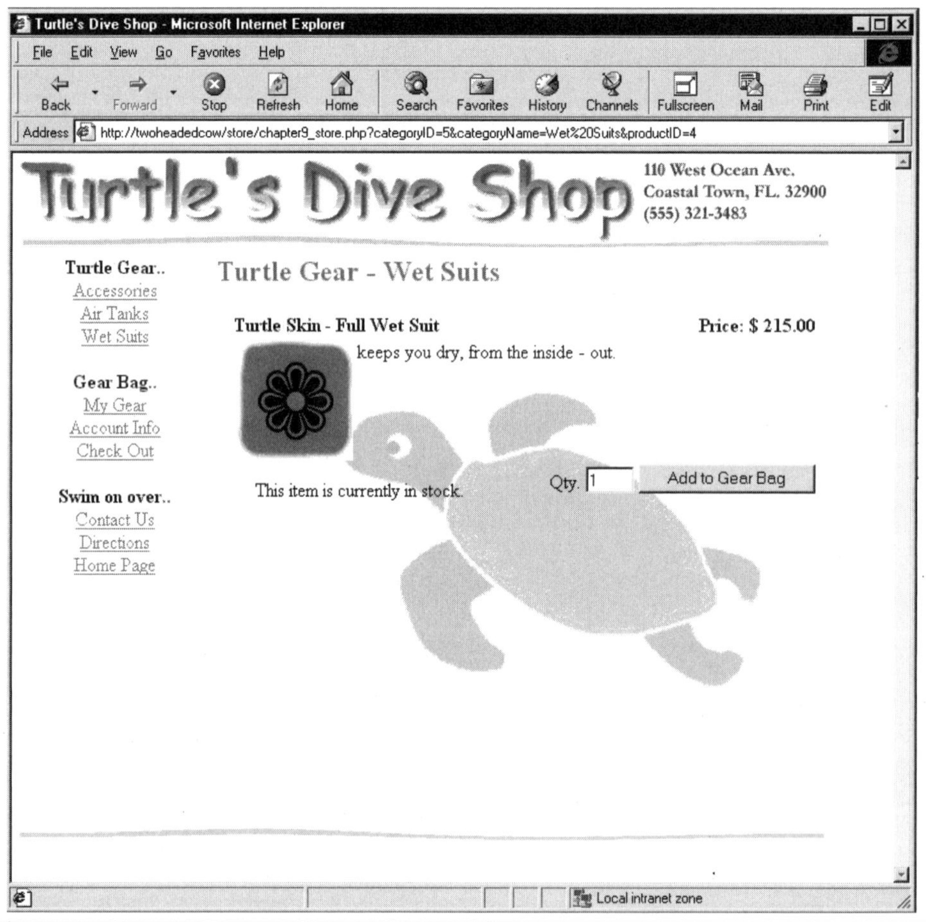

Figure 9-6 *PHP online store shopping cart—viewing a product*

```
printf("<h2><font color=\"#2FB472\">Turtle Gear - %s</font></h2>",
$categoryName);
print("<table width=\"500\" align=\"center\" border=\"0\"
cellpadding=\"0\" cellspacing=\"3\">");
print("<tr>\n");
print("<td>\n");
printf("<b>%s</b><br>", $row[1]);
print("</td>\n");
print("<td align=\"right\">\n");
printf("<b>Price: $ %s</b>", $row[5]);
print("</td>\n");
print("</tr>\n");
print("<tr>\n");
print("<td valign=\"top\" colspan=\"2\">\n");
```

```
        printf("<img src=\"%s\" align=\"left\">", $row[4]);
        printf("%s", $row[3]);
        print("</td>\n");
        print("</tr>\n");
        print("<tr>\n");
        print("<td align=\"center\"> This item is currently \n");
        if($row[6] <= 0)
        {
           print("out of stock.");
           print("</td>\n");
           print("<td align=\"right\"> </td>\n");
        }
        else
        {
           print("in stock.");
           print("</td>\n");
           print("<td align=\"right\">\n");
           print("<form action=\"./chapter9_store.php\" method=\"get\">");
           print("<input type=\"hidden\" name=\"gearBag\" value=\"Add Gear\">");
           print("Qty. <input type=\"text\" name=\"qty\" value=\"1\"
           size=\"4\" maxsize=\"10\"> ");
           print("<input type=\"submit\" name=\"submit\" value=\"Add to Gear
           Bag\">");
           printf("<input type=\"hidden\" name=\"productID\" value=\"%s\">",
           $row[0]);
           print("</form>");
           print("</td>\n");
        }
        print("</tr>\n");
        print("</table\n");
}
?>
```

In that code, you made provisions to allow the customer to enter a quantity and add the product to their shopping cart. Let's go ahead and code this next. The result will be along the lines of what is pictured in Figure 9-7.

chapter9_storeCartAdd.php

```
<?
include("./chapter8_dbconnect.php");
$query = "select * from storeOrders where orderCustomerID = '$custID' and
orderStatus = 'Pending'";
$mysql_result = mysql_query($query, $mysql_link);
$recordCount = 0;
$recordCount = mysql_affected_rows ($mysql_link);
if($recordCount == 0)
{
   srand(time());
```

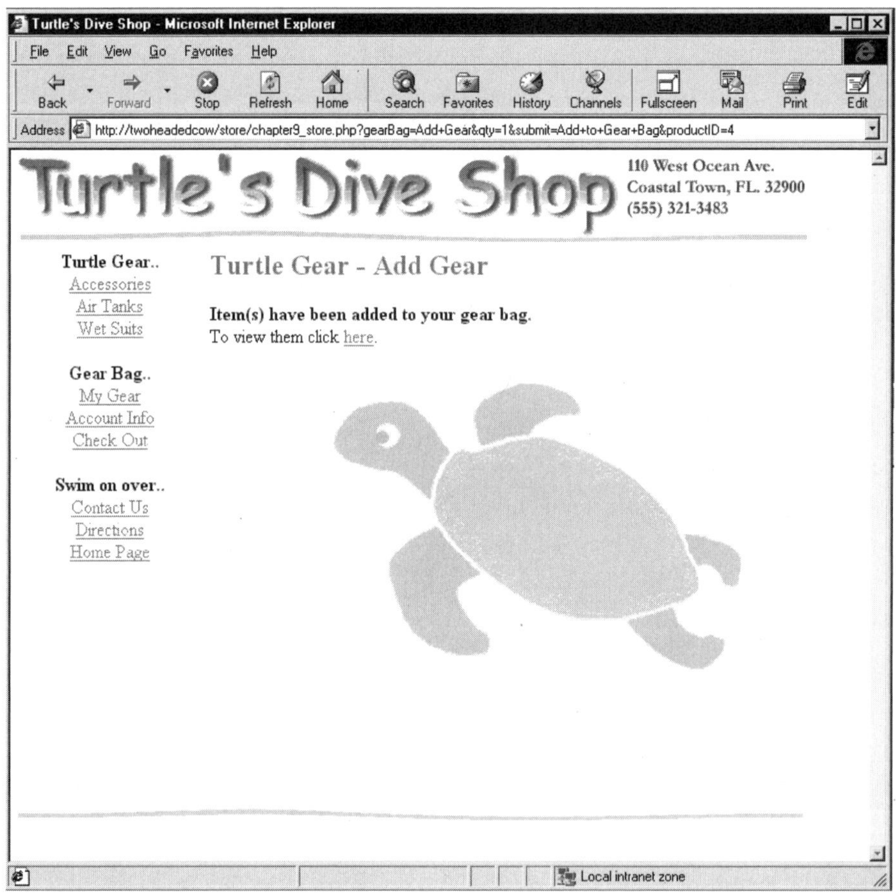

Figure 9-7 *PHP online store shopping cart—adding to the shopping cart*

```
   $orderNumber = (rand()%10000)+1;
}
else
{
   while($row = mysql_fetch_row($mysql_result)) { $orderNumber = $row[1]; }
}
$query = "insert into storeOrders
 (orderNumber, orderStatus, orderCustomerID, orderProductID, orderQuantity)
 values";
$query .= " ('$orderNumber', 'Pending', '$custID', '$productID', '$qty') ";
$mysql_result = mysql_query($query, $mysql_link);
include("./chapter8_dbdisconnect.php");
print("<p><b>Item(s) have been added to your gear bag.</b><br>");
print("To view them click <a
href=\"./chapter9_store.php?gearBag=My+Gear\">here</a>.");
?>
```

Did we lose you on the previous code? As you may have noticed, we are doing a little finagling here. You need a way to create an order number for the customer to reference, but only if they don't already have an existing order pending. So you look into the orders table, and if there are no pending orders, generate a random number as the order number. If the customer already has items in their shopping cart and the order status has not been changed yet, you use the existing order number and append the item they have chosen to that order.

All of this shopping is wearing your customers out! Let's code a way for them to view what's in their shopping cart, and perhaps coax them into checking out. The end result is pictured in Figure 9-8.

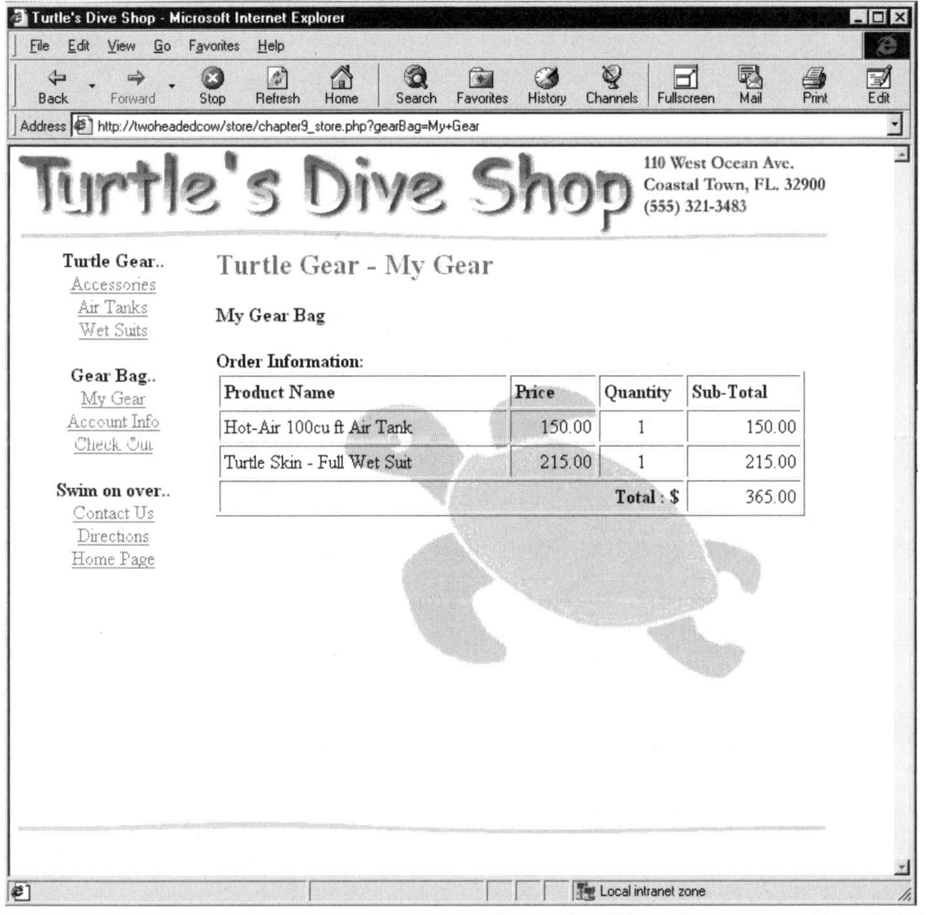

Figure 9-8 *PHP online store shopping cart—viewing cart*

chapter9_storeCartView.php

```
<?
print("<b>My Gear Bag</b><br>\n");
include("./chapter8_dbconnect.php");
$orderTotal = 0;
print("<p><b>Order Information:</b>");
$query = "select * from storeOrders, storeProduct where
 orderCustomerID = '$custID' and orderStatus = 'Pending'
 and orderProductID = productID";
$mysql_result = mysql_query($query, $mysql_link);
print("<table width=\"500\" border=\"1\" cellpadding=\"3\">\n");
print("<tr><td width=\"50%\"><b>Product Name</b></td>
<td width=\"15%\"><b>Price</b></td><td width=\"15%\">
<b>Quantity</b></td><td width=\"20%\"><b>Sub-Total</b>
</td></tr>\n");
while($row = mysql_fetch_row($mysql_result))
{
   $itemSubTotal = ($row[11] * $row[5]);
   $itemSubTotal = number_format($itemSubTotal, 2, '.', '');
   $orderTotal = ($orderTotal + $itemSubTotal);
   $orderTotal = number_format($orderTotal, 2, '.', '');
   print("<tr>\n");
   printf("<td>%s</td><td align=\"right\">%s</td><td
align=\"center\">%s</td><td align=\"right\">%s</td>", $row[7], $row[11],
$row[5], $itemSubTotal);
   print("</tr>\n");
}
printf("<tr><td colspan=\"3\" align=\"right\"><b>Total : $</b></td>
<td align=\"right\">%s</td></tr>", $orderTotal);
print("</table>\n");
include("./chapter8_dbdisconnect.php");
?>
```

And rounding out your online store is the ability for customers to check out and eventually get all the neat stuff they ordered. The resulting output will be similar to Figure 9-9.

chapter9_storeCartCheckOut.php

```
<?
print("<b>Checking Out...</b><br>\n");
include("./chapter8_dbconnect.php");
$query = "update storeOrders set orderStatus = 'Open'
```

```
 where orderCustomerID = '$custID' and orderStatus = 'Pending'";
$mysql_result = mysql_query($query, $mysql_link);
print("<b>Your order is now being processed. You should receive it
shortly.</b><br>\n");
include("./chapter8_dbdisconnect.php");
?>
```

The code to check out was very simple. Once the order has been set to open, it's up to the store administrator to view and process the order. The functionality of this was covered in Chapter 8.

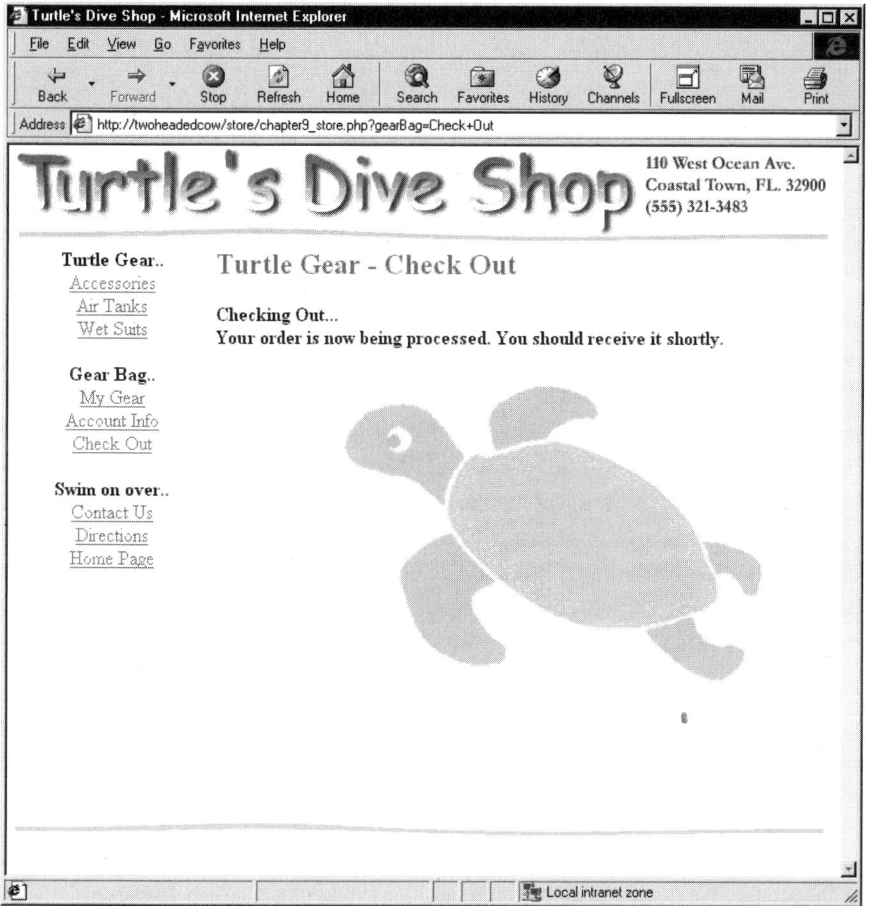

Figure 9-9 *PHP online store shopping cart—checking out*

Implementing Your Store

Since your database was completed in Chapter 8, along with all of the product information, you should be able to place all of the files we've covered in this chapter into the same directory. You can then call upon your store via a web browser with the URL http://twoheadedcow/store/chapter9_store.php. From there, you can browse the products offered; and if you're ready to buy, create an account and add the items you like to your shopping cart. When you've finished, you can check out and let the store owner process your order.

Testing and Debugging the Online Store

Just as in the previous chapter, things like error checking for code and input information are limited at best. There are also other aspects of online stores that were not covered in this chapter. The more common and important features were covered to give you an idea of the whole ordering and shopping cart process.

Limitations and Additional Features

Just as in the last chapter, there are many additional features you can tailor to your exact wants and needs. As you may have noticed, there was no additional code in place to check for errors in any of the inputs for adding and editing your store information. This is one area for you to work on if you'd like. Another step you could take in this project would be to run this application via a web server using Secure Socket Layers (SSL) to improve security for your online store. Take a look at how some other online stores work for additional ideas.

What to Take Away

Now that you have created both sides of an online store, you should be familiar with the basic coding it takes to run such a store. While the functionality was simplistic, you should be able to walk away with the general idea of associating product information with orders and with customer information. There are many aspects that go beyond what has been covered in this chapter, and entire books are devoted to the subject of online stores and e-commerce. By completing this chapter, however, you should now have a sense of how many different aspects of an online store there are.

PART

V

PHP and Operating Systems

OBJECTIVES

- Develop Web-based interface for end users to perform operations on the file and directory systems of the host machine
- Become familiar with the available PHP directory and file system functions
- Understand reusable display, file, and directory operation classes
- Provide PHP administrators with a simple web-based interface to view information about the PHP environment and the PHP ini file itself
- Become familiar with the available PHP options and information functions
- Develop a basic class for examining the contents of a file
- Develop a generic framework for menu processing and HTML output

CHAPTER

10

Administrative Tools

IN THIS CHAPTER:

chapter10_common.php—Common set of functions used for displaying result sets as HTML tables along with the main menu for the application

chapter10_dirActions.php—dirActions class whose methods work with directories. Also processes the dirMenu form and displays the corresponding output

chapter10_dirMenu.php—Provides directory options as selection list with dynamically changing text input boxes

chapter10_fileActions.php—fileActions class whose methods perform actions on files. Also processes the fileActions form and displays the corresponding output

chapter10_fileMenu.php—Provides file options as selection list with dynamically changing text input boxes

chapter10_getProps.php—getFileProps class whose methods retrieve information about files. Also processes the getProps form and displays the corresponding output

chapter10_setProps.php—setFileProps class whose methods specify properties for a file. Also processes the setProps form and displays the corresponding output

The project for this chapter is to develop a Web-based system administration application, which allows an end user to work with files and directories on the host computer. The capabilities of the application are constrained by the privileges that the user the PHP engine is running under has. The code presented in this chapter does not significantly address the many security considerations that should be taken into account when developing this type of application; therefore, it should not be implemented on an actual live site without further security enhancements. The scope of the code in this chapter is limited to demonstrating how PHP can interact with the host operating system and does not implement any of the necessary security mechanisms.

Application Requirements

The basic requirements for the application can be broken down into two segments: working with directories and working with files. Each of these segments has many subcomponents, which are comprised of the typical operations a user would perform on a file or directory.

Directory Listing Requirements

The directories segment includes most of the operations an end user would perform with a directory on the file system. These include creating a new directory, removing an existing directory, renaming a directory, listing the contents of a directory, and checking the available free space for a directory.

File System Requirements

The file portion of the application contains most of the file operations likely to be needed by an end user. The file operations can be further broken down into three main headings: getting information about a file, setting properties for a file, and performing an action on a file. The information available for retrieval for a file includes file type, file properties, examining hard and symbolic links, and checking for available disk space. The properties that can be set for files include the file's owner, the file's group, the file's permissions, the umask, and setting a hard or symbolic link for a file. Finally, the file actions available are copying a file, moving a file, removing a file, renaming a file, unlinking a file, and touching a file.

Application Design

We begin building on the requirements by outlining what information we need to gather from the user, as well as what information will be returned to the user.

Application Inputs

The first step in designing the application is to determine what information will need to be gathered from the user for each of the aforementioned operations. Each operation for files and directories could potentially have a different set of inputs needed.

Directory Inputs

We'll begin by examining the directory inputs. The first requirement for the directory operations is to be able to create a new directory. All that is required for this operation is the name of the new directory that should be created. Next comes the ability to remove a directory, which also requires only the name of the directory. The option to rename a directory requires both the old name for a directory and the new name for the directory. In order to display the contents of a directory you'll need the name of the directory. In the case of examining the amount of free space available, you'll look at either a directory name or a file system path.

Get File Inputs

Again let's break the file operations into three separate units, the first of which deals with getting information about a file. When determining a file type, all that is needed is the file's name. This is also true when retrieving a file's properties. When examining links, the user should input the name of the link in question. When asking the file system for its umask (the default permissions given to a file), no other input is needed.

Set File Inputs

The next set of input operations to look at is the set file properties operations. In order to set a file's owner or group, you will need two inputs: the filename and either the owner or group that the file should be set to. In the case of file permissions, the user should input the filename, as well as a permission mask. For umask, the user only needs to input a permissions mask—no filename is necessary since the umask applies to any new file that is created. In order to set a link for a file, the user must input the name of the file, as well as the name of the hard or symbolic link to be used.

File Action Inputs

The last set of input operations to examine is the file actions operations. The first file action that requires input is the copy file option. This requires both a source filename and a destination filename. The same is also true when requesting to move a file. All that is necessary to input when removing a file is the name of the file to be removed. Since unlinking a file is the same as removing a file, the same holds true for it as well. When you are touching a file, you are updating its last modified and accessed times. If a time is explicitly supplied, its modification time will be changed to it. In the case of Windows machines, the time will be set to 12/31/1969; and for *nix machines, the time will be the current time if no time parameter is specified.

Application Outputs

The outputs for this application all follow a similar design. After each operation, the user should be presented with the results of the operation, including the results from the corresponding function and a status message indicating either success or failure of the operation.

Application Modules

In order to have fast, efficient, easy-to-debug code, we will divide the application into several smaller modules. Each module will be contained in a separate file. We'll start with a common module that will contain code that is used repeatedly throughout the application. The next set of modules to create are the menu modules. There will be a separate menu module for the directory operations and the file operations. The directory menu module will call the directory actions module. The file menu will contain three submenus: one for getting information about files, one for setting properties of files, and one for performing actions on files. Each of these submenus will call a corresponding module to actually perform the operation. Altogether, there are two menu modules, one common module, and four operation modules. Each of the operation modules is designed so it can be incorporated into larger applications if needed. Also, as other file or directory operations become necessary, each module can be expanded without impacting the existing code.

Application Implementation

The coding of the application is broken down into three sections. The first is a common section of code that is used repeatedly throughout the application. The second section is the menu section that includes menus for file and directory operations. The last section is an actions section that includes code to handle the processing of the menu action selected by the user.

Common Functions

You begin actual coding of the application with development of those functions that will be used repeatedly within the application. The first common function we'll look at is the echoLine() function. This is a very basic function whose sole purpose is to save a little typing when outputting lines of HTML code. The input parameter is a string and the output is the same string with a new line appended to the end of the string. Any time the application writes out HTML text, this function is used. In general, spacing and line feeds don't matter in HTML; however, adding linefeeds and carriage returns makes it much easier for the user if they view the source of the HTML document.

chapter10_common.php

```
<?php

//#################################################################
//##        Function:    echoLine                               ##
//##      Parameters:    string                                 ##
//##     Description:    Outputs a single line including lf & cr  ##
//#################################################################
function echoLine ($inputstring)
   {
   echo $inputstring."\n";
   }
```

The next function we examine is the mainMenu() function. It should be called any time in the application when you want to output the top-level menu for the application.

The top-level menu currently only has two options: file operations and directory operations. Of course, if you choose to expand this application with other options, such as system administration operations, having to change the menu in only one place makes your coding task much easier. As you can see below, the mainMenu is implemented as a class with its constructor method actually creating the menu in HTML. Any time you need the main menu to appear, you just instantiate the class with code similar to the following:

```
$myMainMenu = new mainMenu();
```

This class's functionality could easily be expanded to handle any type of menu, where you would pass parameters for the menu at the time of creation. This would allow you to change the look and feel of all the menus used throughout the application in just one block of code.

```
//################################################################
//##    Class:           mainMenu                                ##
//##    Description:     Present user with file and directory    ##
//##                     operation options                       ##
//################################################################
class mainMenu
   {
   //constructor
   function mainMenu ()
      {
      echoLine ("<center>");
      echoLine ("<a href=\"chapter10_filemenu.php\"");
      echoLine (">File Operations</a>");
      echoLine ("<a href=\"chapter10_dirmenu.php\"");
      echoLine (">Directory Operations</a>");
      echoLine ("<br><br><br>");
      echoLine ("</center>");
      }
   }
```

The next common function to look at is called display2ColumnTable(). Its purpose is to take a two-dimensional associative array and turn it into a two-column HTML table. This is handy code for any time you need to display several key=values pairs. The first section of this code checks to make sure the array passed to the function has values, and, if not, it just writes out a simple HTML message indicating no results were present. Next, the code draws a table with each row having two data elements. The first element is the key from the associative array, and the second element in the row is the value that corresponds to that key. The code iterates through the array until all the values have been output, and then it closes the table and returns control to the calling routine.

```
//###################################################################
//##         Function:           display2ColumnTable               ##
//##       Parameters:           2D associative array              ##
//##      Description:     Outputs a 2 dimensional array in an HTML ##
//##                       table. The first row contains the        ##
//##                       column names                             ##
//###################################################################
function display2ColumnTable($results)
   {
   //Indicate if the resultset is empty
   if (empty($results))
      {
      echoLine ("<center>");
      echoLine ("<br>");
      echoLine ("Action Returned No Results!");
      echoLine ("</center>");
      return ;
      }

   echoLine ("<br>");
   echoLine ("<center>");
   echoLine ("<table cellspacing=5 cellpadding=5 border=3");
   echoLine ("bordercolor=\"0000FF\" >");
   echoLine ("<thead>");
   echoLine ("<tr>");

   while (list ($key, $value) = each ($results))
      {
      echoLine ("<td>$key</td><td>$value</td></tr>");
      }
   echoLine ("</tr>");
   echoLine ("</table>");
   echoLine ("</center>");
   }
```

The displayArray() function is used to display the contents of a simple one-dimensional array as a single-column HTML table. The parameters to the function are the array and a string that represents a heading for the table. As with the previous function, you first must check that the array passed has data in it. Next, you output the start of a table, with the first row being the heading for the table. Each subsequent row has one table data element in it, which is the value from the array.

```
//###################################################################
//##        Function:           displayArray                       ##
//##      Parameters:           1D array                           ##
//##     Description:    Outputs a 1 dimensional array as an HTML  ##
//##                     table. The first row is the heading for   ##
//##                     the array                                 ##
//###################################################################
function displayArray($heading,$resultset)
   {
   //Indicate if the resultset is empty
   if (empty($resultset))
      {
      echoLine ("<center>");
      echoLine ("<br>");
      echoLine ("Action Returned No Rows!");
      echoLine ("</center>");
      return ;
      }
   //The first row is names the results
   echoLine ("<br>");
   echoLine ("<center>");
   echoLine ("<table cellspacing=5 cellpadding=5 border=3 ");
   echoLine ("bordercolor=\"0000FF\" >");
   echoLine ("<thead>");
   echoLine ("<tr>");
   echoLine ("<th>");
   echoLine ($heading);
   echoLine ("</th>");
   echoLine ("</tr>");
   echoLine ("</thead>");

   //Display a new row for each element of the input array
   $itemcount = sizeof ($resultset);
   for($rowCounter = 0; $rowCounter < $itemcount; $rowCounter++)
      {
      echoLine ("<tr>");
      echoLine ("<td>");
      echoLine (" ");
      echoLine ($resultset[$rowCounter]);
      echoLine (" ");
      echoLine ("</td>");
      }
   echoLine ("</tr>");
```

```
    echoLine ("</table>");
    echoLine ("</center>");
    }
?>
```

Directory Menu

The code module that we'll examine next is the directory menu. The purpose of this code is to provide the user with a list of possible operations that they can perform on directories on the host file system. The module is almost entirely HTML and is comprised of a form within a table structure. The file starts off by including your common functions and then presenting the main menu in case the user would rather switch back to the file operations.

chapter10_dirMenu.php

```
<?php

include ('chapter10_common.php');
?>

<!doctype html public -//W3C//DTD HTML 4.0 >
<html>
<head>
<title></title>
</head>
<body>

<?php
$myMainMenu = new mainMenu();
?>
```

The next section of code in the directory menu module contains some JavaScript, which allows the form options to change dynamically depending on what directory operation the user wishes to perform. The HTML form includes a single-selection drop-down list and two text input boxes. The label for the text input boxes changes according to the option that is currently selected in the drop-down list. As you can see, we are altering the inner text property of the labels for the text boxes. There are many possible ways to implement a dynamic menu, so feel free to experiment with this code. In the interest of simplicity, if only one of the input boxes is necessary, the text in the label is set to empty. Ideally, the input box itself would be removed as well. The JavaScript code to do this is as follows:

```
<script language="Javascript">
function onChangeDir (formObj)
  {
  var selIndex = formObj.options.selectedIndex;
  var value = formObj.options[selIndex].value;
  if (value == 1)
     {
     DIRLABEL1.innerText = "DIRECTORY NAME";
     DIRLABEL2.innerText = "MODE";
     }
  else if (value == 3)
     {
     DIRLABEL1.innerText = "OLD NAME";
     DIRLABEL2.innerText = "NEW NAME";
     }
  else
     {
     DIRLABEL1.innerText = "DIRECTORY NAME";
     DIRLABEL2.innerText = "";
     }
  }
</script>
```

After the JavaScript functions are presented, the actual table with its form is drawn. Notice that the labels have been given specific IDs and are assigned using the for statement to the IDs of the text input boxes, not the names of the text boxes themselves, which can be a source of confusion. The code for this form is as follows:

```
<center>
<table cellspacing=5 cellpadding=5 border=3
 bordercolor="0000FF" >
<tr><td>
<form name="DIRACTIONS" action="chapter10_dirActions.php"
 method="POST">
<select name="DIRACTION" SIZE="1"
 onchange="return onChangeDir(this);">
<option value="1" selected>Create Directory
<option value="2">Remove Directory
<option value="3">Rename Directory
```

```
<option value="4">List Contents Of Directory
<option value="5">Check Free Space
</select>
</td></Ttr>
<tr><td>
<label id="DIRLABEL1" for="IDDIRBOX1">DIRECTORY NAME</label>
<br>
<input name="DIRBOX1" id="IDDIRBOX1" type=TEXT >
</td></tr>
<tr><td>
<label id="DIRLABEL2" for="IDDIRBOX2">MODE</label>
<br>
<input name="DIRBOX2" id="IDDIRBOX2" type=TEXT >
</td></tr>
<tr><td>
<input type="SUBMIT" value="OK">
</form>
</td></tr>
</table>
</center>

</body>
</html>
```

File Menu

The file menu module is very similar to the directory menu module. The only difference is that the file operations are broken down into three sets. The first is getting file properties. The next is setting file properties, and the last is acting on files. Each of these sets has their own form and action pages. The code starts by including the common functions module and then writing out the main menu.

chapter10_fileMenu.php

```
<?php
include ('chapter10_common.php');
?>

<!doctype html public -//W3C//DTD HTML 4.0 >
<html>
<head>
<title></title>
```

```
</head>
<body>

<?php
$myMainMenu = new mainMenu();
?>
```

Next are three JavaScript functions that handle dynamically changing the input text box labels based on the selections made by the user, as shown here:

```
<script language="Javascript">
function onChangeSFP (formObj)
  {
  var selIndex = formObj.options.selectedIndex;
  var value = formObj.options[selIndex].value;
  if (value == 1)
     {
     SFPLABEL1.innerText = "FILE NAME ";
     SFPLABEL2.innerText = "OWNER";
     }
  else if (value == 2)
     {
     SFPLABEL1.innerText = "FILE NAME ";
     SFPLABEL2.innerText = "GROUP";
     }
  else if (value == 3)
     {
     SFPLABEL1.innerText = "FILE NAME ";
     SFPLABEL2.innerText = "PERMISSIONS";
     }
  else if (value == 4)
     {
     SFPLABEL1.innerText = " ";
     SFPLABEL2.innerText = "UMASK";
     }
  else if (value == 5 || value == 6)
     {
     SFPLABEL1.innerText = "FILE NAME ";
     SFPLABEL2.innerText = "LINK NAME";
     }
  }
```

```
function onChangeGFP (formObj)
   {
   var selIndex = formObj.options.selectedIndex;
   var value = formObj.options[selIndex].value;
   if (value == 3 || value == 4)
     GFPLABEL1.innerText = "LINK NAME";
   else
     GFPLABEL1.innerText = "FILE NAME";
   }

function onChangePFA (formObj)
   {
   var selIndex = formObj.options.selectedIndex;
   var value = formObj.options[selIndex].value;
   if (value == 1 || value == 2 )
     {
     PFALABEL1.innerText = "SOURCE";
     PFALABEL2.innerText = "DESTINATION";
     }
   else if (value == 3 || value == 5 )
     {
     PFALABEL1.innerText = "FILE NAME";
     PFALABEL2.innerText = "";
     }
   else if (value == 4)
     {
     PFALABEL1.innerText = "OLD FILE NAME";
     PFALABEL2.innerText = "NEW FILE NAME";
     }
   else if (value == 6)
     {
     PFALABEL1.innerText = "FILE NAME";
     PFALABEL2.innerText = "TIME";
     }
   }
</script>
```

Now the HTML begins. The file operations menu is comprised of three forms with a table in each form, and all three forms inside one large table (see Figure 10-1). The tables are used to help position the forms and their elements in a consistent manner. Again, there are multiple ways to present the file operations menu, so consider expanding the menu's look and feel to improve the end user's experience.

The menu code is as follows:

```
<center>
<table cellspacing=5 cellpadding=5 border=3 bordercolor="0000FF">
<tr><td>
Get File Properties
</td><td>
Set File Properties
</td><td>
Perform File Actions
</td></tr>
<tr><td>
<form name="GETPROPERTIES" action="chapter10_getprops.php"
 method="POST">
<table>
<td><tr>
<select name="PROPERTIES" SIZE="1"
 onchange="return onChangeGFP(this);">
<option value="1" SELECTED>Get File Type
<option value="2">Get File Properties
<option value="3">Examine Hard Link
<option value="4">Examine Symbolic Link
<option value="5">Get Umask
</select>
</td></tr>
<tr><td>
<label id="GFPLABEL1" for="IDGFPBOX1">FILE NAME</label>
<br>
<input name="GFPBOX1" id="IDGFPBOX1" type=TEXT >
</td></tr>
<tr><td>
 
</td></tr>
<tr><td>
 
</td></tr>
<tr><td>
<input type="SUBMIT" value="OK">
</form>
</td></tr>
</table>
</td><td>
<form name="SETPROPERTIES" action="chapter10_setprops.php"
 method="POST">
<table>
```

```
<td><tr>
<select name="PROPERTIES" SIZE="1"
 onchange="return onChangeSFP(this);">
<option value="1" selected>Set File Owner
<option value="2" >Set File Group
<option value="3" >Set File Permissions
<option value="4" >Set Umask
<option value="5" >Set A Hard Link
<option value="6" >Set A Symbolic Link
</select>
</td></tr>
<tr><td>
<label id="SFPLABEL1" for="IDSFPBOX1">FILE NAME</label>
<br>
<input name="SFPBOX1" id="IDSFPBOX1" type=TEXT >
</td></tr>
<tr><td>
<label id="SFPLABEL2" for="IDSFPBOX2"> OWNER</label>
<br>
<input name="SFPBOX2" id="IDSFPBOX2" type=TEXT >
</td></tr>
<tr><td>
<input type="SUBMIT" value="OK">
</form>
</td></tr>
</table>
</td><td>
<form name="UTILITIES" action="chapter10_fileactions.php"
 method="POST">
<table>
<td><tr>
<select name="UTILITIES" size="1"
 onchange="return onChangePFA(this);">
<option value="1" SELECTED>Copy File
<option value="2">Move File
<option value="3">Remove File
<option value="4">Rename File
<option value="5">Unlink A File
<option value="6">Touch File
</select>
</td></tr>
<tr><td>
<label id="PFALABEL1" for="IDPFABOX1">SOURCE</label>
<br>
<input name="PFABOX1" id="IDPFABOX1" type=TEXT >
```

```
</td></tr>
<tr><td>
<label id="PFALABEL2" for="IDPFABOX2"> DESTINATION</label>
<br>
<input name="PFABOX2" id="IDPFABOX2" type=TEXT >
</td></tr>
<tr><td>
<input type="SUBMIT" value="OK">
</form>
</td></tr>
</table>
</td></tr>
</table>
</center>

</body>
</html>
```

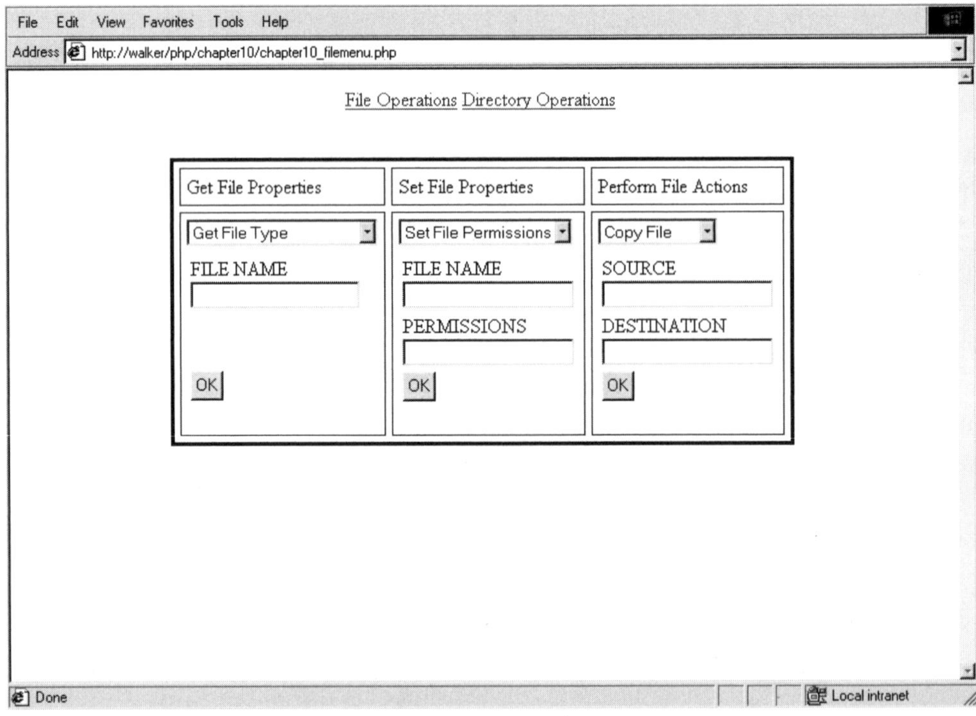

Figure 10-1 *The file operations menu*

Directory Actions

The next code module to discuss is the directory actions module. This is what the directory operations form calls, and it includes all of the PHP methods used to work with directories along with the code to process the form and display the appropriate output.

We begin by including the common functions used throughout the application. Next, we define the dirActions class, which contains the methods used to work with directories on the file system. To instantiate a dirActions class, just create a new object and pass a directory name to the constructor.

chapter10_dirActions.php

```
<?php


include ('chapter10_common.php');

//####################################################################
//##    Class:          dirActions                                 ##
//##    Description:    Class for manipulating directories          ##
//####################################################################
class dirActions
   {
   //member variables
   var $dir;

//####################################################################
//##    Constructor:    dirActions                                 ##
//##    Parameters:     dir                                        ##
//##    Return value:   Instance of dirActions class               ##
//####################################################################
   function dirActions ($dir)
      {
         $this->dir = $dir;
      }
```

The first method we'll look at in the dirActions class is the createDir() method. Figure 10-2 shows the form used in conjunction with the createDir() method. This method takes one argument: the mode the directory should be created with. It uses the mode along with the directory name supplied in the constructor of the class to call PHP's mkdir() function. The mode represents what permission should be

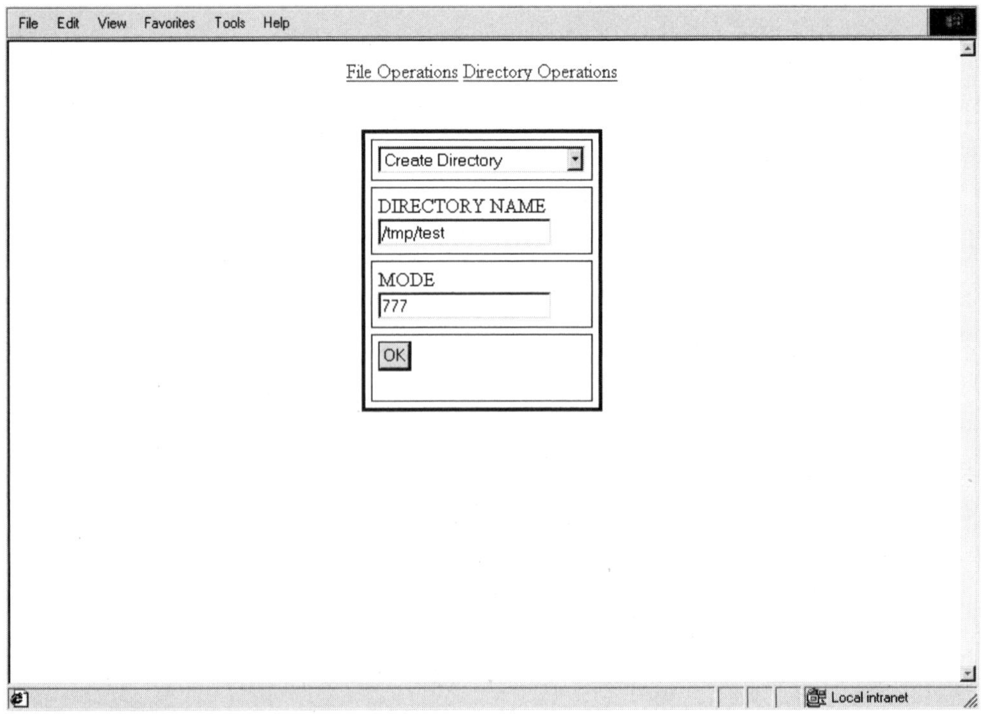

Figure 10-2 *The Create Directory form*

assigned to the directory upon creation and is represented by an octal number. The number is comprised of three masks representing the user, the group, and the other or world's permissions. The masks indicate read, write, and execute permission, with 1 corresponding to execute, 2 corresponding to write, and 4 corresponding to read. In order to combine these options, just add them together, such as execute and write equals 1 plus 2, or 3. Therefore, to give the user all permissions, the group read and writes, and the world read permissions, you would specify a mode of 0764. The mode applies to all files in the directory if permissions are not explicitly defined. Note that this mode is not supported on Windows machines.

```
//####################################################################
//##    Method:          createDir                                  ##
//##    Parameters:      Mode                                       ##
//##    Return value:    array with return code and status msg      ##
//####################################################################
```

```
    function createDir ($mode)
        {
        $rc = mkdir ($this->dir,$mode);
            if ($rc == 1)
                {
                $results = array("rc" => $rc,
                                 "Directory" => $this->dir,
                                 "Created With Mode" => $mode);
                }
            else
                {
                $results = array("rc" => $rc,
                "Directory" => $this->dir,
                "Could Not Be Created With Mode" => $mode);
                }

        return $results;
        }
```

For each of the methods of the dirActions class, the return value is an associative array, which includes the return code from the corresponding PHP function along with a message regarding the success or failure of the operation. This allows the calling routine to decide what information it wants to present to the user—the return code, the message, or both.

The next method removes a directory from the file system utilizing PHP's rmdir() function and acts on the directory that was supplied to the constructor.

```
//#####################################################################
//##    Method:           removeDir                                 ##
//##    Parameters:       none                                      ##
//##    Return value:     array with return code and status msg     ##
//#####################################################################
    function removeDir()
        {
        $rc = rmdir ($this->dir);
            if ($rc == 1)
                {
                $results = array("rc" => $rc,
                                 "Removed Directory" => $this->dir);
                }
            else
```

```
            {
            $results = array("rc" => $rc,
                    "Could Not Remove Directory" => $this->dir);
            }
      return $results;
      }
```

The rename directory method renameDir() takes the directory supplied with the constructor and attempts to rename it to the supplied parameter using PHP's rename function.

```
//####################################################################
//##    Method:           renameDir                                ##
//##    Parameters:       new name                                 ##
//##    Return value:     array with return code and status msg    ##
//####################################################################
   function renameDir($newName)
      {
      $rc = rename ($this->dir,$newName);
      if ($rc == 1)
        {
       $results = array("rc" => $rc,
        "Directory" => $this->dir,
       "Was Renamed To" => $newName);
        }
      else
        {
            $results = array("rc" => $rc,
                             "Directory" => $this->dir,
                             "Could Not Be Renamed To" => $newName);

       }

      return $results;
      }
```

The listContents() method provides a very basic directory listing. It only returns the names of the files and directories located within the directory supplied with the constructor. It places each of the files/directories into a single-dimensional array so that they can be listed out by the calling routine. A logical next step for this routine would be to return more detailed information about each of the items returned in the array, such as which are files and which are directories, along with timestamps and sizes for each.

```
//#####################################################################
//##    Method:          listContents                                ##
//##    Parameters:      none                                        ##
//##    Return value:    array with contents(files) in directory     ##
//#####################################################################
   function listContents()
      {
      $dh = dir ($this->dir);
      $results = array();
      while ($file = $dh->read())
         {
         array_push($results,$file);
         }
      return $results;
      }
```

The checkFree() method reports how much space is available on a disk, and is measured in bytes. For Windows, the user should enter the drive and path; and for *nix, the user just needs to enter a path. The amount of free space is returned in an array for easy display.

```
//#####################################################################
//##    Method:          checkFree                                   ##
//##    Parameters:      none                                        ##
//##    Return value:    array with amount of free space available ##
//#####################################################################
   function checkFree()
      {
      $results = array();
      array_push($results,diskfreespace($this->dir));
      return $results;
      }
   }//end of dirActions class
```

Handling the Directory Operations Form

The first step in handling the directory operations form is to retrieve the form variables from PHP, as follows:

```
//Retrieve input variables from HTTP get or post
$userinfo = strtolower($REQUEST_METHOD) == 'get'
   ? $HTTP_GET_VARS : $HTTP_POST_VARS;
```

Next, generate the main menu so that after a user views the results they can perform subsequent actions, as shown here:

```
$myMainMenu = new mainMenu();
```

Next, the code examines what operation the user requested and then calls the corresponding directory action based on their choice. When creating, removing, or renaming a directory, the results of the associative array are displayed using the display2ColumnTable method found in the common module. When displaying the directory contents and free space available, the displayArray() method is used to show the heading, and then the file list or the free space, respectively. The code to handle the directory actions is as follows:

```
//Perform Directory Actions
switch($userinfo[DIRACTION])
   {
   case '1':
      {
      $myDirActions = new dirActions($userinfo[DIRBOX1]);
      $results = $myDirActions->createDir($userinfo[DIRBOX2]);
      display2ColumnTable($results);
      break;
      }
   case '2':
      {
      $myDirActions = new dirActions($userinfo[DIRBOX1]);
      $results = $myDirActions->removeDir();
      display2ColumnTable($results);
      break;
      }
   case '3':
      {
      $myDirActions = new dirActions($userinfo[DIRBOX1]);
      $results = $myDirActions->renameDir($userinfo[DIRBOX2]);
      display2ColumnTable($results);
      break;
      }
   case '4':
      {
      $myDirActions = new dirActions($userinfo[DIRBOX1]);
      $results = $myDirActions->listContents();
      displayArray("Files",$results);
      break;
      }
```

```
    case '5':
        {
        $myDirActions = new dirActions($userinfo[DIRBOX1]);
        $results = $myDirActions->checkFree();
        displayArray("Free Space",$results);
        break;
        }
    }
?>
</body>
</html>
```

File Operations

Now we'll move on to the file operations modules of the application. The file operations are split into three separate modules that correspond to the three forms on the fileMenu module. The first file operation module we'll look at is the fileActions module.

File Actions

The fileActions module handles all requests that affect a file's name or location. This includes copying, moving, renaming, touching, and so on. The module begins by including the common module and then defining a fileActions class that will comprise all of the methods necessary for this module. The constructor for the fileActions class includes a file name parameter that becomes a member variable of the class and is used by most of the methods in the class.

chapter10_fileActions.php

```
<?php

include ('chapter10_common.php');

//####################################################################
//##    Class:          fileActions                                 ##
//##    Description:    Class for acting on file                    ##
//####################################################################
class fileActions
    {
    //member variables
    var $file;
```

```
//####################################################################
//##    Constructor:    fileActions                                ##
//##    Parameters:     file                                       ##
//##    Return value:   Instance of fileActions class              ##
//####################################################################
   function fileActions ($file)
      {
         $this->file = $file;
      }
```

The first method of the fileActions class we'll examine is the copyFile() method, which simply copies a file from a source to a destination location. The return value is an associative array with the return code from the PHP copy function along with a status message on whether the copy was successful.

```
//####################################################################
//##    Method:         copyFile                                   ##
//##    Parameters:     New Location                               ##
//##    Return value:   array with return code and status msg      ##
//####################################################################
   function copyFile($dest)
      {
      if (file_exists($this->file))
         {
         $rc = copy ($this->file,$dest);
         if ($rc == 1)
            {
            $results = array("rc" => $rc,
                             "File" => $this->file,
                             "Copied To" => $dest);
            }
         else
            {
            $results = array("rc" => $rc,
                             "File" => $this->file,
                             "Could Not Be Copied To" => $dest);
            }
         }
      return $results;
      }
```

The moveFile() method is identical to the copyFile() method, except that the status message refers to moving instead of copying. The moveFile() method just copies the file at this point and leaves it up to the calling routine to determine whether the file should be deleted from the original location—however, you may want to move that code into this method as well.

```
//######################################################################
//##    Method:           moveFile                                    ##
//##    Parameters:       New Location                                ##
//##    Return value:     array with return code and status msg       ##
//######################################################################
   function moveFile($dest)
      {
      if (file_exists($this->file))
         {
         $rc = copy ($this->file,$dest);
         if ($rc == 1)
            {
            $results = array("rc" => $rc,
                             "File" => $this->file,
                             "Moved To" => $dest);
            }
         else
            {
            $results = array("rc" => $rc,
                             "File" => $this->file,
                             "Could Not Be Move To" => $dest);
            }
         }
      return $results;
      }
```

The removeFile() method does just that—it deletes a file from the file system. The delete is permanent, there is no confirmation request, and the file is not moved into the recycle bin as on Windows machines, so use this method carefully.

```
//######################################################################
//##    Method:           removeFile                                  ##
//##    Parameters:       none                                        ##
//##    Return value:     array with return code and status msg       ##
//######################################################################
   function removeFile()
      {
      if (file_exists($this->file))
         {
         $rc = unlink ($this->file);
         if ($rc == 1)
```

```
            {
            $results = array("rc" => $rc,
                             "File" => $this->file,
                             "Status:" => "Was Removed");
            }
         else
            {
            $results = array("rc" => $rc,
                             "File" => $this->file,
                             "Status:" => "Could Not Be Removed");
            }
         }
      return $results;
      }
```

Renaming a file is done using the renameFile() method and changes a file's name to the new one, assuming the file exists in the first place. This method will not rename a file to a name that already exists on the file system. (See Figure 10-3.)

```
//####################################################################
//##    Method:          renameFile                                  ##
//##    Parameters:      New File Name                               ##
//##    Return value:    array with return code and status msg       ##
//####################################################################
   function renameFile($newName)
      {
      if (file_exists($this->file))
         {
         $rc = rename ($this->file,$newName);
         if ($rc == 1)
            {
            $results = array("rc" => $rc,
                             "File" => $this->file,
                             "Was Renamed To" => $newName);
            }
         else
            {
            $results = array("rc" => $rc,
                             "File" => $this->file,
                             "Could Not Be Renamed To" => $newName);
            }
         }
      return $results;
      }
```

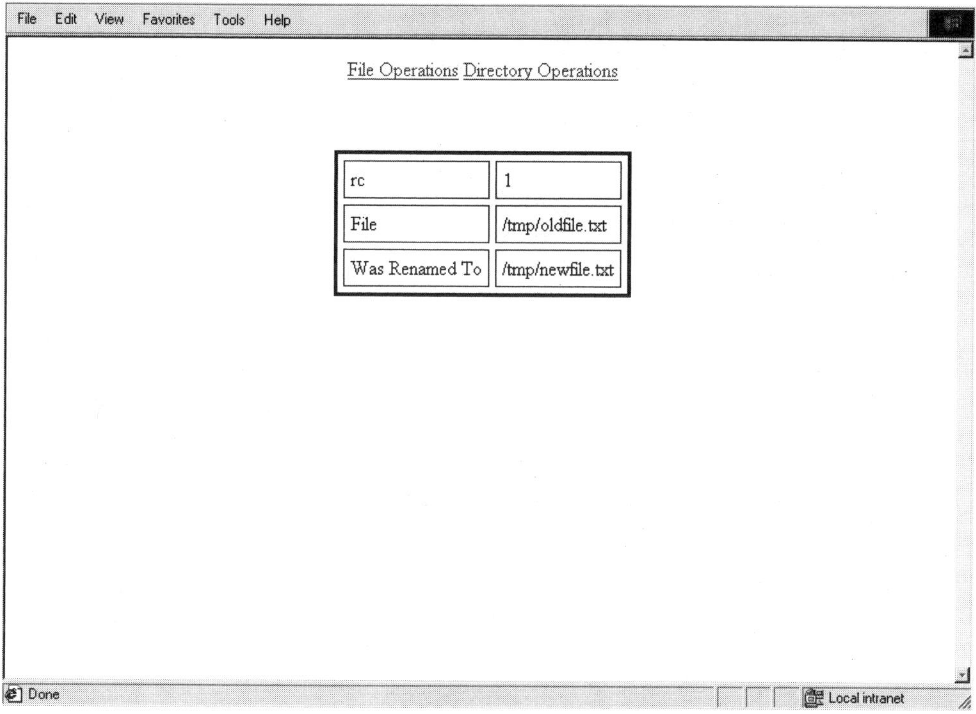

Figure 10-3 *Sample renamed file output*

As you may already know, unlinking a file is equivalent to removing a file. Since not everyone is aware of this, however, two methods exist—one with a remove status message and one with an unlink status message.

```
//####################################################################
//##    Method:          unlinkFile                                  ##
//##    Parameters:      none                                        ##
//##    Return value:    array with return code and status msg       ##
//####################################################################
   function unlinkFile()
      {
      if (file_exists($this->file))
         {
         $rc = unlink ($this->file);
         if ($rc == 1)
            {
```

```
            $results = array("rc" => $rc,
                                "File" => $this->file,
                                "Status:" => "Was UnLinked");
            }
        else
            {
            $results = array("rc" => $rc,
                                "File" => $this->file,
                                "Status:" => "Could Not Be Unlinked");
            }
        }
    return $results;
    }
```

The purpose of touching a file is to update its last accessed and last modified times. This is often used as a sort of flag letting other shell scripts or applications recognize if work needs to be done with the file. The touchFile() method includes a time parameter, which indicates what the new times should be. The time is the offset from the start of the system clock, which works out to be 12-31-1969 on Windows machines. On *nix machines, no time parameter will cause the access and modified times to change to the current time.

```
//####################################################################
//##    Method:         touchFile                                  ##
//##    Parameters:     time                                       ##
//##    Return value:   array with return code and status msg      ##
//####################################################################
   function touchFile($time)
    {
    if (file_exists($this->file))
        {
        $rc = touch ($this->file,$time);
        if ($rc == TRUE)
            {
            $results = array("rc" => $rc,
                                "File" => $this->file,
                                "Status:" => "Was Touched");
            }
        else
            {
            $results = array("rc" => $rc,
                                "File" => $this->file,
                                "Status:" => "Could Not Be Touched");
```

```
            }
        }
    return $results;
    }
}//end of fileActions class
```

Handling the File Actions Form

After defining the file action class and its methods, the next step is to actually handle the file actions form call from the file menu page. You'll start by retrieving the form variables from PHP and then outputting the main menu so that the user can return to the application after viewing the results, as shown here:

```
//Retrieve input variables from HTTP get or post
$userinfo = strtolower($REQUEST_METHOD) == 'get'
   ? $HTTP_GET_VARS : $HTTP_POST_VARS;


$myMainMenu = new mainMenu();
```

Then you examine the form variables to determine which action the user selected. For each operation, you create a fileActions object and then call the method that corresponds to the action chosen. After the method call, you display the results to the user using the display2ColumnTable function from the common module. Notice that for the moveFile() method, we chose to delete the file at the original location within this section of code, since it is not implemented in the fileActions class. The code to handle the file actions is as follows:

```
//Perform File Actions
switch($userinfo[UTILITIES])
   {
   case '1':
      {
      $myFileActions = new fileActions($userinfo[PFABOX1]);
      $results = $myFileActions->copyFile($userinfo[PFABOX2]);
      display2ColumnTable($results);
      break;
      }
   case '2':
      {
      $myFileActions = new fileActions($userinfo[PFABOX1]);
      $results = $myFileActions->moveFile($userinfo[PFABOX2]);
      display2ColumnTable($results);
      if ($results[rc] == 1)
```

```
            {
            $removeresults =
            $myFileActions->removeFile($userinfo[PFABOX1]);
            echoLine ("<br><br>");
            display2ColumnTable($removeresults);
            }
        break;
        }
    case '3':
        {
        $myFileActions = new fileActions($userinfo[PFABOX1]);
        $results = $myFileActions->removeFile();
        display2ColumnTable($results);
        break;
        }
    case '4':
        {
        $myFileActions = new fileActions($userinfo[PFABOX1]);
        $results = $myFileActions->renameFile($userinfo[PFABOX2]);
        display2ColumnTable($results);
        break;
        }
    case '5':
        {
        $myFileActions = new fileActions($userinfo[PFABOX1]);
        $results = $myFileActions->unlinkFile();
        display2ColumnTable($results);
        break;
        }
    case '6':
        {
        $myFileActions = new fileActions($userinfo[PFABOX1]);
        $results = $myFileActions->touchFile($userinfo[PFABOX2]);
        display2ColumnTable($results);
        break;
        }
    }
?>
</body>
</html>
```

The Get File Properties Class

The getFileProps class contains all of the methods needed to learn more about a file. To use this class, create a getFileProps object and pass it a filename you want to learn more about. Then call the appropriate method. The return value will be an array with a status code for the PHP function that was used along with a status message, which can be displayed for the user. Keep in mind that the properties available on a Windows machine will differ from those available on a *nix machine, so you will want to do some experimenting between the two. Also keep in mind that links, which provide alternate names for a file, have no meaning on Windows machines. For the umask property no filename is necessary, which is why the code doesn't check for file existence in the constructor of the class, but instead waits until the particular methods that require file existence are called. The clearstatcache() function is used before each test for file existence because PHP tends to cache file information–related requests to help improve performance. However, for the methods defined here, the test needs to be performed each time.

chapter10_getProps.php

```
<?php

include ('chapter10_common.php');

//####################################################################
//##    Class:          getFileProps                                ##
//##    Description:    Class for retrieving file properties        ##
//####################################################################
class getFileProps
   {
   //member variables
   var $file;

//####################################################################
//##    Constructor:    getFileProps                                ##
//##    Parameters:     file                                        ##
//##    Return value:   Instance of getFileProps class              ##
//####################################################################
   function getFileProps ($file)
      {
```

```
        $this->file = $file;
        }

//####################################################################
//##    Method:         getFileType                                ##
//##    Parameters:     none                                       ##
//##    Return value:   array with file and type                   ##
//####################################################################
    function getFileType()
        {
        clearstatcache();
        if (file_exists($this->file))
            {
            $fileType = filetype($this->file);
            $results = array("File" => $this->file ,"File Type" =>
            $fileType);
            }
        else
            {
            $results = array("File" => $this->file,
                            "Error" => "Does Not Exist");
            }
        return $results;
        }

//####################################################################
//##    Method:         getFileProperties                          ##
//##    Parameters:     none                                       ##
//##    Return value:   array with file and properties             ##
//####################################################################
    function getFileProperties()
        {
        clearstatcache();
       if (file_exists($this->file))
            {
            $filePermissions = fileperms($this->file);
            $fileOwner = fileowner($this->file);
            $fileGroup = filegroup($this->file);
            $fileSize = filesize ($this->file);
            $fileATime = fileatime($this->file);
            $fileCTime = filectime($this->file);
            $fileMTime = filemtime($this->file);
            $fileInode = fileinode($this->file);
```

```
        $results = array("File" => $this->file,
                         "Permissions" => $filePermissions,
                         "Owner" => $fileOwner,
                         "Group" => $fileGroup,
                         "Size" => $filesize,
                         "Last Access Time" => $fileATime,
                         "Last Change Time" => $fileCTime,
                         "Last Modified Time" => $fileMTime,
                         "Inode" => $fileInode);
        }
      else
        {
        $results = array("File" => $this->file,
                          "Error" => "Does Not Exist");
        }
      return $results;
      }

//######################################################################
//##    Method:         getFileHardLink                               ##
//##    Parameters:     none                                          ##
//##    Return value:   array with return code and status msgs       ##
//######################################################################
   function getFileHardLink()
      {
      clearstatcache();
      if (file_exists($this->file))
        {
        $rc = linkinfo ($this->file);
        if ($rc == 0)
          {
          $results = array("rc" => $rc,
                           "Link" => $this->file,
                           "Status:" => "Exists");
          }
        else
          {
          $results = array("rc" => $rc,
                           "Link" => $this->file,
                           "Status:" => "Does Not Exist");
          }
        }
      return $results;
      }
```

```
//####################################################################
//##    Method:         getFileSymLink                              ##
//##    Parameters:     none                                        ##
//##    Return value:   array with return code and status msgs      ##
//####################################################################
   function getFileSymLink()
      {
      clearstatcache();
      if (file_exists($this->file))
         {
         $contents = readlink ($this->file);
         if ($contents != FALSE)
            {
            $results = array("rc" => $rc,
                             "Link" => $this->file,
                             "Points To" => $contents);
            }
         else
            {
            $results = array("rc" => $rc,
                             "Link" => $this->file,
                             "Status" => "Does Not Exist");
            }
         }
      return $results;
      }

//####################################################################
//##    Method:         getFileUmask                                ##
//##    Parameters:     none                                        ##
//##    Return value:   array with return code and status msgs      ##
//####################################################################
   function getFileUmask()
      {
      $umask = umask ();
      if ($umask != FALSE)
         {
         $results = array("Umask" => $umask);
         }
      else
         {
         $results = array("Umask" => "Could Not Be Determined");
         }
```

```
        return $results;
        }
    }//end of getFileProps class
```

Handling the Get File Properties Form

Now that you have the fileProps class in place, you can process the incoming get file properties form and display the corresponding output. For each get operation, create a fileProps object and then call the corresponding method of the object. Then display the results as an HTML table using the display2ColumnTable function that was created with the common module. The code to handle the file actions follows:

```
//Retrieve input variables from HTTP get or post
$userinfo = strtolower($REQUEST_METHOD) == 'get'
    ? $HTTP_GET_VARS : $HTTP_POST_VARS;

$myMainMenu = new mainMenu();

switch($userinfo[PROPERTIES])
    {
    case '1':
        {
        $myGetFileProps = new getFileProps($userinfo[GFPBOX1]);
        $results = $myGetFileProps->getFileType();
        display2ColumnTable($results);
        break;
        }
    case '2':
        {
        $myGetFileProps = new getFileProps($userinfo[GFPBOX1]);
        $results = $myGetFileProps->getFileProperties();
        display2ColumnTable($results);
        break;
        }
    case '3':
        {
        $myGetFileProps = new getFileProps($userinfo[GFPBOX1]);
        $results = $myGetFileProps->getFileHardLink();
        display2ColumnTable($results);
        break;
        }
    case '4':
```

```
        {

  $myGetFileProps = new getFileProps($userinfo[GFPBOX1]);
        $results = $myGetFileProps->getFileSymLink();
        display2ColumnTable($results);
        break;
        }
    case '5':
        {
        $myGetFileProps = new getFileProps($userinfo[GFPBOX1]);
        $results = $myGetFileProps->getFileUmask();
        display2ColumnTable($results);
        break;
        }
    }
?>
</body>
</html>
```

The Set File Properties Class

The last portion of code we'll examine is the set file properties class. This class defines all the methods needed to modify a file's properties, such as owner, group, permissions, and so on. Similar to the get file properties class, the methods have different meanings on Windows machines versus *nix machines, so it is best to do some experimenting to be sure you get the results you would expect. Also, remember that links are not used on Windows systems.

chapter10_setProps.php

```
<?php

include ('chapter10_common.php');

//####################################################################
//##    Class:          setFileProps                               ##
//##    Description:    Class for setting file properties          ##
//####################################################################
class setFileProps
    {
    //member variables
    var $file;
```

```
//#####################################################################
//##    Constructor:    setFileProps                                 ##
//##    Parameters:     file                                         ##
//##    Return value:   Instance of setFileProps class               ##
//#####################################################################
   function setFileProps ($file)
      {
         $this->file = $file;
      }

//#####################################################################
//##    Method:         setFileOwner                                 ##
//##    Parameters:     New Owner                                    ##
//##    Return value:   array with return code and status msg        ##
//#####################################################################
   function setFileOwner($owner)
      {
      clearstatcache();
      if (file_exists($this->file))
         {
         $rc = chown ($this->file,$owner);
         if ($rc == 0)
            {
            $results = array("rc" => $rc,
                             "File" => $this->file,
                             "Now Owned By" => $owner);
            }
         else
            {
            $results = array("rc" => $rc,
                             "File" => $this->file,
                             "Cannot Be Owned By" => $owner);
            }
         }
         return $results;
      }

//#####################################################################
//##    Method:         setFileGroup                                 ##
//##    Parameters:     New Group                                    ##
//##    Return value:   array with return code and status msg        ##
//#####################################################################
```

```
    function setFileGroup($group)
       {
       clearstatcache();
       if (file_exists($this->file))
          {
          $rc = chgrp ($this->file,$group);
          if ($rc == 0)
             {
             $results = array("rc" => $rc,
                              "File" => $this->file,
                              "Now Belongs To Group" => $group);
             }
          else
             {
             $results = array("rc" => $rc,
                              "File" => $this->file,
                              "Cannot Belong To Group" => $group);
             }
          }
          return $results;
       }

//#####################################################################
//##    Method:          setFilePermissions                         ##
//##    Parameters:      Permission object                          ##
//##    Return value:    array with return code and status msg      ##
//#####################################################################
    function setFilePermissions($mode)
       {
       clearstatcache();
       if (file_exists($this->file))
          {
          $rc = chmod ($this->file,$mode);
          if ($rc == 0)
             {
             $results = array("rc" => $rc,
                              "File" => $this->file,
                              "Permissions Set To" => $mode);
             }
          else
             {
             $results = array("rc" => $rc,
                              "File" => $this->file,
                              "Permissions Can't Be Set To" => $mode);
```

```
            }
        }
      return $results;
      }



//####################################################################
//##    Method:          setFileHardLink                             ##
//##    Parameters:      link object                                 ##
//##    Return value:    array with return code and status msg       ##
//####################################################################
   function setFileHardLink($linkName)
      {
      clearstatcache();
      if (file_exists($this->file))
         {
         $rc = link ($this->file,$linkName);
         if ($rc == 0)
            {
            $results = array("rc" => $rc,
                             "File" => $this->file,
                             "Was Linked To" => $linkName);
            }
         else
            {
            $results = array("rc" => $rc,
                             "File" => $this->file,
                             "Could Not Be Linked To" => $linkName);
            }
         }
      return $results;
      }

//####################################################################
//##    Method:          setFileSymLink                              ##
//##    Parameters:      Link Name                                   ##
//##    Return value:    array with return code and status msg       ##
//####################################################################
   function setFileSymLink($linkName)
      {
      clearstatcache();
      if (file_exists($this->file))
         {
```

```
          $rc = symlink ($this->file,$linkName);
          if ($rc == 0)
             {
             $results = array("rc" => $rc,
                              "File" => $this->file,
                              "Was Symbolically Linked To" =>
$linkName);
             }
          else
             {
             $results = array("rc" => $rc,
                              "File" => $this->file,
                              "Could Not Be Symbolically Linked To" =>
$linkName);
             }
          }
       return $results;
       }

//####################################################################
//##    Method:          setFileUmask                               ##
//##    Parameters:      Umask                                      ##
//##    Return value:    array with return code and status msg      ##
//####################################################################
    function setFileUmask($mask)
       {
       $rc = umask ($mask);
       if ($rc == 0)
          {
          $results = array("rc" => $rc,
                           "Umask Set To" => $mask);
          }
       else
          {
          $results = array("rc" => $rc,
                           "Umask Could Not Be Set To" => $mask);
          }
       return $results;
       }
    }//end of fileActions class
```

Handling the Set File Properties Form

In the same way you have already handled the other file and directory operation forms, you'll now process the set file properties form. In typical style, you instantiate the setFileProps class, call the corresponding methods, and then display the results array as a two-column HTML table. By now, this code should look very familiar:

```
//Retrieve input variables from HTTP get or post
$userinfo = strtolower($REQUEST_METHOD) == 'get'
   ? $HTTP_GET_VARS : $HTTP_POST_VARS;


$myMainMenu = new mainMenu();

//Set File Properties
switch($userinfo[PROPERTIES])
   {
   case '1':
      {
      $mySetFileProps = new setFileProps($userinfo[SFPBOX1]);
      $results = $mySetFileProps->setFileOwner($userinfo[SFPBOX2]);
      display2ColumnTable($results);
      break;
      }
   case '2':
      {
      $mySetFileProps = new setFileProps($userinfo[SFPBOX1]);
      $results = $mySetFileProps->setFileGroup($userinfo[SFPBOX2]);
      display2ColumnTable($results);
      break;
      }
   case '3':
      {
      $mySetFileProps = new setFileProps($userinfo[SFPBOX1]);
      $results =
      $mySetFileProps->setFilePermissions($userinfo[SFPBOX2]);
      display2ColumnTable($results);
      break;
      }
```

```
    case '4':
        {
        $mySetFileProps = new setFileProps($userinfo[SFPBOX1]);
        $results = $mySetFileProps->setFileUmask($userinfo[SFPBOX2]);
        display2ColumnTable($results);
        break;
        }
    case '5':
        {
        $mySetFileProps = new setFileProps($userinfo[SFPBOX1]);
        $results =
        $mySetFileProps->setFileHardLink($userinfo[SFPBOX2]);
        display2ColumnTable($results);
        break;
        }
    case '6':
        {
        $mySetFileProps = new setFileProps($userinfo[SFPBOX1]);
        $results = $mySetFileProps->setFileSymLink($userinfo[SFPBOX2]);
        display2ColumnTable($results);
        break;
        }
    }
//}
?>
</body>
</html>
```

Testing the Application

Once you have the application coded and your environment set up correctly, you can begin working with the application. A very important concept to keep in mind when using the application is how Windows and *nix file systems differ. Many of the functions within the application will have no effect on a Windows system, so don't be surprised to see this behavior. Another important point is that you are performing these operations as the user under which PHP is running. This means that your permissions are based on this user and may be too narrow or too broad. Because of this, be very careful who has access to the application, as it could be very easy for someone to do harm whether that is their intent or not. The application is not really intended for use as it stands currently, but instead lays the groundwork for allowing users to do file and directory operations through a web browser.

Next Steps

The application presented in this chapter covers file and directory operations that are likely to be only a subset of what a user would like to perform on a remote system through a web browser. Next steps for this application are to include its functionality into a larger application that encompasses all the features a remote user is likely to need. A key part of this is implementing a strong, robust security mechanism that allows the user the appropriate amount of freedom while still maintaining tight control over the host system.

The actual layout of the application could definitely be tailored differently as well. The menus and forms were designed with a minimal amount of HTML in order to focus on the PHP code behind the application. Depending on if and how you choose to apply the code developed in this application, you will likely want to improve on the look and feel of the interfaces to the operations.

What to Take Away

This application provided an insight into many of the PHP functions that are available for working directly with directories and the file system. This chapter will likely best be used as a foundation for creating other applications that need to interact with the file system. The application has already logically grouped the type of operations a user needs to do with files and directories. Its results format (associative arrays with both return codes and status messages) should make it easy to reuse the code for other applications.

CHAPTER 11

PHP Information Console

IN THIS CHAPTER:

chapter11_common.php—Contains functions used throughout the application, including printing a single line of output and printing a two-column table of results in HTML

chapter11_getPHP.php —Executes a user's request for PHP information and returns output to the lower frame of the main page

chapter11_main.php—Divides page into two frames: a menu selection frame and an output frame

chapter11_menu.php—Appears in top frame of main page, and provides user with selection list menus for retrieving parameters and working with the PHP ini file

chapter11_viewPHP.php —Handles a user's request for viewing the PHP ini file and places the output in the lower frame of the main page

The project for this chapter is to develop a web-based PHP information console. This project includes determining how the PHP engine has been configured, examining the currently running PHP process settings, and viewing PHP's ini file. The application will utilize the existing PHP options and information functions along with some new HTML output functions to provide the user with the desired information. The application's functions are designed to be easily expandable and reusable.

Application Requirements

The first step in designing the PHP console application is to determine the requirements. The basic requirements for this chapter's project are as follows:

- Allow the user to view how PHP has been configured.
- Allow the user to view the current operating parameters.
- Allow the user to examine the PHP ini file directly.

This project can be divided into two segments: presenting a menu of options and displaying the output of the user's menu selection.

Menu Options

Begin by examining the list of choices that should be available to the user to examine the PHP settings and process. The first choice is examining an assertion. An *assertion* is a test that is added to code, typically for debugging purposes. A program should not be dependent on assertion testing because it causes extra overhead, and assertion testing may not even be turned on. Assertions are used to add debugging code to an application that can be easily turned on or off as needed. Often assertions are used to test conditions that should theoretically always be true and only be otherwise if a programming flaw has occurred or the environment was set up incorrectly. PHP allows a user to turn assertion testing on or off along with setting the appropriate action that should occur when an assertion fails. These options are outlined in the following table.

Assertion Setting	Description
ASSERT_ACTIVE	Enable an assert() evaluation to occur.
ASSERT_WARNING	Issue a PHP warning for each time an assertion test fails.

Assertion Setting	Description
ASSERT_BAIL	Terminate the execution of the PHP script if any assertion test fails.
ASSERT_QUIET_EVAL	Do assertion test, but don't report the errors.
ASSERT_CALLBACK	Provide a mechanism for a particular function to be called if an assertion fails.

The next choice presented to the user is examining an environment variable. There are several environment variables available to a PHP script. The exact variables that are available will depend on the web server and operating system, but they typically include PATH_INFO, QUERY_STRING, REMOTE_HOST, SERVER_NAME, and so on. Details about these variables can be found at http://hoohoo.ncsa.uiuc.edu/cgi/env.html, which is part of the CGI (Common Gateway Interface) specification.

Next comes the ability for the user to query what a configuration option is set to. The configuration options are contained in the php.ini file, which is read by PHP on startup of the web server when implemented as a SAPI module, or read on each execution when implemented as a cgi process. The configuration options that can be retrieved by a PHP script are only those that can be set in the php.ini file, and do not include those set at compile time or in any of Apache's configuration files. Note that PHP will run without a php.ini file, causing the default values for all settings to be used. A simple check of whether an ini file exists is to check the cfg_file_path value.

Next we look at the runtime properties for the PHP engine. The first one available is the current user. This is just what user the PHP script is running as. Similar operations include determining the PID (process ID) and UID (user ID) that PHP is running as.

The next operation available to the user is examining the Magic Quotes settings. Magic Quotes can be turned on or off for two different scenarios. The first is GPC, which stands for GetPostCookie and refers to information that is available from a form submission that used a Get or Post action, along with any data that is read in from a cookie. Having this setting on causes all single quotes, double quotes, and backslashes to have an escape character (the backslash "\") applied to them. Another Magic Quotes setting is runtime, which causes data from any external source to be escaped as well. Turning on Magic Quotes often makes it easier to work functions that depend on these characters as delimiters.

Resource information is another option available to PHP administrators. The information available comes from the getrusage system call and will vary by operating system. More information can be found in your system's man pages for the **getrusage** command.

The next operation details information about the creators of the PHP software itself. The credit information available is outlined in the following table:

Name	Description
CREDITS_ALL	All of the credits available
CREDITS_DOCS	Documentation credits
CREDITS_GENERAL	Includes language designers, PHP 4.0 authors, and the Web Server API extension
CREDITS_GROUP	The core PHP developers
CREDITS_MODULES	A listing of the extension modules and their corresponding developers
CREDITS_SAPI	A listing of the Web Server API modules and their developers

Another choice for the user should be the PHP information option, which includes properties such as credits, modules, configuration, variables, license, and environment.

Next are the operations that provide details on the PHP engine. These include version numbers for PHP and Zend, and uname, which is what operating system the server is running on. You can view the GUIDs for PHP and Zend, which allows you to then request a logo for each of these from the PHP engine. GUID stands for globally unique identifier, and is typically used as a unique signature—theoretically across all space and time. Finally, you may determine whether PHP is running as a server module or as a cgi process.

The next set of operations detail the use of extensions to the core PHP engine. There are options to examine which extensions are loaded, along with what functions are present in each extension. (See Figure 11-1.)

The final set of menu options pertain to the PHP ini file itself. The application should allow the file to be displayed either in whole or in part. This includes looking at the first or last *n* number of lines. The user should also have the ability to display any lines that match regular expression criteria the user provides.

Output Requirements

Each of the menu operations has a result set that should be displayed back to the user. The interface should be divided into a top and bottom half, with the menu options displayed in the top portion and the results in the bottom. The results should be displayed as a two-column HTML table when they contain keys and values, and as a single-column table when the results are a list of items. Last, when displaying portions of the ini file, line numbers should be provided.

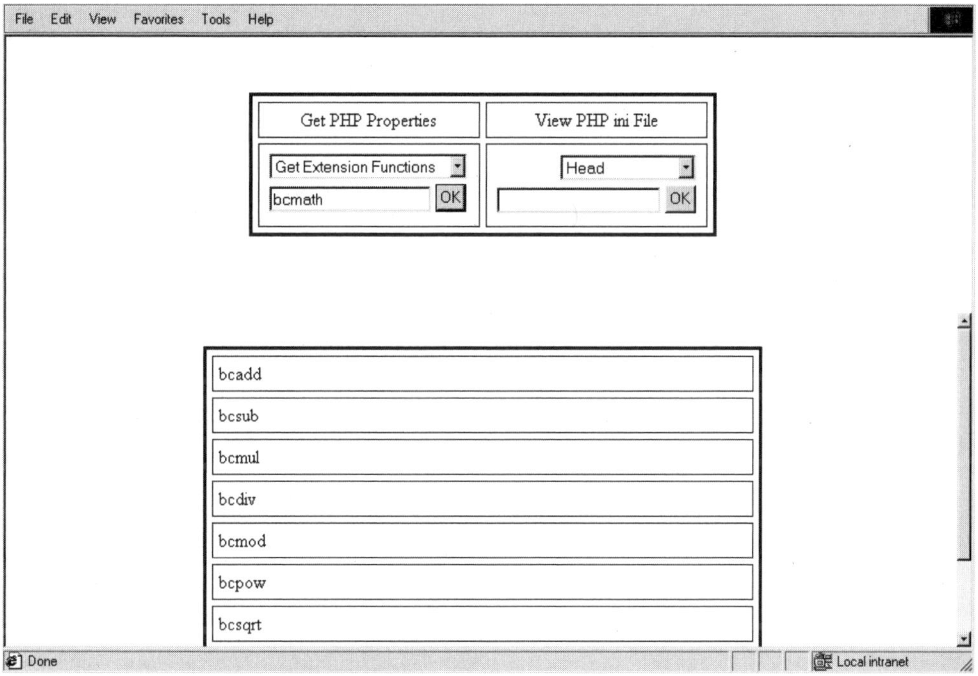

Figure 11-1 *Sample get extensions output*

Application Design

The design of an application is broken out into two parts: namely, what information needs to be retrieved from the user, and what information should be returned to the user.

Application Inputs

The necessary inputs for this project are fairly basic. The user must first be able to choose which operation they want to perform and then, second, supply the appropriate parameter as needed. Each of the previously mentioned operations requires either one or zero parameters (see Figure 11-2).

Application Outputs

The outputs for this project will be the result set from the operation displayed as a table or list depending on whether the results have keys along with values. For

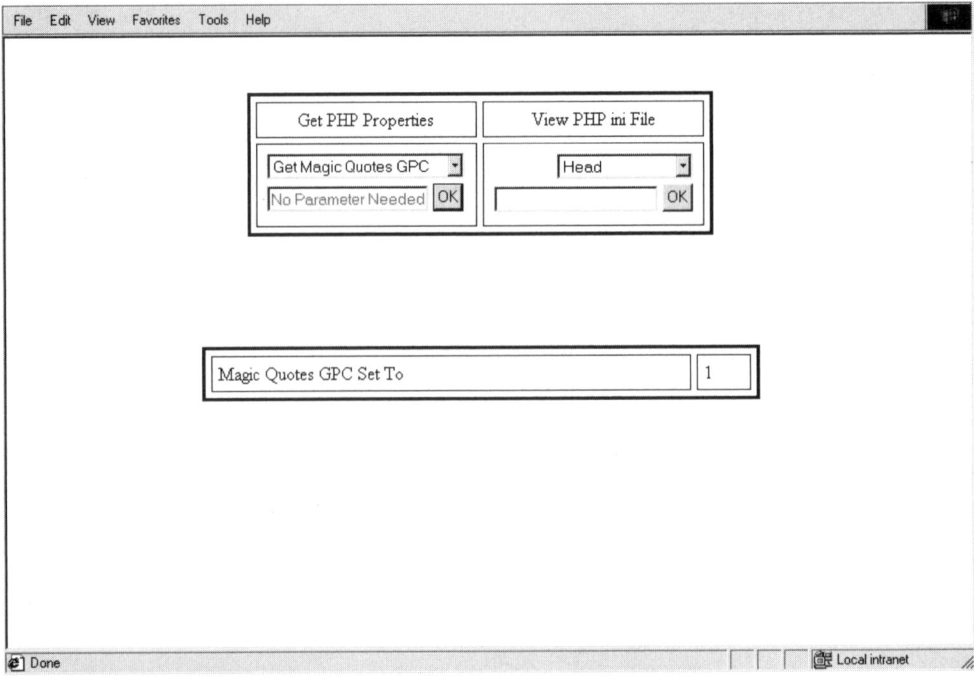

Figure 11-2 *An example where no parameter is needed*

displaying the ini file, the key is the line number, and the value is the line itself. (See Figure 11-3.)

Application Implementation

The application is implemented as a collection of PHP scripts, each serving its unique purpose. In general, the presentation code is separated from the execution code in order to provide greater flexibility to the look and feel of the application.

Main Page

We begin development of the project with the main page. This is the page to which a user would go to access the management console. The main page is just a simple HTML page that divides the window into two frames. The top frame holds the two sets of menu options and the bottom frame contains the output from the operation.

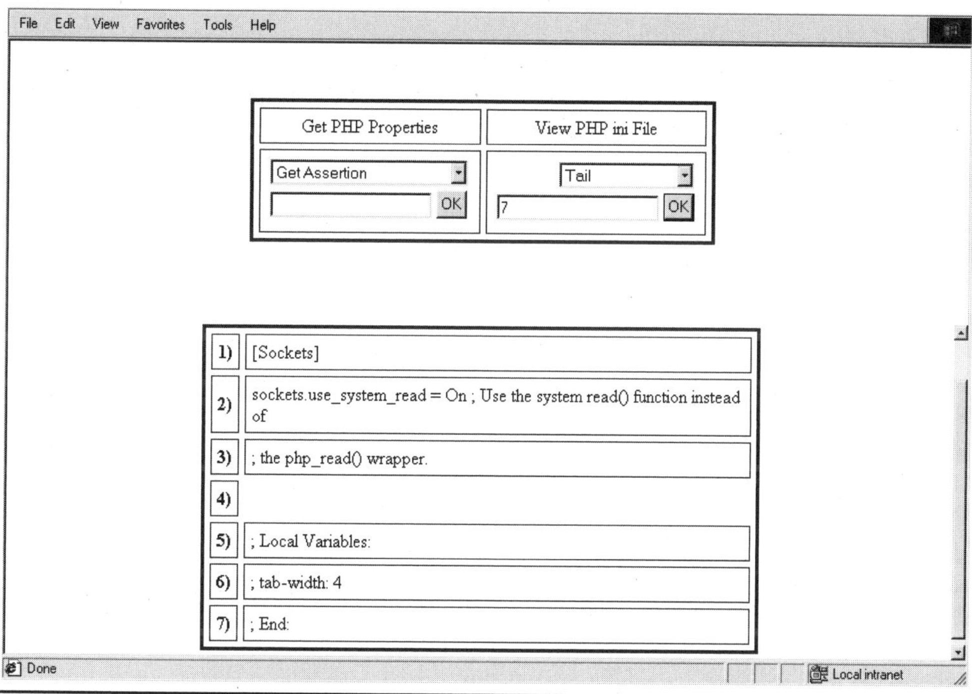

Figure 11-3 *Sample ini file output*

chapter11_main.php

```
<!DOCTYPE HTML PUBLIC "-//W3C//DTD HTML 4.0 Transitional//EN">

<html>
<head>
    <title>Chapter 11 Main Menu</title>
</head>
<!-- frames -->
<frameset  rows="45%,*">
    <frame name="Menu" src="chapter11_menu.php" marginwidth="10"
    marginheight="10" scrolling="auto" frameborder="0">
    <frame name="Results" src="" marginwidth="10" marginheight="10"
    scrolling="auto" frameborder="0">
</frameset>
</html>
```

Menu Page

The next piece of code is the menu portion of the console. It provides the available operations, along with a text input box for the corresponding parameter.

chapter11_menu.php

```
<!DOCTYPE HTML PUBLIC "-//W3C//DTD HTML 4.0 Transitional//EN">

<html>
<head>
      <title>Chapter 11 Menu</title>
</head>

<body>
```

The menu page is composed of two forms that contain selection lists of operations, along with a text input field for the corresponding parameter when needed. The following block of code is JavaScript; it checks to see whether a parameter needs to be supplied. The code identifies what operation is selected and then looks at its value. If the value starts with a 0, no parameter is needed. If it starts with a 1, a parameter is required. If a parameter is required, the text box is enabled (it may already be enabled), and focus is given to the text box. If no parameter is required, the text box is disabled and a "No Parameter Needed" message is placed into the box instead. There are two nearly identical functions, one for the get options and one for the view options. The JavaScript code used to do this is as follows:

```
<script language="JavaScript">
function onGetChangeSelection(formObj)
   {
   var selIndex = formObj.options.selectedIndex;
   var value = formObj.options[selIndex].value;
   if (value.substr(0,1) == 1)
      {
      document.GetMenu.GETPARM1.disabled = false;
      document.GetMenu.GETPARM1.focus();
      document.GetMenu.GETPARM1.value = "";

      }
   else
      {
      document.GetMenu.GETPARM1.disabled = true;
```

```
        document.GetMenu.GETPARM1.value = "No Parameter Needed";
        }
    }
function onViewChangeSelection(formObj)
    {
    var selIndex = formObj.options.selectedIndex;
    var value = formObj.options[selIndex].value;
    if (value.substr(0,1) == 1)
        {
        document.ViewMenu.VIEWPARM1.disabled = false;
        document.ViewMenu.VIEWPARM1.focus();
        document.ViewMenu.VIEWPARM1.value = "";

        }
    else
        {
        document.ViewMenu.VIEWPARM1.disabled = true;
        document.ViewMenu.VIEWPARM1.value = "No Parameter Needed";
        }
    }
```

The next JavaScript function looks at the text input field and makes sure a value is present if one is required. Again, by examining the first position of the value field from the selection list, you are able to determine whether a parameter is required. This function will be called any time the user tries to submit the form. If a parameter is required and missing, the user will be alerted through a pop-up box and returned to the form to correct the problem. There are separate functions for the get and view operation forms, as shown here:

```
function onGetSubmitForm()
    {
    if (document.GetMenu.GetMenuOption.value.substr(0,1) == 1)
        {
        if (document.GetMenu.GETPARM1.value == "")
            {
            alert ("Parameter Required For This Action");
            return false;
            }
        }
    }
function onViewSubmitForm()
    {
```

```
    if (document.ViewMenu.ViewMenuOption.value.substr(0,1) == 1)
        {
        if (document.ViewMenu.VIEWPARM1.value == "")
            {
            alert ("Parameter Required For This Action");
            return false;
            }
        }
    }

</script>
```

The next portion of code sets up the menus as two forms inside a table that is used for alignment purposes. Notice that the forms have JavaScript functions assigned to their onSubmit event to verify that the parameter field is filled in when appropriate. The code used to generate the forms is as follows:

```
<br><br>
<table cellspacing=5 cellpadding=5
 border=3 bordercolor="0000FF" width=50% align="center">
<tr><td align="center">
Get PHP Properties
</td><td align="center">
View PHP ini File
</td></tr>
<tr><td align="center">
<table align="center">
<tr><td>
<form action="chapter11_getPHP.php"
      target="Results"
      method="post"
      name="GetMenu"
      id="GetMenu"
      align="center"
      onSubmit="return onGetSubmitForm();">
```

The get and view forms include a single-selection drop-down list box that allows the user to choose which operation to perform. Each time the user selects a different operation, the JavaScript function is executed to see whether the text input parameter box should be available for input. As you have already seen, the number preceding the value is used to determine whether a parameter is necessary for the operation. Later in the project, you will see how the naming of the values for the selection list can be used as a shortcut. The selection list code is as follows:

```
<select name="GetMenuOption"
        id="GetMenuOption"
        size="1"
        align="right"
        onchange="return onGetChangeSelection(this);">
<option value="1getAssertion" SELECTED>Get Assertion</option>
<option value="1getEnvVar">Get Environment Variable</option>
<option value="1getConfigOption">Get Configuration Option</option>
<option value="0getCurrentUser">Get Current User</option>
<option value="0getMagicQuotesGPC">Get Magic Quotes GPC</option>
<option value="0getMagicQuotesRT">Get Magic Quotes RT</option>
<option value="0getPHPPID">Get PHP Process Id</option>
<option value="0getPHPUID">Get PHP User Id</option>
<option value="0getResourceUsage">Get Resource Usage</option>
<option value="1getIniValue">Get Ini Value</option>
<option value="1getPHPCredits">Get PHP Credits</option>
<option value="1getPHPInfo">Get PHP Info</option>
<option value="0getPHPVersion">Get PHP Version</option>
<option value="0getLogoGuid">Get Logo Guid</option>
<option value="0getSapiName">Get Sapi Name</option>
<option value="1getExtensionLoaded">Get Extension Loaded</option>
<option value="0getPHPUname">Get PHP Uname</option>
<option value="0getZendGuid">Get Zend Guid</option>
<option value="0getLoadedExtensions">Get Loaded Extensions</option>
<option value="1getExtensionFunctions">Get Extension Functions</option>
<option value="0getZendVersion">Get Zend Version</option>
</select>
</td></tr>
<tr><td>
<input name="GETPARM1" id="IDGETPARM1" align="center" type=text size="20">
<input type="submit" align="center" value="OK">
</td><tr>
</form>
</table>
</td><td align="center">
<table align="center">
<tr><td>
<form action="chapter11_viewPHP.php"
      target="Results"
      method="post"
      name="ViewMenu"
      id="ViewMenu"
      align="center"
```

```
      onSubmit="return onViewSubmitForm();">

<select name="ViewMenuOption"
        id="ViewMenuOption"
        size="1"
        align="right"
        onchange="return onViewChangeSelection(this);">
<option value="0displayFile">Display</option>
<option value="1headFile" SELECTED>Head</option>
<option value="1tailFile">Tail</option>
<option value="1eregFile">Reg Expression</option>
</select>
</td></tr>
<tr><td>
<input name="VIEWPARM1" id="IDVIEWPARM1"  align="center" type=text size="20">
<input type="submit" value="OK" align="center">
</td></tr>
</form>
</table>
</tr>
</table>
</body>
</html>
```

Common Page

Next we'll look at a couple of functions that are useful for HTML output and are used repeatedly in the project. The first one simply takes a string as an argument and outputs it as a single line in an HTML file. This shortcut is particularly useful when someone wants to view the source of the generated HTML file. Although spacing doesn't matter in an HTML file, introducing line breaks can greatly improve readability.

chapter11_common.php

```
//####################################################################
//##        Function:    echoLine                                    ##
//##      Parameters:    string                                      ##
//##     Description:    Outputs a single line including lf & cr     ##
//####################################################################
function echoLine ($inputstring)
   {
   echo $inputstring."\n";
   }
```

The next function is display2ColumnTable, which takes an associative array as a parameter and outputs it as an HTML table with two columns. The first column in the table is the key from the array, and the second is its corresponding value. A couple of additional checks are part of this code, which include checking for an empty array being passed in or one that doesn't contain any keys. Finally, this function will not output values for the keys of rc or rv, which represent return code or return value, respectively.

```
//#################################################################
//##        Function:          display2ColumnTable              ##
//##      Parameters:          2D associative array             ##
//##     Description:    Outputs a 2 dimensional array in an HTML ##
//##                     table. The first row contains the        ##
//##                     column names                             ##
//#################################################################
function display2ColumnTable($results)
   {
   //Indicate if the resultset is empty
   if (empty($results))
      {
      echoLine ("<CENTER>");
      echoLine ("<BR>");
      echoLine ("Action Returned No Results!");
      echoLine ("</CENTER>");
      return ;
      }

   echoLine ("<BR>");
   echoLine ("<CENTER>");
   echoLine ("<TABLE CELLSPACING=5 CELLPADDING=5 BORDER=3 width=60%");
   echoLine ("BORDERCOLOR=\"0000FF\" >");
   echoLine ("<THEAD>");
   echoLine ("<TR>");

   while (list ($key, $value) = each ($results))
      {
      if (is_numeric($key))
         echoLine ("<TD>$value</TD></TR>");
      else if ($key != "rc" && $key != "rv")
         echoLine ("<TD>$key</TD><TD>$value</TD></TR>");
      }
   echoLine ("</TR>");
```

```
   echoLine ("</TABLE>");
   echoLine ("</CENTER>");
   }

?>
```

getPHP Page

Next, we move to the piece of code that handles each of the get menu operations. This code page contains function wrappers for each of the PHP functions used to execute the menu operations. For each function, the results are placed into an associative array, which includes a return code or value when available, along with a message and the results of the function call. The return codes and values are not used in this application, but are left in because they might be needed in a future application.

chapter11_getPHP.php

```
<!DOCTYPE HTML PUBLIC "-//W3C//DTD HTML 4.0 Transitional//EN">
<html>
<head>
     <title>Chapter 11 Get PHP Settings</title>
</head>
<body>
<?php
include ('chapter11_common.php');

//#################################################################
//##    Method:          getAssertion                          ##
//##    Parameters:      option - can be ASSERT_ACTIVE,        ##
//##                     ASSERT_WARNING,ASSERT_BAIL,           ##
//##                     ASSERT_QUIET_EVAL,ASSERT_CALLBACK     ##
//##    Return value:    array with return code and assertion  ##
//##                     option and value                      ##
//#################################################################
   function getAssertion($option)
      {
      $rc = assert_options($option);
      $results = array("rc" => $rc,
                       "Assertion Option" => $option,
                       "Set To" => $rc);
      return $results;
      }
```

```
//##################################################################
//##    Method:         getEnvVar                                ##
//##    Parameters:     Environment Variable                     ##
//##    Return value:   array with return value and environment  ##
//##                    option and value                         ##
//##################################################################
   function getEnvVar($envVar)
      {
      $rv = getenv($envVar);
      $results = array("rv" => $rv,
                       "Environment Variable" => $envVar,
                       "Set To" => $rv);
      return $results;
      }

//##################################################################
//##    Method:         getConfigOption                          ##
//##    Parameters:     Configuration Option                     ##
//##    Return value:   array with return value and configuration ##
//##                    option and value                         ##
//##################################################################
   function getConfigOption($configOption)
      {
      $rv = get_cfg_var($configOption);
      $results = array("rv" => $rv,
                       "Configuration Option" => $configOption,
                       "Set To" => $rv);
      return $results;
      }

//##################################################################
//##    Method:         getCurrentUser                           ##
//##    Parameters:     None                                     ##
//##    Return value:   array with return code and user name     ##
//##################################################################
   function getCurrentUser()
      {
      $rv = get_current_user();
      $results = array("rv" => $rv,
                       "Current User Set To" => $rv);
      return $results;
      }
```

```
//##################################################################
//##    Method:          getMagicQuotesGPC                       ##
//##    Parameters:      none                                    ##
//##    Return value:    array with return value and setting for ##
//##                     magic quotes GPC                        ##
//##################################################################
   function getMagicQuotesGPC()
      {
      $rv = get_magic_quotes_gpc ();
      $results = array("rv" => $rv,
                       "Magic Quotes GPC Set To" => $rv);
      return $results;
      }

//##################################################################
//##    Method:          getMagicQuotesRT                        ##
//##    Parameters:      none                                    ##
//##    Return value:    array with return value and setting for ##
//##                     magic quotes GPC                        ##
//##################################################################
   function getMagicQuotesRT()
      {
      $rv = get_magic_quotes_runtime();
      $results = array("rv" => $rv,
                       "Magic Quotes Runtime Set To" => $rv);
      return $results;
      }

//##################################################################
//##    Method:          getPHPPID                               ##
//##    Parameters:      none                                    ##
//##    Return value:    array with return value and PHP process id##
//##################################################################
   function getPHPPID()
      {
      $rv = getmypid();
      $results = array("rv" => $rv,
                       "PHP Process ID" => $rv);
      return $results;
      }
```

```
//###################################################################
//##    Method:          getPHPUID                                 ##
//##    Parameters:      none                                      ##
//##    Return value:    array with return code and PHP user id    ##
//###################################################################
   function getPHPUID()
      {
      $rv = getmyuid ();
      $results = array("rv" => $rv,
                       "PHP User ID" => $rv);
      return $results;
      }

//###################################################################
//##    Method:          getResourceUsage                          ##
//##    Parameters:      none                                      ##
//##    Return value:    array with output from system call        ##
//###################################################################
   function getResourceUsage()
      {
      $results = array("Resource Usage"=>getrusage());
      return $results;
      }

//###################################################################
//##    Method:          getIniValue                               ##
//##    Parameters:      Ini Name                                  ##
//##    Return value:    array with return value and ini option    ##
//##                     and value                                 ##
//###################################################################
   function getIniValue($iniName)
      {
      $rv = ini_get($iniName);
      $results = array("rv" => $rv,
                       "Ini Option" => $iniName,
                       "Set To" => $rv);
      return $results;
      }

//###################################################################
//##    Method:          getPHPCredits                             ##
//##    Parameters:      flag indicating what credits should be    ##
//##                     displayed                                 ##
```

```
//##                      Flag values include: CREDITS_ALL,         ##
//## CREDITS_DOCS, CREDITS_FULLPAGE, CREDITS_GENERAL,               ##
//## CREDITS_GROUP, CREDITS_MODULES, CREDITS_SAPI                   ##
//##    Return value:   None - credits printed from routine         ##
//####################################################################
   function getPHPCredits($flag)
      {
      switch($flag)
         {
         case 'CREDITS_DOCS':
            {
            phpcredits(CREDITS_DOCS);
            }
         case 'CREDITS_FULLPAGE':
            {
            phpcredits(CREDITS_FULLPAGE);
            }
         case 'CREDITS_GENERAL':
            {
            phpcredits(CREDITS_GENERAL);
            }
         case 'CREDITS_GROUP':
            {
            phpcredits(CREDITS_GROUP);
            }
         case 'CREDITS_MODULES':
            {
            phpcredits(CREDITS_MODULES);
            }
         case 'CREDITS_SAPI ':
            {
            phpcredits(CREDITS_SAPI );
            }
         }
      return 0;
      }

//####################################################################
//##    Method:         getPHPInfo                                  ##
//##    Parameters:     flag                                        ##
//##                    Flag values include: INFO_GENERAL,          ##
//## INFO_CREDITS, INFO_CONFIGURATION, INFO_MODULES,                ##
```

```
//## INFO_ENVIRONMENT, INFO_VARIABLES, INFO_LICENSE,INFO_ALL      ##
//##    Return value:   None - prints info directly                ##
//##################################################################
   function getPHPInfo($flag)
      {
      switch($flag)
         {
         case 'INFO_CREDITS':
            {
            phpinfo(INFO_CREDITS);
            }
         case 'INFO_CONFIGURATION':
            {
            phpinfo(INFO_CONFIGURATION);
            }
         case 'INFO_MODULES':
            {
            phpinfo(INFO_MODULES);
            }
         case 'INFO_ENVIRONMENT':
            {
            phpinfo(INFO_ENVIRONMENT);
            }
         case 'INFO_VARIABLES':
            {
            phpinfo(INFO_MODULES);
            }
         case 'INFO_LICENSE':
            {
            phpinfo(INFO_ENVIRONMENT);
            }
         case 'INFO_ALL':
            {
            phpinfo(INFO_ALL);
            }
         }
      return 0;
      }

//##################################################################
//##    Method:         getPHPVersion                               ##
//##    Parameters:     none                                        ##
//##    Return value:   array with return code and PHP Version #    ##
//##################################################################
```

```
   function getPHPVersion()
      {
      $rv = phpversion ();
      $results = array("rv" => $rv,
                       "PHP Version" => $rv);
      return $results;
      }

//#################################################################
//##    Method:         getLogoGuid                             ##
//##    Parameters:     none                                    ##
//##    Return value:   array with return code and PHP logo GUID ##
//#################################################################
   function getLogoGuid()
      {
      $rv = php_logo_guid ();
      $results = array("rv" => $rv,
                       "PHP Logo Guid" => $rv);
      return $results;
      }

//*** see http://www.php.net/manual/en/function.php-sapi-name.php for use

//#################################################################
//##    Method:         getSapiName                             ##
//##    Parameters:     none                                    ##
//##    Return value:   array with return code and SAPI name    ##
//#################################################################
   function getSapiName()
      {
      $rv = php_sapi_name ();
      $results = array("rv" => $rv,
                       "PHP Sapi Name" => $rv);
      return $results;
      }

//#################################################################
//##    Method:         getExtensionLoaded                      ##
//##    Parameters:     name                                    ##
//##    Return value:   array with return code and status on    ##
//##    whether a particular extension has been loaded or not   ##
//#################################################################
```

```
   function getExtensionLoaded($name)
      {
      $rc = extension_loaded ($name);
      $results = array("rc" => $rc,
                       "Extension" => $name,
                       "Loaded" => $rc);
       return $results;
      }

//####################################################################
//##    Method:          getPHPUname                                ##
//##    Parameters:      none                                       ##
//##    Return value:    array with return code and Uname details   ##
//##    from the Operating System                                   ##
//####################################################################
   function getPHPUname()
      {
      $results = array("Uname" =>php_uname());
      return $results;
      }

//####################################################################
//##    Method:          getZendGuid                                ##
//##    Parameters:      none                                       ##
//##    Return value:    array with return code and Zend Guid       ##
//####################################################################
   function getZendGuid()
      {
      $rv = zend_logo_guid ();
      $results = array("rv" => $rv,
                       "PHP Zend Logo Guid" => $rv);
      return $results;
      }

//####################################################################
//##    Method:          getLoadedExtensions                        ##
//##    Parameters:      none                                       ##
//##    Return value:    array with loaded extensions               ##
//####################################################################
   function getLoadedExtensions()
      {
      $results = get_loaded_extensions();
      return $results;
      }
```

```
//####################################################################
//##    Method:         getExtensionFunctions                      ##
//##    Parameters:     module_name                                ##
//##    Return value:   array with functions in module             ##
//####################################################################
   function getExtensionFunctions($module_name)
      {
      $results = get_extension_funcs($module_name);
      return $results;
      }

//####################################################################
//##    Method:         getZendVersion                             ##
//##    Parameters:     none                                       ##
//##    Return value:   array with return code and status msg      ##
//####################################################################
   function getZendVersion()
      {
      $results = array("Zend Version" =>zend_version());
      return $results;
      }
```

That completes the functions used to query PHP for options and information. Now you'll actually process the form data and call the appropriate function. First, retrieve the form variables and place them into the userinfo variable. Next, look at the first character of the value parameter that came over from the drop-down list box. This tells you whether you should expect a parameter with the function call. Finally, you extract the appropriate function name from the selection value and call the corresponding wrapper function, as shown here:

```
//Retrieve input variables from HTTP get or post
$userinfo = strtolower($REQUEST_METHOD) == 'get'
   ? $HTTP_GET_VARS : $HTTP_POST_VARS;

$parmNumber = substr ($userinfo[GetMenuOption],0,1);
$functionName = substr ($userinfo[GetMenuOption],1);

if ($parmNumber == 1)
   {
   $results = call_user_func ($functionName,$userinfo[GETPARM1]);
   }
else
```

```
    {
    $results = call_user_func ($functionName);
    }
```

The return value from the function is examined to see whether it is in an array format that indicates that its contents should be displayed as an HTML table (see Figure 11-4). The condition where the return value is not an array indicates the function that was called already handled the output to the results window, as shown here:

```
if (is_array($results))
    {
    display2ColumnTable($results);
    }
?>
</body>
</html>
```

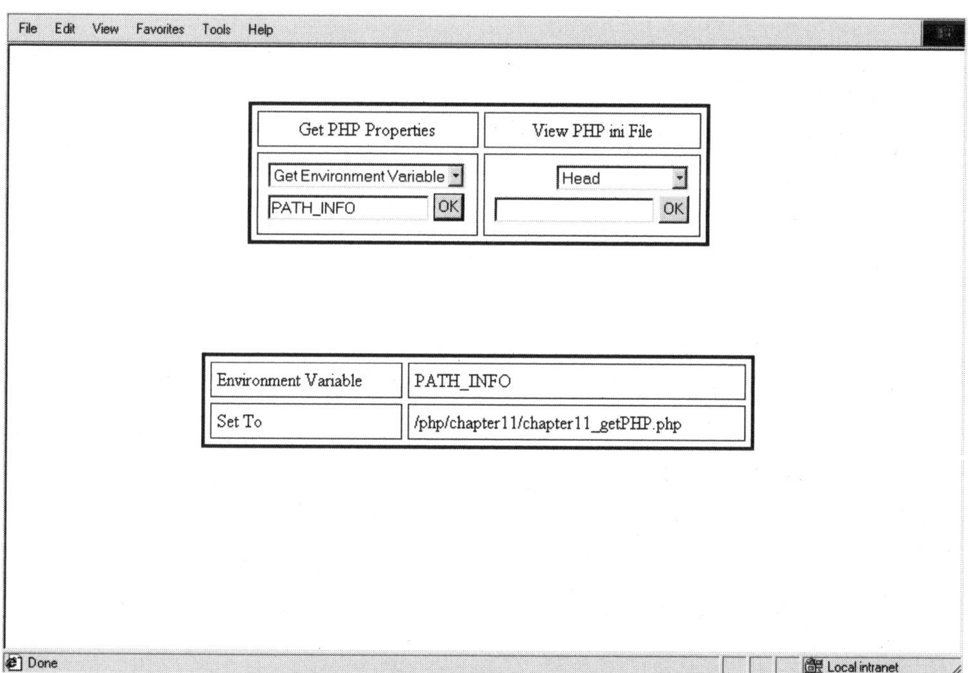

Figure 11-4 *Sample environment variable output*

viewPHP Page

The last page of code to examine is the piece that handles displaying the PHP ini file. To accomplish this task, we created a fileActions class that contains the following methods: displayFile(), eregFile(), headFile(), and tailFile().

Begin by defining the fileActions class. The fileActions class takes as its sole parameter a file. The parameter should include the full path to the file to ensure the correct file is operated on.

chapter11_viewPHP.php

```
<!DOCTYPE HTML PUBLIC "-//W3C//DTD HTML 4.0 Transitional//EN">
<html>
<head>
     <title>Chapter 11 View PHP INI</title>
</head>
<body>
<?php
include ('chapter11_common.php');

//####################################################################
//##    Class:              fileActions                            ##
//##    Description:        Class for acting on file               ##
//####################################################################
class fileActions
   {
   //member variables
   var $file;

//####################################################################
//##    Constructor:        fileActions                            ##
//##    Parameters:         location of php.ini file               ##
//##    Return value:       Instance of fileActions class          ##
//####################################################################
   function fileActions ($iniFile)
      {
         $this->iniFile = $iniFile;

      }
```

Once the fileActions class has been defined, you can begin to add the necessary methods to it. The first one is displayFile(). The purpose for this method is to display the entire contents of the file specified with creation of the fileActions class. This method attempts to open the file for reading and, if unsuccessful, outputs a message directly to the page. Next, it writes the HTML tag <pre>, which tells the browser that the following text has already been formatted. Finally, it attempts to close the file since it is no longer needed. The displayFile method is show here:

```
//####################################################################
//##    Method:          displayFile                                ##
//##    Parameters:      none                                       ##
//##    Return value:    direct output of file contents             ##
//##                     option and value                           ##
//####################################################################
   function displayFile()
      {
      @$fp = fopen($this->iniFile,"r") or
      die("php.ini file could not be opened!");
      echoLine("<pre>");
      fpassthru($fp);
      @fclose($fp);
      echoLine("</pre>");
      }
```

The next method is the eregFile() method. Its purpose is to display lines from the file that correspond to the given regular expression (see Figure 11-5). A few simple examples of regular expressions are as follows:

- **[aA]** Matches lines with a lower- or uppercase *A*
- **[0-9]** Matches lines with a number in them
- **[a-z]** Matches lines with any lowercase letter

For more information on regular expressions, consult the PHP manual. We use the file function to place the contents of the php.ini file into an array, and then iterate through the array, outputting lines that the regular expression matches on.

```
//####################################################################
//##    Method:          eregFile                                   ##
//##    Parameters:      grep arguments                             ##
//##    Return value:    direct output of grep command on the file ##
//####################################################################
   function eregFile($args)
      {
      $fileContents = file ($this->iniFile);
```

```
echoLine ("<table cellspacing=5 cellpadding=5 border=3 ");
echoLine ("align=\"center\" width=60%");
echoLine ("BORDERCOLOR=\"0000FF\" >");
$ctr = 1;
foreach ($fileContents as $line)
   {
   if (ereg ($args,$line))
      {
      echoLine ("<tr><td><strong>".$ctr.") </strong></td>");
      echoLine ("<td>".$line."</td></tr>");
      }
   $ctr ++;
   }
echoLine("</table>");
return;
}
```

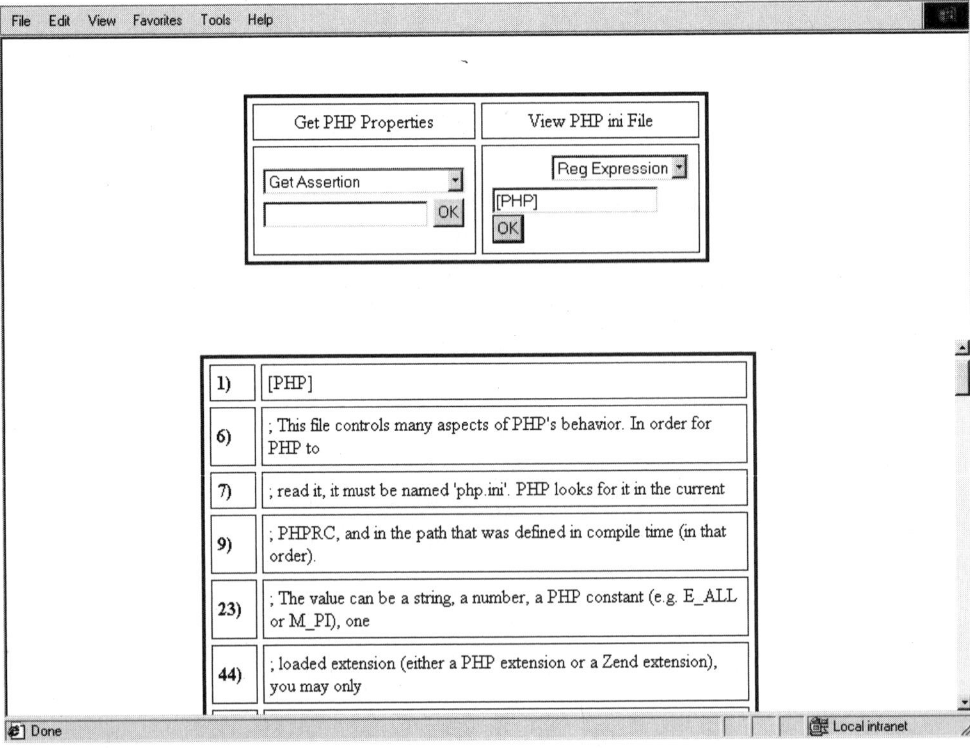

Figure 11-5 *Sample regular expression output*

The headFile() method again takes the contents of the file and places them into an array. Next, it outputs each line up to the number of lines specified by the user from the form. It outputs the lines as an HTML table with the first column as the line number and the second column the contents of the line.

```
//#################################################################
//##    Method:           headFile                               ##
//##    Parameters:       head parameters                        ##
//##    Return value:     output of head command on file         ##
//#################################################################
   function headFile($lines)
      {
       $fileContents = file ($this->iniFile);
       echoLine ("<table cellspacing=5 cellpadding=5 border=3 ");
       echoLine ("align=\"center\" width=60%");
       echoLine ("BORDERCOLOR=\"0000FF\" >");
      for ($ctr = 1;$ctr <= $lines;$ctr++)
         {
         echoLine ("<tr><td><strong>".$ctr.") </strong></td>");
         echoLine ("<td>".$fileContents[$ctr-1]."</td></tr>");
         }
      echoLine("</table>");
      return;
      }
```

The tailFile() method is similar to the headFile() method, except that the file is reversed before iterating through the lines. Also, the lines are displayed from the highest number (equal to the number of lines requested) down to 1, which marks the beginning of the reversed file. This results in the lines being displayed in the order in which they appear in the file.

```
//#################################################################
//##    Method:           tailFile                               ##
//##    Parameters:       tail parameters                        ##
//##    Return value:     output of tail command on file         ##
//#################################################################
function tailFile($lines)
      {
      $fileContents = array_reverse(file ($this->iniFile));
      echoLine ("<table cellspacing=5 cellpadding=5 border=3 ");
      echoLine ("align=\"center\" width=60%");
      echoLine ("bordercolor=\"0000FF\" >");
```

```
        for ($ctr = $lines-1;$ctr >= 0;$ctr--)
            {
            echoLine ("<tr><td><strong>".($lines-$ctr).") </strong></td>");
            echoLine ("<td>".$fileContents[$ctr]."</td></tr>");
            }
        echoLine("</table>");
        return;
        }
    }//end of viewPHP class
```

After all of the methods have been defined for the fileActions class, you handle the form submission and return the output. The first step in handling the form submission is to retrieve the menu option and corresponding parameter from the appropriate global variable, as follows:

```
//Retrieve input variables from HTTP get or post
$userinfo = strtolower($REQUEST_METHOD) == 'get'
    ? $HTTP_GET_VARS : $HTTP_POST_VARS;
```

Next, locate the PHP ini file and, if one doesn't exist, output the appropriate message and end the application, as follows:

```
$iniFile = get_cfg_var(cfg_file_path);

echoLine ("<div align=\"center\"><strong>iniFile = ");
echoLine ($iniFile."</strong></div><br>");
clearstatcache();
if (!file_exists($iniFile))
    {
    echoLine("<strong>php.ini file doesn't exist!</strong>");
    return $false;
    }
```

If the PHP ini file does exist, use it to create an instance of the fileActions class, as shown here:

```
$myFileActions = new fileActions($iniFile);
```

You then check to see whether the operation requested requires a parameter and retrieve the name of the method that corresponds to the request, as follows:

```
$parmNumber = substr ($userinfo[ViewMenuOption],0,1);
$functionName = substr ($userinfo[ViewMenuOption],1);
```

Finally, call the corresponding method of the fileActions class, passing the parameter if one exists, as shown here:

```
if ($parmNumber == 1)
    {
    $results = call_user_method
($functionName,$myFileActions,$userinfo[VIEWPARM1]);
    }
else
    {
    $results = call_user_method ($functionName,$myFileActions);
    }

?>
</body>
</html>
```

Testing the Project

Upon completion of the coding of the project, you can run through the various operations to see vast amount of information that is available about your PHP installation. If you're working with multiple operating systems, you will notice that the results will vary between them. Also, some of the operations used in this chapter are not available in early versions of PHP 4 and, therefore, may not be available in the version you are using.

Next Steps

The logical next step for this project is to provide the ability to alter all the settings you are able to view through this interface. Other possibilities include providing subsets of available options for each operation, such as the possible credits parameters that are available, as opposed to the user having to enter them.

What to Take Away

This application demonstrates the use of the many PHP functions available for learning more about the system you are running on. It demonstrates how variable names and values can represent method or function names and the number of parameters that are necessary. This application demonstrates the use of JavaScript to handle dynamic menu needs in an application. It also focuses on separating the presentation of the data from the code used to retrieve the data, which allows you to alter the look of the application without having to change the underlying code. Finally, it shows how to utilize user-defined functions, which are based on variable values.

PART

VI

PHP and Socket Communications

OBJECTIVES

- Develop web-based Usenet newsreader
- Examine the PHP functions used for socket communications
- Examine the commands and responses used to communicate with a Usenet news server
- Develop a message board application that handles multiple users and multiple topic threads
- Become familiar with data retrieval from a MySQL database
- Use session data to maintain user login credentials

CHAPTER

12

NNTP Server Communications

IN THIS CHAPTER:

chapter12_article.php—The page that displays the body of the article

chapter12_index.php—The initial page that lists the groups available

chapter12_listarticles.php—The page that lists the articles in the group selected

chapter12_nntp.conf—The Usenet newsreader configuration file

chapter12_nntplib.inc—The library of functions to communicate with the NNTP server

The project for this chapter is to develop a web-based Usenet newsreader. The application that will be reviewed is simple, but is designed to introduce the topic of client/server socket-level communications. You will also learn about communicating with a Network News Transport Protocol (NNTP) server. The basic NNTP server commands and responses will be discussed along with status and error codes.

Application Requirements

The requirements for this application are simple. The initial page needs to list the newsgroups you are interested in monitoring. Subsequent pages will list the article in the selected group and the body of the selected article. The configuration options should be kept to a minimum and allow the user to input the news server address, the news server port, username and password information, and the groups to be monitored.

PHP does not have built-in functions for communicating with an NNTP server. You will create your own functions and package them in a library that will be used throughout the applications. These functions will initiate communication with the NNTP server, request NNTP group information, request the article header information and the article body, and close the NNTP server connection.

Application Design

In this chapter, you will learn how to use a newsreader to interact with an NNTP server. We will also discuss the NNTP server commands necessary when communicating with the server. This section will discuss the NNTP server basics you will need to know to understand the code presented in this chapter.

NNTP Communication Basics

NNTP servers use TCP sockets to communicate between the client and the server. The default NNTP socket that has been defined is port 119. The client will open port 119 to the NNTP server and send a command stream requesting some information. These commands, which are not case sensitive, must not be more than 512 characters in length. The server will reply with either a text response or a status response. This response stream will always contain the numeric status first, followed by the text message. The text is sent as a stream that can contain carriage returns and line feeds. The server will indicate the end of a text stream with a single line containing only a period.

The NNTP server status responses are textual lines that begin with a three-digit numeric code. These responses will alert the client program to communication or syntax problems. Other responses will alert the client program that text will be available in a following stream.

The following table details the high-level responses that can be received from the NNTP server.

1xx	Informational message
2xx	Command successful
3xx	The initial command was successful; the server is looking for additional commands
4xx	Command error
5xx	Command syntax error or the command was not understood by the server

The entire NNTP server specification is contained in RFC 977. This can be reviewed online at http://www.w3.org/Protocols/rfc977/rfc977.html.

We will now look at the five commands that will be used in this application. These commands are used to request information from the NNTP server. We will show you the syntax of the command and give an example response. We will then dissect the response and describe the elements that are received from the server.

BODY

The BODY command tells the server to send the body of the message that has been selected. The message is selected by using either the HEAD or NEXT command, as follows:

```
CLIENT REQUEST: BODY
SERVER RESPONSE: 222 11196 <992m6d$1fi$1@aunews.duc.auburn.edu>
article retrieved - body follows
If baseball is so easy, why couldn't Michael Jordan
hit a curve ball?
  David Swanger
Office of Information Technology
Auburn University, ALswangdb@mail.auburn.edu
```

The server response elements are

Element	Description
222	Successfully retrieved body
11196	Article number
<992m6d$1fi$1@aunews.duc.auburn.edu>	Message ID

There are error codes and descriptions that may be returned if the request is not successful:

Error Code	Description
412	No newsgroup has been selected
420	No current article has been selected
423	No such article number in this group
430	No such article found

LISTGROUP

The LISTGROUP command lists all the article numbers for the selected group. The client/server communication example that follows lists all the articles in the alt.sports.baseball newsgroup:

```
CLIENT REQUEST: LISTGROUP alt.sports.baseball
SERVER RESPONSE: 211 article list follows
11191 11192 11193 11194 11195 11196 11197 11198 11199 11200 11201
11202 11203 11204 11205 11206 11207 11208 11209 11210 11211 11212
11213 11214 11215 11216 11217 11218 11219 11220 11221 11222 11223
11224 11225 11226 11227 11228 11229 11230 11231 11232 11233 11234
11235 11236 11237 11239 11240 11241 11242 11243 11244 11245 11246
11247 11248 11249 11250 11251 11252 11253 11254 11255 11256 11257
11258 11259 11260 11261 11262 11263 11264 11265 11266 11267 11268
11269 11270 11271 11272 11273 11274 11275 11276 11277 11278 11279
11280 11281 11282 11283 11284 11285 11286 11287 11288 11289 11290
11291 11292 11293 11294 11295 11296 11297 11298 11299 11300 11301
11302 11303 11304 11305 11306 11307 11308 11309 11310 11311 11312
11313 11314 11315 11316 11317 11318 11319 11320 11321 11322 11323
11324 11325 11326 11327 11328 11329 11330 11331 11332 11333 11334
11335 11336 11338 11339 11340 11341 11342 11343 11344 11345 11346
```

Element	Description
211	Successfully selected group

To retrieve all the information from the LISTGROUP request, you must call the fgets() function twice. The first time will get the information shown in the preceding table; the second time will retrieve the entire list of articles. The server indicates the end of the transmission with a single line containing only a period.

The error code that may be returned by this command is

Error Code	Description
411	No such newsgroup

GROUP

The GROUP command will select the group that is passed in with the command. In the example request that follows, the group alt.sports.baseball is selected:

```
CLIENT REQUEST: GROUP alt.sports.baseball
SERVER RESPONSE: 211 722 11186 11907 alt.sports.baseball group
selected
```

Element	Description
211	Successfully selected group
722	Number of articles in the group
11186	First article number in the group
11907	Last article number in the group
alt.sports.baseball	Name of the group

The error code that may be returned by this command is

Error Code	Description
411	No such newsgroup

HEAD

The HEAD command will return the header information of the selected article. An example request and response is shown here:

```
CLIENT REQUEST: HEAD
SERVER RESPONSE: 221 11188 <3AB24217.5A51DF70@mighty.com> article retrieved -
 head follows
Path:

sn-us!sn-xit-01!supernews.com!feeder.qis.net!europa.netcrusader.net!208.184.7.
66!newsfeed.skycache.com!Cidera!cyclone-0.nyroc.rr.com!cyclone-out.nyroc.rr.
com!typhoon.nyroc.rr.com.POSTED!not-for-mail
Message-ID: <3AB24217.5A51DF70@mighty.com>
From: "Quinn M. Mann"
Reply-To: info@mighty.com
```

```
Organization: Mighty Eskimo
X-Mailer: Mozilla 4.7 (Macintosh; U; PPC)
X-Accept-Language: en
MIME-Version: 1.0
Newsgroups:
rec.photo.marketplace,alt.sports.baseball,alt.sports.baseball.memorabilia,rec.
collecting.sport.baseball
Subject: eBay: 1890s CORNELL UNIVERSITY BASEBALL REAL PHOTO
Content-Type: text/plain; charset=us-ascii; x-mac-type="54455854";
x-mac-creator="4D4F5353"
Content-Transfer-Encoding: 7bit
Lines: 22
Date: Fri, 16 Mar 2001 16:38:10 GMT
NNTP-Posting-Host: 24.24.23.223
X-Complaints-To: abuse@twcny.rr.com
X-Trace: typhoon.nyroc.rr.com 984760690 24.24.23.223 (Fri, 16 Mar 2001
11:38:10 EST)
NNTP-Posting-Date: Fri, 16 Mar 2001 11:38:10 EST
Xref: sn-us rec.photo.marketplace:240791 alt.sports.baseball:11188
alt.sports.baseball.memorabilia:6088 rec.collecting.sport.baseball:1111714
```

Element	Description
221	Command successful
11188	Article number
<1390-3AB1CB85-113@storefull-227.iap.bryant.webtv.net>	Message ID

To retrieve all the information from the HEAD request, you must call the fgets() function twice. The first time will get the information in the preceding table; the second time will retrieve the entire text of the header. The server indicates the end of the header with a single line containing only a period.

The error codes that can be returned by this command are

Error Code	Description
412	No newsgroup has been selected
420	No current article has been selected
423	No such article number in this group
430	No such article found

NEXT

The NEXT command will select the next article in the group. An example request and response is shown here:

```
CLIENT REQUEST: NEXT
SERVER RESPONSE: 223 11196 <992m6d$1fi$1@aunews.duc.auburn.edu>
article retrieved - request text separately
```

Element	Description
223	Successfully retrieved next article
11196	Article number
<992m6d$1fi$1@aunews.duc.auburn.edu>	Message ID

Note that the response indicates that the text of the article is to be retrieved separately. This is done by using the BODY command described earlier in this section.

The error codes that may be returned by the NEXT command are

Error Code	Description
412	No newsgroup selected
420	No current article has been selected
421	No next article in this group

QUIT

The QUIT command will terminate the NNTP session with the server, as shown here:

```
CLIENT REQUEST: QUIT
SERVER RESPONSE: 205 closing connection - goodbye!
```

Element	Description
205	Connection successfully closed

You should be familiar with some general error codes. These error codes indicate syntax errors, command errors, or other general communication failures:

Error Codes	Description
400	Service discontinued
500	Command not recognized
501	Command syntax error
502	Access restriction or permission denied
503	Program fault—command not performed

Implementation

The first thing you need to know about NNTP or socket-level communications is that the interaction between the application (or client) and the server is much the same as writing or interacting with files. The functions that are used for this interaction are fsockopen(), fputs(), fgets(), and fclose().

The fsockopen() function opens an Internet or Unix socket connection. In our application, the following parameters are to be used with the fsockopen() function:

```
int fsockopen(string hostname, int port);
```

The first parameter is hostname. This string will contain the Internet address of the NNTP server. In our example application, this parameter is included in the configuration file and can be changed at any time.

The second parameter is the port that is to be used. The port is passed the fsockopen() function as an integer. NNTP servers almost exclusively use port 119 on which to communicate. This parameter is also included in the configuration file.

The fsockopen() function will return an integer that is referred to as the file pointer. This file pointer will be used with other socket read, write, and close operations.

The fputs() function will write a string to a file pointer. In our application the following parameters will be used:

```
int fputs(int fp, string str);
```

The first parameter is the integer file pointer that was returned from the successful completion of the fsockopen() function. The second parameter is the string that is to be written to the port. In our application, this function will be used to issue commands to the NNTP server. For instance, to send the GROUP command to the server, the fputs() function would be used like this:

```
fputs($ns, "GROUP alt.php\r\n");
```

The $ns parameter is the file handle of the NNTP server, and the remainder is the string to be sent to the NNTP server. The \r\n at the end of the string is a carriage-return/line-feed pair signifying to the server that the transmission has ended.

The fgets() function reads a stream of data from the file handle and returns the data as a string. The format of the fgets() function looks like this:

```
string fgets(int fp, int length);
```

The first parameter should be familiar to you by now; it is the file pointer to the NNTP server's port. The second parameter is the length of data to be read from the port. The fgets() function will read data from the file pointer until length –1 bytes have been read or until the end of file (EOF), whichever comes first. In our application the fgets() function will be used like this:

```
$response = fgets($ns, 1024);
```

If the fgets() function is successful, variable $response will contain the string read from the NNTP server.

The last function we will cover before we look at some code is fclose(). The fclose() function is used to simply close the file pointer to the NNTP server. The usage is

```
int fclose(int fp);
```

The only parameter that is passed to this function is the file pointer that is to be closed. The fclose() function returns a 1 if the function is successful and the port is closed.

The configuration file looks like a regular PHP file and is used to set a series of PHP variables. These variables tell the application what news server to use, the news server port, the username and password, and the groups. Notice that the groups are arranged in array format. These array elements must start at [0], but can contain as many groups as you would like (however, they must be in sequential order). The code is as follows:

chapter12_nntp.conf

```
<?
  $server = 'news.mynewsserver.com';
  $port = '119';
  $username="myusername";
  $password="mypassword";
  $group[0]="alt.sports.baseball";
  $group[1]="alt.php";
  $group[2]="alt.php.sql";
  $group[3]="alt.os.linux";
  $group[4]="alt.linux";
?>
```

The most important file in this application is the NNTP library. This file will be included in all PHP pages, and the functions that are contained in this file will be called to perform the NNTP specific functions. We will break this library up and discuss the functions individually.

The first function is called openNNTPconnection() and is used to initiate the connection with the NNTP server. The parameters that are passed to this function are the NNTP server address, the NNTP server port, the username, and the password. The NNTP server address and port are used in the fsockopen() function to open a socket to the news server. If the function is successful, the $ns variable will contain the socket's file handle. This variable will be used throughout the application when the NNTP server's socket is referenced.

Once the socket is open, the server status is checked by reading data from the socket. The fgets() function is used to do this, and the server's initial string is placed in the $response PHP variable. The $response variable is checked for a successful response. If the response is successful, the fputs() function is used to change the communication mode to READER. The last two tasks this function performs are to send the username and password to the NNTP server. If the authentication codes that are returned indicate success, the function returns the $ns file handle. If the function is not successful, –1 is returned. The code is as follows:

chapter12_nntplib.inc

```
<?
include "chapter12_nntp.conf";
//
// This function opens the NNTP server connection,
// the parameters accepted are:
// server = news.server.com
// port = 119
// username = [the news server username]
// password = [the news server password]
//
// The news server file handle is returned if the connection is successful.
// If the connection is not successful, -1 is returned.
//
function openNNTPConnection($server,$port,$username,$password)
{
  $ns = fsockopen($server, $port);
  if (!$ns)
  {
    echo "ERROR: Could not open connection to server: $server";
    return -1;
  }

  $response = fgets($ns, 1024);

// If the response is not OK
  if (substr($response, 0, 2) != "20")
```

```
  {
    echo "ERROR: There was a problem communicating with the server: $server";
    return -1;
  }

// Sets the communication mode to READER
  fputs($ns, "MODE READER\r\n");
  $response = fgets($ns, 1024);
  if (substr($response, 0, 2) != "20")
  {
    echo "ERROR: There was a problem setting the mode to READER on server:
    $server";
    return -1;
  }

// Sends the username to the server
  fputs($ns, "authinfo user $username\r\n");
  $response = fgets($ns, 1024);
  if (substr($response, 0, 3) != "381")
  {
    echo "ERROR: There was a problem with username: $username on server:
    $server";
    return -1;
  }

// Sends the password to the server
  fputs($ns,"authinfo pass $password\r\n");
  $response = fgets($ns, 1024);
  if (substr($response, 0, 3) != "281")
  {
    echo "ERROR: There was a problem with password: $password on server:
    $server";
    return -1;
  }
  return $ns;
}
```

The next function closes the NNTP server socket. The fputs() function is used to send the disconnect string to the news server. The disconnect string in this case is quit\r\n. After this string is sent, the file handle is closed. The code is as follows:

```
//
// This function closes the NNTP server connection,
// the parameters accepted are:
// ns = the nntp server file handle
//
```

```
function closeNNTPConnection($ns)
{
  fputs($ns,"quit\r\n");
  fclose($ns);
}
```

The getSingleNNTPGroup() function is used to return information about the group that is passed to the function. The information that will be gathered will be the response code, the number of articles in the group, the name of the group, the first article number, and the last article number. You will notice that once the response is retrieved from the server the PHP function strtok() is called. This function will take the string and tokenize it or split it into pieces. The delimiter in this case is the space character. This means that the string that is returned from the server will be split into words. The strtok() function will be used throughout this library to tokenize the response strings from the server. If this function is successful, these items will be returned in an array called $info[]. The code is as follows:

```
//
// This function selects a single NNTP group,
// the parameters accepted are:
// ns = news server file handle
// group = the group that is to be selected
//
// The news server group information is returned if the
// connection is successful.
// If the connection is not successful, -1 is returned.
//
function getSingleNNTPGroup($ns, $group)
{
   fputs($ns, "GROUP $group\r\n");
   $response = fgets($ns, 1024);
   $tok = strtok($response, " ");

   $info["code"] = $tok;
   $tok = strtok(" ");

   if($info["code"] == "411")
   {
      echo "ERROR: $group - This group does not exist on this server";
      return -1;
   }
   if ($info["code"] != "211")
   {
      echo "ERROR: There was a problem retrieving group: $group";
```

```
        return -1;
    }

      $info["number"] = $tok;
      $tok = strtok(" ");

      $info["first"] = $tok;
      $tok = strtok(" ");

      $info["last"] = $tok;
      $tok = strtok(" ");

      $info["name"] = $tok;
      $tok = strtok(" ");

      return $info;
}
```

The getNNTPArticlesFromGroup() function retrieves all the articles from the selected group. This is done by using the LISTGROUP command. As we discussed previously, the LISTGROUP command gathers all the article numbers from the selected group. These article numbers and the total number of array elements are read into an array called $article[] and then passed back to the calling code, as follows:

```
//
// This function gets the articles from the specific group,
// the parameters accepted are:
// ns = news server file handle
// group = the group the article is in
//
// An array is returned that contains the group data.
// If the connection is not successful, -1 is returned.
//
function getNNTPArticlesFromGroup($ns,$group)
{
   fputs($ns, "LISTGROUP $group\r\n"),
   $response = fgets($ns, 1024);
   $tok = strtok($response, " ");

   $info["code"] = $tok;
   $tok = strtok(" ");
   $i=0;
   if($info["code"] == "411")
   {
      echo "ERROR: $group - This group does not exist on this server";
      return -1;
```

```
    }
    if ($info["code"] == "211")
    {
       while ((substr($response = fgets($ns, 1024), 0, 1) != ".")) {
          $article[$i]["number"] = trim($response);
          $i++;
       }
    }
    else
    {
       echo "ERROR: There was a problem retrieving group: $group";
       return -1;
       }

    $article["count"] = $i;
    return $article;
}
```

The getNNTPArticleBody() function retrieves the body of the article referenced by the $article and $body parameters. This function calls getSingleNNTPGroup to select the group. If this function is not called before you call the getAllNNTPArticleHead() function, you will get an error back from the NNTP server stating that the group has not been selected. Once the group is selected, the getAllNNTPArticleHead() function will retrieve the header information and place the variables in the $head[] array. The elements of this array are printed out to the web page.

This function then communicates with the news server again and retrieves the body of the article. The body of this article is returned line by line in an array called $body[]. The code is as follows:

```
//
// This function gets the body of the article from the specific group,
// the parameters accepted are:
// ns = news server file handle
// article = the article number
// group = the group the article is in
//
// An array is returned that contains the body data.
// If the connection is not successful, -1 is returned.
//
function getNNTPArticleBody($ns,$article,$group)
{
   getSingleNNTPGroup($ns,$group);

   $head = getAllNNTPArticleHead($ns,$article);
```

```
    if($head)
    {
        echo "Article Number: ".$article."<br>";
        echo "Subject: ".$head["subject"]."<br>";
        echo "Date: ".$head["date"]."<br>";
        echo "From: ".$head["from"]."<br>";
    }

    fputs($ns, "BODY $article\r\n");
    $response = fgets($ns, 1024);
    $tok = strtok($response, " ");

    $info["code"] = $tok;
    $tok = strtok(" ");
    $i=0;
    if($info["code"] == "423")
    {
        echo "ERROR: $article - This article does not exist on this server";
        return -1;
    }
    if ($info["code"] == "222")
    {
        while ((substr($response = fgets($ns, 1024), 0, 1) != ".")) {
            $body[$i] = $response."<br>";
            $i++;
        }
    }
    else
    {
        echo "ERROR: There was a problem retrieving the article: $article";
        return -1;
        }

    $body["count"] = $i;
    return $body;
}
```

The getAllNNTPArticleHead() function retrieves the header for the selected article. This entire header is returned from the server, but this function parses through the returned text and gathers the important information. An example of the returned header is given in the description of the HEAD command earlier in this chapter. You can see from this example header that there is an abundance of information that is returned. Much of the information is not useful in this application. The useful items are the subject of the article, the date the article was posted, and the author of the article. After these items are parsed from the header, they are stored in an array called

$head[]. The elements of the array are $head["subject"], $head["date"], $head["from"], and $head["all"]. The subject, date, and from items are obvious, but the $head["all"] element may not be. This element preserves the entire text of the header and may be used as needed. The code is as follows:

```
//
// This function gets the article heads from the specific group,
// the parameters accepted are:
// ns = news server file handle
// article = the article number
//
// An array is returned that contains the heading data.
// If the connection is not successful, -1 is returned.
//
function getAllNNTPArticleHead($ns, $article)
{
   fputs($ns, "HEAD $article\r\n");
   $response = fgets($ns, 1024);
   $tok = strtok($response, " ");

   $head["code"] = $tok;
   $tok = strtok(" ");

   if($head["code"] == "411")
   {
      echo "ERROR: $article - This article does not exist on this server";
      return -1;
   }
   if ($head["code"] == "221")
   {
      $head["all"] = "";
      while ((substr($response = fgets($ns, 1024), 0, 1) != ".")) {
         $head["all"] = $head["all"].$response."<br>";
            if(substr($response, 0, 9) == "Subject: ")
               $head["subject"] = ereg_replace("Subject: ", "", $response);
            if(substr($response, 0, 6) == "Date: ")
               $head["date"] = ereg_replace("Date: ", "", $response);
            if(substr($response, 0, 6) == "From: ")
               $head["from"] = ereg_replace("From: ", "", $response);
         $i++;
      }
   }
   else
   {
      echo "ERROR: There was a problem retrieving head: $article";
      return -1;
```

```
        }

    $head["count"] = $i;
    return $head;
}
```

The get20NNTPArticlesFromGroup() function is used in this application to gather the article heads for display in the web page. The initial lines of code select the group, which is passed in as an argument. From there, the header is requested and parsed into subject, date, and from variables, as we discussed earlier in this chapter. These variables are placed into a multidimensional array called $article[][].

The NEXT command is sent to the server, which will cause the server to increment the article number. The HEAD is then issued again, which will retrieve the new header information. This new information is subsequently parsed and placed into the $article[][] array as before. This procedure is looped through 20 times, and 20 sets of headers are retrieved and stored in the array. The code is as follows:

```
//
// This function gets the first 20 article heads from the specific group,
// the parameters accepted are:
// ns = news server file handle
// group = the group the article is in
//
// An array is returned that contains the article data.
// If the connection is not successful, -1 is returned.
//
function get20NNTPArticlesFromGroup($ns, $group)
{
   $i = 0;
   $response = "";
   fputs($ns, "GROUP $group\r\n");
   $response - fgets($ns, 1024);
   $tok = strtok($response, " ");
   $tok = strtok(" ");
   $tok = strtok(" ");
   $article[$i]["number"] = $tok;
   $response = "";
   fputs($ns, "HEAD\r\n");
   $response = fgets($ns, 1024);
   $tok = strtok($response, " ");
   $head["code"] = $tok;
   $tok = strtok(" ");

   if($head["code"] == "411")
   {
```

```
        echo "ERROR: $article - This article does not exist on this server";
        return -1;
    }
    if ($head["code"] == "221")
    {

    while($line = fgets($ns,1024)) {
      $line = chop($line);
      if($line == ".") { break; }
        if(ereg("^(.*):(.*)$",$line,$ph)) {
          if (substr($ph[1], 0, 7) == "Subject" )
            $article[$i]["subject"] = trim($ph[2]);
            if (substr($ph[1], 0, 6) == "Date: ")
              $article[$i]["date"] = ereg_replace("Date: ", "", $ph[1]);
              if (substr($ph[1], 0, 4) == "From")
                $article[$i]["from"] = trim(ereg_replace("\"", "",$ph[2]));
          }
      }
    }
    else
    {
        echo "ERROR: There was a problem retrieving head: $article";
        return -1;
        }
        $i++;

while ($i < 20 ){

    $response = "";
    fputs($ns, "NEXT \r\n");
    $response = fgets($ns, 1024);
    $tok = strtok($response, " ");
    $tok = strtok($response, " ");
    $tok = strtok(" ");
    $article[$i]["number"] = $tok;

    $response = "";
    fputs($ns, "HEAD\r\n");
    $response = fgets($ns, 1024);
    $tok = strtok($response, " ");
    $head["code"] = $tok;
    $tok = strtok(" ");

    if($head["code"] == "411")
    {
        echo "ERROR: $article - This article does not exist on this server";
        return -1;
```

```
    }
    if ($head["code"] == "221")
    {

    while($line = fgets($ns,1024)) {
      $line = chop($line);
      if($line == ".") { break; }
      if(ereg("^(.*):(.*)$",$line,$ph)) {
        if (substr($ph[1], 0, 7) == "Subject" )
          $article[$i]["subject"] = trim($ph[2]);
          if (substr($ph[1], 0, 6) == "Date: ")
            $article[$i]["date"] = ereg_replace("Date: ", "", $ph[1]);
            if (substr($ph[1], 0, 4) == "From")
              $article[$i]["from"] = trim(ereg_replace("\"", "",$ph[2]));
          }
      }
    }
    else
    {
       echo "ERROR: There was a problem retrieving head: $article";
       return -1;
       }
   $i++;
  }
    return $article;
}
?>
```

The next three files are the PHP files that will display the NNTP information in a web browser. The first file, chapter12_index.php, begins with normal HTML tags to set up the title of the page along with a simple style sheet.

The first two PHP instructions include the configuration file (chapter12_nntp.conf) and the library (chapter12_nntplib.inc) that we discussed in the preceding paragraphs. At this point the library functions are called. The first, openNNTPConnection(), opens the connection to the news server and returns the file handle. The group variables that are defined in the configuration file are used in the getSingleNNTPGroup() function to retrieve the details of each group. The variables that are returned are displayed in a table. The group name is defined as a hyperlink and will take the user to the chapter12_listarticles.php page. The code is as follows:

chapter12_index.php

```
<html>
<head>
      <title>NNTP Communications</title>
```

```
</head>

<body>
<STYLE TYPE="TEXT/CSS">
TH      {color: #ffcc99; background-color: #000000;}
TD, TH {FONT-SIZE: 8pt; FONT-FAMILY: verdana, arial, sans-serif;}
</STYLE>

<?
// Include the nntp library and the configuration file
include "chapter12_nntplib.inc";
include " chapter12_nntp.conf";

// Open the NNTP server connection
$ns = openNNTPConnection($server,$port,$username,$password);
if (!$ns)
{
   exit;
}

// Get the groups from the configuration file and gather the information
// from the nntp server.
$i=0;
while($group[$i]!=NULL){
   $groupinfo[$i] = getSingleNNTPGroup($ns,$group[$i]);
   $i++;
}

echo "<table align=center>";
echo "<tr><td>Articles</td><td>Group
Name</td><td>Start</td><td>End</td></tr>";

// Print out the group information to the browser
$i=0;
while ($group[$i] != NULL)
{
   echo "<tr><td>".$groupinfo[$i]["number"]."</td>";
   echo "<td><A
   HREF=\"chapter12_listarticles.php?group=".$groupinfo[$i]["name"]."\">".
   $groupinfo[$i]["name"]."</A></td>";
   echo "<td>".$groupinfo[$i]["first"]."</td>";
   echo "<td>".$groupinfo[$i]["last"]."</td></tr>\n";
   $i++;
}
echo "</table>";

// Close the connection
```

```
closeNNTPConnection($ns);
?>

</body>
</html>
```

This will produce a page that looks similar to Figure 12-1.

The next file in the sequence is chapter12_listarticles.php. This file is passed the group as a GET variable from the previous page. This GET variable is transferred to a PHP variable and is used in the get20NNTPArticlesFromGroup() function. Once again, this function is contained in the file called chapter12_nntplib.inc and will return 20 article headers from the news server. These headers will be returned in a multidimensional array called $article. This array is traversed and the elements are placed in a table. The items that are displayed include the article number, the subject of the article, the date the article was posted, and the author of the article.

The article headers are limited to 20 in this application for a couple of reasons. The main reason is simply the time it takes to download all the articles in the group.

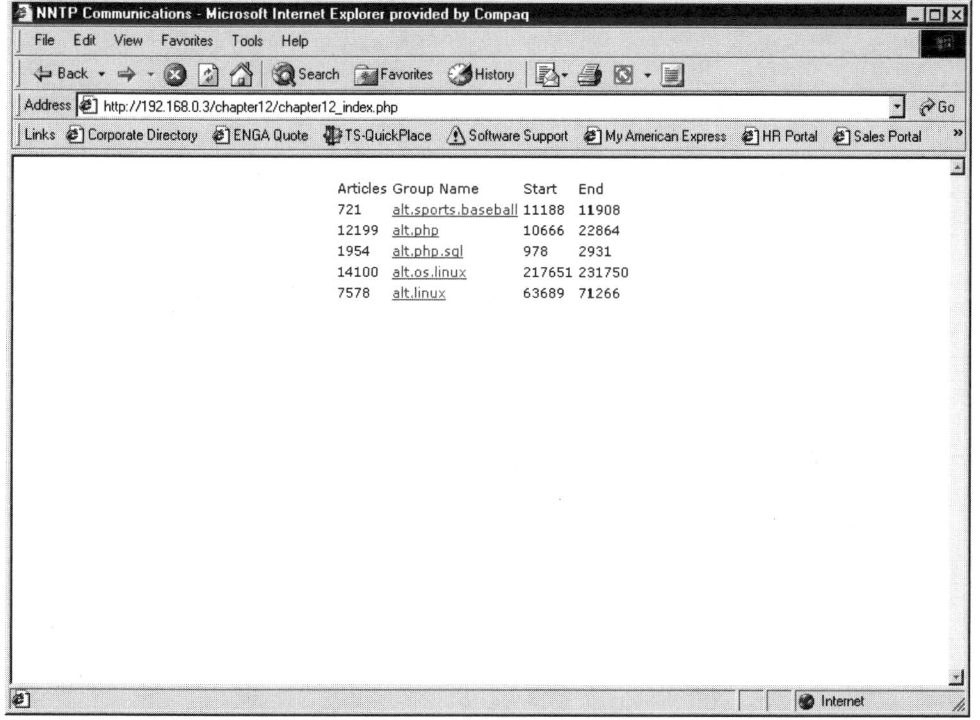

Figure 12-1 *NNTP client main page*

If all the article headers are gathered from the server, the web server will often time out, giving a "page cannot be displayed" error. The timeout can be adjusted on the web server; however, the time to download will still be excessive. Remember, the goal of this chapter is to teach NNTP server- and socket-level communications. You will still accomplish this goal even though the headers retrieved are limited to 20. The code is as follows:

chapter12_listarticles.php

```
<html>
<head>
      <title>NNTP List Articles</title>
</head>

<body>
<STYLE TYPE="TEXT/CSS">
TH      {color: #ffcc99; background-color: #000000;}
TD, TH {FONT-SIZE: 8pt; FONT-FAMILY: verdana, arial, sans-serif;}
</STYLE>

<?
// Include the nntp library and the configuration file
include "chapter12_nntplib.inc";
include "chapter12_nntp.conf";

// Transfer the query string variable to a PHP variable
if (isset($HTTP_GET_VARS[group]) )
   $group = $HTTP_GET_VARS[group];
else
   $group=NULL;

echo "GROUP: ".$group."<BR>";

// Open the NNTP server connection
$ns = openNNTPConnection($server,$port,$username,$password);
if (!$ns)
{
   exit;
}

// Retrieve 20 articles from the selected group
$article = get20NNTPArticlesFromGroup($ns,$group);
$i=0;

// Create a table and place the retrieved data in the table.
```

```
echo "<table>";
echo
"<tr><td>Article<br>Number</td><td>Subject</td><td>Date</td><td>From</td></tr>";
while ($i < 21)
{
   echo "<tr><td>".$article[$i]["number"]."</td>";
   echo "<td><A
   HREF=\"chapter12_article.php?group=".$group."&article=".$article[$i]
   ["number"]."\">".$article[$i]["subject"]."</A></td>";
   echo "<td>".$article[$i]["date"]."</td>";
   echo "<td>".$article[$i]["from"]."</td></tr>\n";
   $i++;
}
echo "</table>";

// Close the connection
closeNNTPConnection($ns);

?>
```

This page will look like Figure 12-2. Notice that the article subject is displayed as a hyperlink. Clicking on the subject will take you to the next page and display the body of the article.

The final source file that is included in this chapter is instrumental in displaying the body of the article in the browser. The chapter12_article.php file is passed two variables from the previous page, group and article. Again, both of these parameters need to be passed into the getNNTPArticleBody() to retrieve the appropriate body. The body of the article is placed in an array called $body[], and then the array is printed out to the browser. The code is as follows:

chapter12_article.php

```
<html>
<head>
      <title>NNTP Article</title>
</head>

<body>
<STYLE TYPE="TEXT/CSS">
TH     {color: #ffcc99; background-color: #000000;}
TD, TH {FONT-SIZE: 8pt; FONT-FAMILY: verdana, arial, sans-serif;}
</STYLE>

<?
```

```
// Include the nntp library and the configuration file
include "chapter12_nntplib.inc";
include "chapter12_nntp.conf";

if (isset($HTTP_GET_VARS[group]) ){
   $group = $HTTP_GET_VARS[group];
   $article = $HTTP_GET_VARS[article];
   }

// Open the NNTP server connection
$ns = openNNTPConnection($server,$port,$username,$password);
if (!$ns)
{
   exit;
}

// Get the body of the article
$body = getNNTPArticleBody($ns,$article,$group);

// Echo the article to the browser.
$i=0;
while ($i < $body["count"])
{
   echo $body[$i];
   $i++;
}

// Close the connection
closeNNTPConnection($ns);
?>

</body>
</html>
```

This page, like the others, is very simple and displays only the important information. This page will look similar to Figure 12-3.

Next Steps

This application is a good start toward creating a fully functional Usenet newsreader application. Now that you know the basics for communicating with the NNTP server

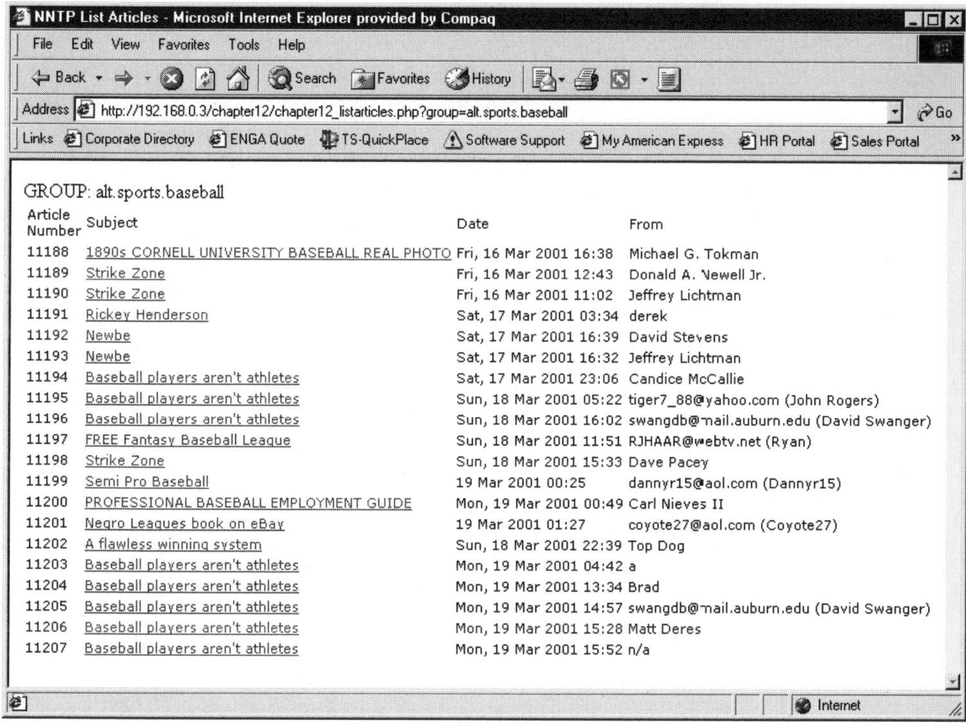

Figure 12-2 *Listing the articles in the newsgroup*

through PHP, you should be able to take the next step and provide the code to post to a Usenet newsgroup. RFC 977, which was mentioned at the beginning of this chapter, will provide the syntax and further details on the POST command. You should already have the software functions and tools needed to add this functionality.

Other feature upgrades that can be implemented to provide further functionality can include integrating this application with a MySQL database. With the articles stored in a database, this would reduce repetitive server communications and allow for other enhancements such as searching and archiving.

As with any software development project, your imagination is the only limit to what can be done with the code. Many newsgroups contain attachments or uuencoded binary information. An interesting exercise would be to uudecode the information and save it to a file.

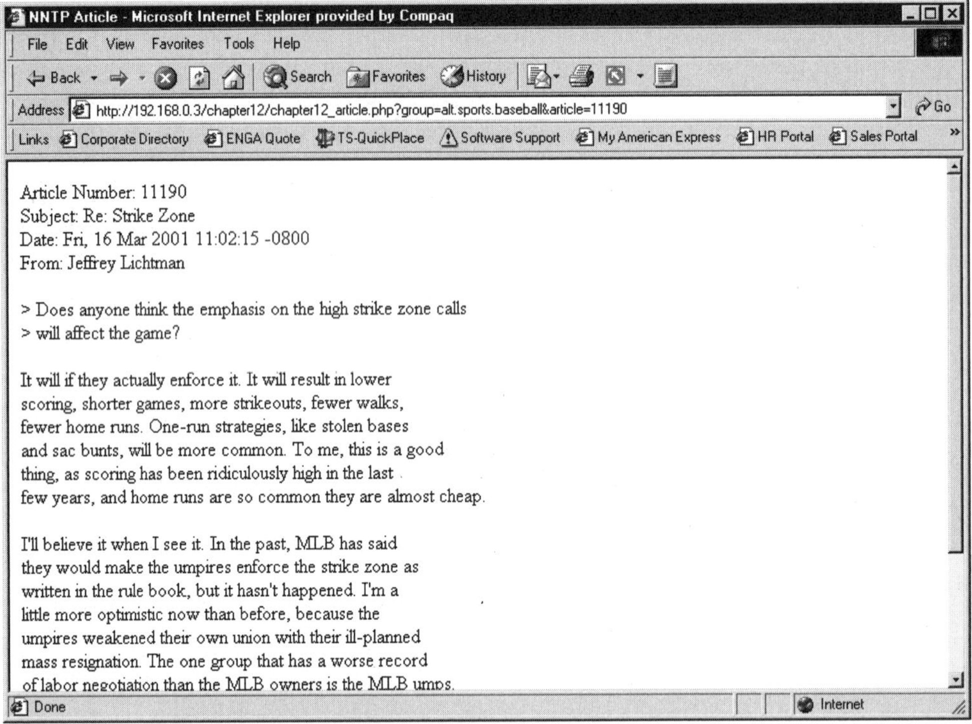

Figure 12-3 *Displaying the body of the article*

What to Take Away

This chapter was intended to give the beginner an overall view of basic socket-level communications and provide examples of this communication. The method that was chosen to illustrate this functionality was the Usenet news server system. This system uses TCP sockets to communicate and pass requests and responses between the client and server. We looked at the NNTP communication specification and created an application based on this specification. This chapter should give you the tools you need to understand and continue developing using TCP sockets. You can use the techniques that were introduced here and modify them to fit your needs and the needs of your application.

CHAPTER 13

Message Board Application

IN THIS CHAPTER:

chapter13.sql—Contains SQL statements for creating a message board database

chapter13_checklogin.php—Code to verify user is logged in to application

chapter13_common.php—Contains commonly used functions for the application

chapter13_login.php—Presents a login form for the user

chapter13_message.php—Contains message class for handling messages such as displaying contents of a message or creating a new message

chapter13_messageForm.php—Presents user with a form for entering a new message

chapter13_topics.php—Contains topics class for handling topics, such as listing or creating new ones

chapter13_user.php—Contains user class for handling the creation and display of user information and so on

chapter13_userForm.php—Presents user with a form for entering or editing profile information

The project for Chapter 13 is to develop a message board application. This application is very similar to those found on financial sites for posting comments about various stocks. The application is built on a MySQL database, but it should be straightforward to adapt the application to other databases, as only the basic SQL statements are used. The application is not specific to any subject matter, and therefore can be adapted for use in any type of web site.

Application Requirements

The first stage in development of this project is to examine all of the requirements and then divide them into logical groupings.

Requirements Analysis

The basic requirement for this chapter's project is to develop an interactive message board application where users can post comments on various topics and read others' comments on each topic.

Requirements Detail

The project's requirements can be broken down into three main groups: topics, users, and messages. Each of these groups has several subcomponents, outlined as follows.

Topics The application must allow for several topic threads to exist. Each topic can have one or more subtopics, such as *Sports – Basketball – Men's* and *Sports – Basketball – Women's*. The application should allow the user to create a topic at any level in the hierarchy, not just at the lowest level. The list of topics may continually grow as a user makes use of the application.

Users Each person who uses the application will be required to register. During this process, the user will be instructed to enter the following pieces of data: login name, password, first name, last name, phone number, e-mail address, city, state, zip code, country, and birth date. In addition to these fields being recorded, the date the user signed up will also be stored and a unique ID is generated for the user. Once the user is registered they can log in to the application and post messages for a given topic. Finally, other users will be able to view the information entered about the user when viewing a post from the user.

Messages Messages are the heart of this application. Each message that is posted will have a corresponding subject and body text. In addition to these fields, each message will have associated with it the ID of the person who posted it, the ID of the message it is in reply to (if applicable), the topic under which it was posted, and the date and time when it was posted. Each message will also have a unique ID that will allow it to be retrieved more easily later.

Application Design

During the application design phase we'll break the application into its input and output requirements and then further divide the application into groups of related functionality.

Application Inputs

Following the structure of the requirements, we'll divide the application's inputs into three sections.

Topics

The only input required for a topic is selecting a particular topic or creating a new one. There is not a requirement to delete a topic or rename it because of all the messages linked to it. The handling of topic selection is discussed in the application's output design. When the user chooses to create a new topic, they will first need to navigate to the appropriate point in the hierarchy tree and then fill in a form to create the new topic (see Figure 13-1). The topic name can be up to 20 characters.

Users

The input required for a user is twofold. First, a user should be presented with a login dialog box that asks for the login name and password. If the user has not already registered with the application, they will be presented with a link to a registration form, which contains the fields mentioned in the requirements section. Once they have registered, they can use the same form later to edit their personal information.

Messages

For each message, a user can supply a subject and a body. The subject is limited to 20 characters and the body is limited to 255 characters. This limit was chosen

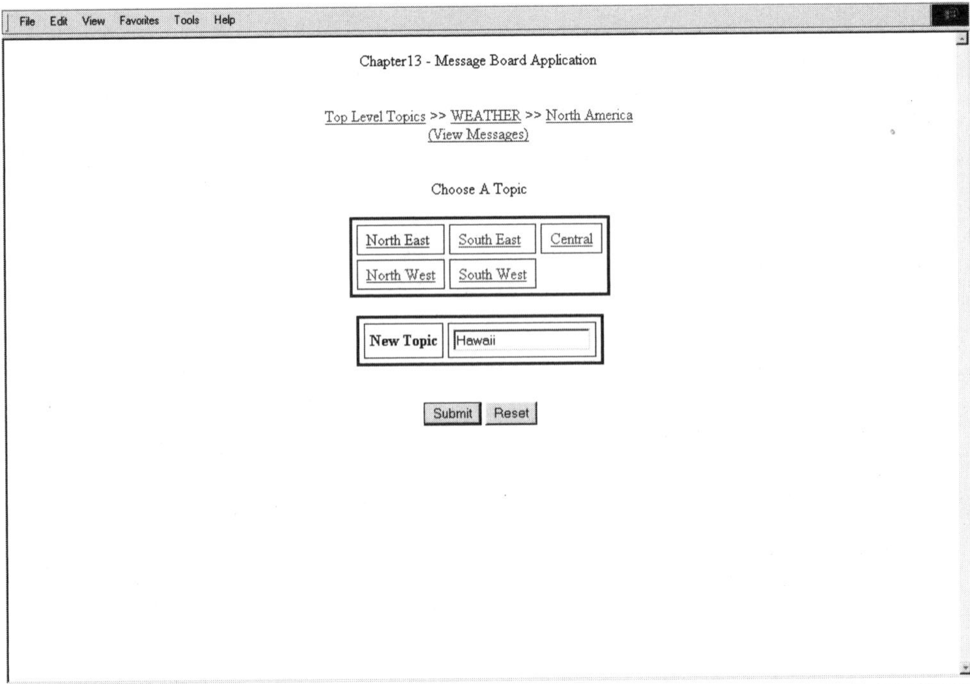

Figure 13-1 *Adding a new topic to the hierarchy*

because it is a safe number for most databases; a larger number of characters often requires support for a blob (binary large object) database field that not all databases support. When viewing a message, the application user can click the name of the person who posted the message to see their personal information. Also the user can click links to take them to the next or previous message.

Application Outputs

The applications output requirements are fairly vague as far as look and feel of the interface so that they may be adapted to fit the rest of a site. The requirements that must be met are outlined as follows.

Topics

The user will begin with a list of top-level topics. Once they have chosen a top-level topic they will be presented with all of the next level subtopics for that topic along with the option to view recent messages associated with that topic. This can best be presented as a list containing the topic and its subtopics that are all clickable to get to each level of the hierarchy. At each level of the hierarchy, all the subtopics should be displayed so the user can either move up the hierarchy or down the hierarchy as desired.

Users

The only user information that is output is when someone clicks a user's name to view more information about the user. This is the same information that the user filled out to register for the site, minus the password field, and with the addition of the sign-up date.

Messages

When an application user clicks View Messages for a particular topic, they will be presented with a list of the last five messages posted for this topic. This list includes who posted the message, what the message was in reply to, when it was posted, the message ID, and its subject. If the user clicks the message ID or subject, they will be taken to another screen, which displays further detail for the message. This screen indicates who posted the message, what it is in reply to, the subject, body, creation date, creation time, and links to the previous and next message.

Application Implementation

The next step in the development process is to begin writing the code. This phase is broken out by setup, common functions, and the individual modules that make up the application.

Setup

The first step in developing this application is to prepare the database to store the necessary information. The SQL statement syntax presented here corresponds to using a MySQL database. The first step was to create a database to house the data. For the application, we created a database called chapter13. The script checks for existence of the table and drops it before creating it again, which allows the script to be run over and over. The script used to build the user table is as follows:

chapter13.sql

```
USE CHAPTER13;
DROP TABLE IF EXISTS user;
CREATE TABLE user (userid int AUTO_INCREMENT PRIMARY KEY,
```

```
login VARCHAR(20) NOT NULL UNIQUE,
password VARCHAR(20) NOT NULL,
fname VARCHAR(20) NOT NULL,
lname VARCHAR(20) NOT NULL,
phone VARCHAR(20) NULL,
email VARCHAR(30) NULL,
address1 VARCHAR(30) NULL,
address2 VARCHAR(30) NULL,
city VARCHAR(20) NULL,
state CHAR(20) NULL,
zip CHAR(5) NULL,
country VARCHAR(20) NULL,
bdate VARCHAR(20) NULL,
cdate DATE NOT NULL);
```

For the userid column, we set auto increment, which causes the database to generate a unique ID for each user inserted into the database. Another method would be to issue the first user an ID of 1, and then select max and add 1 for each additional user that is created. The login field is specified as unique to not allow multiple users with the same login name, as it would be impossible to determine whose ID was whose. All of the fields other than login, password, and cdate (creation date) are set to NULL, which means that they are optional to the user. The message and user table also use the auto_increment feature of MySQL to generate unique IDs for each message. Use the following SQL to create the message and topic tables:

```
DROP TABLE IF EXISTS message;

CREATE TABLE message (msgid int AUTO_INCREMENT PRIMARY KEY,
                      topicid int NOT NULL,
                      posterid int NOT NULL,
                      replytoid int NULL,
                      subject VARCHAR(20) NOT NULL,
                      body VARCHAR (255) NOT NULL,
                      ctime TIME NOT NULL,
                      cdate DATE NOT NULL);

DROP TABLE IF EXISTS topic;

CREATE TABLE topic (topicid int AUTO_INCREMENT PRIMARY KEY,
                    topicname VARCHAR(20) NOT NULL,
                    parentid int NULL,
                    cdate DATE NOT NULL);
```

Common Functions

Next, we move on to common functions, which are used throughout the application. The first thing is to turn on sessionizing so a user's login, password, and user ID can be stored and retrieved as the user navigates through the application, as follows:

chapter13_common.php

```
<?php
session_start();
session_register("sessiondata");
```

The echoLine() function is defined next. This is used to make writing HTML to the page with a carriage return at the end of each line a little easier. Since white space generally doesn't matter in HTML (or in PHP, for that matter), it is not required to do this, but it makes viewing the source of the HTML page much easier on the eyes. The echoLine() function is shown here:

```
//#################################################################
//##        Function:    echoLine                                ##
//##      Parameters:    string                                  ##
//##     Description:    Outputs a single line including lf & cr ##
//#################################################################
function echoLine ($inputstring)
   {
   echo $inputstring."\n";
   }
```

The next function in the common file is used to establish a connection to the MySQL database. This function is used throughout the application any time a database handle is needed. The DBConnection class looks like this:

```
//#################################################################
//##     Function:           DBConnection                        ##
//##     Description:    Establishes a connection to the database ##
//#################################################################
function dbConnect()
   {
   $database="chapter13";
   $username="root";
   $hostname="walker";
   $password=NULL;
```

```
$linkID =
mysql_pconnect ($hostname,$username, $password);
if ($linkID)
    {
    $linkID =
    mysql_connect ($hostname,$username,$password);
    }
mysql_query("use $database",$linkID);
echo mysql_error($linkID);
return $linkID;
}
```

The displayUser() function is used in conjunction with the userForm file to fill in the registration form if the user has already signed up and is simply editing their information (see Figure 13-2). The displayUser() function is shown here:

```
//##################################################################
//##        Function:    displayUser                              ##
//##      Parameters:    arrray of user info                      ##
//##     Description:    Outputs the user information as an       ##
//##                     HTML table                               ##
//##                                                              ##
//##################################################################
function displayUser($userInfo)
    {
    //Indicate if the resultset is empty
    if (empty($userInfo))
        {
        echo "<center>\n";
        echo "<BR>\n";
        echo "User Not Found!";
        echo "</center>\n";
        return ;
        }

    echo "<center>User Details For<br><b>$userInfo[login]<b><center>";
    echo "<br><br>";
    echo "<table cellspacing=5 cellpadding=5 border=3 ";
    echo "bordercolor=\"0000FF\" align=\"center\">\n";

    //Display a new row for each element of the input array
    $itemcount = sizeof ($resultset);
    while (list ($key,$value) = each ($userInfo))
```

```
    {
    echoLine ("<tr><td>");
    switch($key)
        {
        case 'login':
            {$key = "Login Name"; break;}
        case 'fname':
            {$key = "First Name"; break;}
        case 'lname':
            {$key = "Last Name";  break;}
        case 'phone':
            {$key = "Phone"; break;}
        case 'email':
            {$key = "Email"; break;}
        case 'address1':
            {$key = "Address"; break;}
        case 'address2':
            {$key = "Address"; break;}
        case 'city':
            {$key = "City"; break;}
        case 'state':
            {$key = "State"; break;}
        case 'zip':
            {$key = "Zip"; break;}
        case 'country':
            {$key = "Country"; break;}
        case 'bdate':
            {$key = "Birth Date"; break;}
        case 'cdate':
            {$key = "Sign Up Date"; break;}
        }
    echo $key;
    echoLine ("</td><td>");
    echo $value;
    echoLine ("</td></tr>");
    }
  echoLine ("</table>");
  echo "<br><br><br>";
  echo "<a href=\"#\" onclick=\"window.close();\">Close Window</a>";
  }

?>
```

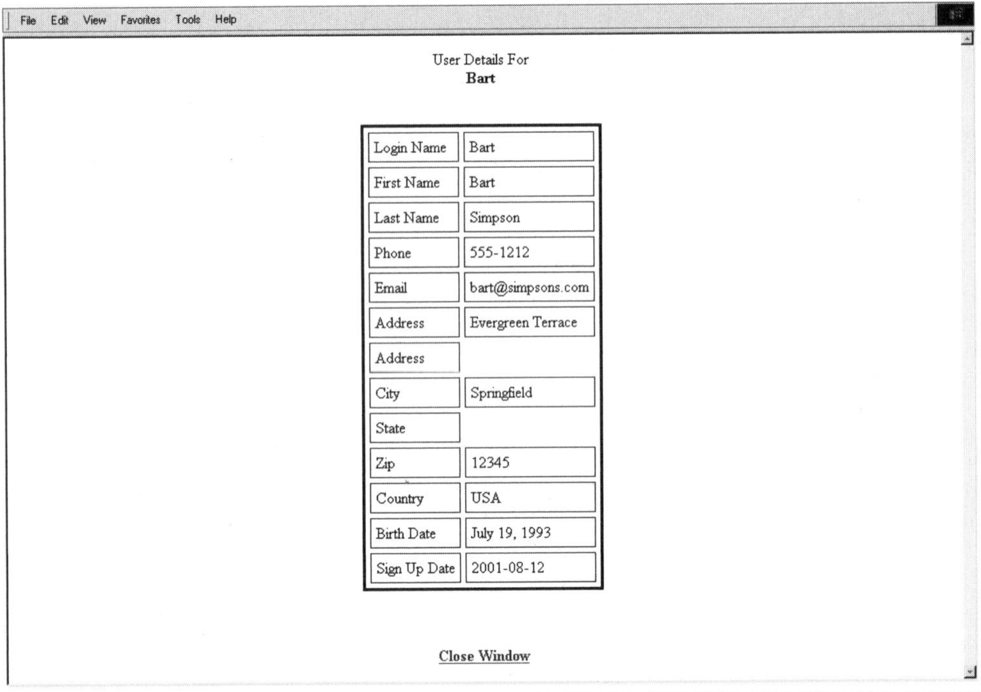

Figure 13-2 *The display user form*

Login

The next section of code we'll look at gathers the user's login credentials. The code begins by including the common functions and then setting the user's session data login value to NULL, which effectively logs them out if they happen to have already logged in and their session was still active. The following code presents the login screen:

chapter13_login.php

```
<?php
include ('chapter13_common.php');
$sessiondata[login] = NULL;
?>

<!doctype html public "-//W3C//DTD HTML 4.0 //EN">
<html>
<head>
<title>Instant PHP4 Chapter13 - Message Board Application</title>
</head>
```

```
</body>
<center>Chapter13 - Message Board Application </center>
<br><br>
<center><a href="chapter13_userform.php?action=new">
 Click Here To Register</a></center>
<br><br>
<form action="chapter13_topics.php" method="POST">
<table cellspacing=5 cellpadding=5 border=3
align="center" borderCOLOR="0000FF" >
<tr><td>Login</td><td>
<input type="TEXT" name="in_login" size="30" maxlength="20"
selected=true><br>
</td></tr>
<tr><td>Password</td><td>
<input type="password" name="in_password" size="30" maxlength="20">
</td></tr>
</table>
<br><br>
<center>
```

The form includes some hidden data fields that tell the resulting page how to behave. Basically, if you log in successfully, you will be presented with a list of the top-level topics. In this case, we display the subtopics for topicID=0, which results in the top-level topics being displayed, as shown here:

```
<input type="hidden" name="action" value="subtopic">
<input type="hidden" name="topicID" value="0">
<input type="submit" value="Login">
<input type="reset" value="Reset">
</center>
</form>
</body>
```

Verifying Login

We now examine the code that is used to verify that a user has indeed logged in to the application successfully:

chapter13_checkLogin.php

```
</html><!doctype html public "-//W3C//DTD HTML 4.0 //EN">
<html>
<head>
<title>Instant PHP4 Chapter13 - Message Board Application</title>
```

```
</head>
</body>
<center>Chapter13 - Message Board Application</center>
<br><br>
```

After displaying the top of an HTML page, we next retrieve the user's session variables and check that they have a login ID. If they do not have a login ID, we present them with the appropriate message and a link to log in or register for the application. The code to retrieve the form variables and verify login is as follows:

```
<?php
//Retrieve input variables from HTTP get or post
$userinfo = strtolower($REQUEST_METHOD) == 'get'
   ? $HTTP_GET_VARS : $HTTP_POST_VARS;

$loggedin = TRUE;

//If no username in sessiondata or form data then they are not
//logged in and are not trying to

if ($userinfo[in_login] == NULL && empty($sessiondata[login]))
   {
   echoLine ("<center>");
   echoLine ("<br><br><br>");
   echoLine ("You are not logged in!");
   echoLine ("<br>");
   echoLine ("<a href=\"chapter13_login.php\">Click Here
              To Log In</a>");
   echoLine ("<br>");
   echoLine ("<a href=\"chapter13_userform.php?action=new\">
              Click Here To Register</a>");
   echoLine ("</center>");
   $loggedin = FALSE;
   }
```

If they are logging in to begin their session, we add their login credentials to their session data so that they don't have to log in to each page. Again, if their login fails, we display the links for them to login again or register. This is the code that actually looks at the database to verify the supplied credentials:

```
//If they are logging in, set the session data
else if (!empty($userinfo[in_login]))
   {
   $sessiondata[login] = $userinfo[in_login];
   $sessiondata[password] = $userinfo[in_password];
   }

   $linkid = mysql_connect ('walker','root',NULL);
   $sqlstmt =
   "select userid
      from user
     where login =\"".$sessiondata[login]."\"
       and password = \"".$sessiondata[password]."\"";
   $resultid =
   mysql_db_query ('chapter13',$sqlstmt,$linkid);
   $results =
            mysql_fetch_array ($resultid, MYSQL_ASSOC);
   $userID = $results[userid];
   if (is_Null($userID))
      {
      echoLine ("<center>");
      echoLine ("<br><br><br>");
      echoLine ("Login Failed!<br>");
      echoLine ("<a href=\"chapter13_login.php\">Click Here
                 To Log In</a>");
      echoLine ("<br>");
      echoLine ("<a href=\"chapter13_userform.php?action=new\">
                 Click Here To Register</a>");
      echoLine ("</center>");
      $loggedin = FALSE;
      }
   else
      {
      $sessiondata[userID] = $userID;
      }
?>
```

User Data

The next section of code we'll cover is the processing of user data. This code provides a form for the user to either enter or update their personal data. We begin by including the common functions, as shown here:

chapter13_userForm.php

```
<?php

include ('chapter13_common.php');
?>

<!DOCTYPE HTML PUBLIC "-//W3C//DTD HTML 4.0 Transitional//EN">

<html>
<head>
    <title>Instant PHP4 Chapter13 - Registration</title>
</head>


<?php
```

The action variable is used to determine whether a new user is signing up or a person is editing their data. We retrieve the action variable from the form data as shown here:

```
//Retrieve input variables from HTTP get or post
$userinfo = strtolower($REQUEST_METHOD) == 'get'
   ? $HTTP_GET_VARS : $HTTP_POST_VARS;

switch($userinfo[action])
   {
   case 'new':
      {
      echoLine ("<body>");
      break;
      }
```

In the case that they are updating their data, we retrieve the data already entered into the database and use it to pre-populate the form. The popForm() function is defined in JavaScript and is called on load of the document to fill in the form. Case statements are used to turn each column name into a user-friendly name for output. The Javascript code to populate the form is as follows:

```
case 'update'
      {
      $linkid = mysql_connect ('walker','root',NULL);
      $sqlstmt =
      "select *
         from user
        where userid =".$userinfo[userID];
      $resultid =
      mysql_db_query ('chapter13',$sqlstmt,$linkid);
      $user =
      mysql_fetch_array ($resultid, MYSQL_ASSOC);

      echoLine ("<script language=\"JavaScript\">");
      echoLine ("<!--");
      echoLine ("function popForm()");
      echoLine ("    {");
      echo       "    document.userForm.login.value =";
      echoLine ("\"$user[login]\"");
      echo       "    document.userForm.password.value =";
      echoLine ("\"$user[password]\"");
      echo       "    document.userForm.fname.value =";
      echoLine ("\"$user[fname]\"");
      echo       "    document.userForm.lname.value =";
      echoLine ("\"$user[lname]\"");
      echo       "    document.userForm.phone.value =";
      echoLine ("\"$user[phone]\"");
      echo       "    document.userForm.email.value =";
      echoLine ("\"$user[email]\"");
      echo       "    document.userForm.addr1.value =";
      echoLine ("\"$user[address1]\"");
      echo       "    document.userForm.addr2.value =";
      echoLine ("\"$user[address2]\"");
      echo       "    document.userForm.city.value =";
      echoLine ("\"$user[city]\"");
      echo       "    document.userForm.state.value =";
      echoLine ("\"$user[state]\"");
      echo       "    document.userForm.zip.value =";
      echoLine ("\"$user[zip]\"");
      echo       "    document.userForm.country.value =";
      echoLine ("\"$user[country]\"");
```

```
        echo       "   document.userForm.bdate.value =";
        echoLine ("\"$user[bdate]\"");
        echo       "   document.userForm.action.value =";
        echoLine ("\"update\"");

        echoLine ("    }");
        echoLine ("//-->");
        echoLine ("</script>");
        echoLine ("<body onLoad=\"popForm()\">");
        break;
        }
    }
?>

<form name="userForm" action="chapter13_user.php" method="POST">
<table cellspacing=5 cellpadding=5 align="center" border=3
 bordercolor="0000FF">
<tr>
<td><b>Login</b></td>
<td><input type="text" name="login" size="30"
         maxlength="20" selected=true></td>
</tr><tr>
<td><b>Password</b></td>
<td><input type="password" name="password" size="30"
         maxlength="20"></td>
</tr><tr>
<td>First Name</td>
<td><input type="text" name="fname" size="30"
         maxlength="20"</td>
</tr><tr>
<td>Last Name</td>
<td><input type="text" name="lname" size="30"
         maxlength="20" </td>
</tr><tr>
<td>Phone Number</td>
<td><input type="text" name="phone" size="30"
        maxlength="20" </td>
</tr><tr>
<td>Email Address</td>
<td><input type="text" name="email" size="30"
         maxlength="30" </td>
```

```
</tr><tr>
<td>Address Line 1</td>
<td><input type="text" name="address1" size="30"
          maxlength="30" </td>
</tr><tr>
<td>Address Line 2</td>
<td><input type="text" name="address2" size="30"
          maxlength="30" </td>
</tr><tr>
<td>City</td>
<td><input type="text" name="city" size="30"
          maxlength="20" </td>
</tr><tr>
<td>State</td>
<td><input type="text" name="state" size="30"
          maxlength="20" </td>
</tr><tr>
<td>Zip</td>
<td><input type="text" name="zip" size="30"
          maxlength="5" </td>
</tr><tr>
<td>Country</td>
<td><input type="text" name="country" size="30"
          maxlength="20" </td>
</tr><tr>
<td>Birthdate</td>
<td><input type="text" name="bdate" size="30"
          maxlength="20" </td>
</tr>
</table>
<br><br>
<center>
<input type="hidden" NAME="action" VALUE="create">
<input type="submit" value="Submit">
   
<input type="reset" value="Reset">
</form>
</center>

<body>
</html>
```

User Handling

Now that you have forms for signing up and logging in users, we need to develop functions to work with the users. These functions are part of the user class. Since most of the user functions involve access to the database, the constructor for this class establishes that connection. The user class definition is shown here:

chapter13_user.php

```
<?php

include ('chapter13_common.php');

//##################################################################
//##    Class:          user                                     ##
//##    Description:    registration handler                     ##
//##################################################################
class user
   {
   //member variables
   var $toplevelid;
   var $toplevelname;
   var $sqlstmt;
   var $linkid;
   var $resultid;

    //constructor
   function user()
      {
      //establish dbconnection
      $this->linkid = dbConnect();
      }
```

The newUser() method is called whenever a new user should be added to the database. It first checks that someone is not already using that login name. The code to check whether the user already exists is as follows:

```
//##################################################################
//##    Method:         newUser                                  ##
//##    Return value:   none                                     ##
//##################################################################
   function newUser($login,$password,$fname,$lname,$phone,$email,
                    $address1,$address2,$city,$state,$zip,$country,
```

```
                $bdate)
  {
  //check that someone with username doesn't already exist
  $this->sqlstmt =
  "select userid
     from user
    where login = \"".$login."\"";
  $this->resultid =
  mysql_db_query ('chapter13',$this->sqlstmt,$this->linkid);
  echo mysql_error($this->linkid);
  $count =  mysql_numrows($this->resultid);
  if ($count > 0)
    {
    echo "<center>Login Name Already Exists";
    echo "- Try Again</center>";
           return -1;
    }
```

If no one is using that name, the user is added to the database and a message is displayed indicating so, as shown here:

```
$this->sqlstmt =
"insert into user values (0,\""
.$login."\",\""
.$password."\",\""
.$fname."\",\""
.$lname."\",\""
.$phone."\",\""
.$email."\",\""
.$address1."\",\""
.$address2."\",\""
.$city."\",\""
.$state."\",\""
.$zip."\",\""
.$country."\",\""
.$bdate."\",now())";
$this->resultid =
mysql_db_query ('chapter13',$this->sqlstmt,$this->linkid);
$error = mysql_error ($this->linkid);
if (empty($error))
   {
   echo "<center>User <b>$login</b> was added.<br>\n";
   echo "<a href=\"chapter13_login.php\">Click Here To Login</A></center>";
   }
return;
}
```

The getUser() method is used by other methods within this class whenever further information is required about a user. The method is retrieved based on the user's ID in the database, and is shown here:

```
//###################################################################
//##    Method:          getUser                                     ##
//##    Return value:    associative array of user info             ##
//###################################################################
    function getUser($userID)
        {
           $this->sqlstmt =
           "select *
              from user
             where userid =".$userID;
        $this->resultid =
        mysql_db_query ('chapter13',$this->sqlstmt,$this->linkid);
        $user =
           mysql_fetch_array ($this->resultid, MYSQL_ASSOC);
        return $user;
    }
```

The updateUser() method is called after the user makes changes to their personal information. Here is the code for the updateUser() method:

```
//###################################################################
//##    Method:          updateUser                                  ##
//##    Return value:    none                                        ##
//###################################################################
   function updateUser($login,$password,$fname,$lname,$phone,$email,
                       $address1,$address2,$city,$state,$zip,$country,
                       $bdate)
      {
      $this->sqlstmt =
      "update user set
      password = \"".$password."\",
      fname    = \"".$fname."\",
      lname    = \"".$lname."\",
      phone    = \"".$phone."\",
      email    = \"".$email."\",
      address1 = \"".$address1."\",
      address2 = \"".$address2."\",
      city     = \"".$city."\",
      state    = \"".$state."\",
```

```
    zip      = \"".$zip."\",
    country  = \"".$country."\",
    bdate    = \"".$bdate."\"
    where login = \"".$login."\"";
    $this->resultid =
    mysql_db_query ('chapter13',$this->sqlstmt,$this->linkid);
    echo mysql_error($this->linkid);
    return;
    }

  }//end of message class
```

The rest of this file is used to handle various user actions such as create, update, or view. In each case, the action variable is examined to determine which action is necessary. For create and update, the user's information is retrieved from the form variables and passed to the appropriate create or update method. When viewing a user, all that is necessary is a user's ID. The code for processing the code related to user handling is as follows:

```
//Retrieve input variables from HTTP get or post
$userinfo = strtolower($REQUEST_METHOD) == 'get'
   ? $HTTP_GET_VARS : $HTTP_POST_VARS;

$myUser = new user();
switch($userinfo[action])
   {
   case 'create':
      {
      $myUser->newUser($userinfo[login],$userinfo[password],
                       $userinfo[fname],$userinfo[lname],
                       $userinfo[phone],$userinfo[email],
                       $userinfo[addr1],$userinfo[addr2],
                       $userinfo[city], $userinfo[state],
                       $userinfo[zip], $userinfo[country],
                       $userinfo[bdate]);
      break;
      }
   case 'update':
      {
      $myUser->updateUser($userinfo[login],$userinfo[password],
                          $userinfo[fname],$userinfo[lname],
                          $userinfo[phone],$userinfo[email],
```

```
                                    $userinfo[addr1],$userinfo[addr2],
                                    $userinfo[city], $userinfo[state],
                                    $userinfo[zip], $userinfo[country],
                                    $userinfo[bdate]);
        break;
        }
      case 'view':
        {
        $user =$myUser->getUser($userinfo[userID]);
        unset($user[userid]);
        unset($user[password]);
        displayUser($user);
         break;
        }
    }
?>
</BODY>
</HTML>
```

Topic Handling

We will now examine the code used for managing the topics the user can choose from. First, we create a topics class whose constructor establishes the database connection, similar to how the user class was set up. The code that defines the topics class and its constructor is shown here:

chapter13_topics.php

```
<?php

include ('chapter13_common.php');

//###################################################################
//##    Class:          topics                                     ##
//##    Description:    topic list handler                         ##
//###################################################################
class topics
   {
   //member variables
   var $toplevelid;
   var $toplevelname;
```

```
   var $sqlstmt;
   var $linkid;
   var $resultid;

    //constructor
   function topics()
      {
      //establish dbconnection
      $this->linkid = dbConnect();
      }
```

The first method we look at in the topics class is getTopic(). It is used by other methods within this class whenever topic details need to be retrieved from the database, and is as follows:

```
//####################################################################
//##    Method:          getTopic                                    ##
//##    Parameters:      topicID                                     ##
//##    Return value:    associative array of topic info             ##
//####################################################################
   function getTopic($topicID)
      {
         $this->sqlstmt =
         "select *
            from topic
           where topicid =".$topicID;
      $this->resultid =
      mysql_ query (this->sqlstmt,$this->linkid);
      $topic =
         mysql_fetch_array ($this->resultid, MYSQL_ASSOC);
      return $topic;
      }
```

The getParent() method is similar to the getTopic() method, except that the information is retrieved for topic that is the parent for the topic ID that is given, as shown here:

```
//####################################################################
//##    Method:          getParent                                   ##
//##    Parameters:      topicID                                     ##
//##    Return value:    associative array of parent info            ##
//####################################################################
```

```
function getParent($topicID)
   {
   $this->sqlstmt =
   "select parentid
      from topic
     where topicid =".$topicID;
   echo $this->sqlstmt;
   $this->resultid =
   mysql_query ($this->sqlstmt,$this->linkid);
   $topicInfo =
      mysql_fetch_array ($this->resultid, MYSQL_ASSOC);
   $parentId = $topicInfo[parentid];
   if (is_Null($parentID))
      {
      echo "<br>parent is null<br>";
      return 0;
      }
   else
      {
      $parent = $this->getTopic($parentID);
      return $parent;
      }
   }
```

The listSubTopics() method of the topics class returns an associative array of subtopics for a particular parent topic ID that is passed in. If the passed-in value is NULL, it is assumed that the top level of topics should be returned. The listSubtopics() method is as follows:

```
//################################################################
//##    Method:          listSubTopics                          ##
//##    Parameters:      parentID                               ##
//##    Return value:    associative array of subtopics (id,name) ##
//################################################################
   function listSubTopics($parentID=0)
      {
      if ($parentID == 0)
         {
         $this->sqlstmt =
         "select topicid, topicname
            from topic
           where parentid is NULL
```

```
        order by topicid";
      }
   else
      {
      $this->sqlstmt =
      "select topicid, topicname
         from topic
        where parentid = $parentID
        order by topicid";
      }

   $this->resultid =
   mysql_query ($this->sqlstmt,$this->linkid);
   $count =  mysql_numrows($this->resultid);
   for ($i=0;$i < $count;$i++)
      {
      $subTopics[$i] =
      mysql_fetch_array ($this->resultid, MYSQL_ASSOC);
      }
   return $subTopics;
   }
```

The displayTopicList() method is used to actually display the subtopics that are determined in the listSubTopics() method. It retrieves the topic IDs and the corresponding topic name from the database and displays them in an HTML table. The table has three columns, and we use the bcmod() function to recognize that we have shown a multiple of three topics and should start a new row. The code for displayTopicList() is as follows:

```
//###################################################################
//##        Function:          displayTopicList                    ##
//##      Parameters:          2D associative array                ##
//##     Description:    Outputs the list of topics as a 3         ##
//##                      column HTML table                        ##
//###################################################################
function displayTopicList($topicList)
   {
   //Indicate if the resultset is empty
   if (empty($topicList))
      {
      echo "<CENTER>\n";
      echo "<BR>\n";
```

```
        echo "No Further Sub Topics Exist";
        echo "</CENTER>\n";
        return 0;
        }

    echoLine ("<br><center>");
    echoLine ("Choose A Topic</center><br>");
    echo "<table cellspacing=5 cellpadding=5 border=3 ";
    echo "bordercolor=\"0000FF\" align=\"center\">\n";

    $keycount = 0;
    //Output each key as a column heading
    while (list ($key,$value) = each($topicList[0]))
        {
        $keycount++;
        }
    echo "</tr>\n";
    echo "</thead>\n";

    //Output each value as elements of a table starting a new row
    //each time the key number of columns is reached
    $rowcount = sizeof ($topicList);

    for($rowCounter = 0;$rowCounter  < $rowcount;
        $rowCounter++)
        {
        $valuesarray = array_values($topicList[$rowCounter]);
        if (bcmod ($rowCounter,3) == 0 )
            {
            echo "<tr>\n";
            }
        for($colCounter = 0; $colCounter < $keycount; $colCounter+=2)
            {
            echo "<td>\n";
            echo " ";
            echo "<a href=\"chapter13_topics?action=subtopic&topicID";
            echo "=$valuesarray[$colCounter]\">";
            echo $valuesarray[$colCounter+1]."</a>";
            echo " ";
            echo "</td>\n";
            }
        }
    echo "</tr>\n";
```

```
echo "</table>\n";
echo "</center>\n";
echo "<br>\n";
```

After displaying the list of topics, a form is displayed that allows the user to create a new topic. The topicID is passed to the form method that indicates what level of the hierarchy the user is trying to add the topic to, as follows:

```
$parentID = $valuesarray[colCounter];
if (is_null($parentID))
   {
   $parentID = 0;
   }

}
```

The displayCreateTopicForm() method is called from the displayTopicList() method to present the user with a form for adding a new topic. The new topic will be added beneath the topic that is indicated by the parentID parameter. The parentID and action create are passed along as hidden values in the form. Use the following code to display the create topic form:

```
//####################################################################
//##    Method:         displayCreateTopicForm                      ##
//##    Parameters:     parent topic id                             ##
//##    Return value:   none                                        ##
//####################################################################
   function displayCreateTopicForm($parentID=0)
      {
      echoLine ("<form action=\"chapter13_topics.php\" ");
      echoLine ("method=\"POST\">");
      echoLine ("<table cellspacing=5 cellpadding=5");
      echoLine ("align=\"center\" border=3 bordercolor=\"0000FF\">");
      echoLine ("<tr><td><b>New Topic</b></td>");
      echoLine ("<td><input type=\"text\" name=\"topicName\" ");
      echoLine ("size=\"20\" maxlength=\"20\" selected=true></td>");
      echoLine ("</tr></table><center><br><br>");
      echoLine ("<input type=\"hidden\" NAME=\"action\" ");
      echoLine ("value=\"create\">");
      echoLine ("<input type=\"hidden\" NAME=\"parentID\" ");
      echoLine ("value=\"$parentID\">");
      echoLine ("<input type=\"submit\" value=\"Submit\"> ");
```

```
    echoLine ("<input type=\"reset\" value=\"Reset\">");
    echoLine ("</form></center>");
    return 0;
    }
```

The createTopic() method is called when the user submits the form from the displayTopicForm() method. It first verifies the topic doesn't already exist at this level, and if not, it proceeds to add it to the database. The code used to create a new topic is shown here:

```
//##################################################################
//##    Method:         createTopic                                ##
//##    Parameters:     parent topic id                            ##
//##    Return value:   new topic id and name                      ##
//##################################################################
   function createTopic($topicName,$parentID=0)
      {
      //check that this topic doesn't already exist for this parent
      if ($parentID == 0)
         {
         $this->sqlstmt =
         "select topicid
            from topic
          where topicName = \"".$topicName."\"
              and parentid is NULL";
         }
      else
         {
         $this->sqlstmt =
         "select topicid
            from topic
          where topicName = \"".$topicName."\"
              and parentid = ".$parentID;
         }

      $this->resultid =
      mysql_query ($this->sqlstmt,$this->linkid);
      echo mysql_error($this->linkid);
      $count =  mysql_numrows($this->resultid);
      if ($count > 0)
         {
         echoLine ("<center>Topic Already Exists</center><br>");
         return -1;
         }

      if ($parentID == 0)
```

```
        {
        $this->sqlstmt =
        "insert into topic values (0,\"".$topicName."\",NULL,now())";
        }
      else
         {
         $this->sqlstmt =
         "insert into topic values (0,\"".$topicName."\",".$parentID.",now())";
         }
      $this->resultid =
      mysql_query ($this->sqlstmt,$this->linkid);
      $error = mysql_error($this->linkid);
      if (empty($error))
         {
         echo "<center>Topic $topicName was added</center>";
         }
      }
```

The displayParentTree() method is used to display the current topic hierarchy to the user so they can always tell where they are in the tree. The code locates the parent ID given a topic ID, and adds it to the tree. It continues doing this until it reaches the top of the tree. It always adds the top-level topics to the tree since all topics must start from that point. The code used to display the tree is as follows:

```
//#################################################################
//##    Method:          displayParentTree                      ##
//##    Parameters:      topicID                                ##
//##    Return value:    none (Tree is Displayed)               ##
//#################################################################
   function displayParentTree($topicID)
      {
      if ($topicID < 1)
         {
         $topicID=0;
         }      $topicInfo = $this->getTopic($topicID);
          $topicTree =
     "<a href=\"chapter13_topics.php?action=subtopic"
     ."&topicID=$topicID\">$topicInfo[topicname]</a>";
     $msgTopicID = $topicID;
     $topicID = $topicInfo[parentid];
     while ($topicID > 0 || (!(is_Null($topicID))))
        {
        $parentInfo = $this->getTopic($topicID);
        $topicTree =
```

```
            "<a href=\"chapter13_topics.php?action=subtopic"
            ."&topicID=$topicID\">$parentInfo[topicname]</a>"
            ." &gt&gt ".$topicTree;
            $msgTopicID = $topicID;
            $topicID = $parentInfo[parentid];
            }

        $topicTree = $topicTree
        ."<br><a href=\"chapter13_message.php?action=lastntopic"
        ."&topicID=$msgTopicID\">  (View Messages)</a>";

        $topicTree =
        "<a href=\"chapter13_topics.php?action=subtopic"
        ."&topicID=0\">Top Level Topics</a>"
        ." &gt&gt ".$topicTree;

        return $topicTree;
        }

    }//end of topics class
```

Now that we have defined all of the topic-handling methods, let's look at the code that decides which method to call. As usual, we first verify the user has logged in correctly. We then examine the action variable to see what we need to do next. If the action is subtop, we display the parent tree and then all of the topics at the current topic level. The code to handle the appropriate topic action is as follows:

```
include ('chapter13_checklogin.php');

if ($loggedin == TRUE)
    {

$myTopics = new topics();

switch($userinfo[action])
    {
    case 'subtopic':
        {
        if ($userinfo[topicID] >0)
            {
            $parentTree =
            $myTopics->displayParentTree($userinfo[topicID]);
```

```
            echoLine ("<center>$parentTree</center><br>");
            }
        $toparray = $myTopics->listSubTopics($userinfo[topicID]);
        $myTopics->displayTopicList($toparray);
        $myTopics->displayCreateTopicForm($userinfo[topicID]);
        break;
        }
```

If the action is create, we add the new topic to the database and then display where we are at in the topic tree, as follows:

```
    case 'create':
        {
        $newTopicID =
        $myTopics->createTopic($userinfo[topicName],$userinfo[parentID]);
        $parentTree = $myTopics->displayParentTree($newTopicID);
        echoLine ("<center>$parentTree</center><br>");
        break;
        }
    }
}
?>
</BODY>
</HTML>
```

Message Form

The next block of code handles the displaying of the form used to fill in a message. The form prompts the user for the subject and body text, and uses the session data that was passed to this page to populate the other pertinent fields, such as poster ID, reply to ID, and topic ID. Use the following code to display a new message form:

chapter13_messageForm.php

```
<?php

include ('chapter13_common.php');
?>

<!DOCTYPE HTML PUBLIC "-//W3C//DTD HTML 4.0 Transitional//EN">
```

```
<html>
<head><title>Chapter13 - Message Board Application</title>
</head>
<center>Chapter13 - Message Board Application - Post Message</center>
<br><br>

<form name="messageForm" action="chapter13_message.php"
      method="POST">
<table cellspacing=5 cellpadding=5 align="center"
border=3 bordercolor="0000FF">
<tr>
<td><b>Subject</b></td>
<td><input type="text" name="subject" size="20"
maxlength="20" selected=true></td>
</tr><tr>
<td><b>Body</b></td>
<td><textarea name="body" cols=50 rows=5 wrap="soft"></textarea>
</td></tr>
</table>
<br><br>
<center><input type="hidden" NAME="action" VALUE="create">

<?php

//Retrieve input variables from HTTP get or post
$userinfo = strtolower($REQUEST_METHOD) == 'get'
   ? $HTTP_GET_VARS : $HTTP_POST_VARS;

echoLine ("<input type=\"hidden\" name=\"topicID\"");
echoLine ("value=\"$userinfo[topicID]\">");
echoLine ("<input type=\"hidden\" name=\"posterID\"");
//echoLine ("value=\"$userinfo[userID]\">");
echoLine ("value=\"$sessiondata[userID]\">");
echoLine ("<input type=\"hidden\" name=\"replyToID\"");
echoLine ("value=\"$userinfo[replyToID]\">");

?>
<input type="submit" value="Submit">
<input type="reset" value="Reset">
</form>
</center>

<body>
</html>
```

Message Handling

Message handing is done with the message class. The constructor of the message class establishes the link to the database for use by the methods within the class, as shown here:

chapter13_message.php

```
<?php

include ('chapter13_common.php');

//######################################################################
//##    Class:          message                                       ##
//##    Description:    methods for handling messages                 ##
//######################################################################
class message
   {
   //member variables
   var $sqlstmt;
   var $linkid;
   var $resultid;

    //constructor
   function message()
      {
      //establish dbconnection
      $this->linkid = dbConnect();
      }
```

The getMessage() method is called by other methods within this class whenever a database lookup is needed to retrieve all the attributes of a message. The getMessage() code is as follows:

```
//######################################################################
//##    Method:         getMessage                                    ##
//##    Parameters:     message ID                                    ##
//##    Return value:   associative array of message detail           ##
//######################################################################
   function getMessage($msgID)
      {
      $this->sqlstmt =
```

```
"select msgid,message.topicid,posterid,replytoid,subject,
        body,ctime,message.cdate,login, topicname
   from message,user,topic
  where msgid =".$msgID."
    and message.posterid = user.userid
    and message.topicid = topic.topicid";
echo mysql_error();
$this->resultid =
mysql_query ($this->sqlstmt,$this->linkid);
$msg =
   mysql_fetch_array ($this->resultid, MYSQL_ASSOC);
return $msg;
}
```

The getNext() method is used to determine the next message that was posted after the one the user is currently viewing. If there are no further messages within that topic, the user will be displayed the current message again. The code to retrieve the next message is as follows:

```
//##################################################################
//##    Method:          getNext                                 ##
//##    Parameters:      message ID,topic ID                     ##
//##    Return value:    id of next msg                          ##
//##################################################################
    function getNext($msgID,$topicID)
      {
      $this->sqlstmt =
      "select msgid
         from message
        where msgid > ".$msgID."
          and message.topicid = $topicID";
      echo mysql_error();
      $this->resultid =
      mysql_query ($this->sqlstmt,$this->linkid);
      $count =  mysql_numrows($this->resultid);
      if ($count > 0)
         {
         $msgInfo =
         mysql_fetch_array ($this->resultid, MYSQL_ASSOC);
         }
      else
         {
```

```
      $msgInfo[msgid] = $msgID;
      }
   return $msgInfo[msgid];
  }
```

The getPrevious() method is just like the getNext() method except that it looks back in time to find the message before the one the user is currently reading, as shown here:

```
//#################################################################
//##    Method:          getPrevious                             ##
//##    Parameters:      message ID,topic ID                     ##
//##    Return value:    id of previous msg                      ##
//#################################################################
   function getPrevious($msgID,$topicID)
      {
      $this->sqlstmt =
      "select msgid
         from message
        where msgid < ".$msgID."
          and message.topicid = $topicID
          order by msgid desc";
        echo mysql_error();
      $this->resultid =
      mysql_query ($this->sqlstmt,$this->linkid);
      $count =  mysql_numrows($this->resultid);
      if ($count > 0)
         {
         $msgInfo =
         mysql_fetch_array ($this->resultid, MYSQL_ASSOC);
         }
      else
         {
         $msgInfo[msgid] = $msgID;
         }
      return $msgInfo[msgid];
  }
```

The displayMsgList() method takes an array of message IDs and displays the list so the user can choose which message they would like to see (as shown in Figure 13-3). It displays the following for each message: poster, reply to ID, message ID, and subject. The code is as follows:

```
//#################################################################
//##        Function:    displayMsgList                          ##
//##      Parameters:    array of msg ids                        ##
//##     Description:    a clickable row for each message        ##
//#################################################################
function displayMsgList($msgList,$topicID)
   {
   echoLine ("<center>Messages</center><br><br>");
   if (empty($msgList))
      {
      echoLine ("<center>");
      echoLine ("<b>No Messages</b><br><br>");
      echo "<a href=\"chapter13_topics?action=subtopic&topicID=0\"";
      echo ">Return To Top-Level Topics</a><br><br>";
      echoLine ("<a href=\"chapter13_messageForm.php?topicID=");
      echoLine ("$topicID&replyToID=0\">");
      echoLine ("New Message</a><br><br>");

      echoLine ("</center>");
      return 0;
      }

   foreach ($msgList as $key => $value)
      {
      $msgInfo = $this->getMessage($value[msgid]);
      echoLine ("<table cellspacing=\"5\" cellpadding=\"5\" ");
      echoLine ("border=\"1\" bordercolor=\"0000FF\" ");
      echoLine ("align=\"center\">");
      echoLine ("<tr><td width=200>");
      echo "<a href=\"chapter13_user?action=view&userID=";
      echo "$msgInfo[posterid]\" target=\"_blank\">";
      echoLine ("From: $msgInfo[login]</a>");
      echoLine ("</td><td width=200>");
      if ($msgInfo[replytoid] > 0)
        {
         echo "<a href=\"chapter13_message?action=view&msgID=";
         echoLine ("$msgInfo[replytoid]\">Reply To: #$msgInfo[replytoid]</a>");
         }
      echoLine ("</td><td width=250>");
```

```
    echo "<a href=\"chapter13_message?action=view&msgID=";
    echoLine ("$msgInfo[msgid]\">MSG: #$msgInfo[msgid]");
    echoLine (" Subject: $msgInfo[subject] </a><br>");
    echoLine ("</td><tr>");
    echoLine ("</table>");
    }
echoLine ("<center><br><br>");
echo "<a href=\"chapter13_topics?action=subtopic&topicID=0\"";
echo ">Return To Top-Level Topics</a><br><br>";
echoLine ("<a href=\"chapter13_messageForm.php?topicID=");
echoLine ("$topicID&replyToID=0\">");
echoLine ("Post New Message</a>");
echoLine ("</center>");
}
```

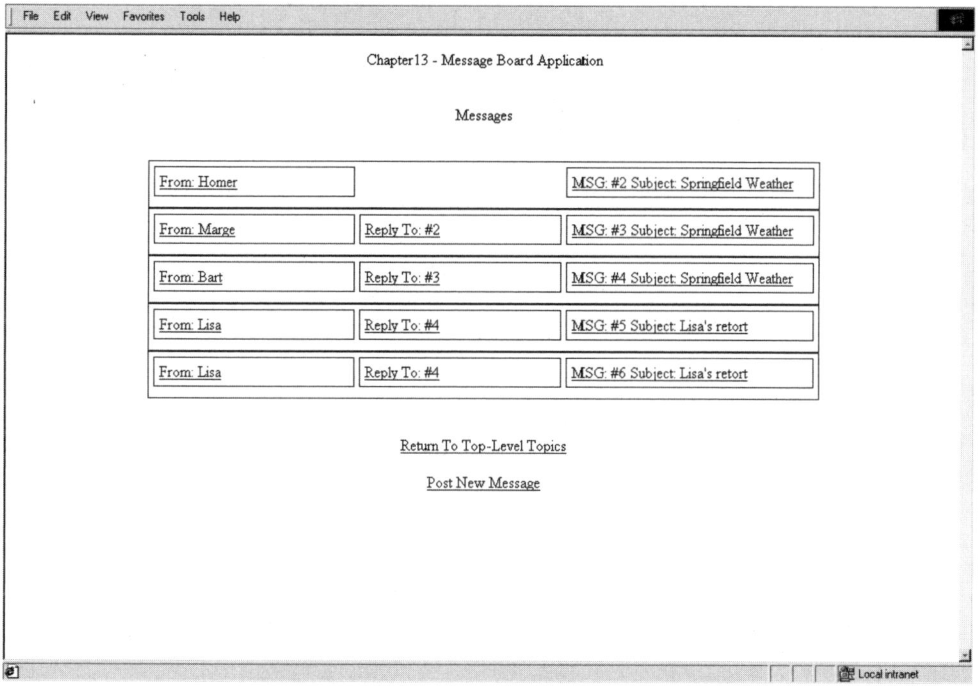

Figure 13-3 *A sample message list*

The displayMsg() method is used to display the actual contents of a message. It displays all the attributes of the message along with the current topic, a link to respond to the message, and links to navigate to the next or previous message (see Figure 13-4). The displayMsg() method is coded as follows:

```
//##################################################################
//##        Function:    displayMsg                              ##
//##      Parameters:    array of msg ids                        ##
//##     Description:    a clickable row for each message        ##
//##################################################################
function displayMsg($msgID)
   {
   $msgInfo = $this->getMessage($msgID);
   echoLine ("<center><b>Topic: ");
   echoLine ("<a href=\"chapter13_topics.php?action=subtopic");
   echoLine
   ("&topicID=$msgInfo[topicid]\">$msgInfo[topicname]</b>");
   echoLine ("</a><br>");
   echo "<table cellspacing=10 cellpadding=10 border=1 ";
   echo "bordercolor=\"0000FF\" >\n";
   echoLine ("<tr><td width=200>");
   echoLine ("<a href=\"chapter13_message.php?action=previous");
   echoLine ("&msgID=$msgInfo[msgid]&topicID=$msgInfo[topicid]\">");
   echoLine ("Previous</a></td>");
   echoLine ("<td width=400>");
   echoLine ("<a href=\"chapter13_messageForm.php?topicID=");
   echoLine ("$msgInfo[topicid]&replyToID=$msgInfo[msgid]\">");
   echoLine ("Respond</a></td>");
   echoLine ("<td width=200>");
   echoLine ("<a href=\"chapter13_message.php?action=next");
   echoLine ("&msgID=$msgInfo[msgid]&topicID=$msgInfo[topicid]\">");
   echoLine ("Next</a></td>");
   echoLine ("<tr><td width=200>");
   echoLine ("<a href=\"chapter13_user?action=view&userID=");
   echoLine ("$msgInfo[posterid]\" target=\"_blank\">");
   echoLine ("By: $msgInfo[login]</a><br>");
   if ($msgInfo[replytoid] > 0)
      {
      echoLine ("<a href=\"chapter13_message?action=view&msgID=");
      echoLine ("$msgInfo[replytoid]\">");
      echoLine ("Reply To: #$msgInfo[replytoid]</a>");
```

```
    }
  echoLine ("</td><td>");
  echoLine ("<a href=\"chapter13_messageForm.php?topicID=");
  echoLine ("$msgInfo[topicid]&replyToID=0\">");
  echoLine ("New Message</a></td>");
  echoLine ("<td>Submitted: $msgInfo[ctime] $msgInfo[cdate]<br>");
  echoLine ("Post #$msgInfo[msgid]</td><tr>");
  echoLine ("<td colspan=3 align=\"left\">");
  echoLine ("<b>Subject:</b> $msgInfo[subject]<br>");
  echoLine ("$msgInfo[body]");
  echoLine ("</td></tr>");
  echoLine ("</table>");
  echoLine ("<br><br>");

  echoLine ("</center>");
}
```

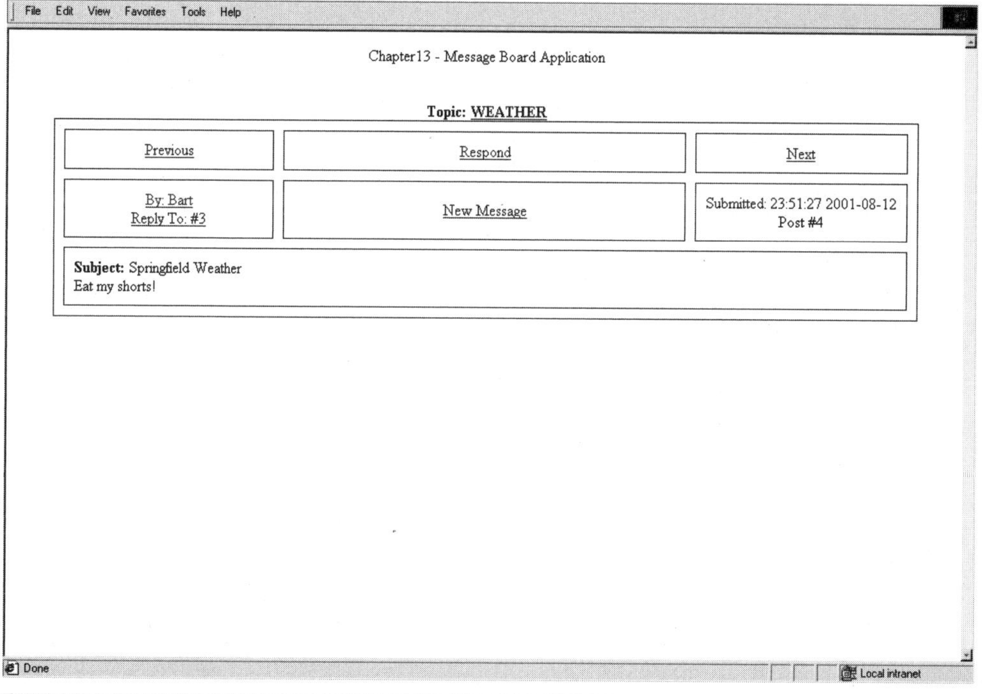

Figure 13-4 *A sample message*

The getLastNUserMsgs() method can be used whenever a user wants to see what posts another user has made. Given a user ID and a number *N* of messages, it will determine the last *N* messages that were posted by the user. The code is as follows:

```
//###################################################################
//##    Method:          getLastNUserMsgs                          ##
//##    Return value:    array of message ids                      ##
//###################################################################
   function getLastNUserMsgs($userID,$n=5)
      {
         $this->sqlstmt =
         "select msgid
            from message
          where posterid =".$userID." order by ctime desc";
      $this->resultid =
      mysql_query ($this->sqlstmt,$this->linkid);
      echo "n=".$n."<br>";
      $this->resultid =
      mysql_query ($this->sqlstmt,$this->linkid);
      $count =  mysql_numrows($this->resultid);
         if ($count < $n)
        {
        $n = $count;
        }

      for ($i=0;$i < $n;$i++)
         {
         $msgArray[$i] =
         mysql_fetch_array ($this->resultid, MYSQL_ASSOC);
         }
      return $msgArray;
      }
```

The getLastNTopicMsgs() method retrieves the last *N* messages that were posted under a particular topic. This is called when a user navigates through the topic hierarchy and clicks View Msgs to display recent messages for that topic. The code is as follows:

```
//###################################################################
//##    Method:          getLastNTopicMsgs                         ##
//##    Return value:    array of message ids                      ##
//###################################################################
```

```
function getLastNTopicMsgs($topicID,$n=5)
   {
      $this->sqlstmt =
      "select msgid
         from message
        where topicid =".$topicID
        ." order by cdate desc, ctime desc";
   $this->resultid =
   mysql_query ($this->sqlstmt,$this->linkid);
   $count =  mysql_numrows($this->resultid);
  if ($count < $n)
     {
     $n = $count;
     }

  if ($n == 0)
     {
     return 0;
     }

   for ($i=0;$i < $n;$i++)
      {
      $msgArray[$i] =
      mysql_fetch_array ($this->resultid, MYSQL_ASSOC);
      }
   return array_reverse($msgArray);
  }
```

The createMessage() method is called after a user fills out the new message form, and is used to add the message to the database (see Figure 13-5). The code used to create a new message is as follows:

```
//####################################################################
//##    Method:          createMessage                              ##
//##    Parameters:      topicID, replyToID, posterID               ##
//##                     subject, body                              ##
//##    Return value:    new topic id and name                      ##
//####################################################################
   function
   createMessage($topicID,$posterID,$replyToID=0,$subject,$body)
      {
      $this->sqlstmt =
       "insert into message values (0,".$topicID.",".$posterID.","
```

```
     .$replyToID.",\"".$subject."\",\"".$body."\",now(),now())";
    $this->resultid =
    mysql_query ($this->sqlstmt,$this->linkid);
    echo mysql_error($this->linkid);
   }

}//end of message class
```

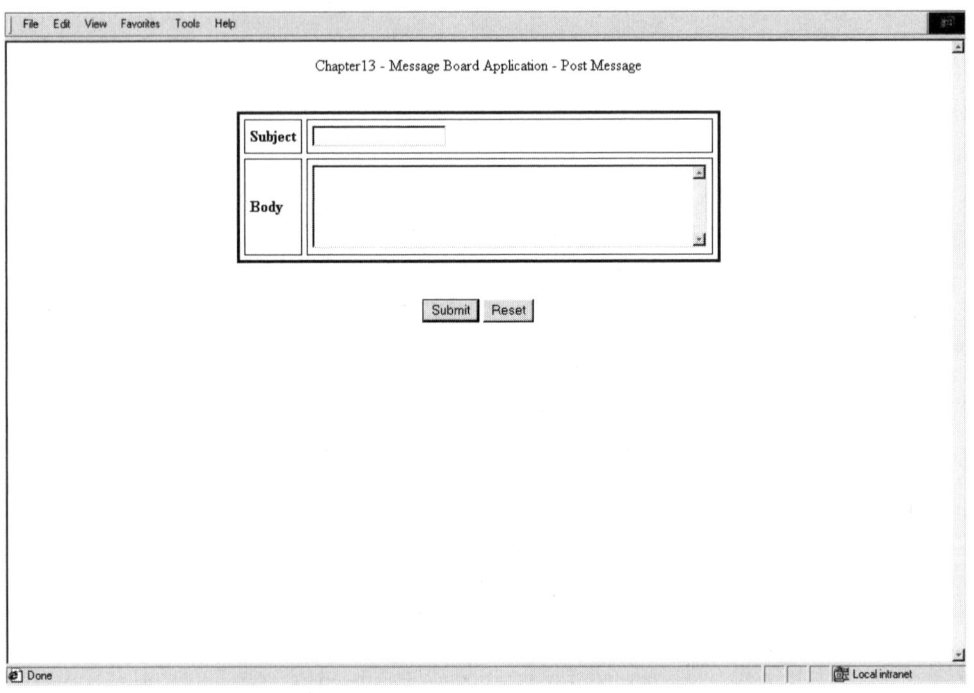

Figure 13-5 *The message input screen*

Now let's look at when the message handler methods are called. The createMessage() method is called when the action value passed in is equal to create. This happens when a user fills in the New Message form and clicks Submit. The code is as follows:

```
include ('chapter13_checklogin.php');
//if ($loggedin == TRUE)

$myMessage = new message();
switch($userinfo[action])
   {
   case 'create':
      {
      $myMessage->
      createMessage($userinfo[topicID],$userinfo[posterID],
      $userinfo[replyToID],$userinfo[subject],
      substr($userinfo[body],0,254));
      $msgList = $myMessage->getLastNTopicMsgs($userinfo[topicID],5);
      $myMessage->displayMsgList($msgList);
      break;
      }
```

The last *N* messages are shown (in this case, 5) whenever a user selects View Msgs from the topic tree, as shown here:

```
   case 'lastntopic':
      {
      $msgList = $myMessage->getLastNTopicMsgs($userinfo[topicID],5);
      $myMessage->displayMsgList($msgList);
      break;
      }
```

The view action is called when a user wishes to see the contents of the message, as follows:

```
   case 'view':
      {
      $myMessage->displayMsg($userinfo[msgID]);
      break;
      }
```

Finally, the next and previous actions are called when a user is viewing a message and they wish to navigate to the next or previous message within the same topic. The code to determine how to navigate to the next or previous message is shown here:

```
    case 'next':
        {
        $nextMsg = $myMessage->getNext($userinfo[msgID],$userinfo[topicID]);
        $myMessage->displayMsg($nextMsg);
        break;
        }
    case 'previous':
        {
        $previousMsg = $myMessage->getPrevious($userinfo[msgID],$userinfo[topicID]);
        $myMessage->displayMsg($previousMsg);
        break;
        }
    }
?>
</BODY>
</HTML>
```

Next Steps

There are several directions in which you can take this project. One interesting option would be to allow the user to create an ignore list to filter out postings from another user. Another option would be to offer a preview and spell check of the message before it is posted. You may also want to add the ability to do free text searches on the messages. Finally, there is plenty of room to improve the "look and feel" of the application as the HTML surrounding the project is done at a minimum level. This chapter provides a good starting point for including a message board on your site, and should be easily adaptable to whatever your site's content is.

What to Take Away

This chapter illustrated many useful PHP programming techniques. The session variables were used to maintain user login credentials. A MySQL database was used to store all of the message board data. Classes were used to logically group related functions. JavaScript was used to promote code reuse. Finally, there were several examples of using post variables to manage the flow of the application.

PART

PHP and WAP

OBJECTIVES

- Learn specifics about WML and WAP
- Discover how to develop WML pages
- Set up Apache to serve WML pages
- Learn how to install and debug using a WAP emulator
- Examine WML language elements and entities
- Understand the settings needed to use PHP with WML
- Further your knowledge of WAP and WML
- Examine, in depth, WML entities and attributes
- Learn how to integrate PHP into WML
- Understand how to integrate WML and MySQL

CHAPTER

14

WML and WAP

IN THIS CHAPTER:

chapter14_example1.wml—Example of decks, cards, and deck-level events

chapter14_example2.wml—Example of the <do> event

chapter14_example3.wml—Example of the <onevent> event

chapter14_example4.wml—Example of the <go> event

chapter14_example5.wml—Example of the <prev> event

chapter14_example6.wml—Example of the <refresh> event

chapter14_example7a.wml—Example of the <postfield> event

chapter14_example7b.php—Displays the variables from the <postfield> event

chapter14_example8.wml—Example of initializing using and displaying variables

chapter14_example9.wml—Example using <option>, <optgroup>, and <select> elements

chapter14_example10.wml—Example of the <input> element

chapter14_example11.wml—Example of the <timer> event

chapter14_example12.wml—Example of the <anchor> element

chapter14_example13.wml—Example of the <a> element

chapter14_example14.wml—Example using <table>, <tr>, and <td> elements

chapter14_example15.wml—Example using text layout properties

chapter14_example16.wml—Example using character entities and escape characters

chapter14_hello.wml—Initial .wml file to introduce the language

This chapter will introduce WAP and WML. We will talk a great deal about the WML language and give basic examples to demonstrate functionality. You will learn how to write WML code and learn the basic syntax and language constructs. We will provide reference material on tags that are used within this chapter and show you how to set up a WAP emulator to test your pages.

The chapter concludes with a discussion on integrating PHP and WML to produce dynamic wireless pages.

Introduction to WAP and WML

Wireless Application Protocol (WAP) is an open specification that defines how information is formatted and displayed on wireless devices such as mobile phones. This specification defines an Internet protocol that is primarily for devices with limited bandwidth. The WAP protocol is an open specification. This means it is not owned by any one organization. The protocol was initially designed and is currently maintained by a democratic group that votes on the features, implementation, versions, and so forth. This group, known as the WAP-forum, was founded in 1997 by Ericsson, Motorola, Nokia, and Phone.com (formerly known as Unwired Planet). The WAP-forum defines itself as "... an industrial co-operation with more than 90 members, who developed the WAP standardizations." One of the main objectives of the WAP-forum is to bring all companies with a business interest in the wireless industry together to exchange ideas and promote the growth of the wireless market.

One of the most important specifications the WAP-forum has produced is the WML (Wireless Markup Language) definition. This markup language, which is part of the WAP specification, is based on XML and looks very much like HTML. In fact, WML and HTML are close cousins. However, since WML is based on XML, it is a much stricter language. WML defines the format and presentation of text and images on wireless devices much as HTML defines format and presentation on personal computers. One obvious difference between the two languages is that WML also defines page hierarchy. In WML, entire screens are called *cards*, and *decks* define the navigation of the cards. In other words, if you have three screens in your application, these screens are called cards. The association of these cards with each other is defined in the deck. It is this deck that usually constitutes an entire WML page.

The WML language is interpreted by a WAP micro-browser just as HTML is interpreted by a regular browser, such as Microsoft's Internet Explorer or Netscape's Navigator. The micro-browser is usually embedded in the WAP-enabled wireless or portable device and is available on many portable operating systems, such as

Windows CE, EPOC, and Palm OS. Aside from interpreting WML, the micro-browser is also designed to interpret WMLScript, which is a simplified version of JavaScript. The latest WAP version at the time of this writing is 1.1. The WAP-forum has announced version WAP 2.0, and on August 1, 2001, they released the WML specification for public review.

WAP-enabled devices have many uses, ranging from checking flight arrivals to weather conditions, and from viewing sports scores to stock information. The beauty of WAP and WML is that the devices are mobile and the information is in the palm of your hand.

The WML Language

When you sit down to design your WAP application, it is useful to know the limitations of the devices and the WML language. If you come from an HTML background, many of the functions you take for granted are not available in WML. For example, there is no mouse or other pointing device in a WML page. User interaction is through the numerical and other keys on the phone. If you require your users to input extended amounts of text, many will become frustrated because of the time and effort it takes to input the information. WML has limited support for tables and graphics. Tables are kept simple, and graphics must be in the .wbmp format. Remember that WAP screens are small, and information must be accessed a bit at a time. WML does not support color or extensive font control. If your application requires any of these items, it may be best not to use WML.

Let's first look at a very simple WML page:

chapter14_hello.wml

```
<?xml version="1.0"?>
<!DOCTYPE wml PUBLIC "-//WAPFORUM//DTD WML 1.1//EN"
"http://www.wapforum.org/DTD/wml_1.1.xml">
<wml>
   <card id="one" title="Card One">
   <p>Hello Wireless World!</p>
   </card>
</wml>
```

Pages that are to be rendered by the WAP micro-browser all end with the .wml extension. As you can see, the first line defines this page as an XML document. The DOCTYPE is defined to be wml, and the DTD (document type definition) is accessed at http://www.wapforum.org/DTD/wml_1.1.xml.

The next line has a <wml> tag. The start of the deck is defined by this tag. Note that WML is very strict about case. The <wml> tag is a valid tag, while <WML> is not, as is the case with all tags in the WML specification. Cards in the deck are defined by the <card>...</card> tags, and the paragraphs are inside the <p>...</p> tags. Note that each card has an ID and a title.

Serving WML Pages

Now that you have a high-level overview of WAP and WML, let's set up a web server and a WAP emulator, and serve some WML pages. In this section, we are going to show you how to set up the Apache web server to serve WML pages. We are also going to set up the UP.SDK and use the emulator to view the pages as if they were on a Nokia cellular phone.

Setting Up Apache for WML

We are going to assume that you already have Apache up and running in your Linux environment. If you have made it this far in this book, you should have an instance set up and serving PHP pages. Now, simply serving a .wml page through Apache like you would a .php or an .html page is not enough. You must tell the micro-browser what type of content it is about to receive. This is done using the server's MIME type extensions, as follows:

1. Edit the httpd.conf file.
2. Find the AddType section of the conf file and add the following lines:

```
# Start Mime Types for WAP
# Definition for PHP
AddType application/x-httpd-php .wml
# Definition for WML pages
AddType text/vnd.wap.wml .wml
# Definition for embedded graphics
AddType image/vnd.wap.wbmp .wbmp
# Definition for WML Script
AddType text/vnd.wap.wmlscript .wmls
# Definition for compiled WML
AddType application/vnd.wap.wmlc .wmlc
# Definition for compiles WML Script
AddType application/vnd.wap.wmlscriptc .wmlsc
# End Mime Types for WAP
```

3. Save the httpd.conf file and restart the Apache server.

Now with these changes to the httpd.conf file, and if your web server is on the Internet and if you have a WAP-compatible phone, you will be able to see your first WML web page. Actually, those are too many "ifs." If you would like to test your page on an internal web server before you place it for the world to see, you need to visit the Openwave web site (http://www.openwave.com/), sign up for their developer's program, and download the Software Developers Kit (http://developer.openwave.com/download/).

The installation of the Openwave WAP emulator is very straightforward. At the time of this writing there are two versions available for download. Version 3.2 emulates phones that are in widespread use in North America, Japan, and Korea. These phones have been in use since 1999 and they will continue to be sold through the end of 2002. The other version is 4.1. These phones are in use in Europe and some Asia-Pacific countries. They are just starting to be shipped in the United States and should be growing in popularity throughout 2001 and into 2002. This book will concentrate on the 3.2 version of the emulator.

Once you have downloaded the software, the setup file is a self-extracting executable called upsdkW32We.exe. Even though the company that distributes the emulator is known as Openwave, you will see references to former companies such as Phone.com, the UP.SDK, and Unwired Planet. All these companies at one time or another maintained the emulator and the SDK that Openwave now distributes.

Go ahead and install the emulator by running the downloaded executable. After installation, launch the emulator and you will see two windows. The first is the generic emulator, which looks like a phone. The second window is an information screen, which will give you information, messages, warnings, and errors. With the emulator running, type the location of your web server and the chapter14_hello.wml file in the GO field and you will see something similar to Figure 14-1. You will also see the output similar to Figure 14-2 in the information screen.

Some additional features are available with the Openwave simulator. To view the source of the WML page, press F5. You will see the source output in the information screen, shown in Figure 14-3.

That's all there is to it. You have now set up an environment in which you can develop, test, and deploy WML pages.

We realize that your knowledge of WML is probably limited at this time. We have also told you that the WML specification is an extension of XML. We will now take the information in the WML DTD and discuss each of the events, elements, and entities. We will discuss each tag, give you an example of its syntax, explain the attributes that are associated with this tag, and then provide simple examples where appropriate.

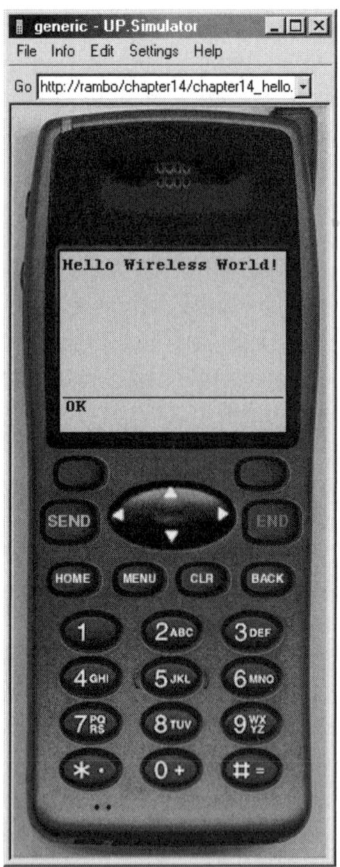

Figure 14-1 *The UP.SDK WAP emulator*

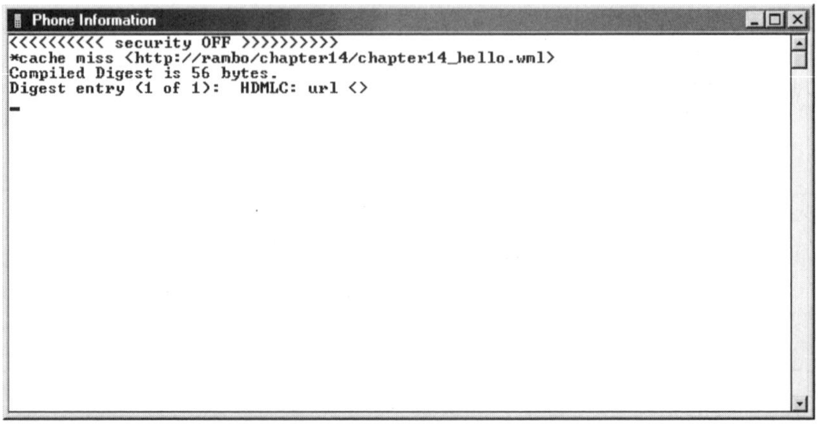

Phone Information

```
<<<<<<<<<< security OFF >>>>>>>>>>
*cache miss <http://rambo/chapter14/chapter14_hello.wml>
Compiled Digest is 56 bytes.
Digest entry (1 of 1):  HDMLC: url <>
```

Figure 14-2 *The UP.SDK WAP information screen*

```
Phone Information
<<<<<<<<<< security OFF >>>>>>>>>>
*cache miss <http://rambo/chapter14/chapter14_hello.wml>
Compiled Digest is 56 bytes.
Digest entry (1 of 1):  HDMLC: url <>

************************ Current WML ******************************************
<?xml version="1.0"?>
<!DOCTYPE wml PUBLIC "-//WAPFORUM//DTD WML 1.1//EN"
"http://www.wapforum.org/DTD/wml_1.1.xml">
<wml>
   <card id="one" title="Card One">
   <p>Hello Wireless World!</p>
   </card>
</wml>

*******************************************************************************
```

Figure 14-3 *Viewing the source of the WML page*

The Prolog

Every WML page must begin with specific lines of code. These specific lines are known as the *prolog*. We discussed these lines earlier, but did not introduce the official name of this section of code. Three lines of code constitute the prolog:

```
<?xml version="1.0"?>
<!DOCTYPE wml PUBLIC "-//WAPFORUM//DTD WML 1.1//EN"
"http://www.wapforum.org/DTD/wml_1.1.xml">
```

The prolog defines the page as an XML document. It then defines the XML version and the DTD to be referenced. Notice that the official DTD resides at the WAP-forum web site.

Decks, Cards, and Deck-Level Events

WML pages are made up of physical decks. These decks, as we have discussed before, usually refer to a WML page. The deck is made up of logical cards, which define what the user sees in the WAP-enabled device. These cards define how the user interacts with the device and the progression of the user through the application. The DTD defines decks and cards in a single section and then deck-level declarations in another section. For the purpose of this book, we have included all these items in one section.

<wml>

The <wml> tag defines a WML deck. The opening and closing <wml> tags contain cards that define the interaction, navigation, and other information about the WML page.

Syntax

```
<wml></wml>
```

Attributes

Attribute	Format	Description
xml:lang	Language	This optional attribute sets the language used in the element. The default for the United States is en-US.
class	Character	This optional attribute defines the class name for the element. This name is case sensitive and can be used in multiple classes. If you use multiple class names, separate them with a space.
id	Unique ID	This optional attribute defines a name for the element. This must be unique for each element in the deck.

<card>

Cards define the path through the deck and the user interaction with the WML application. They can contain text, hyperlinks, input fields, images, and so on. Cards are displayed one at a time and define an entire user screen. A simple example that defines three cards is in chapter14_example1.wml, at the end of this section. The first accepts user input and the second displays the result.

Syntax

```
<card></card>
```

Attributes

Attribute	Format	Description
newcontext	Boolean	This optional attribute defines the browser context. This directs the browser to reinitialize the display of the card when it is loaded. The default value is false, which means no reinitialization.
ordered	Boolean	This optional attribute defines the card order. When set to True, the browser will display the content in a linear sequence. When set to False, users define the order as they navigate through the application. The default value is True.

Attribute	Format	Description
title	Character	This optional attribute defines the title of the card.
xml:lang	Language	This optional attribute sets the language used in the element. The default for the United States is en-US.
onenterbackward	URL string	This optional attribute defines the behavior when the user navigates into a card using a <prev> task.
onenterforward	URL string	This optional attribute defines the behavior when the user navigates into a card using a <go> task.
ontimer	URLstring	This optional attribute defines the URL that is to be loaded into the browser when the <timer> event expires for the current card.
class	Character	This optional attribute defines the class name for the element. This name is case sensitive and can be used in multiple classes. If you use multiple class names, separate them with a space.
id	Unique ID	This optional attribute defines a name for the element. This must be unique for each element in the deck.

<head>

The <head> tag contains information about the entire deck. This information could include access control and <meta> tag details.

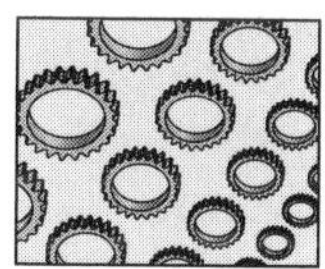

NOTE

The following tags can go in the head element: <access> and <meta>.

Syntax

```
<head></head>
```

Attributes

Attribute	Format	Description
class	Character	This optional attribute defines the class name for the element. This name is case sensitive and can be used in multiple classes. If you use multiple class names, separate them with a space.
id	Unique ID	This optional attribute defines a name for the element. This must be unique for each element in the deck.

<template>

The <template> tag defines a template that is added to all cards in the deck. Only one <template> tag is allowed per deck, and this tag can only contain <do> and <onevent> tags.

The individual card elements can override the behavior specified by the template element. For example, if you define behavior in the <template> tag with a <do> element, that <do> element can be redefined in the individual card only if both elements have the same name.

Syntax

```
<template></template>
```

Attributes

Attribute	Format	Description
onenterbackward	URL string	Occurs when the user navigates into a card using a <prev> task.
onenterforward	URL string	Occurs when the user navigates into a card using a <go> task.
ontimer	URL string	Occurs when the timer expires.
class	Character	This optional attribute defines the class name for the element. This name is case sensitive and can be used in multiple classes. If you use multiple class names, separate them with a space.
id	Unique ID	This optional attribute defines a name for the element. This must be unique for each element in the deck.

<access>

The <access> tag defines information about the access control of a WML deck. This means that the browser checks the current deck to verify that the user can navigate to this deck from the previous deck or domain.

If the <access> tag is not set, any other decks/cards can access the deck. The <access> tag must be within the <head> tags, and each deck can have only one <access> tag.

Syntax

```
<access/>
```

Attributes

Attribute	Format	Description
domain	Character	This optional attribute defines the URL of other decks that can access cards in the current deck.
path	Character	This optional attribute defines the path that must be matched by the previous deck that is requesting access to the current deck.
class	Character	This optional attribute defines the class name for the element. This name is case sensitive and can be used in multiple classes. If you use multiple class names, separate them with a space.
id	Unique ID	This optional attribute defines a name for the element. This must be unique for each element in the deck.

<meta>

The <meta> tag provides meta data or special information about the current WML deck. This special information can include keywords, subjects, topics, and so on. The meta data that is listed in this tag is most often used by Internet search engines.

Meta data contained in this tag is not displayed by the browser and must be contained in the <head> tag. The <meta> tag can also be used with the http-equiv attribute to simulate HTTP headers.

Syntax

```
<meta/>
```

Attributes

Attribute	Format	Description
content	Character	This optional attribute should specify a description of the name attribute.
forua	Boolean	This optional attribute specifies whether the meta data is sent to the browser. If set to true, the meta data must be sent to the browser.
http-equiv	Character	This optional attribute sets whether the content of the <meta> tag is sent as an http response header.

Attribute	Format	Description
name	Character	This optional attribute should specify a name for something you want to describe on the page. This could be "keywords," "author," "topic," and so on.
scheme	Character	This optional attribute specifies the structure used to translate the meta data.
class	Character	This optional attribute defines the class name for the element. This name is case sensitive and can be used in multiple classes. If you use multiple class names, separate them with a space.
id	Unique ID	This optional attribute defines a name for the element. This must be unique for each element in the deck.

<!-- -->

The comment tag is used to insert comments into the WML deck. These comments are usually used to describe functionality and provide future developers with information about your code. Comments are not displayed by the browser.

Syntax

```
<!--  -->
```

Example

chapter14_example1.wml

```
<?xml version="1.0"?>
<!DOCTYPE wml PUBLIC "-//WAPFORUM//DTD WML 1.1//EN"
"http://www.wapforum.org/DTD/wml_1.1.xml">
<!-- This example defines the usage for deck, card and
//   deck level events
//   Specifically this example is for the following WML tags:
//         <wml></wml>
//         <head></head>
//         <access/>
//         <meta/>
//         <template></template>
//         <card></card>   -->
<wml>
```

```
<head>
<!-- Access is limited to other decks/cards in www.wapiscool.com -->
  <access domain="www.wapiscool.com"/>
<!-- Set keyword Meta Tag to WAP -->
  <meta name="keyword" content="WAP"/>
<!-- Set Cache Control Meta Tag to No-Cache -->
  <meta http-equiv="cache-control" content="no-cache"/>
</head>
<template>
   <do type="prev" label="Back">
      <prev/>
   </do>
</template>
<card id="card1" title="Card 1">
   <p><a href="#card2">Go to Card 2</a></p>
</card>
<card id="card2" title="Card 2">
   <p><a href="#card3">Go to Card 3</a></p>
</card>
<card id="card3" title="Card 3">
   <p> Hello Wireless World!</p>
</card>
</wml>
```

Event Bindings

The event bindings in WML refer to elements that perform some kind of action. These actions can transfer variables or other data, or even trigger some process. Events will allow you to interact with your users and capture actions to perform a function or process.

<do>

The <do> tag is how users perform tasks. These tasks are usually performed when users select words or phrases in the browser. The <do> element can be used in the <template> element or be included inside <card> elements.

Syntax

```
<do type="type"></do>
```

Attributes

Attribute	Format	Description
type	accept prev help reset options delete unknown X-* vnd.*	This required attribute defines the type of the <do> element. Formats are described as follows: accept: Acknowledgment of acceptance prev: Backward navigation help: Request for help reset: Clear or reset options: Options or additional operations delete: Delete item unknown: Unknown item X-*: Experimental vnd*: Vendor specific
label	Character	This optional attribute creates a label for the <do> element.
name	Character	This optional attribute defines a name for the <do> element.
optional	Boolean	This is an optional attribute. If set to true, the browser ignores this element. If set to false, the browser does not ignore this element. The default is false.
xml:lang	Language	This optional attribute sets the language used in the element. The default for the United States is en-US.
class	Character	This optional attribute defines the class name for the element. This name is case sensitive and can be used in multiple classes. If you use multiple class names, separate them with a space.
id	Unique ID	This optional attribute defines a name for the element. This must be unique for each element in the deck.

Example

chapter14_example2.wml

```
<?xml version="1.0"?>
<!DOCTYPE wml PUBLIC "-//WAPFORUM//DTD WML 1.1//EN"
"http://www.wapforum.org/DTD/wml_1.1.xml">
<!-- This is an example of the <do> event -->
<wml>
<template>
   <do type="prev" label="Back">
      <prev/>
   </do>
</template>
<card id="card1" title="Card 1">
```

```
   <p><a href="#card2">Go to Card 2</a></p>
</card>
<card id="card2" title="Card 2">
   <p>This is card two</p>
</card>
</wml>
```

<onevent>

The <onevent> tag is processed when one of four events occur. The <onevent> element is associated to the event through the type attribute. The four events are onenterbackward, onenterforward, onpick, and ontimer.

Syntax

```
<onevent type="type"></onevent>
```

Attributes

Attribute	Format	Description
type	onenterbackward onenterforward onpick ontimer	This required attribute specifies the type of the <onevent> element: onenterbackward: This event occurs when a <prev> event navigates back to the previous card. onenterforward: This event occurs when a <go> event navigates to a card. onpick: This event occurs when a user selects or deselects an option. ontimer: This event occurs when the timer expires.
class	Character	This optional attribute defines the class name for the element. This name is case sensitive and can be used in multiple classes. If you use multiple class names, separate them with a space.
id	Unique ID	This optional attribute defines a name for the element. This must be unique for each element in the deck.

Example

chapter14_example3.wml

```
<?xml version="1.0"?>
<!DOCTYPE wml PUBLIC "-//WAPFORUM//DTD WML 1.1//EN"
"http://www.wapforum.org/DTD/wml_1.1.xml">
<!-- This is an example of the <onevent> event  -->
```

```
<wml>
<template>
  <onevent type="onenterbackward">
    <go href="#card2"/>
  </onevent>
</template>
<card id="card1" title="Card 1">
  <p>Card One</p>
</card>
<card id="card2" title="Card 2">
<p>Card Two</p>
</card>
</wml>
```

Task Elements

Task elements in WML provide a mechanism for completing a process. For instance, the <postfield> element must be encapsulated within the <go> tag to tell WML to post the variables to the resulting page. This process is known as a *task*.

<go>

The <go> tag or task is used to navigate to a specific URL. The <go> element can contain one or more <postfield> elements. See the <postfield> element for a description of this tag. The <go> element can also set variables. This is done through the <setvar> element. The <go> tag can contain one or more <setvar> elements. For more information, please refer to the <setvar> element.

Syntax

```
<go href="urltext"></go>
```

Attributes

Attribute	Format	Description
href	URL string	This required attribute contains the destination URL or destination card. Some browsers or servers impose a 255-character limit on this string.
accept-charset	Character	This optional attribute itemizes a comma- or space-separated list of character encoding the server must be able to process. This attribute's default value is "unknown."

Attribute	Format	Description
method	post get	This optional attribute determines how to send the data to the server. The default method is get. The get method sends the data in the query string portion of the URL line. Only a limited amount of data can be sent through this method. The post method sends data in the body of the request and is only limited to the server's environment, which is usually quite large.
sendreferer	Boolean	This optional attribute sends the URL of the current deck with the request. This is sometimes used to perform simple access control on decks.
class	Character	This optional attribute defines the class name for the element. This name is case sensitive and can be used in multiple classes. If you use multiple class names, separate them with a space.
id	Unique ID	This optional attribute defines a name for the element. This must be unique for each element in the deck.

Example

chapter14_example4.wml

```
<?xml version="1.0"?>
<!DOCTYPE wml PUBLIC "-//WAPFORUM//DTD WML 1.1//EN"
"http://www.wapforum.org/DTD/wml_1.1.xml">
<!-- This is an example of the <go> event  -->
<wml>
  <card id="card1" title="Card 1">
    <p>
    <anchor>
      Click to go to Card 2
      <go href="#card2"/>
    </anchor>
    </p>
  </card>
<card id="card2" title="Card 2">
    <p>Card Two</p>
</card>
</wml>
```

<prev>

The <prev> tag is used to navigate back to the previous URL. If there is no previous URL, the <prev> tag has no effect.

The <prev> tag is sometimes referred to as self-closing. The content between the <prev> and </prev> tags is optional. If no content is included you must use the single <prev/> tag, which has no closing tag.

Syntax

```
<prev></prev>
```

Attributes

Attribute	Format	Description
class	Character	This optional attribute defines the class name for the element. This name is case sensitive and can be used in multiple classes. If you use multiple class names, separate them with a space.
id	Unique ID	This optional attribute defines a name for the element. This must be unique for each element in the deck.

Example

chapter14_example5.wml

```
<?xml version="1.0"?>
<!DOCTYPE wml PUBLIC "-//WAPFORUM//DTD WML 1.1//EN"
"http://www.wapforum.org/DTD/wml_1.1.xml">
<!-- This is an example of the <prev> event  -->
<wml>
<card>
  <p>
  <do type="accept" label="Back">
    <prev>
      <setvar name="varname" value="varvalue"/>
    </prev>
  </do>
  </p>
</card>
</wml>
```

<refresh>

The <refresh> task refreshes the current screen and the card variables that are displayed. The <refresh> tag can only be used inside an <anchor>, <do>, or

<onevent> tag. The <refresh> tag can contain one or more <setvar> elements. For more information, please refer to the <setvar> section.

Syntax

```
<refresh></refresh>
```

Attributes

Attribute	Format	Description
class	Character	This optional attribute defines the class name for the element. This name is case sensitive and can be used in multiple classes. If you use multiple class names, separate them with a space.
id	Unique ID	This optional attribute defines a name for the element. This must be unique for each element in the deck.

Example

chapter14_example6.wml

```
<?xml version="1.0"?>
<!DOCTYPE wml PUBLIC "-//WAPFORUM//DTD WML 1.1//EN"
"http://www.wapforum.org/DTD/wml_1.1.xml">
<!-- This is an example of the <refresh> event  -->
<wml>
<card>
<p>
  <anchor>
  This is a refresh example
  <go href="chapter14_hello.wml"/>
    <refresh>
      <setvar name="varname" value="varvalue"/>
    </refresh>
  </anchor>
</p>
</card>
</wml>
```

<noop>

The <noop> (short for "no operation") tag is used when no task is to be performed. It is used to override operations from deck-level elements such as those used in the <template> tag. The <noop> tag can only be used inside a <do> or <onevent> tag.

Syntax

```
<noop/>
```

Attributes

Attribute	Format	Description
class	Character	This optional attribute defines the class name for the element. This name is case sensitive and can be used in multiple classes. If you use multiple class names, separate them with a space.
id	Unique ID	This optional attribute defines a name for the element. This must be unique for each element in the deck.

Postfield

In HTML, the form submit defines whether the variables will be transferred to the resulting page as GET variables or POST variables. In WML, the <postfield> tag performs this function. The variables that are included in this tag are transferred to the resulting page as POST variables. To pass variables to the resulting page as GET variables, they must be passed in the query string of the URL. The query string is anything after the question mark of the URL.

<postfield/>

The <postfield> tag contains variable information that is sent to the server when a request is made. This information is sent as a name/value pair. The name is set by the name attribute and is accompanied by a value attribute. The <go> tag can contain one or more <postfield> elements. The <postfield> element is a self-closing tag. This means that there is no closing </postfield> tag.

Syntax

```
<postfield name="somename" value="somevalue"/>
```

Attributes

Attribute	Format	Description
name	Character	This required attribute contains the name of the field.
value	Character	This required attribute contains the value of the attribute defined in the name field.

Attribute	Format	Description
class	Character	This optional attribute defines the class name for the element. This name is case sensitive and can be used in multiple classes. If you use multiple class names, separate them with a space.
id	Unique ID	This optional attribute defines a name for the element. This must be unique for each element in the deck.

Example

chapter14_example7a.wml

```
<?xml version="1.0"?>
<!DOCTYPE wml PUBLIC "-//WAPFORUM//DTD WML 1.1//EN"
"http://www.wapforum.org/DTD/wml_1.1.xml">
<!-- This is an example of the <postfield> entity.
//   Note that the 'get' method can also be used with the
//   <go> tag to pass variables to the resulting page. -->
<wml>
<card>
<p>
OK Sends the
variables to PHP
<do type="accept">
  <go href="chapter14_example7b.php" method="post">
   <postfield name="variable1" value="one"/>
   <postfield name="variable2" value="two"/>
  </go>
</do>
</p>
</card>
</wml>
```

chapter14_example7b.php

```
<?
header("Content-type: text/vnd.wap.wml");
echo("<?xml version=\"1.0\"?>\n");
echo("<!DOCTYPE wml PUBLIC \"-//WAPFORUM//DTD WML 1.1//EN\"
\"http://www.wapforum.org/DTD/wml_1.1.xml\">\n\n");
?>
<wml>
<card id="card1" title="variables">
```

```
  <p>
<?
    echo("variable1: ".$variable1."<br/>\n"); // variable 1
    echo("variable2: ".$variable2."<br/>\n"); // variable 2
?>
  </p>
</card>
</wml>
```

Variables

Variable names in WML begin with a dollar sign and behave like variables in any other programming language. Variable names can contain uppercase or lowercase letters, numbers, or underscores. Other characters are illegal and their use will generate an error. Variable names are case sensitive and can be assigned values through using the <setvar> or <postfield> elements.

<setvar/>

The <setvar> tag is used to assign a value to a variable. The tag uses a name attribute to define the name of the variable and the value attribute to assign its value. Multiple <setvar> tags can be used, but they all must only be nested in the <go>, <prev>, and <refresh> tags. The <setvar> tag is self-closing. This means that there is no closing </setvar> tag.

Syntax

```
<setvar name="somename" value="somevalue"/>
```

Attributes

Attribute	Format	Description
name	Character	This required attribute contains the name of the variable.
value	Character	This required attribute contains the value of the variable defined in the name field.
class	Character	This optional attribute defines the class name for the element. This name is case sensitive and can be used in multiple classes. If you use multiple class names, separate them with a space.
id	Unique ID	This optional attribute defines a name for the element. This must be unique for each element in the deck.

Example

chapter14_example8.wml

```
<?xml version="1.0"?>
<!DOCTYPE wml PUBLIC "-//WAPFORUM//DTD WML 1.1//EN"
"http://www.wapforum.org/DTD/wml_1.1.xml">
<!-- This is an example initializing, using, and displaying
//   variables   -->
<wml>
<card id="card1" title="Card 1">
  <p>
  OK Sends the
  variables
  <do type="accept">
    <go href="#card2">
      <setvar name="variable1" value="one"/>
      <setvar name="variable2" value="two"/>
    </go>
  </do>
  </p>
</card>
<card id="card2" title="Card 2">
  <p>
  variable1 = $variable1
  variable2 = $variable2
  </p>
</card>
</wml>
```

Card Fields

In WML, *card fields* are elements that can be included within each individual card. These include elements to select items, input variables, and generally interact with the user.

<select>

The <select> tag is used to create a list of selectable items. This list is a selection of choices from which the user may choose one or more items. This tag defines the beginning and end of the select list. Within the beginning and ending <select> tags are one or more <option> elements. These <option> elements contain items to be displayed in the list. If these options are related, you can group them into sublistings using the <optgroup> element. For further information, please refer to the <option> and <optgroup> sections.

Syntax

```
<select></select>
```

Attributes

Attribute	Format	Description
iname	Character	This optional attribute specifies the name the variable that is set when a selection is made. This attribute contains the position of the selected item in the select list. If multiple selections are permitted, the index result is a semicolon-delimited list of the indices.
ivalue	Character	This optional attribute specifies the default value for the iname attribute. This attribute is ignored if the iname attribute already has a value.
multiple	Boolean	This optional attribute determines whether multiple items can be selected. The default value is false, which means only one item can be selected.
name	Character	This required attribute defines the name of the variable that is set with the result of the selection.
tabindex	Number	This optional attribute sets the tabbing order for the current element.
title	Character	This optional attribute sets the title for the list.
value	Character	This optional attribute sets the default value of the variable in the “name” attribute.
xml:lang	Language	This optional attribute sets the language used in the element. The default for the United States is en-US.
class	Character	This optional attribute defines the class name for the element. This name is case sensitive and can be used in multiple classes. If you use multiple class names, separate them with a space.
id	Unique ID	This optional attribute defines a name for the element. This must be unique for each element in the deck.

<optgroup>

The <optgroup> tag is used to group related <option> elements in a select list. This tag defines the beginning and end of the group. It contains the collection of <option>

elements that are related. Each <option> element defines an item to be displayed in the select list.

Syntax

```
<select></select>
```

Attributes

Attribute	Format	Description
title	Character	This optional attribute sets the title for the optgroup element.
xml:lang	Language	This optional attribute sets the language used in the element. The default for the United States is en-US.
class	Character	This optional attribute defines the class name for the element. This name is case sensitive and can be used in multiple classes. If you use multiple class names, separate them with a space.
id	Unique ID	This optional attribute defines a name for the element. This must be unique for each element in the deck.

<option>

The <option> tag defines the items that are available to the user in a select list. The user is able to select one or more items depending on the application. Text describing the item is defined between the opening and closing <option> tags. Related items in the select list can be grouped together using the <optgroup> tag.

Syntax

```
<option></option>
```

Attributes

Attribute	Format	Description
onpick	URL string	This optional attribute sets the action when the user selects an item.
title	Character	This optional attribute defines the title for the option.
value	Character	This optional attribute sets the value to be used if this item is selected. If this <option> element is selected, the value is assigned to the variable named by the name attribute of the <select> element.
xml:lang	Language	This optional attribute sets the language used in the element. The default for the United States is en-US.

Attribute	Format	Description
class	Character	This optional attribute defines the class name for the element. This name is case sensitive and can be used in multiple classes. If you use multiple class names, separate them with a space.
id	Unique ID	This optional attribute defines a name for the element. This must be unique for each element in the deck.

Example

chapter14_example9.wml

```
<?xml version="1.0"?>
<!DOCTYPE wml PUBLIC "-//WAPFORUM//DTD WML 1.1//EN"
"http://www.wapforum.org/DTD/wml_1.1.xml">
<!-- This example defines the usage for the select, option,
//   and optgroup elements
//   Specifically this example is for the following WML tags:
//        <select></select>
//        <option></option>
//        <optgroup></optgroup>     -->
<wml>
<card id="card1" title="Selectable List">
  <p>
  <select name="variable">
    <optgroup title="Option Group 1">
      <option onpick="#card2" value="Option 1">Option 1</option>
      <option onpick="#card2" value="Option 2">Option 2</option>
      <option onpick="#card2" value="Option 3">Option 3</option>
    </optgroup>
    <optgroup title="Option Group 2">
      <option onpick="#card2" value="Option 4">Option 4</option>
      <option onpick="#card2" value="Option 5">Option 5</option>
      <option onpick="#card2" value="Option 6">Option 6</option>
    </optgroup>
  </select>
  </p>
</card>
<card id="card2" title="Card 2">
  <p>
    You Chose $variable
  </p>
</card>
</wml>
```

<input>

The <input> tag is a mechanism to capture data that is entered by the user. When the <input> field is selected, a text box is displayed that allows the user to enter information. The information in the text window can be checked based on an input mask. If the data is valid, it will be assigned to the variable defined by the name attribute. An invalid entry will be rejected by the browser. If the type attribute is defined as password, the characters that are entered will be displayed as asterisks. The emptyok attribute will allow the <input> field to be submitted with no data even if an input mask is defined.

Syntax

```
<input name="inputvariable"/>
```

Attributes

Attribute	Format	Description
name	Character	This required attribute defines the name of the variable that is set with the result of the user's input.
emptyok	Boolean	This optional attribute determines whether the field can be left empty or whether input is required. The default value is false.
format	AaNXxMm*fnf	This optional attribute determines the data format for the input field. The input mask details the alphanumeric and other characters that can be entered. The mask also defines the order in which they must be entered. The default value is "*M". A: Any uppercase alphabetic or punctuation character a: Any lowercase alphabetic or punctuation character N: Any numeric character *N: Any number of any numeric characters X: Any uppercase character x: Any lowercase character M: Any character, but is treated as uppercase for data entry *M: Any number of any characters, but is treated as uppercase for data entry m: Any character, but is treated as lowercase for data entry *f: Any number of any type of characters *n*f: Any *n* integer number of any characters \c: Display the character after the slash in the display

Attribute	Format	Description
maxlength	Number	This optional attribute defines the maximum number of characters that will be accepted by the <input> tag.
size	Number	This optional attribute determines the width of the input field.
tabindex	Number	This optional attribute defines the tabbing order for the input field.
title	Character	This optional attribute defines the title for the input field.
type	Text Password	This optional attribute defines the type of input field. The two valid values are text and password. The password type displays asterisks instead of the actual characters. The default value is "text."
value	Character	This optional attribute defines the default value of the variable in the name attribute. This value will appear in the input field in the browser.
xml:lang	Language	This optional attribute sets the language used in the element. The default for the United States is en-US.
class	Character	This optional attribute defines the class name for the element. This name is case sensitive and can be used in multiple classes. If you use multiple class names, separate them with a space.
id	Unique ID	This optional attribute defines a name for the element. This must be unique for each element in the deck.

<fieldset>

The <fieldset> tag is used to logically group related elements in a card. These related elements can include text, tables, select elements, links, input elements, images, and so on. This permits the browser to optimize the layout and navigation. <fieldset> elements can be nested inside each other.

Syntax

```
<fieldset></fieldset>
```

Attributes

Attribute	Format	Description
title	Character	This optional attribute defines the title for the <fieldset> tag.

Attribute	Format	Description
xml:lang	Language	This optional attribute sets the language used in the element. The default for the US is en-US.
class	Character	This optional attribute defines the class name for the element. This name is case sensitive and can be used in multiple classes. If you use multiple class names, separate them with a space.
id	Unique ID	This optional attribute defines a name for the element. This must be unique for each element in the deck.

Example

chapter14_example10.wml

```
<?xml version="1.0"?>
<!DOCTYPE wml PUBLIC "-//WAPFORUM//DTD WML 1.1//EN"
"http://www.wapforum.org/DTD/wml_1.1.xml">
<!-- This example defines the usage for the <input> tag -->
<wml>
  <card id="card1" title="Fieldset">
    <do type="accept" label="submit">
      <go href="#card2"/>
    </do>
    <p>
      First Name: <input name="FName" type="text"/><br/>
      Last Name: <input name="LName" type="text"/>
    </p>
  </card>
  <card id="card2" title="Card 2">
    <p>
      First Name = $FName
      Last Name = $LName
    </p>
  </card>
</wml>
```

<timer>

The <timer> tag is a timer for a card. The timer begins when the card is displayed and stops when the card is exited. Only one timer is allowed per card, and the time is preset using the value attribute. The value can be defined to .1 (1/10th) seconds. Usually, when the timer reaches zero, an event is launched using the <onevent> or <template> elements.

Syntax

```
<timer value="somevalue"/>
```

Attributes

Attribute	Format	Description
value	Character	This required attribute defines the initial time, in seconds, that is entered into the <timer> event.
name	Character	This optional attribute defines the name of the variable that can be set with the result of the value attribute.
class	Character	This optional attribute defines the class name for the element. This name is case sensitive and can be used in multiple classes. If you use multiple class names, separate them with a space.
id	Unique ID	This optional attribute defines a name for the element. This must be unique for each element in the deck.

Example

chapter14_example11.wml

```
<?xml version="1.0"?>
<!DOCTYPE wml PUBLIC "-//WAPFORUM//DTD WML 1.1//EN"
"http://www.wapforum.org/DTD/wml_1.1.xml">
<!-- This is an example of the <timer> event  -->
<wml>
<card ontimer="chapter14_hello.wml">
  <timer value="30"/>
    <p>Wait...</p>
</card>
</wml>
```

Images

Images in WML/WAP are required to be in a specific format. This format is called WBMP (wireless bitmap). WBMP currently supports only uncompressed black-and-white images.

The WBMP is a binary format that defines a series of octets, which are translated into black and white. WBMP images begin with a header definition, which defines the type of WBMP. Currently, there is only a type 0 WBMP format. Because of this, the first octet will always be 0. The next octets define the width of the image followed by the height of the image. These width and height definitions are in multibyte integer format. A multibyte integer can consist of one or more bytes. The first bit of every octet in a multibyte integer defines whether the next bytes that follow are part of the same multibyte integer. If the first bit of an octet is 0, there will be no other octets in this multibyte integer. If the first bit of an octet is 1, more octets will follow.

The next sequences of octets contain the image data. Since the WBMP width and height are set in the header, this means that the next octets will define the image. For instance, if the width is 96 pixels, then the first 12 octets of image data ($12 \times 8 = 96$ bits) form one row. All subsequent octets will form sets of 12 octets each, with each octet representing one row. If the height is 40 pixels, there should be 40 such sets of octets. A 0 defines a black pixel and a 1 defines a white pixel.

Programs are available that can convert images from standard formats to the WBMP format.

<img>

The <img> tag defines the placement of a WBMP image.

Syntax

```
<img src="filename.wbmp" alt="alternate text"/>
```

Attributes

Attribute	Format	Description
align	top middle bottom	This optional attribute defines the alignment of the image. The default alignment is bottom.
alt	Character	This mandatory attribute sets the alternate text that is to be displayed if the image cannot be rendered.
height	Number	This optional attribute defines the height of the image. The number is the height in pixels.
hspace	Number	This optional attribute defines the spacing on either side of the image. The number is the spacing in pixels; the default is 0.
localsrc	Character	This optional attribute sets the alternate substitution for the image. If this attribute is set, the browser will use it instead of the information defined in the src attribute.

Attribute	Format	Description
src	URL string	This mandatory attribute defines the path to the image.
vspace	Number	This optional attribute defines the spacing above and below the image. The number is the spacing in pixels.
width	Number	This optional attribute defines the width of the image. The number is the width in pixels.
xml:lang	Language	This optional attribute sets the language used in the element. The default for the US is en-US.
class	Character	This optional attribute defines the class name for the element. This name is case sensitive and can be used in multiple classes. If you use multiple class names, separate them with a space.
id	Unique ID	This optional attribute defines a name for the element. This must be unique for each element in the deck.

Anchor

There are two types of tags that can be referred to as anchor tags: the <anchor> tag and the <a> tag. Both of these tags make it possible to link pages together with hyperlinks. The <anchor> tag is more cumbersome to use since it must be coupled with the <go> tag to provide the hyperlink.

<anchor>

The <anchor> tag defines a navigation link. This hyperlink enables navigation from one card or deck to another. The <anchor> tag must always be used with the <go>, <prev>, or <refresh> task. The <a> tag should be used instead of the <anchor> tag. The <anchor> tag is included for backward compatibility.

Syntax

```
<anchor></anchor>
```

Attributes

Attribute	Format	Description
title	Character	This optional attribute defines the text identifying the link.
xml:lang	Language	This optional attribute sets the language used in the element. The default for the US is en-US.

Attribute	Format	Description
class	Character	This optional attribute defines the class name for the element. This name is case sensitive and can be used in multiple classes. If you use multiple class names, separate them with a space.
id	Unique ID	This optional attribute defines a name for the element. This must be unique for each element in the deck.

Example

chapter14_example12.wml

```
<?xml version="1.0"?>
<!DOCTYPE wml PUBLIC "-//WAPFORUM//DTD WML 1.1//EN"
"http://www.wapforum.org/DTD/wml_1.1.xml">
<!-- This is an example of the <anchor> element   -->
<wml>
  <card title="Anchor Tag">
  <p>
    <anchor>Next
      <go href="chapter14_hello.wml"/>
    </anchor>
  </p>
</card>
</wml>
```

<a>

The <a> tag in conjunction with the href attribute defines a hyperlink that allows you to jump from one card or deck to another.

Syntax

```
<a href="urltext"></a>
```

Attributes

Attribute	Format	Description
href	Character	This mandatory attribute defines the destination address when the user selects the link.
title	Character	This optional attribute defines the text that identifies the link.

Attribute	Format	Description
xml:lang	Language	This optional attribute sets the language used in the element. The default for the US is en-US.
class	Character	This optional attribute defines the class name for the element. This name is case sensitive and can be used in multiple classes. If you use multiple class names, separate them with a space.
id	Unique ID	This optional attribute defines a name for the element. This must be unique for each element in the deck.

Example

chapter14_example13.wml

```
<?xml version="1.0"?>
<!DOCTYPE wml PUBLIC "-//WAPFORUM//DTD WML 1.1//EN"
"http://www.wapforum.org/DTD/wml_1.1.xml">
<!-- This is an example of the <a> tag   -->
<wml>
  <card>
  <p>
    <a href="chapter14_hello.wml">Next</a>
  </p>
</card>
</wml>
```

Tables

Tables in WML only provide basic table structure. The syntax is similar to HTML, but only simplistic options and attributes are available. For instance, the column attribute in the <table> tag is required and a value of zero is not valid. If you declare too few columns, the extra columns represented by the <td> tag will be combined together in the last column. If you declare too many columns, blank columns may be used to pad the table. There are no borders in WML tables, and the default is to display the information in the table from left to right. However, depending on the xml:lang attribute, the information may be displayed from right to left. WML does not allow nesting tables. This means that the <table> tag cannot contain other <table> tags.

<table>

The <table> tag defines a table. A WML table contains rows and columns defined by specific tags. The cells in the table can contain data in the form of text, numbers, strings, links, images, and so on.

Syntax

```
<table columns="number"></table>
```

Attributes

Attribute	Format	Description
columns	Number	This mandatory attribute defines the number of columns in the table.
align	c l r	This optional attribute aligns the text in a column. Valid values for this attribute are c: Center l: Left r: Right
title	Character	This optional attribute defines the title for the table.
xml:lang	Language	This optional attribute sets the language used in the element. The default for the US is en-US.
class	Character	This optional attribute defines the class name for the element. This name is case sensitive and can be used in multiple classes. If you use multiple class names, separate them with a space.
id	Unique ID	This optional attribute defines a name for the element. This must be unique for each element in the deck.

<tr>

The <tr> tag defines a table row. Each row can contain one or more data elements represented by the <td> tag. This tag must be enclosed within <table></table> tags; however, there can be multiple rows per table.

Syntax

```
<tr></tr>
```

Attributes

Attribute	Format	Description
class	Character	This optional attribute defines the class name for the element. This name is case sensitive and can be used in multiple classes. If you use multiple class names, separate them with a space.
id	Unique ID	This optional attribute defines a name for the element. This must be unique for each element in the deck.

<td>

The <td> tag defines a table data cell. This cell can contain images, text, links, and so on. This tag must be enclosed within <tr></tr> tags, but there can be multiple data elements per row. Usually, the number of <td> pairs will equal the columns attribute in the <table> element.

Syntax

```
<td></td>
```

Attributes

Attribute	Format	Description
xml:lang	Language	This optional attribute sets the language used in the element. The default for the US is en-US.
class	Character	This optional attribute defines the class name for the element. This name is case sensitive and can be used in multiple classes. If you use multiple class names, separate them with a space.
id	Unique ID	This optional attribute defines a name for the element. This must be unique for each element in the deck.

Example

chapter14_example14.wml

```
<?xml version="1.0"?>
<!DOCTYPE wml PUBLIC "-//WAPFORUM//DTD WML 1.1//EN"
"http://www.wapforum.org/DTD/wml_1.1.xml">
<!-- This is an example of the table creation elements
```

```
//   Specifically this example is for the following WML tags:
//        <table></table>
//        <tr></tr>
//        <td></td>    -->
<wml>
<card title="Table">
  <p>
  <table columns="3">
  <tr>
    <td>C1</td>
    <td>C2</td>
    <td>C3</td>
  </tr>
  <tr>
    <td>C4</td>
    <td>C5</td>
    <td>C6</td>
  </tr>
  <tr>
    <td>C7</td>
    <td>C8</td>
    <td>C9</td>
  </tr>
  </table>
</p>
</card>
</wml>
```

Text Layout

WML offers tags that affect the layout of a text. These, again, are limited compared to their HTML counterparts. The following table describes the elements that control the text format. The second table defines the attributes that are available with each of these text-layout elements.

WML Element	Description
<b>	This element defines bold text.
<big>	This element defines text that is larger than the normal text.
<em>	This element defines emphasized text. The appearance of this text is browser dependent.

WML Element	Description
<i>	This element defines italicized text.
<small>	This element defines text that is smaller than the normal text.
<strong>	This element defines strong text. The appearance of this text is browser dependent.
<u>	This element defines underlined text.

Attributes

Attribute	Format	Description
xml:lang	Language	This optional attribute sets the language used in the element. The default for the US is en-US.
class	Character	This optional attribute defines the class name for the element. This name is case sensitive and can be used in multiple classes. If you use multiple class names, separate them with a space.
id	Unique ID	This optional attribute defines a name for the element. This must be unique for each element in the deck.

Example

chapter14_example15.wml

```
<?xml version="1.0"?>
<!DOCTYPE wml PUBLIC "-//WAPFORUM//DTD WML 1.1//EN"
"http://www.wapforum.org/DTD/wml_1.1.xml">
<!-- This is an example of text formatting elements
//   Specifically this example is for the following WML tags:
//        <em></em>
//        <strong></strong>
//        <b></b>
//        <i></i>
//        <u></u>
//        <big></big>
//        <small></small>   -->
<wml>
<card>
  <p>
  normal<br/>
  <em>emphasized</em><br/>
  <strong>strong</strong><br/>
```

```
  <b>bold</b><br/>
  <i>italic</i><br/>
  <u>underline</u><br/>
  <big>big</big><br/>
  <small>small</small>
  </p>
</card>
</wml>
```

Character Entities

WML offers certain characters by default that can be represented by an entity name or entity number. These characters are described in the following table.

Symbol	Description	Entity Name	Entity Number
&	Ampersand	&	&
'	Apostrophe	'	'
>	Greater than	>	>
<	Less than	<	<
	Non-breaking space		
"	Quotation mark	"	"
-	Soft hyphen		

Other characters are also supported, but they must be escaped. For example, the word resumé would be written as resumé, where decimal character 233 (E9h) in the ISO-10646 character set is the letter é. For additional information and character/code charts, please visit http://www.unicode.org/charts/.

Example

chapter14_example16.wml

```
<?xml version="1.0"?>
<!DOCTYPE wml PUBLIC "-//WAPFORUM//DTD WML 1.1//EN"
"http://www.wapforum.org/DTD/wml_1.1.xml">
<!-- This is an example of character entities and escape characters -->
<wml>
<card>
  <p>
  <table columns="2">
  <tr>
```

```
      <td>ampersand</td>
      <td>&amp;</td>
    </tr>
    <tr>
      <td>apostrophe</td>
      <td>&apos;</td>
    </tr>
    <tr>
      <td>greater than</td>
      <td>&gt;</td>
    </tr>
    <tr>
      <td>less than</td>
      <td>&lt;</td>
    </tr>
    <tr>
      <td>non-breaking space</td>
      <td> </td>
    </tr>
    <tr>
      <td>quotation mark</td>
      <td>&quot;</td>
    </tr>
    <tr>
      <td>soft hyphen</td>
      <td>&shy;</td>
    </tr>
    <tr>
      <td>cent</td>
      <td>&#162;</td>
    </tr>
    <tr>
      <td>copyright</td>
      <td>&#169;</td>
    </tr>
   </table>
   </p>
  </card>
  </wml>
```

Coding PHP Pages for WAP

At the beginning of this chapter, we discussed the settings needed to integrate WAP and PHP with Apache. The items that were discussed dealt with the configuration settings needed to deliver the proper mime type to the browser. With these settings in place, you are now ready to code pages in PHP to deliver to WAP devices.

You were given a taste of this in chapter14_example7b.php in the previous pages. You will notice that the initial lines of this example look like this:

```
<?
header("Content-type: text/vnd.wap.wml");
echo("<?xml version=\"1.0\"?>\n");
echo("<!DOCTYPE wml PUBLIC \"-//WAPFORUM//DTD WML 1.1//EN\"
\"http://www.wapforum.org/DTD/wml_1.1.xml\">\n\n");
?>
```

It is important that these lines be in place in all the PHP pages you want to deliver to WAP devices. These lines set the content type in the header() function and then deliver the prolog as discussed previously. From here, you must use the proper WML syntax and the appropriate PHP functions to create your application.

The next chapter will illustrate in more depth how to create an application using PHP and WML. We will also show you how to integrate MySQL into the application for a dynamic, database-driven, wireless solution. These three technologies (PHP, MySQL, and WAP) will create a powerful trio on which to build.

Next Steps

Now that you know the basics about the WML language and how to code pages to be displayed to WAP devices, the next step is to practice. This chapter detailed the entire WML language and discussed the options and attributes for each entity. There were numerous examples that illustrated how the language should be used. These examples should be the groundwork for your future projects.

From here, you are equipped with the tools you need to explore the WML language further. Many applications can be used as personal projects to continue to acquaint you with the syntax and usage.

What to Take Away

This chapter was intended to give the beginner an overall view of the WML language. There were discussions about WAP emulators, as well as web server setup and configuration. We also touched on integration processes needed to use WML with PHP. All these items will be extremely useful as you continue with the next chapter and with your experimentation with WAP and WML.

CHAPTER

15

WML-Enabled Address Book

IN THIS CHAPTER:

chapter15_addinfo.php—Allows you to add the details

chapter15_addname.php—Allows you to add the first and last names

chapter15_browse.php—Queries the database and displays all records

chapter15_change.php—Allows you to change the selected information

chapter15_confirm.php—Deletes the record from the database

chapter15_commit.php—Inserts the changes in the database

chapter15_delete.php—Asks whether the record is to be deleted

chapter15_details.php—Queries and displays the details of the selected record

chapter15_edit.php—Allows you to select the information to be edited

chapter15_lookup.php—Queries and displays specific records

chapter15_main.wml—The initial .wml displaying the lookup, browse, and add options

This chapter takes the database schema and design that you did in Chapter 7 and WAP-enables the address book. This chapter assumes that you already have the database set up and functional. You will learn how to use WML in an application and how to pass variables, integrate with PHP and MySQL, and present data to the user. This chapter is designed to show you the basics of WML and PHP. It is not given as an example of a professional application. You will notice that we have left out some error checking and data validation. We felt that these items, while important, would impede your understanding of WML and PHP.

WML Address Book Design

The address book design is simplistic. The basic database operations are made available. You are able to add, update, and delete information from the database. You are also given the option to query the database for matching last names, or any part thereof, and the application will return the appropriate results. You can also browse all the records in the database.

The challenge you will have during any WML design process is the best use of screen space. Realize that not all WAP-enabled phones are created equal, and all WAP browsers will display information in their own format. Some screens will display more lines than others, some give you access to more fonts, and some provide access to buttons and other action. We have tried to only use WML that is available to all browsers. If you set this example application up in your environment and do not see information exactly as displayed in the figures that follow, do not despair—it is not your fault or the fault of the application. Remember that WML and WAP are emerging technologies, and as the technology matures, so will the browsers and the functions that are associated with them.

The WML Main Page

The main page of our application is simple WML. You will notice that this file is the only one in the entire application that ends with the .wml extension. This also means that this is the only page that is not dynamically generated by PHP. The main page gives the user three options, illustrated in Figure 15-1. The first is the ability to look up information from the database. The second allows the user to browse all the records, in alphabetical order. The third option gives the user the ability to add an entry to the database.

Figure 15-1 *The main WML address book page*

Let's look at the logic behind this page in detail. The first thing you should notice is that the page begins with <?xml version="1.0"?> and a reference to the DTD at http://www.wapforum.org/. These must be the first lines of the document; other items, comments, code, and so on, come after these lines. You will notice that the PHP pages have comments as the first few lines. This is because PHP will parse the page initially and then pass the final information, without the comments, to the WAP browser. Thus, you achieve the same results as if this was a basic WML page.

If the user chooses the first option, to look up data in the database, the next card is in this deck. This is referenced by the onpick="#lookup" code in the option tag. This tells the main card to go to the lookup card if this option is chosen. The lookup card simply prompts the user for a string. When the user has finished inputting the string, the resulting page, chapter15_lookup.php, will use this string to pull records from the database. For instance, if you put in the letter **S** as the string, all records with a last name beginning with S will be returned. Likewise, if you enter a string like **Sm**, this will return records beginning with the letters *Sm*. Note that this information is passed to the next page in the query string of the URL. The query string of the URL is anything after the question mark.

The second option allows the user to browse all records in the database. If this option is chosen, the user is taken to chapter15_browse.php, which queries the database and returns all records.

The last option allows the user to add a record to the database. This is done in two steps. The first step is done in this deck. The user is prompted to enter the first and last name of the contact. When the user submits this information, the page chapter15_addname.php is called with the entered information passed as POST variables. This is done through using the postfield tag to pass the variables along to the resulting page. We will show you how to use these variables later in this chapter.

chapter15_main.wml

```
<?xml version="1.0"?>
<!DOCTYPE wml PUBLIC "-//WAPFORUM//DTD WML 1.1//EN"
 "http://www.wapforum.org/DTD/wml_1.1.xml">
```

```
<!--=========================================================
//      This page is the Online Address Book's main page.
//      The user is given three options from this page. They
//      can look up information based on a string, they can
//      browse all the records in the database, and they can
//      add a new record to the database.
//=========================================================
//
//  Produce the standard WAP header and reference the
//  appropriate DTD at www.wapforum.org -->
<wml>
<template>
  <do type='prev' label='Back'>
    <prev/>
  </do>
</template>
<!-- This is start of the WML card -->
<!-- This card displays the three options available to the user; lookup,
browse, and add -->
<card title="Main">
<p align="center">
<b>WAP Address</b></p>
<p align="center">
<b>Home</b>
</p>
<p>
  <select name="task">
    <option onpick="#lookup" value="Lookup">Lookup</option>
    <option onpick="chapter15_browse.php" value="Browse">Browse</option>
    <option onpick="#add" value="Add">Add</option>
  </select>
</p>
</card>
<!-- This is start of the WML card -->
<!-- This card allows the user to input the Last Name information to be
looked up -->
<card id="lookup" title="Lookup">
<p align="center">
<b>WAP Address</b></p>
<p align="center">
<b>$task</b>
</p>
<do type="accept" label="submit">
 <go href="chapter15_lookup.php?str=$str"/>
</do>
```

```
<p>
   Last Name: <input name="str" type="text"/>
</p>
</card>
<!-- This is start of the WML card -->
<!-- This card allows the user to input the first and last name to be added -->
<card id="add" title="Add">
<p align="center">
<b>WAP Address</b></p>
<p align="center">
<b>$task</b></p>
<do type="accept" label="submit">
  <go href="chapter15_addname.php">
    <postfield name="fname" value="$fname"/>
    <postfield name="lname" value="$lname"/>
  </go>
</do>
<p>
   First Name: <input name="fname" type="text"/>
   Last Name: <input name="lname" type="text"/>
</p>
</card>
</wml>
```

This is the entire code listing for the main page. This listing page used WML variables, multiple cards, and multiple actions to achieve a menu scheme that enables the user to navigate through the application. We will now look at the rest of the application that interacts with the database and displays information.

Looking Up Information

The most used feature of any database is the ability to look up information. In our application, this lookup feature is limited to last name, but could be extended to other database fields as necessary. For the lookup functionality to work properly, you must have a variable that contains the string to be queried, and the results of that query. The main page, chapter15_main.wml, contains the code to produce the input field. This should look something like Figure 15-2 when rendered by a WAP browser.

Once the input is complete and the user submits the information, the chapter15_ lookup.php page is called and a variable named str is passed to that page with a value. The next section examines this resulting page.

Figure 15-2 *The lookup portion of the main page*

The WML Lookup Page

This page is called with a string variable called str. The first thing this code does is check for the existence of the str variable. Since this variable is passed using the GET method, you can access this variable by using the $HTTP_GET_VARS array and referencing the str variable. The value of this array variable is assigned to the PHP variable named $str.

You will notice that all the PHP pages that access the database contain similar code to connect to MySQL and select the proper database. We could have created a function and moved this code into its own file. We then could have referenced this library function in all our code. We decided not to do this because of the size of the application. If this application was any bigger or more involved, our recommendation would be to move all similar code to its own file and its own function. You would then include this file in each page that is to call the function.

The str variable is used in the MySQL query to look up information by last name. Notice that the query returns the contactID and contactLastName based on str%. The percent sign in this query is a wildcard. This tells MySQL to match the string contained in str with anything that begins with the string. In other words, if **Sm** was passed in, it would match with Smith, Smuthers, Small, Smedly, and so on. The entire listing of chapter15_lookup.php is included as follows:

chapter15_lookup.php

```
<?
//=========================================================
//     This page connects to the database and selects all of
//     the last names and IDs from the databases.
//     This information is displayed with hyperlinks that
//     allow the user to select the record to display.
//=========================================================
//
//  Produce the standard WAP header and reference the
//  appropriate DTD at www.wapforum.org
```

```
header("Content-type: text/vnd.wap.wml");
echo("<?xml version=\"1.0\"?>\n");
echo("<!DOCTYPE wml PUBLIC \"-//WAPFORUM//DTD WML 1.1//EN\"
\"http://www.wapforum.org/DTD/wml_1.1.xml\">\n\n");
if (isset($HTTP_GET_VARS[str]) )
   $str = $HTTP_GET_VARS[str];
else
   $str=NULL;

// Connect to MySql and select the oab database
$link = mysql_pconnect( "localhost", "webuser", "abc123" );
    if ( ! $link )
        die( "Couldn't connect to MySQL" );
    mysql_select_db( "oab", $link )
        or die ( "Couldn't open database: ".mysql_error($link) );
?>
<!-- This is start of the WML card -->
<!-- This card looks up records matching the criteria and displays the
results -->
<wml>
<card id="lookup" title="Lookup">
<p align="center">
<b>WAP Address</b></p>
<p align="center">
<b>Lookup - <? print $str ?></b><br/>
<?
   $qid=mysql_db_query("oab","select contactID, contactLastName from oabContacts
   where contactLastName like '$str%' order by contactLastName
   ASC") or die("Database Query Error");
   while($row=mysql_fetch_row($qid)) {
      print "<a href=\"chapter15_details.php?id=$row[0]\">".$row[1]."</a><br/>";
   }
?>
</p>
</card>
</wml>
```

Once the results are received, the data is placed in an array called row[]. This entire array is then printed out with hyperlinks to a page to view the details of a particular record. The final lookup results page should look something like Figure 15-3.

Notice that you can highlight a last name and click it. This will take you to the chapter15_details.php page. The ID of the record is passed along to this page as a GET variable in the query string of the URL. This page provides examples of the <a> tag and methods for printing PHP variables to the display. We will examine the details page in the next section.

Figure 15-3 *The lookup results page*

WML Details Page

If the user has made it this far, they have searched on a record or, as we will find out later, browsed to a record. They have selected it, and now want to view the details of this record. This page, along with providing a listing of the details, allows the user to edit any information or delete the record from the database.

The resulting page should look something like Figure 15-4.

The variable that is passed to this page is simply the ID of the record to be viewed. Once again, you make a connection to the database and then select all the data for the ID that was passed to this page. The data is then displayed line by line.

Figure 15-4 *Viewing the details*

chapter15_details.php

```
<?
//===========================================================
//     This page connects to the database and then displays
//     the information from the selected record. The user
//     is given the option to edit the record, delete the
//     record, or return to the main page.
//===========================================================
//
//  Produce the standard WAP header and reference the
//  appropriate DTD at www.wapforum.org
header("Content-type: text/vnd.wap.wml");
echo("<?xml version=\"1.0\"?>\n");
echo("<!DOCTYPE wml PUBLIC \"-//WAPFORUM//DTD WML 1.1//EN\"
\"http://www.wapforum.org/DTD/wml_1.1.xml\">\n\n");
if (isset($HTTP_GET_VARS[id]) )
   $id = $HTTP_GET_VARS[id];
elseif (isset($HTTP_POST_VARS[id]) )
   $id = $HTTP_POST_VARS[id];
else
   $id=NULL;

// Connect to MySql and select the oab database
$link = mysql_pconnect( "localhost", "webuser", "abc123" );
    if ( ! $link )
        die( "Couldn't connect to MySQL" );
    mysql_select_db( "oab", $link )
        or die ( "Couldn't open database: ".mysql_error($link) );
$qid=mysql_db_query("oab","select * from oabContacts, oabInfo where
oabContacts.contactID=oabInfo.contactID and oabContacts.contactID =
$id") or die("Database Query Error");
$row=mysql_fetch_row($qid);
?>
```

```
<!-- This is start of the WML card -->
<!-- This card displays the record's details -->
<wml>
<template>
   <do type="prev" label="Back">
      <prev/>
   </do>
</template>
<card id="lookup" title="Lookup">
<p align="center">
<b>WAP Address</b></p>
<p align="center">
<b><? print $row[2]." ".$row[1] ?></b><br/>
<?
      print $row[9]."<br/>";
if ($row[10]!="")
      print $row[10]."<br/>";
      print $row[11].", ".$row[12]." ".$row[13]."<br/>";
      print "H: ".$row[15]."<br/>";
      print "P: ".$row[16]."<br/>";
      print "C: ".$row[17]."<br/>";
      print "O: ".$row[18]."<br/>";

  print "<select name=\"task\">";
  print "<option onpick=\"chapter15_main.wml\"
  value=\"$id\">Home</option>";
  print "<option onpick=\"chapter15_edit.php?id=$id\"
  value=\"$id\">Edit
  Info</option>";
  print "<option onpick=\"chapter15_delete.php?id=$id\"
  value=\"$id\">Delete
  Entry</option>";
  print "</select>";
?>
</p>
</card>
</wml>
```

When the data is displayed, we give the user three options at the bottom of the page. They can return to the main page, edit any of the information, or delete the record. These options will look like Figure 15-5.

If the user chooses to return to the main page, they are taken back to chapter15_main.wml. If the user chooses to edit or delete the record, they are taken to chapter15_

1 Home
2>Edit Info
3 Delete Entry
OK

Figure 15-5 *Navigation from this deck*

edit.php or chapter15_delete.php, respectively, and the ID of the record to be edited or deleted is passed along as a GET variable. We will now examine the page that is used to update the information in the database.

Updating Information

Updating information requires two operations. First, the user must tell the application what information needs to be changed. Second, the new information must be substituted for the old information. It is customary in database interaction to display the information to be changed and allow the user to erase it and input the new data. In our application, the update action will involve three WML pages. The first allows the user to select the data to be changed, the second allows the user to change the data, and the third allows the user to actually change the data. Let's examine the first of these three pages.

WML Edit Page

The objective of this page is to display all the information in the details page and allow the user to select the field to be updated. The final page should look similar to Figure 15-6.

When we examine the code, we notice that the GET variable that was passed in is placed into a PHP variable and the database is accessed as usual. The query is similar

Figure 15-6 *Selecting the item to edit*

to what you used when displaying the information. This time when the information is displayed, the data is encapsulated within the select and option tags. This allows the user to select the field to be updated.

chapter15_edit.php

```
<?
//===========================================================
//      This page connects to the database and selects the
//      the information to display. Each data item is a
//      hyperlink to allow the user to edit the information.
//===========================================================
//
//  Produce the standard WAP header and reference the
//  appropriate DTD at www.wapforum.org
header("Content-type: text/vnd.wap.wml");
echo("<?xml version=\"1.0\"?>\n");
echo("<!DOCTYPE wml PUBLIC \"-//WAPFORUM//DTD WML 1.1//EN\"
\"http://www.wapforum.org/DTD/wml_1.1.xml\">\n\n");
if (isset($HTTP_GET_VARS[id]) )
   $id = $HTTP_GET_VARS[id];
else
   $id=NULL;

// Connect to MySql and select the oab database
$link = mysql_pconnect( "localhost", "webuser", "abc123" );
    if ( ! $link )
        die( "Couldn't connect to MySQL" );
    mysql_select_db( "oab", $link )
        or die ( "Couldn't open database: ".mysql_error($link) );

$qid=mysql_db_query("oab","select * from oabContacts, oabInfo where
 oabContacts.contactID=oabInfo.contactID and oabContacts.contactID =
 $id") or die("Database Query Error");
$row=mysql_fetch_row($qid);
?>

<!-- This is start of the WML card -->
<!-- This card allows the user to select the information to be edited -->
<wml>
<template>
   <do type="prev" label="Back">
```

```
        <prev/>
    </do>
</template>
<card id="edit" title="Edit">
<p align="center">
<b>WAP Address</b></p>
<p align="center">
<b><? print $row[2]." ".$row[1] ?></b><br/>

  <do type="accept" label="label">
     <go href="chapter15_change.php" method="post">
          <postfield name="field" value="$field" />
          <postfield name="id" value="<? print $row[0]; ?>" />
      </go>
    </do>

<?

  print "<select name=\"field\">";
  print "<option value=\"contactFirstName\">$row[2]</option>";
  print "<option value=\"contactLastName\">$row[1]</option>";
  print "<option value=\"infoAddress1\">$row[9]</option>";
  print "<option value=\"infoAddress2\">$row[10]</option>";
  print "<option value=\"infoCity\">$row[11]</option>";
  print "<option value=\"infoState\">$row[12]</option>";
  print "<option value=\"infoZip\">$row[13]</option>";
  print "<option value=\"infoPhone\">$row[15]</option>";
  print "<option value=\"infoPager\">$row[16]</option>";
  print "<option value=\"infoCell\">$row[17]</option>";
  print "<option value=\"infoOther\">$row[18]</option>";
  print "</select>";

?>
</p>
</card>
</wml>
```

Notice that the next page that is accessed is chapter15_change.php. This page will receive two variables from this select action, the field and the id. The field will tell the next page what data element to change, and the id will tell the next page what record to change. The only thing left to do is allow the user to input the new data. This action will take place in the next section.

WML Change Page

Now that you have determined the field to change and the record that is to be changed, this page will fill in the last piece of data. The data input the user sees in the WAP browser will look like Figure 15-7.

Notice in the following code that the two variables that were sent from the previous page are placed into PHP variables, and the data to be changed is selected from the database. The resulting data is filled into the input tag and allows the user to backspace over the old information to input the new information. The code for this page is as follows:

chapter15_change.php

```
<?
//==========================================================
//     This page connects to the database and selects the
//     appropriate field to be changed from the oabContacts
//     or oabInfo table. The user is shown the information
//     to be changed and given the opportunity to change it.
//==========================================================
//
//  Produce the standard WAP header and reference the
//  appropriate DTD at www.wapforum.org
header("Content-type: text/vnd.wap.wml");
echo("<?xml version=\"1.0\"?>\n");
echo("<!DOCTYPE wml PUBLIC \"-//WAPFORUM//DTD WML 1.1//EN\"
\"http://www.wapforum.org/DTD/wml_1.1.xml\">\n\n");
if (isset($HTTP_POST_VARS[field]) ){
   $field = $HTTP_POST_VARS[field];
   $id = $HTTP_POST_VARS[id];
   }
else
   $id=NULL;

// Connect to MySql and select the oab database
$link = mysql_pconnect( "localhost", "webuser", "abc123" );
    if ( ! $link )
        die( "Couldn't connect to MySQL" );
    mysql_select_db( "oab", $link )
        or die ( "Couldn't open database: ".mysql_error($link) );

// Select the field to be changed from the database
```

```
$qid=mysql_db_query("oab","select $field from oabContacts, oabInfo where
oabContacts.contactID=oabInfo.contactID and oabContacts.contactID = $id") or
die("Database Query Error");
$row=mysql_fetch_row($qid);
?>

<!-- This is start of the WML card -->
<!-- This card displays the information to be changed and allows the user to
change it -->
<wml>
<card id="input" title="input">
<p align="center">
<b>WAP Address</b></p>
<p align="center">
<b>Input</b>
<do type="accept" label="submit">
  <go href="chapter15_commit.php">
    <postfield name="fieldname" value="<? print $field; ?>" />
    <postfield name="id" value="<? print $id; ?>" />
    <postfield name="fieldvalue" value="$newfield" />
  </go>
</do>
   <input name="newfield" type="text" value="<? print $row[0]; ?>"/>
</p>
</card>
</wml>
```

Notice that the next page is chapter15_commit.php. This next page will expect three variables from the current page. These variables will be the name of the field to be changed, the id of the record to be changed, and the new data. The postfield tag is used to pass these variables to the resulting page. The chapter15_commit.php page will be described next.

Figure 15-7 *Changing the information*

WML Commit Page

This is the final step in the update process. This page now has all the data to form the database query to perform the update. The user does not see anything special, but is notified that the update has taken place and is given a link back to the main page. An example of this page is given in Figure 15-8.

The code for this page should look familiar to you by now. The three POST variables that were passed to this page are placed into PHP variables, and the database is selected and a connection established. Since the data about the user is split into two tables, the next bit of code determines which table to update. This is done by comparing the first few characters of the fieldname with the known values of the tables. For instance, if the fieldname starts with "info," you know the data belongs in the oabInfo table, so you use a conditional if-then statement to use the proper query. Likewise for the oabContacts table.

chapter15_commit.php

```
<?
//===========================================================
//     This page connects to the database and updates the
//     the field that was changed for the selected record.
//     A success message is displayed with a link to the
//     main page.
//===========================================================
//
//  Produce the standard WAP header and reference the
//  appropriate DTD at www.wapforum.org
header("Content-type: text/vnd.wap.wml");
echo("<?xml version=\"1.0\"?>\n");
echo("<!DOCTYPE wml PUBLIC \"-//WAPFORUM//DTD WML 1.1//EN\"
\"http://www.wapforum.org/DTD/wml_1.1.xml\">\n\n");

if (isset($HTTP_POST_VARS[id]) ){
   $fieldvalue = $HTTP_POST_VARS[fieldvalue];
   $id = $HTTP_POST_VARS[id];
   $fieldname = $HTTP_POST_VARS[fieldname];
   }
else
   $id=NULL;

// Connect to MySql and select the oab database
$link = mysql_pconnect( "localhost", "webuser", "abc123" );
    if ( ! $link )
        die( "Couldn't connect to MySQL" );
    mysql_select_db( "oab", $link )
```

```
        or die ( "Couldn't open database: ".mysql_error($link) );

if (substr($fieldname,0,4)=="info"){
   $qid=mysql_db_query("oab","update oabInfo set $fieldname = '$fieldvalue'
where contactID = '$id'");
   if ( ! $qid )
      die ( "database fatal error: ".mysql_error() );
}
elseif (substr($fieldname,0,4)=="cont"){
   $qid=mysql_db_query("oab","update oabContacts set $fieldname =
 '$fieldvalue' where contactID = '$id'");
   if ( ! $qid )
      die ( "database fatal error: ".mysql_error() );
}

?>
<!-- This is start of the WML card -->
<!-- This card displays a success message and allows the user return to the
home page -->
<wml>
<card id="commit" title="commit">
  <p align="center">
    <b>WAP Address</b></p>
  <p align="center">
    <b>Update DONE!</b>
  </p>
  <p>
    <a href="chapter15_main.wml">Home</a><br/>
  </p>
</card>
</wml>
```

The operation is successful and the user is given a hyperlink to return to the main WML page.

Figure 15-8 *Making the changes permanent*

Deleting Information

The other operation that the user can perform from the details screen is to delete the record from the database. To do this, the user will select the link similar to that shown in Figure 15-9.

The delete operation is a two-step process. The first step is to ask the user to confirm the deletion of the record, and the second step is to delete the record from the database. The next section will examine the first of these two steps.

WML Delete Page

When the user selects the delete link in the WAP browser, they will be taken to the chapter15_delete.php page. This page looks like Figure 15-10.

The delete page is passed the id of the record to be deleted and the information is queried from the database. The first name and last name of the record are displayed in the WAP browser, and the user is given the option to continue with the delete operation or to return to the details page.

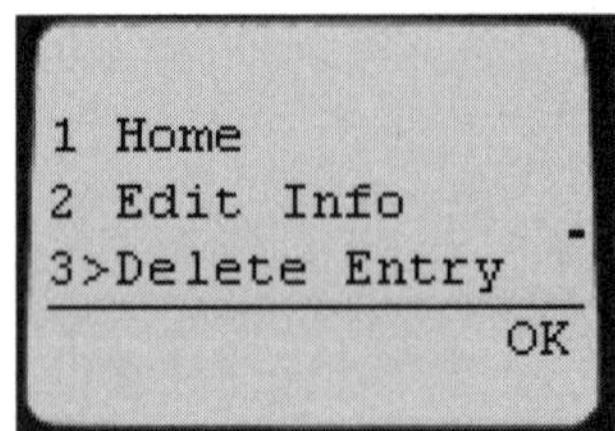

Figure 15-9 *Selecting the delete link*

Figure 15-10 *Deleting the record*

chapter15_delete.php

```
<?
//=============================================================
//     This page connects to the database and selects the
//     information to be deleted. The user is given the
//     option to delete the record or not.
//=============================================================
//
// Produce the standard WAP header and reference the
// appropriate DTD at www.wapforum.org
header("Content-type: text/vnd.wap.wml");
echo("<?xml version=\"1.0\"?>\n");
echo("<!DOCTYPE wml PUBLIC \"-//WAPFORUM//DTD WML 1.1//EN\"
\"http://www.wapforum.org/DTD/wml_1.1.xml\">\n\n");
if (isset($HTTP_GET_VARS[id]) )
   $id = $HTTP_GET_VARS[id];
else
   $id=NULL;

// Connect to MySql and select the oab database
$link = mysql_pconnect( "localhost", "webuser", "abc123" );
    if ( ! $link )
        die( "Couldn't connect to MySQL" );
    mysql_select_db( "oab", $link )
        or die ( "Couldn't open database: ".mysql_error($link) );

$qid=mysql_db_query("oab","select * from oabContacts, oabInfo where
 oabContacts.contactID=oabInfo.contactID and oabContacts.contactID = $id") or
die("Database Query Error");
$row=mysql_fetch_row($qid);

?>
<!-- This is start of the WML card -->
<!-- This card allows the user to select whether the record is to be deleted -->
<wml>
<template>
   <do type="prev" label="Back">
      <prev/>
   </do>
</template>
```

```
<card id="edit" title="Edit">
<p align="center">
<b>WAP Address</b></p>
<p align="center">
<b>DELETE RECORD?</b></p>
<p align="center">
<b><? print $row[2]." ".$row[1] ?></b><br/>

  <do type="accept" label="label">
     <go href="$field" method="post">
          <postfield name="id" value="<? print $row[0]; ?>" />
      </go>
    </do>

<?
  print "<select name=\"field\">";
  print "<option value=\"chapter15_details.php\">No</option>";
  print "<option value=\"chapter15_confirm.php\">Yes</option>";
  print "</select>";
?>
</p>
</card>
</wml>
```

If the user chooses to return to the details page, the id is passed as a POST variable and is used to query the database again for the information to display. If the user chooses to delete the record, the id is still passed as a POST variable to the chapter15_confirm.php page and is used in the delete query to remove the record from the database. This delete operation will be examined in the next section.

WML Confirm Page

The confirm page is actually the page that does the delete operation. This page is similar in function to the commit page during the edit operation. The user sees a success message and is given a link to return to the main page. The browser will look like Figure 15-11.

Figure 15-11 *The completed delete operation*

On the back end, the id is passed to this page and the delete query uses this to remove the information from the two database tables. The code for this page is as follows:

chapter15_confirm.php

```
<?
//=============================================================
//     This page connects to the database and deletes the
//     record from the database. Data is deleted from both
//     the oabInfo and the oabContacts table. The user is
//     given a link back to the main page.
//=============================================================
//
//  Produce the standard WAP header and reference the
//  appropriate DTD at www.wapforum.org
header("Content-type: text/vnd.wap.wml");
echo("<?xml version=\"1.0\"?>\n");
echo("<!DOCTYPE wml PUBLIC \"-//WAPFORUM//DTD WML 1.1//EN\"
\"http://www.wapforum.org/DTD/wml_1.1.xml\">\n\n");

if (isset($HTTP_POST_VARS[id]) ){
   $id = $HTTP_POST_VARS[id];
   }
else
   $id=NULL;

// Connect to MySql and select the oab database
$link = mysql_pconnect( "localhost", "webuser", "abc123" );
    if ( ! $link )
        die( "Couldn't connect to MySQL" );
    mysql_select_db( "oab", $link )
        or die ( "Couldn't open database: ".mysql_error($link) );

// Deletes the data from the oabInfo and the oabContacts table
   $qid=mysql_db_query("oab","delete from oabInfo where contactID =
   '$id'");
   if ( ! $qid )
      die ( "database fatal error: ".mysql_error() );
   $qid=mysql_db_query("oab","delete from oabContacts where contactID =
   $id'");
   if ( ! $qid )
      die ( "database fatal error: ".mysql_error() );
?>

<wml>
```

```
<card id="commit" title="commit">
<p align="center">
<b>WAP Address</b></p>
<p align="center">
<b>Delete DONE!</b>
</p>
<p>
<a href="chapter15_main.wml">Home</a><br/>
</p>
</card>
</wml>
```

The user is then presented with a success message and link to take them back to the main page.

Adding Information

The next main task that this application performs is to allow the user to add information to the database. The first portion of this operation was covered briefly in the discussion about the main page. From the main page, the user has the ability to choose the Add link. This looks similar to Figure 15-12. This link takes the user to another card in that deck and asks them for the first name and the last name of the record to add.

Once the first name and last name is added for this record and the user presses the submit button, they are taken to the chapter15_addname.php page. This page is described in the next section.

WML Add Name Page

Since the detailed information for each first and last name is kept in two separate tables, you will use two input screens to insert the data into the database. Once the first and last names are input into the previous WML page, they are passed as POST variables to the chapter15_addname.php page. From there, these POST variables are placed into PHP variables and inserted as data into the oabContacts table.

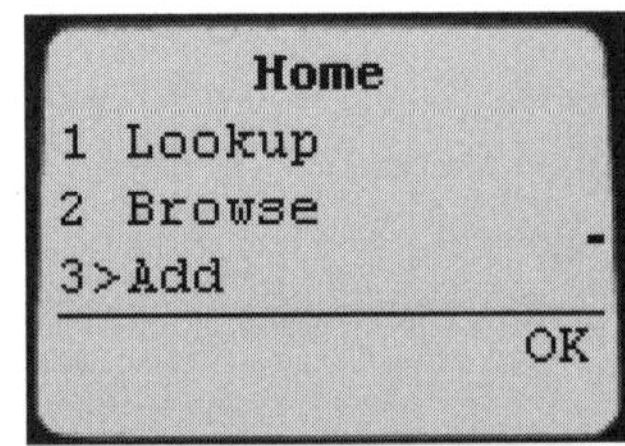

Figure 15-12 *Selecting the Add link and adding the first and last name*

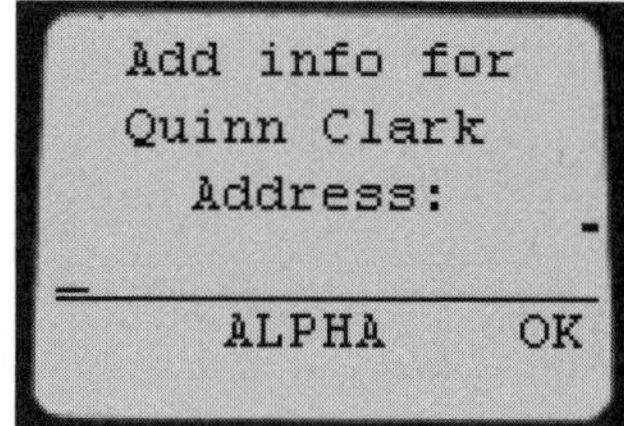

Figure 15-13 *Inputting the additional information*

Once the first name and last name are inserted into the table, the next PHP statement, mysql_insert_id(), will ask the database for the id of the record that was just entered. This id will be passed along with the rest of the data to the next page for insertion into the database.

The user is then prompted to enter additional information into the database. Each data item is entered as an input field and will look similar to Figure 15-13.

The entire code listing for this page is detailed here.

chapter15_addname.php

```
<?
//=============================================================
//      This page connects to the database and inserts the
//      POST variables into the oabContacts table.
//      This page also allows the user to enter additional
//      information to the record.
//=============================================================
//
//   Produce the standard WAP header and reference the
//   appropriate DTD at www.wapforum.org
header("Content-type: text/vnd.wap.wml");
echo("<?xml version=\"1.0\"?>\n");
echo("<!DOCTYPE wml PUBLIC \"-//WAPFORUM//DTD WML 1.1//EN\"
\"http://www.wapforum.org/DTD/wml_1.1.xml\">\n\n");

//  transfer all POST variable into PHP variables
if (isset($HTTP_POST_VARS[fname]) ){
   $fname = $HTTP_POST_VARS[fname];
   $lname = $HTTP_POST_VARS[lname];
   }
else
   $id=NULL;

// Connect to MySql and select the oab database
$link = mysql_pconnect( "localhost", "webuser", "abc123" );
    if ( ! $link )
```

```
        die( "Couldn't connect to MySQL" );
    mysql_select_db( "oab", $link )
        or die ( "Couldn't open database: ".mysql_error($link) );

// Insert the POST variables into the oabContacts table
$qid=mysql_db_query("oab","insert into oabContacts
(contactLastName,contactFirstName) values ('$lname','$fname');") or
 die("Database Query Error");
$id = mysql_insert_id ($link);
?>
<!-- This is start of the WML card -->
<!-- This card allows the user to add the info for the first and last name -->

<wml>
<card id="input" title="input">
<p align="center">
<b>WAP Address</b></p>
<p align="center">
<b>Add</b><br/>
<!-- Submit the entered information to the chapter15_addinfo.php script -->
<do type="accept" label="submit">
  <go href="chapter15_addinfo.php">
    <postfield name="id" value="<? print $id; ?>" />
    <postfield name="address1" value="$address1"/>
    <postfield name="address2" value="$address2"/>
    <postfield name="city" value="$city"/>
    <postfield name="state" value="$state"/>
    <postfield name="zip" value="$zip"/>
    <postfield name="phone" value="$phone"/>
    <postfield name="pager" value="$pager"/>
    <postfield name="cell" value="$cell"/>
    <postfield name="other" value="$other"/>
  </go>
</do>
<!-- Enter the additional information prior to submitting -->
<? print "Add info for $fname $lname"; ?><br/>
   Address: <input name="address1" type="text"/>
```

```
    Address 2: <input name="address2" type="text"/>
    City: <input name="city" type="text"/>
    State: <input name="state" type="text"/>
    Zip: <input name="zip" type="text"/>
    Phone: <input name="phone" type="text"/>
    Pager: <input name="pager" type="text"/>
    Cell: <input name="cell" type="text"/>
    Other: <input name="other" type="text"/>
</p>
</card>
</wml>
```

The data items that are entered into this page are placed into variables and, once again, the postfield tag is used to transfer the variables to the resulting page. There are a total of ten variables that are transferred to the next page to be inserted into the oabInfo table. A discussion of this process is detailed in the next section.

WML Add Info Page

This is the final page of the add process. As we mentioned earlier, these final pages don't interact with the user other than to display a success message. This page will look like Figure 15-14.

However, behind the scenes, the page transfers the POST variables into PHP variables and inserts these final variables into the database. By now, this code should

Figure 15-14 *Adding the information to the database*

look familiar. There is nothing new that is presented in the chapter15_addinfo.php page displayed here.

chapter15_addinfo.php

```
<?
//============================================================
//     This page connects to the database and inserts the
//     POST variables into the oabInfo table.
//     The variables are displayed to the user and
//     a link is provided to navigate back to the home page.
//============================================================
//
//  Produce the standard WAP header and reference the
//  appropriate DTD at www.wapforum.org
header("Content-type: text/vnd.wap.wml");
echo("<?xml version=\"1.0\"?>\n");
echo("<!DOCTYPE wml PUBLIC \"-//WAPFORUM//DTD WML 1.1//EN\"
\"http://www.wapforum.org/DTD/wml_1.1.xml\">\n\n");

//  transfer all POST variable into PHP variables
if (isset($HTTP_POST_VARS[id]) ){
   $id = $HTTP_POST_VARS[id];
   $address1 = $HTTP_POST_VARS[address1];
   $address2 = $HTTP_POST_VARS[address2];
   $city = $HTTP_POST_VARS[city];
   $state = $HTTP_POST_VARS[state];
   $zip = $HTTP_POST_VARS[zip];
   $phone = $HTTP_POST_VARS[phone];
   $pager = $HTTP_POST_VARS[pager];
   $cell = $HTTP_POST_VARS[cell];
   $other = $HTTP_POST_VARS[other];
   }
else
   $id=NULL;

// Connect to MySql and select the oab database
$link = mysql_pconnect( "localhost", "webuser", "abc123" );
    if ( ! $link )
        die( "Couldn't connect to MySQL" );
    mysql_select_db( "oab", $link )
        or die ( "Couldn't open database: ".mysql_error($link) );
```

```
// Insert the POST variables into the oabInfo table
   $qid=mysql_db_query("oab","insert into oabInfo
 (infoAddress1,infoAddress2,infoCity,infoState,infoZip,infoPhone,infoPager,
infoCell,infoPhoneOther,contactID) values
('$address1','$address2','$city','$state','$zip','$phone','$pager','$cell',
'$other','$id');");
   if ( ! $qid )
      die ( "database fatal error: ".mysql_error() );

?>
<!-- This is start of the WML card -->
<!-- This card displays that the ADD is done -->
<wml>
<card id="commit" title="commit">
<p align="center">
<b>WAP Address</b></p>
<p align="center">
<b>Add DONE!</b>
</p>
<p>
<?
// Display the variables
      print "address1: ".$address1."<br/>";
      print "address2: ".$address2."<br/>";
      print "city: ".$city."<br/>";
      print "state: ".$state."<br/>";
      print "zip: ".$zip."<br/>";
      print "phone: ".$phone."<br/>";
      print "pager: ".$pager."<br/>";
      print "cell: ".$cell."<br/>";
      print "other: ".$other."<br/>";
?>
<!— Provide a link back to the Home page —>
<a href="chapter15_main.wml">Home</a><br/>
</p>
</card>
</wml>
```

Notice that, as with the other final pages, the user is presented with a success message, a list of the data that was entered for this record, and a link back to the main page.

Browsing Through Information

The browse function is similar to the lookup function, except that the browse function, as it is defined in this application, will display every record in the database and allow the user to cursor to the desired record and select it to display the details. Figure 15-15 shows the user choosing the Browse link in the application.

WML Browse Page

When the user selects the browse option, the WAP browser will display all the records in the database. The results will look similar to Figure 15-16. The user can then use the up and down arrows to traverse the list and select the record to display.

You will notice that this page is very similar to the lookup page, except that the query statement returns all records, not just records matching a particular string. Once the result set is retrieved, the while loop is used to display all the records and allow the user to select one. The code listing for the browse page is as follows:

chapter15_browse.php

```
<?

//============================================================
//     This page connects to the database and inserts the
//     POST variables into the oabContacts table.
//     This page also allows the user to enter additional
//     information to the record.
//============================================================
//
//  Produce the standard WAP header and reference the
//  appropriate DTD at www.wapforum.org
header("Content-type: text/vnd.wap.wml");
echo("<?xml version=\"1.0\"?>\n");
echo("<!DOCTYPE wml PUBLIC \"-//WAPFORUM//DTD WML 1.1//EN\"
\"http://www.wapforum.org/DTD/wml_1.1.xml\">\n\n");

// Connect to MySql and select the oab database
$link = mysql_pconnect( "localhost", "webuser", "abc123" );
    if ( ! $link )
        die( "Couldn't connect to MySQL" );
    mysql_select_db( "oab", $link )
        or die ( "Couldn't open database: ".mysql_error($link) );
```

```
// Select all the last names and id's from the database and order them
// alphabetically
$qid=mysql_db_query("oab","select contactID, contactLastName from
oabContacts order by contactLastName ASC") or die("Database Query Error");
?>
<!-- This is start of the WML card -->
<!-- This card displays the last name and allows the user to select it for
more details -->
<wml>
<card id="card1" title="Browse">
<p align="center">
<b>WAP Address</b></p>
<p align="center">
<b>Browse</b>
<?
// Loop through the records that were returned from the database
   while($row=mysql_fetch_row($qid)) {
      print "<a href=\"chapter15_details.php?id=$row[0]\">".$row[1]."</a><br/>";
   }
?>

</p>
</card>
</wml>
```

Once a user selects a record, the application will again pass the id as a GET variable to the details page. The details page will behave the same as it did when called from the lookup page. The details will be retrieved from the database and displayed in the browser. The user then has the option to return to the home page, or to delete or edit the record.

Figure 15-15 *Choosing the Browse link*

Figure 15-16 *The browse results*

Next Steps

Chapter 14 took you through the WML language and gave simplistic examples. This chapter took that knowledge to the next level and integrated three technologies that complement each other: WML, PHP, and MySQL. As we have demonstrated in this chapter, using these web technologies can create a very usable, dynamic, database-driven, wireless application.

This chapter's goal was to demonstrate techniques for using WML, PHP, and MySQL together. There are many things you can do to enhance this application. We purposely left out excessive error checking and data validation, as we didn't want this extra code to interfere with the items we were trying to highlight. You can introduce more error checking with the database interaction components and with the PHP functions. You will also find value in validating the data that is put into the database and formatting items like phone numbers and ZIP codes to valid lengths.

Other items to consider when enhancing this application would be the ability to search on other fields besides last name. Another idea for an application enhancement would to add e-mail functionality. An e-mail field could be added, and when the user selects the e-mail link, the application would provide a small text box to send e-mail from your phone.

What to Take Away

This chapter was intended to give the beginner an overall view of the WML language and provide detailed examples of the most popular functions. There are many resources available on the Internet to provide help to the WML developer. Unfortunately, there are not many resources that will give detailed examples and techniques for using WML in a database-driven application. This chapter should give you the tools you need to begin developing WML applications immediately. You can use the techniques that were introduced here and modify them to fit your needs and the needs of your application.

PART VIII

Appendixes

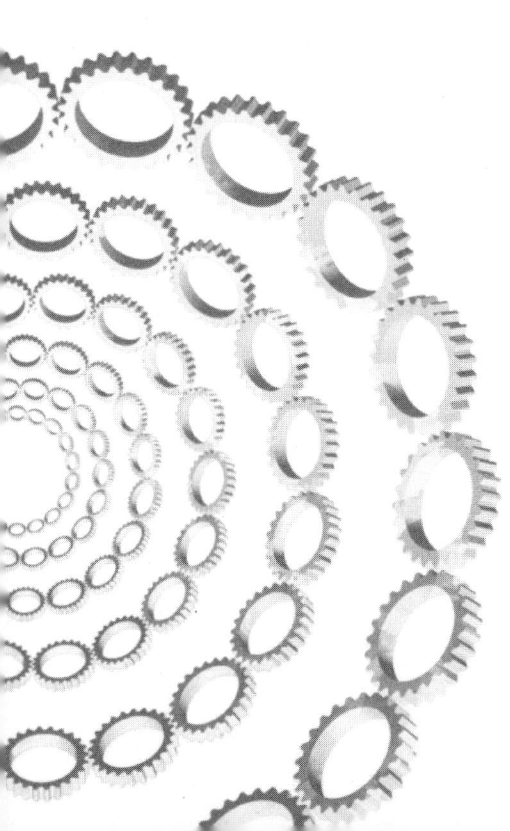

APPENDIX

A

MySQL Database Installation

Throughout this book, we have assumed you are using the Red Hat Linux operating system on the Intel platform. The recommended way to install MySQL on Red Hat Linux is by using an RPM file. There are three files that must be installed for your MySQL distribution to be operational. These three files can be downloaded directly from Red Hat. We will assume that you have Red Hat 7.1 installed, but the steps described here should be similar for prior and future versions of Red Hat Linux.

The RPM files you will want to install are

mysql-version.i386.rpm	MySQL utilities and binaries
mysql-server-version.i386.rpm	MySQL server binaries
mysqlclientversion.i386.rpm	Client programs

Following are the steps you need to follow to download, install, and configure MySQL on your Red Hat Linux 7.1 system.

First, log in to Red Hat's anonymous FTP server and download the appropriate files. Your sequence of commands should look like this, beginning with the login sequence:

```
[root@quinn rcox]# ftp ftp.redhat.com
Connected to ftp.redhat.com.
220 Red Hat FTP server ready. All transfers are logged.
Name (ftp.redhat.com:rcox): anonymous
331 Please specify the password.
Password:
230 Login successful. Have fun.
Remote system type is UNIX.
Using binary mode to transfer files.
```

Next, change to the appropriate directory, as follows:

```
ftp> cd /pub/redhat/linux/7.1/en/os/i386/RedHat/RPMS/
250 Directory successfully changed.
```

Next, list the MySQL files in the current directory, as shown here:

```
ftp> ls mysql*
227 Entering Passive Mode (63,240,14,63,107,195)
150 Here comes the directory listing.
-rw-r--r--    2 0        0         4150937 Apr 08 19:34 mysql-3.23.36-1.i386.rpm
-rw-r--r--    2 0        0          443263 Apr 08 19:34 mysql-devel-3.23.36-1.i386.rpm
-rw-r--r--    2 0        0          932220 Apr 08 19:34 mysql-server-3.23.36-1.i386.rpm
```

```
-rw-r--r--    2 0         0          116371 Apr 08 19:34 mysqlclient9-3.23.22-4.i386.rpm
226 Directory send OK.
```

Now change the mode to binary, like this:

```
ftp> bin
```

Next, get all the files that begin with MySQL (except the development distribution), as follows:

```
ftp> mget mysql*
mget mysql-3.23.36-1.i386.rpm? y
227 Entering Passive Mode (216,148,218,192,106,142)
150 Here comes the data.
226 File send OK.
4150937 bytes received in 201 secs (20 Kbytes/sec)
mget mysql-devel-3.23.36-1.i386.rpm? n
mget mysql-server-3.23.36-1.i386.rpm? y
227 Entering Passive Mode (216,148,218,192,223,33)
150 Here comes the data.
226 File send OK.
932220 bytes received in 43 secs (21 Kbytes/sec)
mget mysqlclient9-3.23.22-4.i386.rpm? y
227 Entering Passive Mode (216,148,218,192,122,137)
150 Here comes the data.
226 File send OK.
116371 bytes received in 3.04 secs (37 Kbytes/sec)
```

Finally, log off the FTP server:

```
ftp> bye
221 Goodbye.
```

Once these three files are on your local Linux machine, you can use the rpm utility to install the MySQL distribution. The -i option tells rpm to install the package and the -vv option describes in detail what the installation is. For the sake of brevity in this appendix, we have not included the entire output of the rpm command, as it is quite extensive. Please note that it really doesn't matter in what order the packages are added. We will install the base MySQL package first.

```
[root@quinn rcox]# rpm -ivv mysql-3.23.36-1.i386.rpm
D: counting packages to install
D: found 1 packages
D: looking for packages to download
D: retrieved 0 packages
D: Expected size:       4150937 = lead(96)+sigs(149)+pad(3)+data(4150689)
```

```
D:   Actual size:      4150937
D: opening db index        /var/lib/rpm/Packages create mode=0x42
D: locked  db index        /var/lib/rpm/Packages
D: found 0 source and 1 binary packages
D: opening db index        /var/lib/rpm/Depends create mode=0x42
D: opening db index        /var/lib/rpm/Basenames create mode=0x42
```

We're deleting the verbose listing of the rpm output, but this listing includes the description of required packages and the listing of files that are added or modified..

```
D: closed  db index        /var/lib/rpm/Depends
D: closed  db index        /var/lib/rpm/Triggername
D: closed  db index        /var/lib/rpm/Conflictname
D: closed  db index        /var/lib/rpm/Providename
D: closed  db index        /var/lib/rpm/Requirename
D: closed  db index        /var/lib/rpm/Group
D: closed  db index        /var/lib/rpm/Basenames
D: closed  db index        /var/lib/rpm/Name
D: closed  db index        /var/lib/rpm/Packages
```

The next item to install is the MySQL client application. Again, the -ivv options are used to install with verbose output. Here's how you install the package:

```
[root@quinn rcox]# rpm -ivv mysqlclient9-3.23.22-4.i386.rpm
D: counting packages to install
D: found 1 packages
D: looking for packages to download
D: retrieved 0 packages
D: Expected size:      116371 = lead(96)+sigs(149)+pad(3)+data(116123)
D:   Actual size:      116371
D: opening db index        /var/lib/rpm/Packages create mode=0x42
D: locked  db index        /var/lib/rpm/Packages
D: found 0 source and 1 binary packages
D: opening db index        /var/lib/rpm/Depends create mode=0x42
D: opening db index        /var/lib/rpm/Basenames create mode=0x42
```

As before, we're deleting the verbose listing of the rpm output. This listing includes the description of required packages , the listing of files that are added or modified , and details of permission changes and users added.

```
D: closed  db index        /var/lib/rpm/Depends
D: closed  db index        /var/lib/rpm/Triggername
D: closed  db index        /var/lib/rpm/Conflictname
D: closed  db index        /var/lib/rpm/Providename
D: closed  db index        /var/lib/rpm/Requirename
D: closed  db index        /var/lib/rpm/Group
```

```
D: closed  db index       /var/lib/rpm/Basenames
D: closed  db index       /var/lib/rpm/Name
D: closed  db index       /var/lib/rpm/Packages
```

The last package we will install is the MySQL server application. This has all the binaries and scripts needed to run the MySQL server daemon on the Linux machine. Installation begins as follows:

```
[root@quinn rcox]# rpm -ivv mysql-server-3.23.36-1.i386.rpm
D: counting packages to install
D: found 1 packages
D: looking for packages to download
D: retrieved 0 packages
D: Expected size:        932220 = lead(96)+sigs(149)+pad(3)+data(931972)
D:   Actual size:        932220
D: opening db index        /var/lib/rpm/Packages create mode=0x42
D: locked  db index        /var/lib/rpm/Packages
D: found 0 source and 1 binary packages
D: opening db index        /var/lib/rpm/Depends create mode=0x42
D: opening db index        /var/lib/rpm/Basenames create mode=0x42
```

The verbose listing of the rpm output is deleted. This listing includes the description of required packages, the listing of files that are added or modified, and the details of permission changes and users added.

```
D: closed  db index       /var/lib/rpm/Depends
D: closed  db index       /var/lib/rpm/Triggername
D: closed  db index       /var/lib/rpm/Conflictname
D: closed  db index       /var/lib/rpm/Providename
D: closed  db index       /var/lib/rpm/Requirename
D: closed  db index       /var/lib/rpm/Group
D: closed  db index       /var/lib/rpm/Basenames
D: closed  db index       /var/lib/rpm/Name
D: closed  db index       /var/lib/rpm/Packages
```

The next thing to do in the installation of MySQL is to set up the initial databases. This is done by using the mysql_install_db script. This script can be found in the /usr/bin directory and the output is as follows:

```
[root@quinn bin]# /usr/bin/mysql_install_db
Preparing db table
Preparing host table
Preparing user table
Preparing func table
Preparing tables_priv table
Preparing columns_priv table
```

```
Installing all prepared tables

To start mysqld at boot time you have to copy support-files/mysql.server
to the right place for your system

PLEASE REMEMBER TO SET A PASSWORD FOR THE MySQL root USER !
This is done with:
/usr/bin/mysqladmin -u root -p password 'new-password'
/usr/bin/mysqladmin -u root -h quinn -p password 'new-password'
See the manual for more instructions.

You can start the MySQL daemon with:
cd /usr ; /usr/bin/safe_mysqld &

You can test the MySQL daemon with the benchmarks in the 'sql-bench'
directory:
cd sql-bench ; run-all-tests

Please report any problems with the /usr/bin/mysqlbug script!

The latest information about MySQL is available on the web at
http://www.mysql.com
Support MySQL by buying support/licenses at https://order.mysql.com
```

Now you should be ready to start mysqld (MySQL daemon) and connect to the server. However, in some instances, if you start the server you will immediately see that the daemon shuts down. The output looks like this:

```
[root@quinn bin]# /usr/bin/safe_mysqld &
[1] 27351
[root@quinn bin]# Starting mysqld daemon with databases from /var/lib/mysql
010819 23:33:14  mysqld ended

[1]+  Done                        /usr/bin/safe_mysqld
```

This points to a permissions problem with your MySQL installation. To remedy this, change all the subdirectories in /var/lib/mysql to be owned by the mysql user and the mysql group. Your command sequence will look like this:

```
[root@quinn mysql]# pwd
/var/lib/mysql
[root@quinn mysql]# chown -R mysql:mysql *
[root@quinn mysql]# ls -la
total 4
drwxr-xr-x    4 mysql    mysql         1024 Aug 19 23:33 .
drwxr-xr-x   11 root     root          1024 Aug 19 23:28 ..
```

```
drwx------     2 mysql    mysql        1024 Aug 19 23:30 mysql
srwxrwxrwx     1 mysql    mysql           0 Aug 19 23:33 mysql.sock
drwx------     2 mysql    mysql        1024 Aug 19 23:30 test
```

Now, if you start the mysqld daemon, it will not die:

```
[root@quinn mysql]# /usr/bin/safe_mysqld &
[1] 27392
[root@quinn mysql]# Starting mysqld daemon with databases from /var/lib/mysql
```

Check for the existence of the mysqld process in the process list, as follows:

```
 [root@quinn mysql]# ps -ef | grep mysqld
root      27392 26935  0 23:35 pts/1    00:00:00 /bin/sh /usr/bin/safe_mysqld
mysql     27415 27392  0 23:35 pts/1    00:00:00 /usr/libexec/mysqld --
basedir=/u
mysql     27417 27415  0 23:36 pts/1    00:00:00 /usr/libexec/mysqld --
basedir=/u
mysql     27418 27417  0 23:36 pts/1    00:00:00 /usr/libexec/mysqld --basedir=/u
mysql     27419 27417  0 23:36 pts/1    00:00:00 /usr/libexec/mysqld --basedir=/u
root      27421 26935  0 23:37 pts/1    00:00:00 grep mysqld
```

The rpm program installs files into the following directories. This table will be useful for administration purposes.

Directory	Components
/usr/bin/	MySQL administration programs
/usr/share/doc/mysql-3.23.36/	Documentation
/usr/share/man/man1/	Manual pages
/usr/share/mysql/	Language and configuration files
/var/lib/mysql/	Databases

APPENDIX B

SQL Help

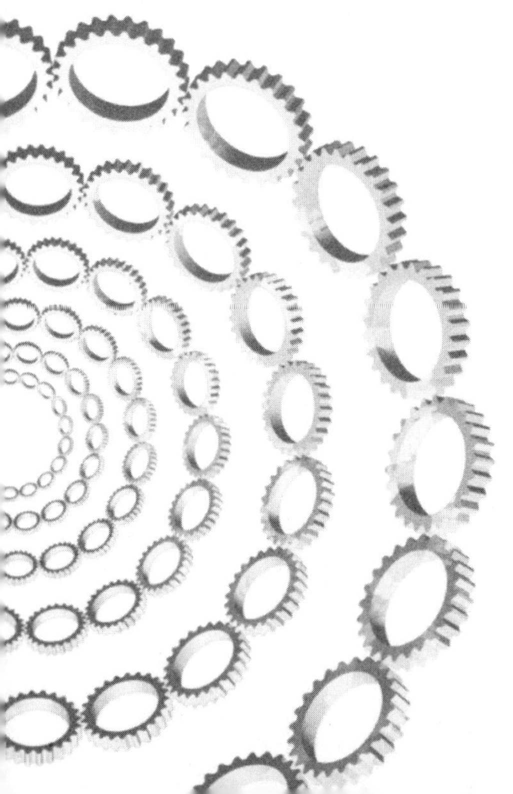

The data in a relational database is stored in groups called *tables*. The table consists of rows and columns. The rows contain data that makes up a database record. The columns contain data that is similar, such as addresses or cities. Each row in the table contains data that, at one time or another, may need to be retrieved from the database. Consider the following two tables, the first called company and the second called contacts.

```
+-----------+---------------------+------------+-------+
|                     company table                    |
+-----------+---------------------+------------+-------+
| companyID | address             | city       | state |
+-----------+---------------------+------------+-------+
|         1 | 540 Breckenridge Ave | Raleigh   | NC    |
|         2 | 123 Warren Ave       | Winslow   | AZ    |
|         3 | 3302 Indian School   | Phoenix   | AZ    |
|         4 | 480 Main St          | Boston    | MA    |
|         5 | 2230 Broadway        | New York  | NY    |
|         6 | 7642 Hill St         | Baltimore | MD    |
|         7 | 1107 Oak Hill Ln     | Atlanta   | GA    |
|         8 | 873 State St         | Seattle   | WA    |
|         9 | 978 South 450 East   | Orem      | UT    |
+-----------+---------------------+------------+-------+

+-----------+-----------+------------+----------+--------------+
|                        contact table                         |
+-----------+-----------+------------+-------------------------+
| contactID | companyID | lastname   | firstname | phone        |
+-----------+-----------+------------+-------------------------+
|         1 |         1 | Sadler     | Wayne     | 919-432-3141 |
|         2 |         2 | Hecht      | Mark      | 520-322-2347 |
|         3 |         3 | Black      | Larry     | 602-145-2458 |
|         4 |         4 | Perry      | Frank     | 978-342-2452 |
|         5 |         5 | Whitt      | Kevin     | 202-234-9771 |
|         6 |         6 | Scott      | Steve     | 543-349-1343 |
|         7 |         7 | Sugrue     | Nancy     | 800-342-2344 |
|         8 |         8 | Kleindienst | Ann      | 283-234-0974 |
|         9 |         9 | Hancock    | Mary      | 432-234-9080 |
+-----------+-----------+------------+----------+--------------+
```

Notice that these two tables are related by a column called companyID. This layout allows multiple contacts to be associated with a single company.

The Select Statement

To retrieve information from the database, you use a select statement. To retrieve selected columns and all rows from a table, the select statement looks like this:

```
select city, state from company;
```

Given the preceding tables, this select statement would return the following result set:

```
+-------------+-------+
| city        | state |
+-------------+-------+
| Raleigh     | NC    |
| Winslow     | AZ    |
| Phoenix     | AZ    |
| Boston      | MA    |
| New York    | NY    |
| Baltimore   | MD    |
| Atlanta     | GA    |
| Seattle     | WA    |
| Orem        | UT    |
+-------------+-------+
```

To return all columns and all rows in a specific table, the select statement would look like this:

```
select * from company;
```

This SQL query would return the following result set:

```
+-----------+----------------------+-----------+-------+
| companyID | address              | city      | state |
+-----------+----------------------+-----------+-------+
|         1 | 540 Breckenridge Ave | Raleigh   | NC    |
|         2 | 123 Warren Ave       | Winslow   | AZ    |
|         3 | 3302 Indian School   | Phoenix   | AZ    |
|         4 | 480 Main St          | Boston    | MA    |
|         5 | 2230 Broadway        | New York  | NY    |
|         6 | 7642 Hill St         | Baltimore | MD    |
|         7 | 1107 Oak Hill Ln     | Atlanta   | GA    |
|         8 | 873 State St         | Seattle   | WA    |
|         9 | 978 South 450 East   | Orem      | UT    |
+-----------+----------------------+-----------+-------+
```

The Conditional Select Statement

Expanding the select statement to return only specific records is done with the WHERE clause and conditional operators. The conditional operators are

=	Equal to
<	Less than
>	Greater than
!= or <>	Not equal to
<=	Less than or equal to
>=	Greater than or equal to

Using the previous example tables, the following is an example of a valid conditional select statement:

```
select city, state from company where state = 'AZ';
```

This statement would return the following results:

```
+---------+-------+
| city    | state |
+---------+-------+
| Winslow | AZ    |
| Phoenix | AZ    |
+---------+-------+
```

More complex select statements can have multiple where clauses separated by Boolean operators. For instance, consider the following select statement:

```
select city, state from company where state = 'AZ' or state = 'NC';
```

Notice that there are two conditional statements. This select statement returns all records where the state column contains AZ or NC. Other columns will not be returned. The result set looks like this:

```
+---------+-------+
| city    | state |
+---------+-------+
| Raleigh | NC    |
| Winslow | AZ    |
| Phoenix | AZ    |
+---------+-------+
```

The Select Statement Using "in," "between," and "like"

Another way to limit the result set is to use the "in," "between," and "like" operators. The "in" operator allows you to specify a set of data. If the set matches rows in the tables, the results will be returned. For instance, in the following query, three last names are specified. If the last names are in the contacts table, the entire row will be returned.

```
select * from contacts where lastname in ('Sadler','Whitt','Perry');
```

The results are

```
+-----------+-----------+----------+-----------+--------------+
| contactID | companyID | lastname | firstname | phone        |
+-----------+-----------+----------+-----------+--------------+
|         1 |         1 | Sadler   | Wayne     | 919-432-3141 |
|         4 |         4 | Perry    | Frank     | 978-342-2452 |
|         5 |         5 | Whitt    | Kevin     | 202-234-9771 |
+-----------+-----------+----------+-----------+--------------+
```

The "between" operator is used to return records between specific boundaries. For instance, the following query will return any record having the contactID 3, 4, 5, 6, 7, or 8:

```
select * from contacts where contactID between 3 and 8;
```

Notice that the results include the boundary records—in this case, the records containing contactIDs 3 and 8. The result set looks like this:

```
+-----------+-----------+-------------+-----------+--------------+
| contactID | companyID | lastname    | firstname | phone        |
+-----------+-----------+-------------+-----------+--------------+
|         3 |         3 | Black       | Larry     | 602-145-2458 |
|         4 |         4 | Perry       | Frank     | 978-342-2452 |
|         5 |         5 | Whitt       | Kevin     | 202-234-9771 |
|         6 |         6 | Scott       | Steve     | 543-349-1343 |
|         7 |         7 | Sugrue      | Nancy     | 800-342-2344 |
|         8 |         8 | Kleindienst | Ann       | 283-234-0974 |
+-----------+-----------+-------------+-----------+--------------+
```

The "like" operator returns records that match the qualifying string. For instance, if you wanted to return all records that start with an *S*, the query would look like this:

```
select * from contacts where lastname like 'S%';
```

This query would return the following results:

```
+-----------+-----------+----------+-----------+--------------+
| contactID | companyID | lastname | firstname | phone        |
+-----------+-----------+----------+-----------+--------------+
|         1 |         1 | Sadler   | Wayne     | 919-432-3141 |
|         6 |         6 | Scott    | Steve     | 543-349-1343 |
|         7 |         7 | Sugrue   | Nancy     | 800-342-2344 |
+-----------+-----------+----------+-----------+--------------+
```

Performing SQL Inner Joins

Joins make it possible to reference data in multiple tables in a single query. Relational databases do this using primary keys and foreign keys. Consider the following two tables:

```
+-----------+----------------------+-------------+-------+
|                      company table                      |
+-----------+----------------------+-------------+-------+
| companyID | address              | city        | state |
+-----------+----------------------+-------------+-------+
|         1 | 540 Breckenridge Ave | Raleigh     | NC    |
|         2 | 123 Warren Ave       | Winslow     | AZ    |
|         3 | 3302 Indian School   | Phoenix     | AZ    |
|         4 | 480 Main St          | Boston      | MA    |
|         5 | 2230 Broadway        | New York    | NY    |
|         6 | 7642 Hill St         | Baltimore   | MD    |
|         7 | 1107 Oak Hill Ln     | Atlanta     | GA    |
|         8 | 873 State St         | Seattle     | WA    |
|         9 | 978 South 450 East   | Orem        | UT    |
+------+-----------+--------------+-------------+-------+
```

```
+-----------+-----------+------------+-----------+--------------+
|                         contact table                         |
+-----------+-----------+------------+-----------+--------------+
| contactID | companyID | lastname   | firstname | phone        |
+-----------+-----------+------------+-----------+--------------+
|         1 |         1 | Sadler     | Wayne     | 919-432-3141 |
```

```
|          2 |          2 | Hecht       | Mark      | 520-322-2347 |
|          3 |          3 | Black       | Larry     | 602-145-2458 |
|          4 |          4 | Perry       | Frank     | 978-342-2452 |
|          5 |          5 | Whitt       | Kevin     | 202-234-9771 |
|          6 |          6 | Scott       | Steve     | 543-349-1343 |
|          7 |          7 | Sugrue      | Nancy     | 800-342-2344 |
|          8 |          8 | Kleindienst | Ann       | 283-234-0974 |
|          9 |          9 | Hancock     | Mary      | 432-234-9080 |
+-----------+-----------+-------------+-----------+--------------+
```

In the company table, the companyID is the primary key. This means there are no other rows in this table that contain this ID, making this column unique. In the contact table, the contactID is the unique primary key for this table. Notice that there is also a companyID in the contact table. This column is referred to as the foreign key. This key doesn't have to be unique, but rather it references a row of data in the company table. For instance, the contact Wayne Sadler belongs to companyID number 1, or 540 Breckenridge Ave. There could be multiple contacts for this companyID; in that case, multiple records in the contacts table would reference the same companyID.

Let's look at a query. If you want to return the first name, last name, address, city, and state from the database, you will have to query data from two tables. The link between these two tables is the field called companyID in the contacts and company tables. The format of the query would look like this:

```
select firstname, lastname, address, city, state from contacts, company
where contacts.companyID=company.companyID;
```

This query is referred to as an inner join and would return the following results:

```
+-----------+-------------+----------------------+-----------+-------+
| firstname | lastname    | address              | city      | state |
+-----------+-------------+----------------------+-----------+-------+
| Wayne     | Sadler      | 540 Breckenridge Ave | Raleigh   | NC    |
| Mark      | Hecht       | 123 Warren Ave       | Winslow   | AZ    |
| Larry     | Black       | 3302 Indian School   | Phoenix   | AZ    |
| Frank     | Perry       | 480 Main St          | Boston    | MA    |
| Kevin     | Whitt       | 2230 Broadway        | New York  | NY    |
| Steve     | Scott       | 7642 Hill St         | Baltimore | MD    |
| Nancy     | Sugrue      | 1107 Oak Hill Ln     | Atlanta   | GA    |
| Ann       | Kleindienst | 873 State St         | Seattle   | WA    |
| Mary      | Hancock     | 978 South 450 East   | Orem      | UT    |
+-----------+-------------+----------------------+-----------+-------+
```

To limit the query to contacts from Arizona, create the join between the two tables and then use the Boolean "and" operator to limit the result set. The query would look like this:

```
select firstname, lastname, address, city, state from contacts,
company where contacts.companyID=company.companyID and state='AZ';
```

The results of this query look like this:

```
+-----------+----------+--------------------+---------+-------+
| firstname | lastname | address            | city    | state |
+-----------+----------+--------------------+---------+-------+
| Mark      | Hecht    | 123 Warren Ave     | Winslow | AZ    |
| Larry     | Black    | 3302 Indian School | Phoenix | AZ    |
+-----------+----------+--------------------+---------+-------+
```

Demo Tables

The next sections assume that four tables exist in a database. The tables are clients, sales, items, and orders. The clients table contains the client name and the clientID:

```
+----------+------------------+
| clientID | name             |
+----------+------------------+
|        3 | Clayton Coggs    |
|        2 | Kites by Keith   |
|        1 | Schrader Suits   |
|        4 | Treichler Trikes |
|        5 | Anders Mints     |
|        6 | Hammond Hammocks |
|        7 | Hard Hats, Inc   |
|        8 | Young Guns       |
|        9 | Sandy Beach Wear |
+----------+------------------+
```

The items table contains the description of the item, the price, and a unique identifier, itemID:

```
+--------+---------------------+-------+
| itemID | description         | price |
+--------+---------------------+-------+
|      1 | Air Anvil           | 29.95 |
|      2 | Ballpeen Bolt       |  0.79 |
```

```
|       3 | Crabbing Cog        |  1.29 |
|       4 | Deep-Sea Drill      | 52.49 |
|       5 | Electric Emeryboard |  1.49 |
|       6 | Fabulous Flypaper   |  2.29 |
|       7 | Grape Gavel         |  8.55 |
|       8 | Hard Hammer         |  9.95 |
|       9 | Inner Icepick       |  3.79 |
+--------+---------------------+-------+
```

The sales table contains information about the sales team. This table contains the first name and last name of the salesperson, along with a unique salesID:

```
+---------+-----------+----------+
| salesID | firstname | lastname |
+---------+-----------+----------+
|       1 | Mike      | Kloss    |
|       2 | Tim       | Hill     |
|       3 | Brian     | McKnight |
+---------+-----------+----------+
```

The orders table contains information about the orders. Notice that this table only contains a salesID linking it to a salesperson in the sales table, a clientID that links it to the client in the clients table, a link to the item in the items table, and the quantity of items ordered. This table layout also has a unique orderID and allows for multiple items to be sold to a single client by a single salesperson. The table is as follows:

```
+---------+---------+----------+--------+----------+
| orderID | salesID | clientID | itemID | quantity |
+---------+---------+----------+--------+----------+
|       6 |       2 |        3 |      1 |        2 |
|       5 |       1 |        2 |      5 |        4 |
|       4 |       1 |        2 |      4 |        2 |
|       3 |       1 |        2 |      3 |        3 |
|       2 |       1 |        1 |      2 |        1 |
|       1 |       1 |        1 |      1 |        2 |
|       7 |       2 |        3 |      6 |        1 |
|       8 |       2 |        4 |      2 |        5 |
|       9 |       2 |        4 |      7 |        5 |
|      10 |       2 |        5 |      3 |        3 |
|      11 |       2 |        5 |      8 |        2 |
|      12 |       3 |        6 |      4 |        5 |
|      13 |       3 |        6 |      3 |        4 |
|      14 |       3 |        6 |      9 |        3 |
|      15 |       3 |        6 |      7 |        7 |
+---------+---------+----------+--------+----------+
```

The following sample queries will use these tables.

Select Distinct and Order By

The distinct operator is used to only return items in a query that are unique. If a query returns multiple rows, some of which are the same, the "distinct" operator can be used to limit the results to unique records. The "order by" operator arranges the results in ascending or descending order. This is done by using the ASC or DESC keyword. If no keyword is present, ASC (ascending) is assumed.

Consider the following query:

```
SELECT clients.clientID, name
FROM clients, orders
WHERE clients.clientID = orders.clientID
ORDER BY name;
```

This query will return only the rows from your database that contain clients that have ordered an item:

```
+----------+------------------+
| clientID | name             |
+----------+------------------+
|        5 | Anders Mints     |
|        5 | Anders Mints     |
|        3 | Clayton Coggs    |
|        3 | Clayton Coggs    |
|        6 | Hammond Hammocks |
|        6 | Hammond Hammocks |
|        6 | Hammond Hammocks |
|        6 | Hammond Hammocks |
|        2 | Kites by Keith   |
|        2 | Kites by Keith   |
|        2 | Kites by Keith   |
|        1 | Schrader Suits   |
|        1 | Schrader Suits   |
|        4 | Treichler Trikes |
|        4 | Treichler Trikes |
+----------+------------------+
```

Unfortunately, since some clients have ordered more than once, they are listed multiple times. The "select distinct" query would look like this:

```
SELECT DISTINCT clients.clientID, name
FROM clients, orders
WHERE clients.clientID = orders.clientID
ORDER BY name;
```

The results set from this query, using the "distinct" and "order by" operators, would look like this:

```
+----------+------------------+
| clientID | name             |
+----------+------------------+
|        5 | Anders Mints     |
|        3 | Clayton Coggs    |
|        6 | Hammond Hammocks |
|        2 | Kites by Keith   |
|        1 | Schrader Suits   |
|        4 | Treichler Trikes |
+----------+------------------+
```

Aliases

Aliases allow the columns referenced in a query to be known by a more familiar name. For instance, if CustomerID makes more sense than clientID, the results can be referenced by CustomerID. Aliases can be used for any column that is returned by the query. The following query has aliases for clientID and name:

```
SELECT DISTINCT clients.clientID CustomerID, name CustomerName
FROM clients, orders
WHERE clients.clientID = orders.clientID
ORDER BY name;
```

When the results of this query are returned, clientID is returned as CustomerID and name is returned as CustomerName. The result set is as follows:

```
+------------+------------------+
| CustomerID | CustomerName     |
+------------+------------------+
|          5 | Anders Mints     |
|          3 | Clayton Coggs    |
|          6 | Hammond Hammocks |
|          2 | Kites by Keith   |
```

```
|          1 | Schrader Suits    |
|          4 | Treichler Trikes |
+-----------+------------------+
```

Subqueries

In SQL, it is possible to include the results of another query within a query. This is known as a subquery. An example of a subquery is shown here:

```
SELECT name, description, quantity
FROM clients, items, orders
WHERE clients.clientID = orders.clientID
AND orders.itemID = items.itemID
AND orders.orderID IN (select orderID from orders where quantity > 4);
```

This query returns all the clients that have bought four items or more. The result set looks like this:

```
+------------------+---------------+----------+
| name             | description   | quantity |
+------------------+---------------+----------+
| Treichler Trikes | Ballpeen Bolt |        5 |
| Treichler Trikes | Grape Gavel   |        5 |
| Hammond Hammocks | Deep-Sea Drill |       5 |
| Hammond Hammocks | Grape Gavel   |        7 |
+------------------+---------------+----------+
```

MySQL will not allow subqueries and will return the following error for the preceding subquery:

```
ERROR 1064: You have an error in your SQL syntax near 'select orderID
from orders where quantity > 4)' at line 5
```

If you need to return the preceding result set and cannot use subqueries, you can always rewrite subqueries into the where clause. A restatement of the subquery is shown here (this query will return the same result set):

```
SELECT name, description, quantity
FROM clients, items, orders
WHERE clients.clientID = orders.clientID
AND orders.itemID = items.itemID
AND orders.quantity > 4;
```

Aggregate Functions

There is a set of functions that are available in the SQL language that allows you to perform simple functions on a returned result set. The following table defines the functions available.

SUM()	Gives the total of all the rows, satisfying any conditions, of the given column, where the given column is numeric
AVG()	Gives the average of the given column
MAX()	Gives the largest figure in the given column
MIN()	Gives the smallest figure in the given column
COUNT(*)	Gives the number of rows satisfying the conditions

To return the customers who have ordered the most items and the number of items they ordered, sorted from most to least, consider the following query:

```
SELECT name, sum(quantity) total
FROM clients, items, orders
WHERE clients.clientID = orders.clientID
AND orders.itemID = items.itemID
GROUP BY name
ORDER BY total DESC;
```

Notice that the first line of the query will select the name from the clients table, sum the quantity from the orders table, and assign that to an alias called total. The next three lines define the tables from which the data is to be pulled and the links between the three tables. The final two lines group the results by name and order it in descending order by total. The final results look like this:

```
+------------------+-------+
| name             | total |
+------------------+-------+
| Hammond Hammocks |    19 |
| Treichler Trikes |    10 |
| Kites by Keith   |     9 |
| Anders Mints     |     5 |
| Clayton Coggs    |     3 |
| Schrader Suits   |     3 |
+------------------+-------+
```

The count function will add up the number of rows that are returned from a query. For instance, if you wanted to know the total number of salespeople or number of clients that are in the database, the query would look like this for the salespeople:

```
select COUNT(*) from sales;
```

and like this for the clients:

```
select COUNT(*) from clients;
```

The results of the first query look like this:

```
+----------+
| COUNT(*) |
+----------+
|        3 |
+----------+
```

and the second query results look like this:

```
+----------+
| COUNT(*) |
+----------+
|        9 |
+----------+
```

The min function is used to return the minimum for the column specified. For instance, the following query will return the minimum order for each client in descending order:

```
SELECT name, min(quantity) total
FROM clients, items, orders
WHERE clients.clientID = orders.clientID
AND orders.itemID = items.itemID
GROUP BY name
ORDER BY total DESC;
```

The results look like this:

```
+------------------+-------+
| name             | total |
+------------------+-------+
| Treichler Trikes |     5 |
```

```
| Hammond Hammocks |     3 |
| Anders Mints     |     2 |
| Kites by Keith   |     2 |
| Clayton Coggs    |     1 |
| Schrader Suits   |     1 |
+------------------+-------+
```

The max function is the exact opposite of the min function and returns the maximum row for the column specified. The example query that follows will return the maximum number of items ordered for each client in descending order:

```
SELECT name, max(quantity) total
FROM clients, items, orders
WHERE clients.clientID = orders.clientID
AND orders.itemID = items.itemID
GROUP BY name
ORDER BY total DESC;
```

The results look like this:

```
+------------------+-------+
| name             | total |
+------------------+-------+
| Hammond Hammocks |     7 |
| Treichler Trikes |     5 |
| Kites by Keith   |     4 |
| Anders Mints     |     3 |
| Clayton  Coggs   |     2 |
| Schrader Suits   |     2 |
+------------------+-------+
```

The avg function averages the column specified and returns the results. The query that follows will average the number of items ordered for each client and return the results in descending order:

```
SELECT name, avg(quantity) total
FROM clients, items, orders
WHERE clients.clientID = orders.clientID
AND orders.itemID = items.itemID
GROUP BY name
ORDER BY total DESC;
```

The results look like this:

```
+------------------+--------+
| name             | total  |
+------------------+--------+
| Treichler Trikes | 5.0000 |
| Hammond Hammocks | 4.7500 |
| Kites by Keith   | 3.0000 |
| Anders Mints     | 2.5000 |
| Clayton  Coggs   | 1.5000 |
| Schrader Suits   | 1.5000 |
+------------------+--------+
```

Creating Tables

Creating tables is standard in the SQL language. To create a table, you must first define the table name and then all the attributes or columns in the table. Each database will have variations of these attribute definitions. You will need to consult the database documentation for further information on these definitions.

The script that follows creates a table called sales, which has its first column defined as salesID. This column is an auto-incrementing integer and is defined as the primary key. The second and third columns are defined as firstname and lastname, respectively. They are initialized as variable characters with a maximum length of 20. The script is as follows:

```
create table sales (salesID int primary key auto_increment, firstname
varchar(20), lastname varchar(20));
```

When the table is created, the definition in MySQL looks like this:

```
+-----------+-------------+------+-----+---------+----------------+
| Field     | Type        | Null | Key | Default | Extra          |
+-----------+-------------+------+-----+---------+----------------+
| salesID   | int(11)     |      | PRI | NULL    | auto_increment |
| firstname | varchar(20) | YES  |     | NULL    |                |
| lastname  | varchar(20) | YES  |     | NULL    |                |
+-----------+-------------+------+-----+---------+----------------+
```

Altering Tables

The alter table command will add or delete columns from a table. First, create a table called items using the following create table command:

```
create table items (itemID int primary key auto_increment,
description varchar(40));
```

The definition looks like this:

```
+-------------+-------------+------+-----+---------+----------------+
| Field       | Type        | Null | Key | Default | Extra          |
+-------------+-------------+------+-----+---------+----------------+
| itemID      | int(11)     |      | PRI | NULL    | auto_increment |
| description | varchar(40) | YES  |     | NULL    |                |
+-------------+-------------+------+-----+---------+----------------+
```

After this table is created, you decide that along with the description, you need to include the price of the item. You have two choices: you can drop and re-create the table, or you can change the table definition using the alter table command. This command would look like this:

```
alter table items add (price decimal(3,2) not null);
```

The table definition would now look like this:

```
+-------------+--------------+------+-----+---------+----------------+
| Field       | Type         | Null | Key | Default | Extra          |
+-------------+--------------+------+-----+---------+----------------+
| itemID      | int(11)      |      | PRI | NULL    | auto_increment |
| description | varchar(40)  | YES  |     | NULL    |                |
| price       | decimal(4,2) |      |     | 0.00    |                |
+-------------+--------------+------+-----+---------+----------------+
```

Adding Data

Adding data to a table is done with the insert query. There are two ways to form the insert query. The first is to only define the values that are to be placed into the table. These values must be ordered the same way they are in the table definition. For instance, in the query that follows, the first entry is the itemID, the second is the description, and the third is the price. If these items are arranged differently, the data types will not match. In this format, all columns must have data associated with them. The query is as follows:

```
insert into items values (1,'Air Anvil',29.95);
```

The second way to form the insert query defines the columns along with the data associated with the column. In this format, the columns and data have to match, but the order does not have to match the table definition. You also don't have to define data for every column, only the columns in the insert query. The query would look like this:

```
insert into clients (clientID, name) values (4,'Treichler Trikes');
```

Updating Data

Changing data in the database is done with the update statement. This statement defines the table, the column, and the data that is to replace the old data. There is usually a where clause that allows only one row to be updated. The following is a query that updates the items table and changes the price of the Deep-Sea Drill to $50.00:

```
update items set price = 50.00 where description = 'Deep-Sea Drill';
```

Deleting Data

Deleting data from a table is done by using the delete query. The following query will delete the Deep-Sea Drill record from the items table:

```
delete from items
where description = 'Deep-Sea Drill';
```

APPENDIX C

CVS Help

Concurrent Versions System (CVS) is a tool commonly used by developers to store the many source files that are brought together as part of a development project. Since the source code is often the key piece of intellectual property for a software company, it is important that it is stored in a safe, reliable, and efficient manner. Because CVS is open-source software, it is typically the tool of choice for developers who work with PHP, MySQL, and the Linux operating system.

Background

The purpose of CVS is to provide a mechanism for recording the history of source files. The CVS concept began as a set of shell scripts written by Dick Grune, who posted these scripts to the Usenet newsgroup comp.sources.unix in December 1986. In April 1989, Brian Berliner went on to design and code CVS based on these scripts. Jeff Polk later helped Brian with the design of the CVS module and vendor branch support. CVS has grown to become the dominant open-source network-transparent version control system. The starting point for more information on CVS is http://www.cvshome.org/. Another useful link is http://www.loria.fr/~molli/cvs-index.html. You may also want to subscribe to the CVS mailing list known as info-cvs. To subscribe to this list, send e-mail to info-cvs-request@gnu.org. Finally, comp.software.config-mgmt is the newsgroup in which CVS is covered, along with other configuration management software.

Overview

Development teams use CVS to store incremental versions of source files in an efficient, reliable, and logical manner. One method of source control is to save a copy of each incremental version of the source file. While this can work, it is not an efficient method for storing source files, because you would have an entire copy of the file for each little change that was made to the file. CVS improves on this by only tracking the changes between each incremental file, conserving considerable disk space. Because CVS tracks each version of the file, a developer can go back to see what changes were made at each step in the development process, which is often important in tracking down when bugs were introduced to a project. In addition to tracking the changes in each file, CVS also helps manage changes made to a single file by multiple developers. It accomplishes this task by providing each developer with a working copy of the file and then managing the merging of changes made by each developer. This is unlike many version control systems, which simply prevent more than one user from accessing a file. The core strength of CVS is the algorithms that handle merging multiple changes into a single file. This process is referred to as *conflict resolution*. CVS is an open-source tool used to manage the multiple versions of source code that are created throughout a project's development process.

In order to understand where CVS fits in a development environment, we'll look at a few of the things CVS is not. First of all, CVS doesn't replace a build system. CVS is only a tree of files and doesn't manage the relationship between the files. Build systems require a mechanism for ensuring that all the dependencies for a source file are met before it is built, and this is not something CVS handles. Typically, developers use the make utility and corresponding make files to ensure that the dependencies are handled. Another important consideration is that CVS doesn't consider code logic across source files when merging multiple developer versions back together. When CVS brings files together, it only looks at the changes for an individual file at a time, and doesn't consider any changes done to other files in the source tree. Finally, CVS does not track multiple files that are checked in together or provide a mechanism for setting the status of a file. These items are left up to the external systems that CVS is tied into. To use CVS effectively, you must understand where CVS fits into a development environment.

Obtaining the Software

CVS is available for many platforms in both binary and source code forms. It has both client/interface and server components. To make the best use of CVS, it is important to understand how it is released and to determine which version is most appropriate for your environment.

Release History

At the time of writing for this book, the current stable version of CVS is 1.11.1p1. Release 1.11, which was released in September of 2000, was the most recent major release and is referred to as SteelHead. The pattern for CVS releases is typically one major release followed by one subsequent minor release. The major releases are generally very stable and often contain notable new features. The minor releases contain fixes for bugs in the major release and are typically the most stable version available.

Platform Availability and File Location

CVS is typically used in a client/server environment. Most often, the CVS server is sitting on a Unix/Linux machine. Work has been done to port the CVS server onto other operating systems; however, none are in widespread use at this point. The CVS client is available for the following platforms: BeOS, Linux, Macintosh, OS2, Unix, VMS, Win9*x*/NT/2000, and DOS—and the list continues to grow. The software is available as both raw source code and precompiled binaries for many of the operating systems mentioned. The primary source for CVS software is ftp://ftp.cvshome.org/pub, although mirror sources exist. The source code is typically distributed as a gzipped tar file, which requires the tar and gzip utilities to uncompress and extract the individual source files.

CVS Interfaces

The core CVS software is a backend tool for version management of files. To make it more robust and simpler to work with, many interfaces have been developed to interact with it.

Client Interfaces

Several client interfaces have been developed to access the CVS server from a variety of platforms. The CVS client/server protocol is documented in the doc/cvsclient.text file in the CVS source distribution. For the most part, it puts the intelligence on the server. It also is designed for low-bandwidth connections and connections that might not be up all the time. There is only one implementation of the server available, but there are many client implementations. The command-line client, which is part of the CVS source distribution, is written in C and is a full-featured client. It is used in conjunction with Emacs, tkCVS, and other Unix/Linux tools. An interface has also been developed for CodeWarrior, which is a development platform most commonly used for Macintosh and Palm development. CVS Coworker is a plug-in developed by Preston L. Bannister that allows CVS to be interfaced with the SCC API. A CVS interface for the RCS library also exists and is covered in Chapter 2 of this book. JCVS, MacCVSClient, and others utilize the CVS remote control. There are DOM (document object model) interfaces available; more information can be found at http://cvshome.org/docs/infodom.html. The RCS command-line interface is documented at http://cvshome.org/dev/softrcs.html. There is a SCC API interface that is accessible by many Windows development systems. Visual Café API from Symantec can interface with CVS as well. Finally, WebDav can interface with CVS, and more information on it can be found at http://www.webdav.org/ and http://cvshome.org/docs/infodav.html.

Graphical User Interfaces

Several graphical user interfaces for CVS servers exist that provide point-and-click interaction with the server. Many of these are documented on the Web at http://cvshome.org/dev/interface.html. gCVS is a user interface that is available for Mac, Windows, and some Unix flavors. It is written in C++ and implemented by incorporating a modified version of the CVS client. jCVS is available for any suitable Java platform, written in Java, and implemented on top of the CVS remote control protocol. Mac CVS/Win CVS is available for Macintosh and Windows operating systems, written in C++, and implemented by incorporating a modified version of the CVS client. Finally, tkCVS is available on Unix and Windows machines, written in tcl/tk, and implemented on top of the CVS command line. There are several graphical user interfaces available for CVS, and you will likely find many that will work in the environment in which you prefer to develop.

Web Interfaces

There are several CVS user interfaces available through an Internet browser. A few of the more common ones are examined here. The CVSweb package allows users to browse the revision history of a CVS tree with a web browser. The Bonsai package is somewhat similar, but focuses on querying CVS to find various kinds of information. A more special-purpose tool is the FAQ-O-Matic, which allows users to edit version-controlled files with a web browser.

Integrated Development Environments

More information on the development environments that have been integrated with CVS can be found at http://cvshome.org/dev/environment.html. The most common ones are Emacs, Microsoft Dev Studio, CodeWarrior, Visual Café, and WipeoutPro.

Working with CVS

Now that you are familiar with the background of CVS, we'll look at actually incorporating it into your development environment.

Setup Recommendations

The main consideration when planning to use CVS is the disk space required. A good baseline to start with is three times the actual size of the code you plan to put under source control. Obviously, as you continue to develop a project you will eventually outgrow this, but it is a good starting point for most development projects.

The Repository

A major concept in working with CVS is the repository. The repository stores a complete copy of all the files and directories that are under version control. Normally, you never access the files directly. You use CVS commands to request a copy of the file to your working directory and then work with the copied file. It is important to note that the repository and working directories are two separate locations altogether. The repository can be either local or remote. When accessing the CVS server, "local" refers to the local file system and "remote" refers to a CVS server you will access across the network, where the network could be your local area network or the Internet.

Setting Up the Repository

There are a couple of different methods to inform the CVS server where you would like the repository to be stored. The first is using the command line. The syntax for this is as follows:

```
cvs -d <directory path>
```

This sets the repository to the specified directory. For example, the following tells CVS to use the /opt/cvsroot directory to store files:

```
cvs -d /opt/cvsroot
```

An alternative method is to set the $CVSROOT environment variable. To set an environment variable using the Bourne (sh) or Bash (bash) shells, add the following to the .profile, .bash_profile, or .bashrc file for the user you are running as

```
CVSROOT=<directory path>;export CVSROOT
```

For C shell (csh) and TC shell (tcsh) users, add the following to the .cshrc or .tcshrc file, respectively:

```
setenv CVSROOT=<directory path>
```

Once you have specified the repository location, it is stored in the CVS/root file of your working directory, so you do not need to specify it for every command. If there is a conflict between repository locations specified by each of the aforementioned methods, the order of precedence is the -d option, followed by the CVS/root file, and then the CVSROOT environment variable, if present. To initialize the repository and have CVS generate the necessary work files, you should execute the **init** command, such as **cvs init**, or combine it with the repository creation, such as **cvs -d /opt/cvsroot init**. Note that reissuing the **init** command will not do any damage to the repository.

Accessing the Repository

The preceding examples assumed that the repository was on the local machine. It is also possible to access repositories that reside on remote machines. The syntax is as follows:

```
:method:[[user][:password]@]hostname[:[port]]/path/to/repository
```

In this case, *method* is either local or remote and assumed to be local if omitted. An alternative to this is omitting the password portion of the command and adding the word *login* to the end of the request. This will cause CVS to prompt you for your password and then save it locally, along with all of your connection information, so you won't have to specify it with each subsequent CVS request. This information is stored in the $HOME/.cvspass file. This file is human-readable; and although the password is encrypted, it would be very easy for someone to decipher it. Therefore, you may want to alter where this file is stored by setting the CVS_PASSFILE environment variable, as well as controlling access to that directory. When you log out of CVS, this file will be cleared automatically.

Restricting Access Inside the Repository

When setting up the repository, you should ensure that the directories inside the repository are writeable by users who have permission to modify the files in that directory. Second, keep in mind that CVS only controls access to files at a directory level.

Repository Maintenance

If you need to move or back up the repository, you should first stop the server. Next, use the normal copy or move command. Although you may need to do some cleanup work, your repository isn't at risk while performing these operations. Keep in mind that if you do move the repository's location, you will need to re-create your working directory in order to access it at the new location.

Using CVS for a Project

When using CVS, related files are grouped together within a project. The following explains the process of setting up a new project for version management.

Setting Up an Empty Project

To set up a project in CVS, you begin by creating an empty directory structure. An example of this would be

```
mkdir project1;mkdir project1/common;mkdir project1/images
```

To begin using this new directory structure, change directory into the project1 directory and then execute the following command:

```
cvs import -m "Begin Project 1" MyProjects/project1 projects start
```

This instructs CVS to place the project1 directory under source control and store it in the repository as MyProjects/project1. The -m flag is used to specify a message to be associated with the import. Alternatively, if you don't specify a message, an editor window will be started and you will be prompted to supply a message. The string *projects* is referred to as the vendor tag and *start* is the release tag. CVS requires that these values be present in the command, but they don't have any significance at this point and will be covered later in this section. The next step is to do a checkout so you can begin working. To do this, execute the following operations:

```
cd ..
cvs checkout MyProjects/project1
```

You may want to go back and delete the original project1 directory (not the one inside MyProjects!) to ensure that you are working in the correct (CVS controlled) directory.

Working with Files and Directories

Now that you have an empty project set up in CVS, you will want to begin adding new source files and directories to the project. A key idea to keep in mind is that you want CVS to track all the changes you make to the project; therefore, all changes must be done using the proper CVS commands.

Adding Files and Directories to a Project

We'll begin by examining what it takes to add files to the directory. You must, of course, first have the directory checked out, which you did already with the **checkout** command. Next, use your preferred editor to create the file in your working copy of the directory. An alternative would be to execute a **touch** command, which creates an empty file, such as **touch source1.php**. Next, use the **add** command to add the file to source control. An example of this is **cvs add source1.php**. If the file were a binary file, you would need to specify the flag -kb after the **add** command. To actually check the file into the repository, which allows others to see the file, you need to execute the **cvs commit** command, such as **cvs commit source1.php**. You can follow the same method to add directories to the project; however, keep in mind that commands cannot include recursive steps. Therefore, to add a directory two levels deep, you would have to do it in two steps, as in the following example:

```
cvs add parentdirectory;cvs add childdirectory
```

If you are trying to add multiple directories with many subdirectories, you are better off using the **import** command instead of the **add** command. Note that the files and directories you are trying to add to the project must already exist before executing the **cvs add** command. For the **add** and **commit** commands, you can specify the **-m "some string"** option, which allows you to associate a message with the action, which will then show up in the history log.

Removing Files from a Project

Over the life of a project you may choose to remove certain files. In order to re-create previous versions of a project, which is often necessary for debugging, you will want to be able to retrieve the files you have removed from the project. The first step is to remove the file from your working directory using the operating system's remove command, such as **rm** or **del**. Next, use a CVS remove command, such as this:

```
cvs remove source1.php
```

Last, execute the **commit** command to confirm the removal:

```
cvs commit source1.php
```

CVS will automatically keep track of the absence of the file, and you can even create a new file with the same name later in the project. Using **remove -f** causes the file to be removed from the file system and removed from CVS in one step. Also, if you want to restore a removed file that the remove hasn't been committed on yet, just add the file back. If you have removed the file using the operating system command, but not the **cvs remove** command, you can use the **cvs update** command to get it back.

Removing Directories from a Project

The concept of removing directories from a project is very similar to that of removing files. The removal of a directory means that you don't want it to show up in your working directory, but still want to be able to track it for version control purposes. The method for removing a directory is to first remove all the files from the directory. Next, you supply the -P option to either the **cvs update** or **cvs checkout** command, which causes the directory to be removed from the working directory. There is no command to remove the directory straightaway. Keep in mind that -P is implied whenever -r or -D are given as flags during a **checkout** command.

Moving or Renaming Files

There are a couple of methods to move or rename files in CVS. The most straightforward method is to use the operating system command to move the old file to the new file, and then ask CVS to remove the old file and add the new file. An example of this is the following:

```
mv myoldfile mynewfile
cvs remove myoldfile
cvs add mynewfile
cvs commit -m "Renamed myoldfile to mynewfile" old new
```

There are also some other advanced methods for moving and renaming files; however, they can prove to be more risky as well. For details on the other methods available, consult the CVS manual.

Moving or Renaming Directories

The typical method for moving a directory is to move each of the files within the directory using the steps mentioned previously to move the files. After you have moved the files, use the -P option on checkout. An alternative method is to rename the directories inside the repository itself, but this is again a risky technique and should be avoided if possible.

Checking Out Files

In order to modify existing files or directories managed by CVS, you must check them out. The syntax of the checkout command is as follows:

```
checkout [options] modules
```

You may also use **get** or **co** in place of the word checkout. The modules option represents either a name for a group of source directories or files, or a path to a set of files or directories in the repository. Files that you retrieve using checkout are able to be modified unless you specify an **-r** option to CVS or the CVSREAD environment variable is set. When you execute a checkout command, a top-level directory is created along with any subdirectories that are part of the module or path you specified. The following common command options are available with checkout: -D date, -f, -k flag, -l, -n, -P, -p, -R, -r tag. These command options are documented later in this appendix. In addition to these common command options, the following are also available with the checkout command:

-A	Resets the dates, sticky flags, or any options that were set with the -k option
-c	Copies the module file to standard output instead of modifying your working directory
-d dir	Overrides the name of the new directory that is created during a checkout command
-s	Similar to the -c option, except that the status of all the modules is reported as well, and the files are sorted by the status string

CVS Command Reference

The following material is presented as a quick reference for working with your CVS environment.

CVS Command Structure

The syntax for a CVS command is as follows:

```
cvs [ cvs_options ] cvs_command [ command_options ] [ command_args ]
```

The components for the CVS commands are outlined in the following table.

cvs	The name of CVS program
cvs_options	An overall CVS option flag that is not specific to any one cvs_command
cvs_command	One of the subcommands available within CVS

command_options	An option flag set for the particular cvs_command
command_args	Parameters passed to the cvs_command

Exit Status

All CVS operations provide an exit status, which is available to the calling environment. How that is accessible will depend on the operating system that CVS is running on. A value of 0 indicates success, while a value greater than 0 will be set on failure. A failure condition will also be accompanied by an error message.

Details for cvs_options

The following is a list of the available cvs_options you are going to encounter most often. For a complete list, consult the CVS documentation.

--allow-root=rootdir	Specifies legal cvsroot directory.
-T tempdir	Uses tempdir as the directory where temporary files are located. Overrides the setting of the $TMPDIR environment variable and any precompiled directory. This parameter should be specified as an absolute pathname.
-d cvs root directory	Uses cvs root directory as the root directory pathname of the repository. Overrides the setting of the $CVSROOT environment variable.
-e editor	Uses editor to enter revision log information. Overrides the setting of the $CVSEDITOR and $EDITOR environment variables.
-H --help	Displays usage information about the specified cvs_command (but do not actually execute the command). If you don't specify a command name, **cvs -H** displays overall help for cvs, including a list of other help options.
-l	Do not log the cvs_command in the command history (but execute it anyway). Do not change any files.
-n	Attempts to execute the cvs_command, but only to issue reports; do not remove, update, or merge any existing files, or create any new files.
-t	Traces program execution; displays messages showing the steps of cvs activity. Particularly useful with -n to explore the potential impact of an unfamiliar command.

-v --version	Displays version and copyright information for cvs.
-w	Makes new working files read-write. Overrides the setting of the $CVSREAD environment variable. Files are created read-write by default, unless $CVSREAD is set or -r is given.

Common command_options

The following table lists some of the key command_options that have similar behavior across multiple CVS commands.

-l	Local; run only in current working directory, rather than recursing through subdirectories.
-m message	Uses message as log information, instead of invoking an editor. Available with the following commands: **add**, **commit**, **import**.
-P	Prunes empty directories.
-p	Pipes the files retrieved from the repository to standard output, rather than writing them in the working directory.
-R	Processes directories recursively. This is on by default. Available with the following commands: **annotate**, **checkout**, **commit**, **diff**, **edit**, **editors**, **export**, **rdiff**, **remove**, **rtag**, **status**, **tag**, **unedit**, **update**, **watch**, **watchers**.
-r tag	Uses the revision specified by the tag argument instead of the default head revision. As well as arbitrary tags defined with the **tag** or **rtag** command, two special tags are always available: **HEAD** refers to the most recent version available in the repository, and **BASE** refers to the revision you last checked out in the current working directory. The tag specification is sticky when you use this with **checkout** or **update** to make your own copy of a file. CVS remembers the tag and continues to use it on future update commands, until you specify otherwise.

Viewing the History of CVS Commands Executed

CVS is able to track when a file checked out, committed, retagged, updated, or released. To have this tracking turned on, the history file must be created in the $CVSROOT/CVSROOT directory. An example of this would be

```
# touch $CVSROOT/cvsroot/history
```

The format of the history command is

```
history [-report] [-flags] [-option args] [files…].
```

The [-report] portion of the command includes the following options:

-c	Generates a report for each time the commit command was used.
-e	Indicates that all (everything) record types should be reported.
-m module	Reports only on a particular module.
-o	Reports only on modules that are checked out and is the default behavior if no report option is specified.
-T	Reports on all tags.
-x type	Reports only on certain record types. See the record type table that follows.

The type values for the [-x type] option are specified as single letters. The following types are available:

F	release
O	checkout
E	export
T	rtag
C	A merge was necessary but collisions occurred, indicating a manual merge is necessary. This is one of the possible record types for an **update** command.
G	A merge was necessary and it was successful. This is one of the possible record types for an **update** command.
U	A working file was copied from the repository. This is one of the possible record types for an **update** command.
W	The working copy of a file was deleted during an update. This is one of the possible record types for an **update** command.
A	A file was added for the first time. This is one of the possible record types for a **commit** command.
M	Indicates that a file was modified. This is one of the possible record types for a **commit** command.
R	Indicates that a file was removed. This is one of the possible record types for a **commit** command.

The [-flags] portion of the command includes the following options:

-a	Shows data for all users. The normal behavior is to only show records for the particular user who is executing the command.
-l	Displays last modification only.

-w	Only shows records from the same working directory from which the **history** command is run.

The [-option args] portion of the command includes the following options:

-b str	Shows records back to the one that contains the given string in the module name, file name, or repository path.
-D date	Shows all records since the date provided.
-f file	Only shows records for the file name given. Multiple files can be specified in one command line.
-n module	Only shows records for the module name given. Multiple modules can be specified in one command line.
-p repository	Only shows records for the repository name given. Multiple repositories can be specified in one command line.
-r rev	Only shows records that refer to revisions since the revision or tag named rev was used in an individual RCS file. All RCS files are searched for the revision or tag.
-u name	Only shows records for the given user name.
-z timezone	When displaying records, uses the time zone specified instead of in UTC format.

Index

Symbols

A

D

E

F

G

H

I

J

L

M

N

O

P

U

V

W

Z

INTERNATIONAL CONTACT INFORMATION

AUSTRALIA
McGraw-Hill Book Company Australia Pty. Ltd.
TEL +61-2-9417-9899
FAX +61-2-9417-5687
http://www.mcgraw-hill.com.au
books-it_sydney@mcgraw-hill.com

CANADA
McGraw-Hill Ryerson Ltd.
TEL +905-430-5000
FAX +905-430-5020
http://www.mcgrawhill.ca

GREECE, MIDDLE EAST, NORTHERN AFRICA
McGraw-Hill Hellas
TEL +30-1-656-0990-3-4
FAX +30-1-654-5525

MEXICO (Also serving Latin America)
McGraw-Hill Interamericana Editores S.A. de C.V.
TEL +525-117-1583
FAX +525-117-1589
http://www.mcgraw-hill.com.mx
fernando_castellanos@mcgraw-hill.com

SINGAPORE (Serving Asia)
McGraw-Hill Book Company
TEL +65-863-1580
FAX +65-862-3354
http://www.mcgraw-hill.com.sg
mghasia@mcgraw-hill.com

SOUTH AFRICA
McGraw-Hill South Africa
TEL +27-11-622-7512
FAX +27-11-622-9045
robyn_swanepoel@mcgraw-hill.com

UNITED KINGDOM & EUROPE (Excluding Southern Europe)
McGraw-Hill Education Europe
TEL +44-1-628-502500
FAX +44-1-628-770224
http://www.mcgraw-hill.co.uk
computing_neurope@mcgraw-hill.com

ALL OTHER INQUIRIES Contact:
Osborne/McGraw-Hill
TEL +1-510-549-6600
FAX +1-510-883-7600
http://www.osborne.com
omg_international@mcgraw-hill.com

About the CD-ROM

The CD-ROM contains the source code, database, and other related files that are used in each chapter of this book. The CD-ROM is organized in chapter-specific directories. So, to find a file used in Chapter 1, you'd look in the chapter1 directory; to find a file used in Chapter 2, look in the chapter2 directory; and so on. Each chapter directory contains a fully functional application, and in some cases contains associated files that are not explicitly referenced in a chapter's text.

LICENSE AGREEMENT

THIS PRODUCT (THE "PRODUCT") CONTAINS PROPRIETARY SOFTWARE, DATA AND INFORMATION (INCLUDING DOCUMENTATION) OWNED BY THE McGRAW-HILL COMPANIES, INC. ("McGRAW-HILL") AND ITS LICENSORS. YOUR RIGHT TO USE THE PRODUCT IS GOVERNED BY THE TERMS AND CONDITIONS OF THIS AGREEMENT.

LICENSE: Throughout this License Agreement, "you" shall mean either the individual or the entity whose agent opens this package. You are granted a non-exclusive and non-transferable license to use the Product subject to the following terms:
(i) If you have licensed a single user version of the Product, the Product may only be used on a single computer (i.e., a single CPU). If you licensed and paid the fee applicable to a local area network or wide area network version of the Product, you are subject to the terms of the following subparagraph (ii).
(ii) If you have licensed a local area network version, you may use the Product on unlimited workstations located in one single building selected by you that is served by such local area network. If you have licensed a wide area network version, you may use the Product on unlimited workstations located in multiple buildings on the same site selected by you that is served by such wide area network; provided, however, that any building will not be considered located in the same site if it is more than five (5) miles away from any building included in such site. In addition, you may only use a local area or wide area network version of the Product on one single server. If you wish to use the Product on more than one server, you must obtain written authorization from McGraw-Hill and pay additional fees.
(iii) You may make one copy of the Product for back-up purposes only and you must maintain an accurate record as to the location of the back-up at all times.

COPYRIGHT; RESTRICTIONS ON USE AND TRANSFER: All rights (including copyright) in and to the Product are owned by McGraw-Hill and its licensors. You are the owner of the enclosed disc on which the Product is recorded. You may not use, copy, decompile, disassemble, reverse engineer, modify, reproduce, create derivative works, transmit, distribute, sublicense, store in a database or retrieval system of any kind, rent or transfer the Product, or any portion thereof, in any form or by any means (including electronically or otherwise) except as expressly provided for in this License Agreement. You must reproduce the copyright notices, trademark notices, legends and logos of McGraw-Hill and its licensors that appear on the Product on the back-up copy of the Product which you are permitted to make hereunder. All rights in the Product not expressly granted herein are reserved by McGraw-Hill and its licensors.

TERM: This License Agreement is effective until terminated. It will terminate if you fail to comply with any term or condition of this License Agreement. Upon termination, you are obligated to return to McGraw-Hill the Product together with all copies thereof and to purge all copies of the Product included in any and all servers and computer facilities.

DISCLAIMER OF WARRANTY: THE PRODUCT AND THE BACK-UP COPY ARE LICENSED "AS IS." McGRAW-HILL, ITS LICENSORS AND THE AUTHORS MAKE NO WARRANTIES, EXPRESS OR IMPLIED, AS TO THE RESULTS TO BE OBTAINED BY ANY PERSON OR ENTITY FROM USE OF THE PRODUCT, ANY INFORMATION OR DATA INCLUDED THEREIN AND/OR ANY TECHNICAL SUPPORT SERVICES PROVIDED HEREUNDER, IF ANY ("TECHNICAL SUPPORT SERVICES"). McGRAW-HILL, ITS LICENSORS AND THE AUTHORS MAKE NO EXPRESS OR IMPLIED WARRANTIES OF MERCHANTABILITY OR FITNESS FOR A PARTICULAR PURPOSE OR USE WITH RESPECT TO THE PRODUCT. McGRAW-HILL, ITS LICENSORS, AND THE AUTHORS MAKE NO GUARANTEE THAT YOU WILL PASS ANY CERTIFICATION EXAM WHATSOEVER BY USING THIS PRODUCT. NEITHER McGRAW-HILL, ANY OF ITS LICENSORS NOR THE AUTHORS WARRANT THAT THE FUNCTIONS CONTAINED IN THE PRODUCT WILL MEET YOUR REQUIREMENTS OR THAT THE OPERATION OF THE PRODUCT WILL BE UNINTERRUPTED OR ERROR FREE. YOU ASSUME THE ENTIRE RISK WITH RESPECT TO THE QUALITY AND PERFORMANCE OF THE PRODUCT.

LIMITED WARRANTY FOR DISC: To the original licensee only, McGraw-Hill warrants that the enclosed disc on which the Product is recorded is free from defects in materials and workmanship under normal use and service for a period of ninety (90) days from the date of purchase. In the event of a defect in the disc covered by the foregoing warranty, McGraw-Hill will replace the disc.

LIMITATION OF LIABILITY: NEITHER McGRAW-HILL, ITS LICENSORS NOR THE AUTHORS SHALL BE LIABLE FOR ANY INDIRECT, SPECIAL OR CONSEQUENTIAL DAMAGES, SUCH AS BUT NOT LIMITED TO, LOSS OF ANTICIPATED PROFITS OR BENEFITS, RESULTING FROM THE USE OR INABILITY TO USE THE PRODUCT EVEN IF ANY OF THEM HAS BEEN ADVISED OF THE POSSIBILITY OF SUCH DAMAGES. THIS LIMITATION OF LIABILITY SHALL APPLY TO ANY CLAIM OR CAUSE WHATSOEVER WHETHER SUCH CLAIM OR CAUSE ARISES IN CONTRACT, TORT, OR OTHERWISE. Some states do not allow the exclusion or limitation of indirect, special or consequential damages, so the above limitation may not apply to you.

U.S. GOVERNMENT RESTRICTED RIGHTS: Any software included in the Product is provided with restricted rights subject to subparagraphs (c), (1) and (2) of the Commercial Computer Software-Restricted Rights clause at 48 C.F.R. 52.227-19. The terms of this Agreement applicable to the use of the data in the Product are those under which the data are generally made available to the general public by McGraw-Hill. Except as provided herein, no reproduction, use, or disclosure rights are granted with respect to the data included in the Product and no right to modify or create derivative works from any such data is hereby granted.

GENERAL: This License Agreement constitutes the entire agreement between the parties relating to the Product. The terms of any Purchase Order shall have no effect on the terms of this License Agreement. Failure of McGraw-Hill to insist at any time on strict compliance with this License Agreement shall not constitute a waiver of any rights under this License Agreement. This License Agreement shall be construed and governed in accordance with the laws of the State of New York. If any provision of this License Agreement is held to be contrary to law, that provision will be enforced to the maximum extent permissible and the remaining provisions will remain in full force and effect.